Blackstone's Guide to the
HUMAN RIGHTS ACT 1998
Second Edition

John Wadham

and

Helen Mountfield

(With a foreword by the Rt Hon. Jack Straw MP,
Secretary of State for Home Affairs)

Royalties from the sale of this book go to support the work
of Liberty (the National Council for Civil Liberties)

BLACKSTONE
PRESS LIMITED

Published by
Blackstone Press Limited
Aldine Place
London
W12 8AA
United Kingdom

Sales enquiries and orders
Telephone +44-(0)-20-8740-2277
Facsimile +44-(0)-20-8743-2292
email: sales@blackstone.demon.co.uk
website: www.blackstonepress.com

ISBN 1-84174-173-6
© J. Wadham and H. Mountfield 2000
First published 1999
Reprinted twice
Second edition 2000
Reprinted 2001

Brtish Library Cataloguing in Publication Data
A catalogue record for this book is available from the British Library

Typeset in 10/11 pt Times by Style Photosetting Ltd, Mayfield, East Sussex
Printed and bound in Great Britain by Ashford Colour Press Ltd,
Gosport, Hampshire

Contents

Contents

Foreword to the First Edition

The Rt Hon. Jack Straw MP

The Human Rights Act 1998 is the most significant statement of human rights in domestic law since the 1689 Bill of Rights. It will strengthen representative and democratic government. It will do so by enabling people to challenge more easily actions of the state if they fail to match the standards set by the European Convention on Human Rights.

Nothing in the Act will take away the freedoms that people already enjoy. But those freedoms alone are not enough: they need to be complemented by positive rights that people can assert when they believe that they have been treated unfairly by the state, or that the state and its institutions have failed properly to protect them. The Act will guarantee to everyone the means to enforce a set of basic civil and political rights, establishing a floor below which standards will not be allowed to fall.

Bringing these rights home will mean that people can rely on their rights in our domestic courts rather than having to incur the cost and delay of taking a case to Strasbourg. It will bring these rights much more fully into the jurisprudence of the courts throughout the United Kingdom, and their interpretation will be far more woven into our common law.

It is important that the effects of the Act are understood not only by lawyers and judges, but also by government officials, local authorities, the police, immigration officers and other public authorities whose actions may be challenged under the Act. In the period before the Act comes into force, it will be important for bodies like these to examine their policies and procedures for compliance with these rights. I also hope that advice agencies, law centres, lawyers and others will help members of the public to understand what their rights are and how to rely on them.

Books on the Act can make an important contribution to the learning process, and I welcome the publication of this Blackstone's Guide. It examines a number of the legal issues arising from the Act, such as the meaning of a public authority and the effect of the Act on the interpretation of legislation. It provides a guide to the wealth of Strasbourg case law on the rights set out in the Act. And, because it will still be possible to go to Strasbourg for human rights breaches which are not remedied under the Act, the book explains how to bring a case under the new procedures introduced at Strasbourg this year.

Liberty has been involved for many years in the campaign to bring home the rights contained in the Convention. It contributed to the debate on the proposals we developed in Opposition and has continued to offer advice during the preparation and Parliamentary passage of the Human Rights Act. This book is the natural result of its close interest in and concern for human rights.

Jack Straw
Home Secretary
October 1998

Preface to the Second Edition

In the preface to the first edition of this book we wrote:

> The Human Rights Act 1998 will have a momentous impact on our legal system
> . . . It will affect every area of law in England and Wales (which is the
> jurisdiction which this book concentrates on) and also Northern Ireland and
> Scotland. No law student or legal practitioner will be able to ignore its effect.

And even before the Act came fully into force in England and Wales, this proved
to be the case. The House of Lords has now decided its first case on the Human
Rights Act 1998. In that case (*R v DPP, ex parte Kebilene* [1999] 3 WLR 972),
Lord Hope said (at para. 838) that:

> although the 1998 Act is not yet in force, the vigorous public debate which
> accompanied its passage through Parliament has already had a profound effect
> on thinking about issues of human rights. It is now plain that the incorporation
> of the European Convention on Human Rights into our domestic law will subject
> the entire legal system to a fundamental process of review and, where necessary,
> reform by the judiciary.

The number of Convention questions which have been raised and determined by
English courts has grown exponentially: every judge has been trained, at least to
a basic level, on the Act and its implications; civil servants and public authorities
have started to examine their practices and procedures to see whether they comply
with the Act. We can also look north, to Scotland, where the Act is in force to see
what the Scottish judiciary has made of the first cases to come before them. So all
lawyers need to understand the way in which the Act will work and to come to
grips with what may at first be new and unfamiliar case law and legal techniques.

Lawyers are the chief audience for this book. But human rights are too important
to be left just to lawyers. We hope that the Act will make an awareness of and
respect for human rights an integral part of our culture. This is an exciting
development and the Act will provide an important tool for creative lawyers to use
on behalf of their clients.

The Human Rights Act 1998 is unique: no other jurisdiction has ever adopted the same approach in giving effect to an international human rights instrument in domestic law. The Act is also unique in British experience: the techniques which it uses are quite different from other 'constitutional' interpretative legislation such as the European Communities Act 1972, and its scope is much broader.

CONTENTS

Chapter 1 provides an overview of the Act's structure and introduces the core provisions of the Human Rights Act 1998, including, in 1.5 a short history of the European Convention on Human Rights and the attempts to incorporate it into English law. Chapter 2 contains the basic legal concepts and core interpretative principles which are used to interpret the European Convention on Human Rights. These two chapters are essential background to understanding the rest of the book and the way in which the Act will operate. The methods of interpreting the Convention are different from traditional English legal techniques, but it is necessary to apply them in all areas where the Human Rights Act 1998 has an impact. Under s. 2 of the Act relevant Strasbourg jurisprudence will be a mandatory consideration in cases concerning Convention rights. As a result, section 2.8 of this book sets out the sources of Convention jurisprudence and Appendix 7 explains how to research Convention case law further and details where references can be found.

Chapters 3 to 6 explain the effect of the Human Rights Act 1998 in English law in more detail. Chapter 3 concerns the important general 'interpretative' obligation introduced by the Act. Chapter 4 turns to the specific new causes of action which the Act creates against public authorities. What type of body constitutes a public authority for these purposes is considered in 4.3, and in 4.4 we consider who may have standing to use the new causes of action, identifying the potential difficulties in public-interest litigation in general and in judicial review proceedings in particular. The forum for these proceedings is considered in 4.5. Chapter 5 is concerned with the remedies which the courts will be able to provide under the Act, including, in 5.2, the innovative 'declaration of incompatibility' and the fast-track procedure which will be available to permit the government to change the law speedily when a declaration of incompatibility has been made. Chapter 6 explains the non-incorporation of Article 13 and the 'special cases' which have been made for the press and the churches. In Chapter 7 we discuss the circumstances in which it is possible to use the Convention as part of European Union law, and why it might be of use to do this even after the Human Rights Act 1998 is in force.

Chapter 8 contains a short outline of each of the rights under the Convention and the most important decided cases in relation to each right. We have included rights, such as Article 13, which will not be incorporated into English law by the Human Rights Act 1998, because they are necessary to understanding the Convention, and because litigants will still be able to use them in cases against the United Kingdom before the European Court of Human Rights in Strasbourg. In relation to each right, we have given a non-exhaustive list of examples of areas in which the Articles may be used in future. These suggestions are necessarily speculative and incomplete. For a more detailed account of the potential uses of the Convention in different areas of practice, see M. Hunt and R. Singh (eds), *A Practitioner's Guide to the Impact of the Human Rights Act 1998* (Oxford: Hart Publishing, 2000).

Chapter 9 deals with the United Kingdom's derogations from and reservations to the Convention, and the procedures available for review. Chapter 10 of the book looks at the institutional framework. This is important in understanding how the Act will effect law-making and the legal and administrative culture. It considers potential functions for a future Human Rights Commission.

This book is primarily concerned with the way in which the Convention can be used in domestic courts and tribunals, but the Convention has not been 'incorporated' in a holistic sense, and there will still be occasions when litigants will have to seek their remedy in Strasbourg. Chapter 11 deals briefly with the procedures for taking a case to the European Court of Human Rights in Strasbourg.

The appendices contain the key materials including the Rules and Directions under the Human Rights Act 1998 available at the time of going to press.

USE OF HANSARD

Since the landmark decision of the House of Lords in *Pepper* v *Hart* [1993] AC 593, Parliamentary statements by ministers may, in certain circumstances, be admissible in order to interpret an Act of Parliament when its meaning is ambiguous, obscure or may lead to an absurdity. The principles are set out in the speech of Lord Browne-Wilkinson at p. 640, namely, that references to Hansard may be admissible where: (a) legislation is obscure or ambiguous or leads to an absurdity; (b) the material relied upon consists of one or more statements by a minister or other promoter of the Bill, and such other material as is necessary to understand such statements and their effect; and (c) the statements relied upon are clear. There has rarely, if ever, been a series of Parliamentary debates in which Members of Parliament have referred quite so repeatedly and self-consciously to the *Pepper* v *Hart* principle. Since there are aspects of the Act which may be ambiguous, we have included relevant Hansard statements, which may be admissible in court when arguing what the Act is intended to mean, and Parliamentary debates, grouped by subject. The question may arise as to the relationship between Hansard statements and the terms of the Convention in interpreting obscurities in legislative provisions. In *R* v *Broadcasting Complaints Commission, ex parte Barclay* [1997] Admin LR 265 at 271–272, Sedley J (as he then was) declined to give Hansard precedence over the Convention. Ultimately, judges not politicians must interpret the law. Some of the Hansard statements are controversial and it is by no means clear that they should be, or will be, regarded as any more persuasive by the courts which will consider them (see *R* v *Deegan* (1998) *The Times,* 17 February, a recent example of a court declining to refer to Hansard).

TIMETABLE FOR IMPLEMENTATION

The Human Rights Act 1998 obtained Royal Assent on 9 November 1998, but its commencement was delayed in order to allow time for a very extensive programme of judicial education to take place. It came into force on 2 October 2000.

The White Paper, *Rights Brought Home* (Appendix 3), and the Bill were published and introduced into the House of Lords on 24 October 1997. The Bill had its second reading on 3 November and the committee stage on 18, 24 and 27 November 1997. The report stage was held on 19 and 29 January 1998, and the third reading on 5 February 1998. The second reading in the Commons was 16 February 1998, the committee stage (on the floor of the House) on 20 May, 3, 17 and 24 June, and 2 July 1998. The report stage and third reading in the House of Commons was 21 October 1998.

Sections 18 (appointment of judges from the United Kingdom to the European Court of Human Rights), 19 (the duty on ministers to produce 'statements of compatibility'), 20 (powers of ministers to make orders under the Act) and 21(5) (substitution of other sentences for the death penalty) came into force on 24 November 1999.

In relation to commencement it is important to note the effect of s. 22 combined with ss. 6 and 7. Section 22(4) provides that s. 7(1)(b) applies to any proceedings 'brought by or at the instigation of a public authority whenever the act in question took place . . .'. This means that any person who is, for instance, a defendant in a civil case (where the claimant is a public authority) or a criminal case will be able to 'rely on the Convention right or rights concerned in any legal proceeding. . .' (s. 7(1)(b)). For instance, defendants in criminal cases whose arrest is before commencement but whose trial or appeal is after that date will nevertheless be able to use the Convention to defend him or herself. In this transition period the Convention can only be used as a shield and not a sword.

For example, if in April 2000 the police gathered evidence against a suspect in violation of Article 8, the right to privacy, it will be open to any defendant to use the Human Rights Act to argue that this evidence is inadmissible at a trial or in any appeal that takes place after October 2000.

The devolution provisions brought the Convention into domestic law before the Human Rights Act itself came into force. In the Northern Ireland Act 1998, s. 6 invalidates any provision of an Act of the Assembly if it is incompatible with a Convention right. Section 24 of that Act makes it *ultra vires* for the Northern Ireland Assembly or a minister or government department to make subordinate legislation which is incompatible with any Convention right. The Scotland Act 1998 introduced similar provisions in respect of the Scottish Parliament and the Scottish Executive (ss. 29 and 57). Lastly, the Government of Wales Act 1998 provided a similar restriction on the Welsh Assembly (s. 107). The first cases raising Convention rights directly have already reached the domestic courts as a result of these provisions rather than from the Human Rights Act itself.

SCOPE OF THE HUMAN RIGHTS ACT 1998

This book talks about the enforcement of 'the Convention rights' in domestic law under the Human Rights Act 1998. It is therefore important to appreciate that the Act 'incorporates' only part of the European Convention on Human Rights. In particular it does not incorporate any of the procedural rights in the Convention, and it does not incorporate Article 13 (the right to an effective remedy). It does, however, include all of the substantive rights: Article 2 (the right to life), Article 3 (freedom from torture), Article 4 (freedom from slavery), Article 5 (freedom from arbitrary arrest and detention), Article 6 (the right to a fair trial), Article 7 (freedom from retrospective penalties), Article 8 (the right to respect for privacy and family life), Article 9 (freedom of thought, conscience and religion), Article 10 (right to free speech), Article 11 (freedom of association), Article 12 (the right to marry and found a family), Article 14 (freedom from discrimination), Article 16 (which restricts the political activity of aliens), Article 17 (prohibition of abuse of rights), and Article 18 (limitation on use of restrictions on rights). In addition the Act incorporates the rights in Protocol 1, Article 1 (the right to peaceful enjoyment of property), Article 2 (the right to education) and Article 3 (the right to free elections).

During the committee stage in the House of Commons it was decided to add the substantive rights in Protocol 6, and these rights were added to those incorporated by the Act. Protocol 6, Article 1 provides for the abolition of the death penalty though the penalty may be used in time of war under Article 2. The White Paper promises that Protocol 7 will be ratified as soon as Parliamentary time can be given to amending the necessary law. Once this happens it is envisaged that the Protocol 7 rights will be incorporated into domestic law by Order under s. 1(4) of the Act. The government's current policy is not to ratify or incorporate the rights contained in Protocol 4. Protocol 12, a substantive equality guarantee, is now open for signature, though the United Kingdom has not yet signed it.

ACKNOWLEDGEMENTS

The list of acknowledgements we ought to make has grown exponentially since the last edition as the 'Human Rights Act debate' has hotted up, and we are enormously grateful to everyone with whom we have discussed the Act.

First, we thank those in other organisations: Francesca Klug (King's College, London), Anne Owers, Jonathan Cooper and Adrian Marshall-Williams (Justice), Andrew Puddephatt and Michele Mitchell (Charter 88), Sarah Spencer (Institute of Public Policy Research), Veena Vasista (the 1990 Trust); and all those colleagues from Liberty and Matrix with whom we have debated our ideas.

We also thank the lawyers who gave their time to Liberty for free during the course of the Bill: Michael Beloff QC, the late Peter Duffy QC, Ben Emmerson QC, Keir Starmer, Rabinder Singh and Murray Hunt; and those in the government service who helped us, particularly Amanda Finlay (Lord Chancellor's Department), Sally Evans, Nigel Varney and James Toon (Home Office).

We would especially like to thank the people who helped to write the book: Jim Murphy (on placement from Boston University) who produced the first drafts of Chapter 8 in the first edition; Janet Arkinstall who wrote the drafts on the protocols in Chapter 9 and checked the text for the first edition; and Anna Edmundson who updated the case law in the second edition, wrote Appendix 7, proof-read and liaised with Blackstone: this was far beyond the call of duty in her job at Liberty or Matrix. We owe them all a very significant debt.

We are also particularly grateful to Justice for allowing us to use their work in dissecting Hansard.

We thank Alistair, David, Heather and Ruth at Blackstone.

Finally we thank Lord Lester of Herne Hill QC for his perennial advocacy of incorporation of the Convention into English law; and the Home Secretary Jack Straw and his team and the Lord Chancellor, Lord Irvine of Lairg, for ensuring that it happened.

The law is up to date as at the end of July 2000.

Any mistakes in the text — of course — are ours.

John Wadham and Helen Mountfield
October 2000

Table of Cases

Table of Statutes

Table of Secondary Legislation

Table of International Conventions

Chapter One
Introduction to the Human Rights Act 1998

1.1 THE EUROPEAN CONVENTION IN UNITED KINGDOM COURTS BEFORE THE 1998 ACT

Even before the Human Rights Act 1998 came into force — indeed, even before the Bill was drafted — it has been possible to use arguments based on the European Convention on Human Rights (referred to in this book as 'the Convention') in English courts. Such arguments have been used in a variety of contexts since the 1970s. The most important pre-Act uses of the Convention have been:

(a) as an aid to the construction of legislation in cases of ambiguity (e.g., *R v Secretary of State for the Home Department, ex parte Brind* [1991] 1 AC 696 at p. 760),

(b) to inform the exercise of judicial (as opposed to administrative) discretion (e.g., *Attorney-General v Guardian Newspapers Ltd* [1987] 1 WLR 1248), and

(c) to establish the scope of the common law (e.g., *Derbyshire County Council v Times Newspapers Ltd* [1992] QB 770 at pp. 812 and 830).

These techniques will continue to be important, and should also still be used in relation to other international Treaties which have not been incorporated into English law. For a more detailed analysis of how this done, see M. Hunt, *Using Human Rights Law in English Courts* (London: Hart Publishing, 1997); M. Beloff and H. Mountfield, 'Unconventional Behaviour? Judicial Uses of the European Convention on Human Rights in England and Wales' [1996] EHRLR 467.

1.2 THE EUROPEAN CONVENTION IN UNITED KINGDOM COURTS AFTER THE 1998 ACT

The Human Rights Act 1998 will make the Convention far more central to the practice of law in Britain.

Until now, there was no overriding presumption that Parliament intended in the past and intends in the future to legislate so as to conform with the rights protected by the Convention. The use of the Convention was limited to cases where the law was ambiguous. Public authorities had no duty to exercise administrative discretions in a manner which complied with the Convention, nor even to have regard to the rights contained in the Convention as 'relevant considerations' when reaching a decision (*R* v *Secretary of State for the Home Department, ex parte Brind* [1991] 1 AC 696) except where they had expressly stated that they would do so (e.g., *Britton* v *Secretary of State for the Environment* [1997] JPL 617).

The Act changed that. Its purpose is to extend the ways in which the Convention can be used before domestic courts while retaining the existing ones. It is described in its long title as 'An Act to give *further* effect' to the rights and freedoms guaranteed under the Convention. The method adopted, however, is a complex one, reflecting a delicate political compromise between 'incorporating' Convention rights, and retaining Parliamentary sovereignty.

The Act creates a statutory general requirement that all legislation (past or future) be read and given effect in a way which is compatible with the Convention. Section 3 provides that all legislation, primary and secondary, whenever enacted, must be read and given effect in a way which is compatible with Convention rights *wherever possible* (see 3.2). Now the Act is in force, it is no longer necessary to find ambiguity in order to use the Convention as an interpretative tool (see Lord Irvine of Lairg, 'The Development of Human Rights Under an Incorporated Convention on Human Rights' [1998] PL 221 at p. 228).

Secondly, s. 6 of the Act requires public authorities — including courts — to act compatibility with the Convention unless they are prevented from doing so by statute. This means that the courts have their own primary statutory duty to give effect to the Convention unless a statute positively prevents this. Section 7 gives the victim of any act of a public authority that is incompatible with the Convention the power to challenge the authority in court using the Convention to found a cause of action or as a defence. However, only persons classified as 'victims' by s. 7 of the Act are able to enforce the duty to act compatibly with the Convention in proceedings against the authority, and only victims will have standing to bring proceedings by way of judicial review. Most private litigants, at least in private law proceedings, will count as victims. Non-victims will be able to rely on s. 3 of the Act, and the common-law approach to Convention obligations.

The way in which the Act can be used by litigants who qualify as 'victims' depends upon whether their opponents are public authorities, quasi-public authorities (see 4.3) or private persons.

1.3   CORE PROVISIONS OF THE ACT

The Human Rights Act 1998 will radically alter the interpretation and use of all other legislation. The overriding objective is to weave the Convention into the existing legal system, so that all courts will consider Convention arguments, and rights which could have been obtained in Strasbourg can be secured in national courts, whilst minimising disruption to the existing legal system. The overall scheme is as follows.

Section 1 and sch. 1 define the 'Convention rights' which have been incorporated, subject to any designated derogations or reservations (see Chapter 9). Article 13 (the right to an effective remedy in a national court) is not specifically designated as a 'Convention right' within this definition. The Secretary of State has power, by order, to amend the list of rights to include Article 13, or in accordance with any protocols to the Convention which the United Kingdom may adopt in future.

Section 2 requires any court or tribunal determining a question which has arisen in connection with a Convention right to take into account the jurisprudence of the Strasbourg organs (the European Court and Commission of Human Rights and the Committee of Ministers). This jurisprudence must be considered 'so far as, in the opinion of the court or tribunal, it is relevant to the proceedings in which that question has arisen', whenever the judgment, decision or opinion to be taken into account was handed down.

Section 3 requires primary and subordinate legislation to be read and given effect in a way which is compatible with Convention rights, so far as it is possible to do so, and whether the legislation in question was enacted before or after the Human Rights Act 1998. Section 3 is a general requirement, presumably addressed to any person reading the legislation, not just to courts.

Section 19 of the Act will assist, in relation to future legislation, with the presumption that legislation is to be (and can be) read compatibly with the Convention. It provides that when legislation is introduced into Parliament for a second reading, the introducing minister must make a statement, either to the effect that, in his or her view, the legislation is compatible with the Convention, or make a statement that although the legislation is not compatible with the Convention, the government still wishes to proceed. It is unlikely that governments will often wish to state publicly that they are acting incompatibly with an internationally binding human rights instrument, but there are limited 'designated derogations and reservations' from the effect of the Convention (ss. 1(2), 14 to 17 and sch. 2 and sch. 3).

If it is not possible to read legislation so as to give effect to the Convention, it is provided in s. 3(2)(b) and (c) that this does not affect the validity, continuing operation or enforcement of the legislation. In such circumstances, however, s. 4 empowers the high courts to make a 'declaration of incompatibility', described in more detail in 5.2. The Crown has a right under s. 5 to intervene in proceedings where such a declaration may be made.

Section 10 and sch. 2 provide a 'fast-track' procedure by which the executive can act to amend legislation in order to remove incompatibility with the Convention where a declaration of incompatibility has been made.

Section 6 makes it unlawful for a public authority to act in a way which is incompatible with a Convention right unless it is required to do so by primary legislation which cannot be interpreted compatibly with the Convention. However, a 'public authority' does not include either House of Parliament, and 'act' does not include a failure to legislate.

Section 6(3)(a) makes courts and tribunals public authorities, and so subject to their own primary duty to act compatibly with the Convention. By virtue of s. 6(3)(b) and (5) a body whose functions are partly public and partly private is a 'public authority' in relation to its functions 'of a public nature' but not in relation to acts which are private in nature. Such bodies are called 'quasi-public' bodies in this book.

Section 7(1)(a) permits a victim of an act by a public authority which infringes a Convention right to bring proceedings 'in the appropriate court or tribunal'. Section 7(1)(b) permits a person to rely on the Convention right or rights concerned in any legal proceedings against the public authority.

Section 7(5) imposes a limitation period for bringing proceedings under s. 7(1)(a). Section 22(4) provides that s. 7(1)(b) can be used as a *defence* whenever the act in question took place, but proceedings may be instigated under s. 7(1)(b) only in relation to acts committed after the section comes into force.

The 'appropriate court or tribunal' for bringing proceedings against public authorities, and incidental jurisdictional matters such as the remedies which such courts or tribunals may provide, have been laid down in rules made by the Secretary of State concerned or the Lord Chancellor (s. 7(2) and (9) to (12)). These are contained in Appendix 2 of this book.

Section 7(1) may only be used by a person who is or would be a 'victim' of the unlawful act, as defined in s. 7(7). Section 7(3) provides that in proceedings brought by way of judicial review, the applicant is to be taken to have a sufficient interest in relation to the unlawful act only if he is, or would be, a victim of it.

Section 8(1) gives a court a wide power to grant such relief, remedies or orders as it considers just and appropriate, provided they are within its existing powers. By virtue of s. 7(11), the powers of existing courts or tribunals may be enlarged by order. To date, no such order has been made. Damages may be awarded in civil proceedings but s. 8(2) provides that such damages may only be awarded by a court which has power to order the payment of damages or compensation in civil proceedings. By virtue of s. 8(3), damages may only be awarded if necessary to afford 'just satisfaction', and s. 8(4) provides that in determining whether to award damages and the amount to award, the court must take account of the principes applied by the European Court of Human Rights in relation to awards of compensation under Article 41 of the Convention.

Section 9 focuses on how the 'public body' provisions operate against courts which have allegedly acted contrary to the Convention. Proceedings in respect of judicial acts under s. 7(1)(a) may only be brought by exercising a right of appeal, or as prescribed by rules. However, awards of damages may be made against the Crown if they are necessary to compensate a person as required by Article 5(5) of the Convention (see 5.1).

Section 11 provides, for the avoidance of doubt, that reliance on Convention rights (as specified in the Act) does not restrict reliance on other legal rights, or procedural methods of enforcing them.

Sections 12 and 13 provide specific assurances as to the respect which will be afforded to freedom of expression and freedom of thought, conscience and religion: these are 'comfort clauses' for sections of the press and certain religious organisations.

1.4 SUMMARY OF THE EFFECTS OF THE ACT

The effect of the Human Rights Act 1998 on English law is the subject of chapters 3 to 6, where the features of the Act are set out in more detail. In summary:

(a) In *all* cases in which Convention rights are in question, the Act gives 'further effect' to the Convention, whether the litigants are private persons or public authorities. It will do this in three ways:

(i)   by obliging courts to decide all cases before them (whether brought under statute or the common law) compatibly with Convention rights unless prevented from doing so either by primary legislation or by provisions made under primary legislation which cannot be read compatibly with the Convention (s. 6(1) to (3));

(ii)   by introducing an obligation upon courts to interpret existing and future legislation in conformity with the Convention wherever possible (s. 3);

(iii)   by requiring courts to take Strasbourg case law into account in all cases, in so far as they consider it is relevant to proceedings before them (s. 2(1)).

(b)   The Act will not make Convention rights *directly* enforceable against a private litigant; nor against a quasi-public body with some public functions if it is acting in a private capacity (see 4.3). But in cases against a private litigant, the Act still has an effect on the outcome, because the court will be obliged to interpret legislation in conformity with the Convention wherever possible; must exercise any judicial discretions compatibly with the Convention; and must ensure that its application of common law or equitable rules is compatible with the Convention.

(c)   Section 7 of the Act will create new, directly enforceable rights against public bodies, and against quasi-public bodies which have some public functions when they are acting in the sphere of those public functions (see 4.3). First, it introduces a new ground of illegality into proceedings brought by way of judicial review, namely, a failure to comply with the Convention rights protected by the Act, subject to a 'statutory obligation' defence. Secondly, it will create a new cause of action against public bodies which fail to act compatibly with the Convention. Thirdly, Convention rights will be available as a ground of defence or appeal in cases brought by public bodies against private bodies (in both criminal and civil cases).

(d)   Even a litigant who cannot challenge a public body's decision using the Act's provisions, because not a victim of the decision, will be able to rely on the court's s. 3 interpretive obligations and use Convention arguments in the circumstances in which this was possible before the Act was brought into force (s. 11).

(e)   The Act will not permit the Convention to be used so as to override primary legislation: if a statute is clear in its terms, and clearly incompatible with the Convention, courts must give it effect. Equally, if the terms of the primary legislation require subordinate legislation made under it (which will usually be in a statutory instrument) to be interpreted in a way which means that the subordinate legislation is incompatible with the Convention, it must still be given effect even though this may result in a breach of a Convention right. To that extent, Parliamentary sovereignty is preserved (s. 3(2)(b) and (c)). But if legislation cannot be read so as to comply with the Convention, the higher courts will have power to issue 'declarations of incompatibility', and a fast-track procedure exists whereby the government can legislate to remedy such incompatibility (ss. 4 and 10 and sch. 2).

(f)   The Act is likely to have a substantial effect in areas of court procedures and procedural rules, particularly with respect to the rules of evidence. It is generally considered that this will have the greatest effects in the criminal courts, but it will also affect civil courts and tribunals.

1.5   HISTORY OF INCORPORATION OF THE CONVENTION

Although the United Kingdom was among the first signatories to the European Convention on Human Rights in 1951, moves to make it part of our domestic law are of more recent origin. Part of the reason for this is the British political and constitutional tradition. 'Freedom' as it has emerged in this tradition rests largely on the (negative) freedom from government interference rather than positive human rights guarantees, enshrined in a written constitution or human rights instrument.

In 1215, England had Magna Carta, which introduced the concepts of due process and trial by jury. In 1688, the Bill of Rights limited the monarch's powers, in most respects, to those permitted by Parliament. In the eighteenth and early nineteenth centuries, many ideas which we regard as central to the rule of law — such as a philosophy of liberty and the notion of the freedom of the press — were developed in the ideas of English thinkers such as Thomas Paine, John Locke and J.S. Mill. But Britain is unusual among developed democracies in having had no written constitution and no positive guarantees of rights. The foundation of our liberties has been a negative one, outlined in nineteenth-century Diceyan theory: we are free to do everything except that which we are forbidden to do by law.

The enormous growth of the power of public and quasi-public bodies over the lives of individuals during the twentieth century has diluted the power of Parliament to scrutinise legislation — if, indeed, it ever had such omniscience. In any case, as J.S. Mill observed in *On Liberty*, democracy is not in itself a guarantee against the tyranny of the majority over unpopular minorities. The negative concept of liberty, so strong in traditional English constitutional thinking, has not been enough to preserve the values enshrined in international rights instruments such as the European Convention on Human Rights.

The Convention was drafted with a significant input from English lawyers and the United Kingdom ratified the Convention in 1951 and recognised the individual right of petition in 1966. But the positive guarantees of 'fundamental rights' contained in the Convention have been found, by the European Court of Human Rights, to have been violated by the United Kingdom in a surprising number of cases (see the list in M. Hunt, *Using Human Rights Law in English Courts* (London: Hart Publishing, 1997, Appendix 1).

Part of the difficulty has been the inability of the judiciary to consider and develop our law consistently with the Convention. Under the dualist principles of English law, the Convention did not have legal effect domestically because it was an international treaty which had not been incorporated into our domestic law by Act of Parliament. 'Parliamentary sovereignty' is the traditional touchstone for accountability in Britain, rather than, as in many European and American jurisdictions, 'the rule of law'. Many thinkers, indeed, have warned against the perils of giving an excess of political power to an unelected and unaccountable judiciary. The best known exponent of this cautious approach to written bills of rights is John Griffith, *The Politics of the Judiciary*, 5th ed. (London: Fontana Press, 1997).

Over the past 30 years, views on the incorporation of the Convention into domestic law have slowly changed, culminating in the Human Rights Act 1998. In 1968, the publication of the Fabian pamphlet, *Democracy and Individual Rights* by Anthony Lester (now Lord Lester of Herne Hill QC), effectively opened the debate in a contemporary context. Anthony Lester was particularly concerned with the role of government in passing a variety of xenophobic Acts during the twentieth century (including the Aliens Act 1905, the Aliens Act 1914, the Commonwealth Immigrants Act 1962 and the Commonwealth Immigrants Act 1968) and how these had affected the rights of people fleeing persecution in their own country or had restricted the rights of New Commonwealth citizens legitimately settling in this country. He also highlighted concern about the power of individual officers of the state, the inability to scrutinise their procedures, and the inadequate machinery for dealing with complaints against the police and other agencies of the state. Lester suggested that incorporating the Convention was only a first step for enshrining human rights guarantees but would be no more than an interim measure.

In subsequent years, the issue of incorporating the Convention was debated a number of times from a variety of political perspectives. Lord Lambton proposed a Bill, from a Conservative perspective, to protect individuals from state intervention. The initiative in promoting a Bill of Rights then passed to the liberal MP John Macdonald (*A Bill of Rights* — Liberal Party Pamphlet) and fellow liberals Lord Wade and Emlyn Hooson introduced motions in the Lords and Commons respectively. The burgeoning power of the executive and the threat to individual freedom from new technology were reasons given for the new need for such a Bill.

An important step was made in 1974 when Sir Leslie Scarman (now Lord Scarman) delivered the first of his Hamlyn lectures (*English Law – The New Dimension*). He spoke of the need for an instrument to challenge the sovereignty of Parliament and to protect basic human rights which could not be adequately protected by the legislature alone. Scarman was in favour of entrenchment. He believed that only by making a Bill of Rights superior to the machinations of Parliament could such fundamental rights be protected.

In the mid 1970s, a Bill of Rights appeared to gain support from all sides of the political spectrum, though support was most vociferous from Conservative sources. In particular, Sir Keith Joseph, concerned by industrial unrest and a Labour Employment Bill, believed that a Bill of Rights could work to protect private property and to challenge the unfettered power of the executive. Other Conservatives, such as Sir Geoffrey Howe (now Lord Howe of Aberavon) and Leon Brittan also supported the idea of a Bill of Rights. Lord Hailsham of St Marylebone, who had previously favoured incorporation of the European Convention into English law shifted his views, and supported a new British Constitution (*The Times*, 9 May 1975). Later in 1975, James Kilfedder MP (an Ulster Unionist) moved that the government establish a Royal Commission to investigate the United Kingdom Bill of Rights question (Hansard HC, 7 July 1975, col. 32) although the motion was withdrawn after being damned with faint praise by the Minister of State from the Home Office, Dr Shirley Summerskill. However, the next week, a Bill of Rights was introduced to the House of Commons by Alan Beith MP, a Liberal, as a 10-minute-rule Bill (Hansard HC, 15 July 1975, cols 1270–3).

In 1975, the Labour Party National Executive Committee unveiled a *Charter of Human Rights*. This document advocated an unentrenched Human Rights Act. This 'unentrenched' proposal was regarded as insufficient by many who considered that such an Act would offer inadequate protection to individual interests against the burgeoning power of the state. In particular, many Tories preferred the concept of a Bill of Rights with entrenched clauses that would prevent even Parliament from granting the executive excessive power over the lives of individuals.

In 1976, Lord Wade (a Liberal Peer) moved a Bill in the Lords which proposed to entrench the Convention as a part of all existing legislation and to make it an entrenched part of all subsequent enactments unless Parliament specifically legislated otherwise (Hansard HL, 25 March 1976, col. 757 et seq.). Lord Wade and Lord Harris continued to be the chief advocates for a Bill of Rights in the Lords. However, they were met with traditional constitutional views, and particularly a concern about the idea of judges deciding 'human rights' cases. The fear was that this would remove the judiciary from its traditionally impartial role, supposedly beyond politics, and embroil it in (party) political questions.

In June 1976, the Home Office published a discussion document drafted by Anthony Lester, which argued in favour of incorporation of the Convention. This was followed by the Highgate House conference, attended by a number of experts in the human rights field from the United Kingdom and abroad (see M. Zander, *A Bill of Rights?* (1997)). Roy Jenkins (now Lord Jenkins of Hillhead), the then Home Secretary, delivered an address in favour of incorporation.

The Society of Conservative Lawyers were on record as favouring incorporation, if not a full Bill of Rights (*Another Bill of Rights* (1976)). In January 1977, Leon

Brittan, then Opposition front-bench spokesman on devolution, promised to table an amendment to the Scotland and Wales Bill that would incorporate the Convention in Scotland and Wales (*The Times*, 15 January 1977). However, the Bill was eventually withdrawn and Opposition amendments not heard. The issue was raised again by Brittan during the committee stage of the Scotland Bill a year later (Hansard HC, 1 February 1978, col. 491). It was opposed by John Smith MP. He stated that the Labour government's position was as outlined in the discussion paper of 1975 but permitted the matter to go to a vote. This was the first occasion a Bill of Rights had been debated in the lower House and the Opposition amendment was defeated by 25 votes.

A few weeks after this, the subject was again raised by Lord Wade in the Lords (Hansard HL, 3 February 1977, col. 973). Lord Hailsham moved that a select committee should be established and it subsequently elicited a wide range of views. The committee eventually reported that whilst it agreed that the Convention should be the basis for any domestic Bill of Rights, it could not reach agreement on whether it was desirable or undesirable to place such a Bill on the statute book. The committee also observed that a Bill of Rights should not be imbued with too many expectations and that ultimately the political climate and nature of the country were of greater importance in the protection of human rights.

Following the change of government in May 1979, Lord Wade continued to move Bills to incorporate the Convention into English law through the Lords, although they were always defeated in the Commons. Despite Conservative support for incorporation whilst in opposition, in government they took no action towards this. In June 1984, however, 107 Tory backbenchers signed an Early Day Motion calling for incorporation. The Thatcher Cabinet did not respond.

In 1985, the Conservative peer Lord Broxbourne (formerly Derek Walker-Smith QC, MP) introduced the Human Rights and Fundamental Freedoms Bill, which called for incorporation of the Convention. Having passed through the Lords, it reached the Commons a year later with cross-party support. It was introduced in the Commons by Sir Edward Gardner QC. However, it was opposed by the front benches of the government and the Labour opposition (Hansard HC, 6 February 1987, col. 1223 et seq.). Once again, the chief objection was that the proposals would result in the politicisation of the judiciary.

The official Labour Party line was still to oppose incorporation of the Convention or the creation of a judicially enforced Bill of Rights (see Roy Hattersley, then Deputy Leader (now Lord Hattersley), writing in *The Guardian*, 12 December 1988). By 1991, however, views within the Labour Party began to alter. In the interim, a number of influential think tanks and pressure groups had published documents supporting a Bill of Rights, including Liberty's consultation document, *A People's Charter — Liberty's Bill of Rights*. The Labour Party produced the *Charter of Rights* which listed 40 'human rights' topics upon which it wished to legislate without mentioning a Bill of Rights (see L. Parratt, 'Unfinished Business?' in Hegarty, A., Leonard S. (eds), *Human Rights in the Twenty First Century*, Cavendish, 1999).

It was not until 1993 that there was a clear shift in Labour Party policy, and the leadership (now under John Smith) started to voice more enthusiasm for a Bill of Rights (see, for instance, Francesca Klug, *A People's Charter: Liberty's Bill of Rights* (1991); Michael Zander, *A Bill of Rights?* (1997)). John Smith gave his support to the incorporation of the Convention in 1993: *The Guardian*, 2 March 1993. Though it was a Labour government which, in 1950, had signed and ratified the Convention and, in January 1966, granted individuals the right to complain to the Commission and Court, the May 1997 election campaign was the first one which Labour fought on the basis of a commitment to incorporate the Convention into domestic law.

The Labour Party conference in October 1993 had adopted a policy supporting a two-stage process to implement mechanisms to enforce rights. The first included the incorporation of the European Convention of Human Rights, entrenching this set of rights by the use of a 'notwithstanding clause' procedure. This was similar to the Canadian Charter of Rights and Freedoms, and would have led to the Convention overriding domestic law. The conference also advocated the establishment of a human rights commission to monitor and promote human rights. The second stage was for a Labour government to set up an all-party commission to consider and draft a home-grown Bill of Rights for future implementation. Graham Allen MP, who was then shadow spokesperson on constitutional affairs, promoted the Human Rights (No. 3) Bill (19 October 1993), which was drafted by Liberty. Tony Blair MP set out his views in *The Guardian*, 16 July 1994, and reaffirmed the need for strengthened incorporation and the idea of a 'notwithstanding clause'.

Lord Lester of Herne Hill continued his human rights work in the Lords by introducing a Bill in November 1994. The Bill did not receive support from the Conservative government. Particular aspects of the proposed Bill were criticised by the Law Lords but they supported incorporation in so far as it allowed United Kingdom judges to interpret human rights away from Strasbourg. The fact that a human rights Bill had received any support from the Law Lords was a significant development.

By December 1996, Jack Straw MP and Paul Boateng MP published a consultation paper, *Bringing Rights Home*, setting out the Labour Party's plans to incorporate the European Convention on Human Rights if they won the election due in 1997. Whereas the 1993 policy had advocated incorporation to be followed by a second stage in the form of a home-grown Bill of Rights, the consultation paper deferred the second stage, and the five key issues posed by the paper only concerned the incorporation of the Convention. Some months earlier, the Society of Labour Lawyers had published *Law Reform for All* (London: Blackstone Press, 1996), which included a chapter written by Lord Irvine of Lairg, then the shadow Lord Chancellor. The part of the chapter relating to human rights reproduced parts of the 1993 policy but omitted completely any reference to a domestic Bill of Rights.

The Liberal Democrats (and before them, the Liberals) have a longer history of support for a Bill of Rights and the incorporation of the Convention (M. Zander,

A Bill of Rights? (1997)). But the 1997 Report of the Joint Consultative Committee on Constitutional Reform, which announced the joint agreement between the Labour Party and the Liberal Democrats, said little about a Bill of Rights beyond the commitment to incorporation of the Convention into British law.

In May 1997, Labour won a landslide victory, on a manifesto which included a commitment to incorporate the European Convention on Human Rights into domestic law. The debate then turned to *how* the Convention should be incorporated and in particular whether it should be permitted to override statutes, subject to a 'notwithstanding' clause. The unique solution adopted in the Human Rights Act 1998 is the subject of chapters 3 to 6 of this book.

Chapter Two
Introduction to the Convention

The European Convention for the Protection of Human Rights and Fundamental Freedoms is a treaty agreed by governments which are members of the Council of Europe. The Council of Europe was established in 1949 as part of the Allies' programme to 'reconstruct durable civilisation on the mainland of Europe'. Today it has over 40 members with a wide variety of political traditions, including many former Communist states from Eastern Europe. The United Kingdom ratified the Convention in 1951 but, unlike many of the other signatories, did not set about incorporating the Convention rights into domestic law. Incorporation was thought to be unnecessary, as it was believed that the rights safeguarded by the Convention already flowed from British common law. The Convention came into force on 3 September 1953.

The unusual feature of the Convention, as an international human rights instrument, is that it provides a mechanism for individuals to enforce it against states which allow the right of 'individual petition', as well as allowing states to bring proceedings against one another. In 1966 the United Kingdom granted the right of individual petition. This has meant that, even before its incorporation into domestic law, the Convention has offered individual litigants in Britain the possibility of redress in international law where their civil liberties have been infringed by the state and where no adequate remedy can be provided by the domestic courts. (It is important to appreciate that as a matter of international law, the Convention creates rights against states, not as against private individuals.)

The Convention originally established three bodies to monitor human rights within the countries that had ratified it. These bodies were the European Commission of Human Rights, the European Court of Human Rights and the Committee of Ministers. All were based in Strasbourg. Until November 1998, these first two bodies heard complaints from individuals about violations of their rights. Protocol 11 to the Convention brought major changes to the Strasbourg mechanisms. From November 1999, the Commission ceased to exist. Instead, all cases are dealt with by the European Court of Human Rights. The procedure for doing this is described in chapter 11. Decisions of the Court are binding on the country concerned.

The Convention's provisions guarantee most, but not all, civil liberties, including the right to life, freedom from torture, freedom from arbitrary arrest, the right to a fair trial, the right to privacy, freedom of religion, freedom of expression, and freedom of assembly and association. The contents of these rights are considered in chapter 8.

The traditional English law has been to adopt a 'black-letter' approach, closely defining the scope and content of a legislative provision. But the Convention is quite unlike a United Kingdom statute, and the Strasbourg organs do not interpret Convention rights in the same way as English judges traditionally construe domestic statutes. Lawyers will have to become accustomed to this different way of working.

2.1 LIMITATIONS AND QUALIFICATIONS ON CONVENTION RIGHTS

The rights protected under the Convention are framed in very wide terms. Some — such as the right to freedom from torture in Article 3 — are absolute. There are no circumstances in which torture can be performed in the interests of the state. There is no balancing of the right against public interest. But most of the core rights are subject to limitations and qualifications.

These are not precise categories, but rather a way of seeking to understand the structures of the Convention rights. By 'limited rights' we mean rights where the content of the right is set out at the beginning of the article itself, but where the text of the article itself contains certain specific limitations on its scope. These include Articles 4(2) and (3) (prohibition on forced labour), Article 5 (right to liberty and security of the person), Article 6 (right to a fair trial), Article 7 (no punishment without law), Article 12 (right to marry), Protocol 1, Article 2 (right to an education), and Article 14 (prohibition on discrimination).

By 'qualified rights', we mean those articles which are set out in two parts in the text. The first sub-paragraph sets out the substantive right, which is then qualified in the second sub-paragraph of the article. For example, Article 8(1) states, 'Everyone has the right to respect for his private and family life, his home and his correspondence.' This is the presumed right, but a number of limitations and exceptions to it are set out in Article 8(2): 'There shall be no interference by a public authority with the exercise of this right except such as is in accordance with the law and is necessary in a democratic society in the interests of national security, public safety or the economic well-being of the country, for the prevention of disorder or crime, for the protection of health or morals, or for the protection of the rights and freedoms of others.' The precise terms of the limitations attached to the different qualified articles vary (contrast, for example, Article 10(2) with Article 8(2)), but the judicial method for considering them is the same.

The qualified rights tend to be those which most obviously raise conflicts with the overall interests of society or the rights of others — for example, the right to respect for private life (Article 8), and the right to freedom of expression (Article

10) may sometimes compete (see, for example, *Kroon* v *Netherlands* (1994) 19 EHRR 263; *Soering* v *UK* (1989) 11 EHRR 439).

Other qualified rights are Article 9 (insofar as it relates to *manifestation* of religious beliefs), Article 11 (freedom of assembly and association) and Protocol 1, Article 1 (right to peaceful enjoyment of possessions).

Except in relation to absolute rights, the Convention permits rights and freedoms to be limited by the state, provided the limitations have a proper legal basis, legitimate objectives and are proportionate. Once a complaint has been shown to engage a primary right, the Strasbourg institutions consider the limitations and qualifications upon it in order to determine whether there has been a violation. There is a presumption that a right identified in the Convention is protected and the limitations and exceptions are subject to this presumption.

The Convention seeks to balance the rights of the individual against other public interests. But the object of human rights jurisprudence in democratic systems is to ensure that democracy does not mean that the tyranny of the majority causes disproportionate interference with the rights of minorities. The Convention therefore seeks to ensure that the limitations which the majority may place upon an individual's protected rights, in the name of the common or competing interests, are imposed only if they are prescribed by law, intended to achieve a legitimate objective, and are necessary in a democratic society (that is, proportionate to the end to be achieved).

Once the prima facie right is engaged, the Strasbourg institutions ask (and, now with the Human Rights Act 1998 in force, domestic courts will ask), 'Is the interference in accordance with or prescribed by law; does it serve a legitimate objective; and is it necessary in a democratic society?'

2.2   THE RULE OF LAW

The concept of the rule of law is a core concept in the Convention. It is described in the preamble to the Convention as part of the 'common heritage' which the signatories share, and is one of the 'fundamental principles of a democratic society' (*Iatridis* v *Greece*, 25 March 1999, para. 62). Rights and freedoms can compete, and states may limit citizens' rights or curtail their freedoms for certain specified and legitimate purposes. But no matter how desirable the end to be achieved, no interference with a right protected under the Convention is permissible unless the citizen knows the basis for the interference because it is set out in an ascertainable law which is accessible and certain. In the absence of such detailed authorisation by the law, any interference, however justified, will violate the Convention. In Strasbourg jurisprudence, a derogation must also have an ascertainable legal basis, that is, be 'prescribed by law' or 'in accordance with the law'.

Article 5 of the European Convention, for example, protects the liberty of the person. It is perhaps best described as protecting individuals from 'arbitrary detention'. Under Article 5 the state can lawfully detain a person in prison following conviction, for contempt of court, on arrest on a criminal charge, because he or she is mentally ill, or in order to deport or to extradite the detained person. But no detention is permitted unless it is 'in accordance with a procedure prescribed by law' — administrative decisions to detain are not sufficient. There are similar limitations on the right to free expression (Article 10) and assembly (Article 11). But, again, any such interference must be 'in accordance with the law' or must be 'prescribed by law'. No such interference can be permitted by executive rules alone.

The phrases 'prescribed by law' or 'in accordance with the law' mean that there must be an ascertainable legal regime governing the interference in question. But they mean more than a simple search for a national legal rule which permits the derogation. To be 'prescribed by law' for Convention purposes, the starting point is that there must be a basis for what is done in national law. But this is no more than a starting point. The idea of a lawful action is also 'imbued with a Convention idea of the essential qualities of law' (Harris, O'Boyle, Warbrick, *The Law of the European Convention on Human Rights*, Butterworths, 1995). A national rule will not constitute a law for Convention purposes unless it has appropriate qualities to make it compatible with the rule of law (see *Kopp* v *Sweden* (1999) 27 EHRR 91, paras 55 and 64).

The Strasbourg court explained the concept in *Sunday Times* v *United Kingdom* (1979) 2 EHRR 245 at para. 49:

> Firstly, the law must be adequately accessible: the citizens must be able to have an indication that is adequate in the circumstances of the legal rules applicable to a given case. Secondly, a norm cannot be regarded as a 'law' unless it is formulated with sufficient precision to enable the citizen to regulate his conduct.

What is sufficiently certain will depend on the circumstances. Internal guidelines from government departments probably do not fulfil the accessibility requirement unless they are published or their content made known (see *Govell* v *United Kingdom* [1999] EHRLR 121). Statute law, secondary legislation, applicable rules of EU law (see *Groppera Radio AG* v *Switzerland* (1990) 12 EHRR 321), ascertainable rules of common law (see *Sunday Times* v *United Kingdom* above) and even the rules of professional bodies (see *Barthold* v *Germany* (1985) 7 EHRR 383) may be sufficient.

In the *Sunday Times* case the Court said that:

> whilst certainty is highly desirable, it may bring in its train excessive rigidity and the law must be able to keep pace with changing circumstances. Accordingly, many laws are inevitably couched in terms which, to a greater or lesser extent, are vague and whose interpretation and application are questions of practice.

In *Wingrove* v *United Kingdom* (1997) 24 EHRR 1 and *Müller* v *Switzerland* (1988) 13 EHRR 212, which were cases involving freedom of expression, the

Court accepted that the concepts of blasphemy and obscenity were not capable of precise definition. In *Kokkinakis v Greece* (1993) 17 EHRR 397, the Court recognised that many statutes were imprecise in their wording. It accepted the need to avoid excessive rigidity and to keep pace with changing circumstances.

Nonetheless, the basic rule is that the legal basis for an interference be ascertainable and certain. It is not acceptable for an interference with a Convention right to occur without any legal regulation (e.g., *Halford v United Kingdom* (1997) 24 EHRR 523, regarding office phone tapping). In *Malone v United Kingdom* (1984) 7 EHRR 14 the applicant's telephone was tapped by the police. At the time this took place the only regulation of the practice was an internal code of guidance produced by the police which was not public. The European Court of Human Rights took the view that Mr Malone was not therefore able to assess whether or not his telephone would be listened in to or what the basis in law for the surveillance might be. The common law was inadequate in this case as was clear from the failure of Mr Malone's proceedings in the High Court (*Malone v Metropolitan Police Commissioner* [1979] Ch 344). Accordingly, the interference violated the Convention because it was not prescribed by law. (The Interception of Communications Act 1985 was introduced as a result of this case.)

The Convention concept of legality is capable of having a substantial effect on the development of English law. It can be used as a powerful democratic tool for accountability: to ensure that the executive legislates accessibly, creating a positive and foreseeable legal basis for its actions, and to strengthen the powers of the courts to restrain interference with fundamental rights.

An example of how Convention case law may affect the English approach is to contrast the European Court of Human Rights judgment in *Amann v Switzerland*, 16 February 2000, with the decision of the English Court of Appeal in *R v Secretary of State for Health, ex parte C* (2000) *The Times*, 1 March, decided a few days later.

In *Amann,* a businessman had a call from a woman in the former Soviet embassy in Berne. The call was intercepted by the Federal Public Prosecutor's office, which made an entry in its security index, noting that Mr Amann was a businessman, a contact with the Russian embassy, and that espionage was established. The European Court held that this interference with Mr Amann's Article 8 rights was not 'in accordance with the law' because the Swiss legal provisions relied upon did not contain specific and detailed provisions on the gathering, recording, storing or destruction of the data to comply with the requirement of foreseeable application, or to permit proper safeguards against abuse. Notwithstanding the existence of a domestic legal basis for it, the interference was held not to be 'in accordance with the law'.

There are some dicta in recent English cases to like effect — see *R v Secretary of State for the Home Department, ex parte Pierson* [1998] AC 539 and *R v Secretary of State for the Home Department, ex parte Simms* [1999] 3 WLR 328, especially per Lord Steyn at 340.

There is a stark contrast, however, between the approach in *Amann* and that adopted by the English Court of Appeal in *ex parte C.* That case concerned a challenge to the legality of an index, which the Department of Health made available to employers, of people about whom there might be doubts as to their suitability to work with children. There is no statutory basis for this index, whose existence is regulated only by Departmental Circular. The Court of Appeal held that the Crown, as a corporation with legal personality, had 'the same capacities and liberties' as a natural person, but could not infringe private rights of others without lawful authority. Since no one had a right to a job (justiciable under Article 6 of the Convention), the index was not unlawful. The concept of legality used in this decision is the Diceyan idea that the Crown can do anything which is not made illegal by some countervailing private right. Using the Convention concept of legality, however, the 'negative freedom' for the Crown to do what it likes is unlikely to provide a sufficient positive legal basis to allow interference with rights (for example, under Article 8 of the Convention).

It is interesting to contrast the decision in *ex parte C* with the decision in *Amann* and to ask whether *ex parte C* would have been decided in the same way if the *Amann* decision had been brought to its attention. It is unlikely that it would have been so decided and, in future cases, the domestic court would have been obliged to take *Amann* into account by virtue of s. 2 of the Human Rights Act 1998 (see further Grosz, Law Society Gazette, May 2000).

One effect of the incorporation of the Convention into English law, therefore, may be to shift our constitutional thinking, so that those exercising executive power, and those scrutinising it, analyse the issue not in terms of the Crown's liberty to act (in a negative sense), but seek instead a positive legal basis for state interference with citizens' freedoms (see further, Mountfield 'The Concept of Legality' in the UCL/Justice Autumn 1999 Seminar Series, Hart, 2000).

2.3   LEGITIMATE AIMS

In order to provide a defence to a claim under the Convention any interference by a public authority with a Convention right capable of qualification must be directed towards an identified legitimate aim. In Articles 8, 9, 10 and 11 the legitimate aims are set out in the second part of each article. The sorts of aims which are legitimate are the interests of public safety, national security, the protection of health and morals and the economic well-being of the country or the protection of the rights and freedoms of others.

The Convention provides a large number of acceptable reasons for restricting rights and they have a wide scope. It is not difficult for a country facing an allegation of a breach of human rights to find a reason relevant to any case. The Strasbourg authorities have had difficulty in assessing allegations made by applicants that the legitimate aim identified by the respondent was not the 'real' aim of the restriction. For example, in *Campbell* v *United Kingdom* (1992) 15 EHRR 137 a prisoner complained about the authorities opening his correspondence with his lawyer. He argued that the real reason was to assess the contents. The government claimed that the interference was for the purposes of the prevention of disorder or crime. More than one aim can be identified by a respondent state although only one is necessary to defeat the claim.

In the case of limited rights the only restrictions on the right that are justified are those set out in the article itself. For example, in connection with Article 5, the limitations on detention must be narrowly interpreted (*Winterwerp* v *Netherlands* (1979) 2 EHRR 387). Whereas in the context of, for example, the restrictions on the right to a public hearing in Article 6, such restrictions are more akin to the qualifications in Articles 8 to 11.

2.4 PROPORTIONALITY

The third important concept which the Strasbourg institutions use when assessing whether a Convention right has been improperly violated is that of proportionality: the test of whether the interference is 'necessary in a democratic society'.

The Convention approach is to decide whether a particular qualification of a right is justified in the sense of being 'proportionate to the legitimate aim pursued' (*Handyside* v *United Kingdom* (1976) 1 EHRR 737). This means that even if a policy which interferes with a Convention right might be aimed at securing a legitimate aim of social policy, for example, the prevention of crime, this will not in itself justify the violation if the means adopted to secure the aim are excessive in the circumstances. The importance of the aim in question and the actual situation which is subject to dispute are important: 'action for the prevention of crime may be directed against homicide or parking offences: the weight of each compared with the right sought to be limited is not the same' (Harris, O'Boyle and Warbrick, p. 297).

The test of proportionality also contains within it its own concept of procedural fairness. An infringement of a qualified right is much less likely to be a proportionate response to a legitimate aim if the person affected by the action were not consulted or not given the right to a hearing than if he or she were given such opportunities. In many cases the more substantial rights set out in Article 6 will apply, but even where they do not the Convention will impose similar duties where possible.

Thus, for instance, a decision to make a place of safety order and to remove a child from its parents may be justified on its merits, but if the parents (and in some circumstances the child) can be consulted and/or attend or be represented at the hearing of the court that takes this decision, then their Article 8 right to family life is less likely to be violated. In such a case Article 6 may not apply because this interim decision is not the 'determination' of the issue. Nevertheless, their right to family life has been interfered with even if only for a temporary period. If it is possible to allow them to participate in the decision-making process, this in itself is more likely to comply with the proportionality test in Article 8 irrespective of the outcome.

In general, as the European Court of Human Rights put it in the case of *Soering* v *United Kingdom* (1989) 11 EHRR 439 at para. 89:

inherent in the whole of the Convention is a search for the fair balance between the demands of the general interest of the community and the requirements of the protection of the individual's human rights.

The test of whether the measure adopted by the member state is 'necessary in a democratic society' or proportionate to the end to be achieved is different from that traditionally used in English law. It will therefore alter the standard of review of the actions of public authorities in cases where Convention rights are engaged.

Before the commencement of the Human Rights Act 1998, the test for challenging the actions of public authorities by way of judicial review was that they must be unlawful or else 'irrational'. In Lord Diplock's often quoted explanation, 'a decision which is so outrageous in its defiance of logic or accepted moral standards that no sensible person who had applied his mind to the question to be decided could have arrived at it'. (*Council of Civil Service Unions* v *Minister for the Civil Service* [1985] AC 375 at p. 410). It is very hard to challenge a decision on this basis, although, in later cases where fundamental rights are at stake, the test has been redefined: see the formulation in *R* v *Ministry of Defence, ex parte Smith* [1996] QB 517.

Where there has been a prima facie violation of a right protected by the Convention, the Strasbourg Court has adopted a more stringent standard in considering whether the state can justify the limitation of that right. Because the Convention starts with a presumption that a right contained in the first part of a Convention article should be respected, it does not require a decision-maker to have 'taken leave of his senses' before the Court can intervene.

Where the Convention allows restrictions on rights it requires them to be justified by a legitimate aim *and* proportional to the need at hand, that is, 'necessary in a democratic society'. The case law interprets this to mean that there must be a 'pressing social need' for the interference. This is a more stringent standard than 'some logical reason': the state's desire to protect a legitimate aim does not allow it to restrict the right of the individual disproportionately — the state cannot use a sledgehammer to crack a nut. The doctrine goes further than the 'sledgehammer' approach. The concept of proportionality requires that if there are two ways of achieving the legitimate aim and one is less likely to infringe a qualified right, that is the approach that should be used. Unnecessary interference is never likely to comply with the 'necessary in a democratic society' test.

An example of the necessity doctrine is contained in the case of *Dudgeon* v *United Kingdom* (1981) 4 EHRR 149. The applicant in that case challenged the law which was then in force in Northern Ireland which made buggery between consenting gay men a criminal offence. The Court accepted that the law in question interfered with the exercise of the applicant's right to privacy as set out in Article 8(1) and was prescribed by law. The Court went on to consider the other issues that arose from Article 8(2), that is, the objectives said to be served by that law, and whether it was a proportionate response to them. It stated that, 'The Court recognises that one of the purposes of the legislation is to afford safeguards for vulnerable members of society, such as the young, against the consequences of homosexual practices' and accepted that this was a legitimate aim. However, it went on to say, at para. 60, that:

> It cannot be maintained in these circumstances that there is a 'pressing social need' to make such acts criminal offences, there being no sufficient justification provided by the risk of harm to vulnerable sections of society requiring protection or by the effects on the public. On the issue of proportionality, the Court considers that such justifications as there are for retaining the law in force unamended are outweighed by the detrimental effects which the very existence of the legislative provisions in question can have on the life of a person of homosexual orientation like the applicant. Although members of the public who regard homosexuality as immoral may be shocked, offended or disturbed by the commission by others of private homosexual acts, this cannot on its own warrant the application of penal sanctions when it is consenting adults alone who are involved.

The concept of proportionality has been filtering into English law for many years. In English courts, judges have generally come across it in the context of European Union law. For example, in *R v Secretary of State for Employment, ex parte Equal Opportunities Commission* [1995] 1 AC 1 the House of Lords, having identified that a particular social measure (different service periods for full-time and part-time workers in order to qualify for the right to claim employment protection) had an effect on a higher proportion of women than men, analysed the evidence which the government had put forward to support the assertion that this was an 'appropriate and necessary' way of advancing the policy objective it had identified (promoting part-time work opportunities). The House of Lords found insufficient evidence of this. The language used in Convention case law is a little different, but the concept of proportionality — and the Continental legal traditions from which it has derived — are very similar in both EU and Convention law.

English judges have found the idea difficult. There is evidence of this difficulty in questions 4 and 5 of the reference to the European Court of Justice in *R v Secretary of State for Employment, ex parte Seymour-Smith* [1997] ICR 371 at p. 381 concerning the time at which justification must be considered, and the evidence required to support a justification defence as a matter of Community law. The European Court of Justice decision in *ex parte Seymour-Smith* (case C–167/97) [1999] 2 AC 554 has now been handed down and the subsequent House of Lords decision is reported at [2000] 1 WLR 435. However, the House of Lords recently applied the proportionality principle in relation to the Prison Service Standing Order 5, made under the Prisons Act 1952. The relevant paragraphs permitted governors to place restrictions on journalists visiting prisoners in their professional capacity, and had been used to prevent journalists visiting two convicted murderers unless they gave an undertaking not to publish the results of their interviews. The House of Lords held that though the relevant paragraphs of the prison rules were not *ultra vires*, they were disproportionate. Lord Steyn said that the provisions were 'exorbitant in width in so far as they would undermine the fundamental rights invoked by the applicants', and Lord Hobhouse said 'this extreme policy is both unreasonable and disproportionate and cannot be justified as a permissible restraint upon the rights of the prisoner'.

2.5 MARGIN OF APPRECIATION

2.5.1 Overview

In essence, this means that a state is allowed a certain freedom to evaluate its public policy decisions, though subject to review by the Strasbourg institutions. For an analysis of some of the issues which arise see Nicholas Lavender, 'The problem of the margin of appreciation' [1997] EHRLR 380.

The phrase has been much used in Strasbourg jurisprudence, and it is important to understand the role it plays in the decision-making of the European Court of Human Rights. However, the concept should not be used by the domestic courts (see below). This is because it is important to understand that Strasbourg case law lays down a minimal 'flow' of human rights protection, not an optimal 'ceiling'. The jurisprudence from Strasbourg will need careful consideration before it is applied by domestic courts because there may be questions in those cases which the Strasbourg organs abstained from deciding but which the domestic courts must decide.

The English courts must themselves apply the doctrine of proportionality. Whilst recognising a discretionary area of judgment, this is not so lax a test as *Wednesbury* unreasonableness (see Hunt, Singh and Demetriou 'Is there a role for the margin of appreciation after incorporation of the ECHR' [1999] EHRLR 15 and Pannick, 'Principles of Interpretation of Convention rights under the Human Rights Act 1998 and the discretionary area of judgment' [1998] Public Law 545).

In the first case on the Human Rights Act to reach the House of Lords (*R v DPP, ex parte Kebilene* [1999] 3 WLR 972) this position seems to have been confirmed. Lord Hope stated that the doctrine of margin of appreciation:

. . . is an integral part of the supervisory jurisdiction which is exercised over state conduct by the international court. By conceding a margin of appreciation to each national system, the court has recognised that the Convention, as a living system, does not need to be applied uniformly by all states but may vary in its application according to local needs and conditions. This technique is not available to the national courts when they are considering Convention issues arising within their own countries. But in the hands of the national courts also the Convention should be seen as an expression of fundamental principles rather than as a set of mere rules. The questions which the courts will have to decide in the application of these principles will involve questions of balance between competing interests and issues of proportionality . . . .

In this area difficult choices may have to be made by the executive or legislature between the rights of the individual and the needs of society. In some circumstances it will be appropriate for the courts to recognise that there is an area of judgment within which the judiciary will defer, on democratic grounds, to the considered opinion of the elected body or person whose act or decision is said to be incompatible with the Convention.

2.5.2   Why the doctrine exists and what it means

The Convention is an international human rights instrument, policed by an international court. The Strasbourg institutions have to be sensitive to the need for 'subsidiarity', that is, to ensuring that the member states' own political and cultural traditions are respected. For example, what may offend religious sensitivities in one country may be an aspect of free speech in another.

When determining whether a social policy aim is legitimate, therefore, or whether the means adopted to achieve it are 'necessary in a democratic society', the Commission and Court have recognised limits to their own competence to judge the issue. They have done this by giving the state a so-called 'margin of appreciation' in assessing the extent to which a signatory has violated the Convention.

The extent of the discretion the Strasbourg institutions will allow the state depends on the policy area involved. States have been allowed a broader margin of appreciation in cases involving national security or public morality, or where there is no general Europe-wide practice, but a narrower one in other types of case.

The Commission explained the margin of appreciation in *Lawless* v *Ireland* (1961) 1 EHRR 1. The Commission suggested that the Court should scrutinise the reasons put forward by the Irish government for claiming that there was a 'state of emergency' for the purpose of anti-terrorist legislation, and should also recognise the limit of its competence to challenge those reasons. The Court did analyse the government's justification, but decided that there was no violation on the basis that 'the existence at the time of a public emergency threatening the life of the nation was *reasonably deduced* by the Irish government'.

The margin of appreciation doctrine was developed by the Court in *Handyside* v *United Kingdom* (1976) 1 EHRR 737. This case concerned the publication in England in 1971 of the *Little Red School Book*, which was intended for children and included a section on sex. The police seized the books and a forfeiture order was obtained on the grounds that the books contravened the Obscene Publications Act 1959. The applicant claimed a violation of Article 10 (freedom of expression) and the government argued that the restriction was necessary for the purpose of the 'protection of morals'. The Court accepted that the limitation was 'prescribed by law' and thus had to decide whether the limitation in question was proportionate and 'necessary in a democratic society'. The Court stated, at paras 48 and 49:

By reason of their direct and continuous contact with the vital forces of their countries, state authorities are in principle in a better position than the international judge to give an opinion on the exact of these requirements as well as on the 'necessity' of a 'restriction' or 'penalty' intended to meet them. . . .

Nevertheless, Article 10(2) does not give the contracting states an unlimited power of appreciation. The Court, which, with the Commission, is responsible for ensuring the observance of those states' engagements (Article 19), is empowered to give the final ruling on whether a 'restriction' or 'penalty' is reconcilable with freedom of expression as protected by Article 10. The domestic margin of appreciation thus goes hand in hand with a European supervision.

The use of this doctrine has sometimes led the Court to draw back from finding violations in cases by holding that the question of the proportionality of a response is within the 'margin of appreciation' of the national institutions. This is particularly so when considering cases under Articles 8 to 11. The doctrine has also been used when the Court has tried to assess the positive obligations in the Convention, for example, in the assessment of evidence by the courts in Article 6, and the right to peaceful enjoyment of property in Article 1 of Protocol 1.

Some commentators see the doctrine as being a necessary aspect of sensitivity to the different democratic traditions in member countries (see P. Mahoney, 'Universality Versus Subsidiarity in the Strasbourg Case Law on Free Speech: Explaining Some Recent Judgments' [1997] EHRLR 364). Others consider that the idea has been used as a sloppy way of refusing to face the question of proportionality (see Lord Lester of Herne Hill QC, 'Universality Versus Subsidiarity: A Reply' [1998] EHRLR 73).

The approach of the Strasbourg court is comparable to the way in which the European Court of Justice sometimes approaches the question of whether derogations from European Union law rights are 'requisite and necessary': it states that this question of proportionality is one for the judgment of the courts of the member states, but is prepared to set out the sort of factors which they should take into account (e.g., in *Nolte* [1975] ECR I-4625; *Keck* [1993] ECR I-6097). It is worth noting that, in European Union law, it is the national courts, not the national executives, which have the power to decide whether derogation from an EU law right is 'necessary'.

2.5.3 The margin of appreciation and the role of the national court

The margin of appreciation should be regarded as an international doctrine. It has no place in domestic arrangements for protecting human rights and should not be used when the Convention is applied by national courts. It was created to allow national judicial bodies a degree of flexibility; to enable an international judicial review system to give due weight to local political and cultural traditions; and to take into account the geographical, cultural, philosophical, historical and intellectual distance between the judges in Strasbourg and local institutions. The local courts do not need the doctrine because this gap does not exist. They can give sufficient deference to the sphere in which there may be policy choices for the executive by use of the concept of proportionality. If domestic courts translate the international law concept of the 'margin of appreciation' into domestic law, the judges are likely to fail in their statutory duty which is to decide for themselves whether a public body's decision constitutes a disproportionate infringement of human rights.

2.6   POSITIVE OBLIGATIONS

Some Convention articles obviously require positive steps to be taken by the state to provide resources needed to protect human rights. For example, to provide free legal assistance in criminal cases under Article 6(3)(c), and, to a certain extent, education under Protocol 1, Article 2. However, it is not just the state which is capable of infringing the rights of others. Even rights which initially look as if they are merely negative freedoms — to stop the state itself infringing human rights — may in fact require the state to take certain positive, protective steps in order to guarantee the essence of the right. For example, in *Plattform 'Ärtze für das Leben'* v *Austria* (1988) 13 EHRR 204, the European Court of Human Rights held that Article 11 (the right to freedom of association) required the state to take positive steps to prevent counter-demonstrators from disrupting a demonstration, since otherwise it would itself inhibit the reality of the right to demonstrate:

   Article 11 sometimes requires positive measures to be taken, even in the sphere
   of relations between states if need be.

The right to life in Article 2 requires the state not only to refrain from taking life intentionally, but to take appropriate steps to safeguard life (see *X* v *United Kingdom* (1979) 14 DR 31). The right to respect for private or family life in Article 8 may require the state to give a person seeking details of his past life in care access to his records in the absence of countervailing considerations (see *Gaskin* v *United Kingdom* (1989) 12 EHRR 36).

The theoretical basis for reading the Convention in a way which imposes positive obligations is not very easy to discern from the case law, but an important factor is Article 1 of the Convention which requires signatory states to *secure* Convention rights to everyone within their jurisdiction. The Convention case law shows that such protection is intended to be 'practical and effective' not merely theoretical. This means more than the state adopting a 'hands off' approach, by which they refrain from interfering with Convention rights, but rather, creating an institutional and juridical structure in which human rights are positively protected from interference whether by state or non-state actors.

2.7 DEROGATIONS

Under Article 15 of the Convention, during 'war or other public emergency threatening the life of the nation', governments can derogate from their obligations under the Convention. This enables them to restrict the exercise of some of the rights and freedoms without violating the Convention. Any derogation must be proportional to the threat and must be necessary to deal with the emergency. Signatories to the European Convention on Human Rights may also enter certain reservations to their agreement to be bound by the Convention. These reservations are open to review.

The derogations and reservations entered into by the United Kingdom, and the review mechanism adopted in relation to them by the Human Rights Act 1998, are considered further in chapter 9.

2.8 CONVENTION JURISPRUDENCE

Now the Human Rights Act 1998 has come into force, courts are under a specific statutory duty under s. 2 to consider Strasbourg jurisprudence in cases concerning Convention concepts. This opens up a whole field of case law and practitioners will have to be aware of it, know how to access it, and how to interpret it. Details of the referencing system used by the authorities in Strasbourg and the practicalities of locating Convention case law, and a number of useful books on the Convention are contained in Appendix 7 of this book.

2.8.1 Interpretation

The Convention is an international treaty and so should be interpreted in accordance with the Vienna Convention on the Law of Treaties 1969. It is intended to be interpreted purposively, that is, to give effect to the Convention's central purposes. These are the protection of individual human rights (*Soering* v *United Kingdom* (1989) 11 EHRR 439) and the ideals and values of a democratic society (see the preamble to the Convention). These suppose pluralism, tolerance and broadmindedness (*Handyside* v *United Kingdom* (1976) 1 EHRR 737). The Convention is intended to guarantee rights which are not merely theoretical and illusory but practical and effective (*Marckx* v *Belgium* (1979) 2 EHRR 330 at para. 31).

The Convention need not — indeed, should not — be interpreted as it would have been by those who drafted it 50 years ago. It is a 'living instrument which . . . must be interpreted in the light of present-day conditions' (*Tyrer* v *United Kingdom* (1978) 2 EHRR 1 at para. 31). As such its meaning will develop over time and new case law will develop in an organic way without old case law being specifically overruled. Thus, when an English court is considering the meaning and effect of a decision of the European Commission of Human Rights or the European Court of Human Rights, it must nevertheless interpret the Convention by the standards of society today, and not when the Convention was drafted. The doctrine of precedent must not be used slavishly in this field and older cases should be treated with caution.

Further, as the margin of appreciation has no part in the domestic application of the Convention (see 2.5), the courts in this country will have to look again at some of the cases decided in Strasbourg. Many cases, for instance, raising issues under Article 10, have not led to a finding of a violation precisely because a margin of appreciation was allowed by the Court. In the absence of such a margin, domestic courts must not use these cases as authority for the proposition that there is no violation. They will have to decide for themselves whether there is a breach of the Convention by undertaking a proper analysis of what, in a domestic context, is 'necessary in a democratic society'.

2.8.2   Weight of authorities

There are a number of factors to be taken into account when considering how much weight should be given to a particular decision from Strasbourg.

- Court judgments are of more importance than decisions of the Commission or the Committee of Ministers and this is particularly true since Protocol 11 which abolished the Commission.
- Judgments of the plenary Court (now the Grand Chamber), or decisions or opinions of the plenary Commission are the most authoritative. Decisions which are unanimous or have large majorities are more likely to be followed or to be influential.
- Recent decisions are more valuable than decisions made some time ago because the Convention is interpreted as a 'living instrument' and the jurisprudence is developed. Previous authorities that conflict may not be specifically set aside.
- Decisions of the Committee of Ministers are made by politicians not judges and without the benefit of legal argument.
- Admissibility decisions rarely set out the Commission's own view and are less helpful than merits decisions which give the Commission's opinion on the law. Whilst the Commission has often decided that cases are inadmissible because they are 'manifestly ill-founded', this is not the same as a finding that the point of law involved is unarguable. It may depend on the facts in issue, or application of the margin of appreciation. Nevertheless a decision that a particular case is inadmissible, on the basis it is manifestly unfounded, may be the only indication of the view of the Strasbourg institutions on the point of law in issue, as such cases never go further. Since there is no strict doctrine of precedence, these decisions need not prevent a well-founded case on the same point being raised in an English Court.
- From November 1998, the Committee of Ministers no longer made decisions on the merits and the Commission has ceased to exist. New learning will emerge only from admissibility decisions and judgments by the chambers and

the Grand Chamber. The Grand Chamber exercises an appeal function so its judgments will command greater authority than the previous plenary court. In the meantime the judgments of the new Court will emerge from chambers which will generally be composed of the same judges each time they sit. This will create the possibility of different chambers taking different views until the matter is resolved by the Grand Chamber.

Chapter Three
Uses of the Act in Any Litigation Concerning Convention Rights

3.1 VERTICAL OR HORIZONTAL EFFECT?

This chapter is concerned with the uses of the Human Rights Act in *all* litigation, whether the parties are public or private. This does not mean that the Convention is 'directly effective' against private litigants.

The Act creates new remedies against public bodies which have breached Articles of the Convention without statutory excuse (unless they have been obliged to do so by other legislation). In litigation concerning purely private bodies, there will be no new cause of action, but in all cases, whatever the nature of the parties, the courts will be under a statutory duty to interpret the law (including the common law) so as to accord with the Convention wherever possible. This means that, for example, in interpreting a statutory right not to be unfairly dismissed, or the common law of trespass, a court or tribunal will be required, if possible, to give an interpretation of the law which gives a result compatible with the Convention.

The Convention itself is an instrument of international law. Its unusual feature as a matter of international law is the right of individual petition to the European Court of Human Rights in Strasbourg; and the rights created under the Convention are enforceable in Strasbourg against the State rather than against individuals. Someone who takes a case to Strasbourg takes it against the government, alleging that it has infringed or failed to take steps to protect some Convention right; even if the failure is a failure to provide some positive protection for the applicant from an infringement of his or her rights by a private third party.

The White Paper introducing the Human Rights Bill was called *Rights Brought Home*, and some commentators take the view that it is those, international law rights which have been brought home: in other words, that the Human Rights Act 1998 is primarily a 'vertically effective' provision that will affect cases between individuals and state or public authorities rather than, in most cases, disputes between private parties. At committee stage in the House of Lords (see Hansard

HL, 24 November 1997, col. 781), Lord Wilberforce said that ministerial statements made it 'perfectly clear . . . that the Bill is aimed entirely at public authorities and not at private individuals'.

Other commentators take the view that the Act effectively incorporates the Convention into domestic law. They argue that as s. 6(3) of the Act makes the courts 'public authorities' which are bound to act in accordance with the Convention in all cases, even between private individuals, the government has effected 'full' incorporation of the Convention, with horizontal effect, so that the distinction which the Act draws between public bodies, semi-public authorities and private bodies is an artificial one. This view is taken by, for example, Sir William Wade QC, 'The United Kingdom's Bill of Rights' in *Constitutional Reforms in the United Kingdom: Practice and Principles* (Oxford: Hart Publishing, 1998).

We consider that the first view is too narrow an approach to the impact of the Act, because of the way in which the courts are obliged to use the Convention in determining cases, whereas the second overlooks some of the subtleties and difficulties in using the Convention against a private body.

To summarise the position, under the Human Rights Act 1998, the articles of the Convention in sch. 1 to the Act will be indirectly rather than directly enforceable against private persons: it will not be possible for one private individual to sue another private legal person for a new tort of 'breach of the Convention'. The Convention will be enforceable against a private legal person only where there is an existing statutory or common law right which can be interpreted so as to accord with the Convention, or where there is a judicial discretion to be exercised which can be exercised so as to give effect to a Convention right. Nevertheless, the Convention creates a positive obligation on public bodies (including courts) to protect individuals from having their rights violated by other private individuals. These 'horizontal' effects of the Human Rights Act are likely to be profound. As Lord Hope said at para. 838 in *R v DPP, ex parte Kebilene* [1999] 3 WLR 972, the first House of Lords case on the Act:

It is now plain that the incorporation of the European Convention on Human Rights into our domestic law will subject the entire legal system to a fundamental process of review and, where necessary, reform by the judiciary.

3.2 INTERPRETATIVE OBLIGATION

3.2.1 A fresh approach to statutory construction

The Act also requires domestic courts and tribunals to interpret legislation, wherever possible, in a manner consistent with the incorporated Convention rights, and requires domestic courts and tribunals to take account of the decisions of the Strasbourg institutions. This will mean that the Convention will potentially be relevant in a large number of cases in which both parties are private persons. As Lord Cooke of Thorndon said during the Parliamentary debates, '. . . the common law approach to statutory interpretation will never be the same again' (Hansard HL, 3 November 1997, col. 1273). Earlier (col. 1272) his lordship had said:

> [Section 3] will require a very different approach to interpretation from that to which the English courts are accustomed. Traditionally, the search has been for the true meaning: now it will be for a possible meaning that would prevent the making of a declaration of incompatibility.

The White Paper, *Rights Brought Home*, says that the new rule of statutory interpretation will go 'far beyond the present rule' (para. 2.7). It might also be said that the judicial approach to interpretation of the common law altogether will also change fundamentally.

Section 3(1) places a duty on the courts to read and give effect to primary legislation so that it complies with the Convention 'so far as it is possible to do so'. This duty requires the courts to seek compatibility in all circumstances and where necessary, to 'read in' the necessary protections into the legislation or to leave out particular words.

Constitutional human rights protections are not to be construed in the same way as other statutes. Such protections must be given 'a generous interpretation avoiding what has been called "the austerity of tabulated legalism", suitable to give to individuals the full measure of the fundamental rights and freedoms referred to' (*Ministry of Home Affairs* v *Fisher* [1980] AC 319 at p. 328; see also *Attorney-General of Gambia* v *Momodou Jobe* [1984] AC 689; *Attorney-General of Hong Kong* v *Lee Kwong-kut* [1993] AC 951; *Vasquez* v *The Queen* [1994] 1 WLR 1304; *Flicklinger* v *Hong Kong* [1991] 1 NZLR 439). The courts need to look for 'the substance and reality of what was involved and should not be over-concerned with what are no more than technicalities' (*Huntley* v *Attorney-General for Jamaica* [1995] 2 AC 1).

The House of Lords has accepted that in interpreting such legislation the courts need to consider authorities from other jurisdictions (*R* v *Khan* [1997] AC 558).

The New Zealand courts have also followed the same approach and given the Bill of Rights there an importance stemming from a broad and purposive approach to interpretation (*Ministry of Transport* v *Noort* [1992] 3 NZLR 260; *R* v *Goodwin (No. 1)* [1993] 2 NZLR 153).

This approach is the same as that adopted by the Commission and Court in Strasbourg to provide for effective, not merely theoretical guarantees.

3.2.2   The Human Rights Act mechanism

A vital feature of the Human Rights Act 1998 is the 'interpretative obligation' in s. 3, and the most frequent use of the Act is likely to be an interpretative one. The Act requires courts to interpret statutory provisions and the common law so as to be compatible with Convention rights wherever possible and regardless of other (perhaps more literal) interpretations or precedents to the contrary. This will affect all cases, civil or criminal, public or private, against private legal persons or public authorities where a Convention right is at stake, regardless of whether the issue is one of statutory construction, declaration of the common law, or involves the exercise of a judicial discretion.

The key to the mechanism adopted by the Human Rights Act 1998 is the interplay between ss. 6, 3 and 2 of the Act, which — though they preserve Parliamentary sovereignty — completely alter both the manner in which courts can scrutinise legislation and the ways in which judges must interpret common law.

3.2.3   Section 6

Section 6(1) makes it unlawful for a public authority to act in a way which is incompatible with a Convention right. Courts and tribunals are defined as public authorities (s. 6(3)(a)) and so they have their own primary duty to act compatibly with the Convention. Parliamentary sovereignty is preserved by s. 6(2), which limits the s. 6(1) duty to the extent that the court or tribunal could not have acted differently as a result of a statutory obligation which cannot be read or given effect to in a way which is compatible with the Convention rights. This is a clever device which places courts and tribunals themselves under a primary obligation to give effect to Convention rights except where they are prevented from doing so by statute.

The obligation to interpret the law so as to accord with the Convention wherever possible will apply to all cases. The consequence is that Convention questions will become pivotal in cases where courts or tribunals are deciding the scope of a statutory provision (even one which regulates the behaviour of one private individual to another); where they are determining what the common law is (in so far as this is within their jurisdiction); or when they are exercising a judicial discretion.

So, for example, a court interpreting existing or future trade union legislation will have to read and apply it, where possible, in conformity with Article 11. A court or tribunal will be under an obligation to give effect to Article 8 of the Convention in deciding whether a failure to respect an employee's private life constitutes a breach of a duty of trust and confidence implied into contract by the common law. Courts considering the scope of the tort of trespass may have to consider whether it creates a positive right to respect for privacy and so on.

3.2.4   Section 3

Section 3(1) of the Act explains how courts will approach their interpretative obligation in relation to primary and secondary legislation. It provides that courts and tribunals *must* read primary and subordinate legislation and give it effect in a way which is compatible with Convention rights 'so far as it is possible to do so'. This section applies to both primary and secondary legislation whenever it was enacted — i.e., whether before or after the enactment of the Human Rights Act 1998.

As was pointed out in the White Paper, this interpretative obligation goes far beyond the pre-incorporation use of the Convention in statutory interpretation. Before the Act, courts were permitted (but did not have to) use the Convention as an interpretative tool where the supposed intention of an Act of Parliament was ambiguous. Now, the courts are under an express statutory duty to interpret legislation so as to accord with the purpose of the Convention if this is at all possible, even if this results in a strained rather than a literal meaning being selected from a range of possible interpretations, or the reading in of additional words so as to give effect to the presumed intended effect of the Convention. In the first House of Lords judgment on the Convention, *R v DPP, ex parte Kebilene* [1999] 3 WLR 972, this was described as a 'strong' interpretative obligation (see Lord Steyn at para. 831 and Lord Cooke at para. 837).

This more purposive approach to statutory construction has already begun to permeate English judicial reasoning because it is required in relation to European Union law. The obligation of domestic courts to comply with the objects and purposes of the underlying EU law provisions has been emphasised in many decisions in the European Court of Justice. It is exemplified in *Marleasing SA v La Comercial Internacional de Alimentación SA* (case C–106/89) [1990] ECR I-4135, in which it was held that where national courts have to interpret national law in a field governed by EU law, they must interpret that law in the light of the wording *and purpose* of the EU legislation, so far as it is possible for them to do so.

The interpretative obligation can have quite far-reaching effects. An example of the way in which this interpretative obligation was used in the United Kingdom in the field of European Union law is *Litster v Forth Dry Dock and Engineering Co. Ltd* [1990] 1 AC 546, in which the House of Lords had to consider the construction of the Transfer of Undertakings (Protection of Employment) Regulations 1981 (SI 1981/1794). The Regulations were intended to implement the Acquired Rights Directive (77/187/EEC), the purpose of which was to protect the workers in an undertaking when its ownership was transferred. But the Regulations only protected those who were employed in the business 'immediately before' the time of the transfer. Mr Litster and other employees had been dismissed just before (and because of) the intended transfer of an undertaking, and did not fall within the scope of the Regulations if they were strictly and literally construed. But the House of Lords enquired into the purpose of the underlying Directive, and interpreted the Regulations so as to accord with that purpose by implying additional words into the Regulations so that they protected workers if they were employed 'immediately before' the time of transfer 'or would have been so employed if [they] had not been unfairly dismissed [by reason of the transfer]'. The Regulations were accordingly much wider than might appear on their face, and the employees won the case.

These principles of purposive construction will probably be transferred relatively easily from the European Union to the European Convention context.

3.2.5   Section 19 and statements of compatibility

The interpretative obligation will apply to legislation whether passed before or after the Human Rights Act 1998. In respect of legislation which post-dates the Act, the task of compliant interpretation will be made easier by reference to the statement which the Act requires a minister to make spelling out whether he or she intends the legislation to comply with the Convention. Section 19 of the Act requires a Minister of the Crown in charge of any Bill, before its second reading, either to make and publish a 'statement of compatibility' or state that the legislation is not compatible with the Convention rights. A 'statement of compatibility' is a statement by the relevant minister to the effect that in his or her view the provisions of that Bill are compatible with the Convention rights. Where such a statement has been made, whether or not in Parliament, it is likely that courts will use it as evidence of Parliamentary intention — as it presently does with statements made by persons introducing legislation under the principle in *Pepper* v *Hart* [1993] AC 593. As Lord Irvine of Lairg, the Lord Chancellor, said in the Tom Sargant Memorial Lecture, 16 December 1997, in relation to future legislation:

. . . it should be clear from the Parliamentary history, and in particular the Ministerial statement of compatibility which will be required by the Act, that Parliament did not intend to cut across a Convention right. Ministerial statements of compatibility will inevitably be a strong spur to the courts to find means of construing statutes compatibly with the Convention.

In assessing whether a particular provision complies with the Act and the Convention, those advising the government have thus far not sought positive guarantees for Convention rights within the text of the statute before giving a 'section 19' statement. Instead, they have assumed that all those public authorities that have to implement the provision will act in compliance with the Convention if they have the power to do so. So, for instance, a Bill which gave wide discretion to the police to act in ways which would clearly violate the Convention would still be assessed as complying with the Convention because the discretion would be constrained by the Human Rights Act. By July 2000 only one Bill (the Local Government Bill 2000) was assessed as having provisions which did not comply with the Convention.

3.2.6   Section 2 — the effect of Strasbourg case law

Section 2 of the Act introduces new 'relevant considerations' which courts must take into account when seeking to interpret domestic law in compliance with the Convention. The Act does not permit courts to decide these questions in accordance only with domestic precedent or their own instincts. Section 2 of the Act provides that a court or tribunal determining a question which has arisen under any

Act in connection with a Convention right *must* take account of any judgment, decision, declaration or advisory opinion of the European Court of Human Rights, opinion or decision of the Commission or decision of the Committee of Ministers, whenever made or given so far as, in the opinion of the court or tribunal, it is relevant to the proceedings in which that question has arisen.

Now, because a United Kingdom court must give effect to the Convention wherever possible, it is also obliged to have regard to the Strasbourg case law so that it has in mind the appropriate principles in deciding what it must give effect to. The obligation to have regard to Strasbourg case law when considering a Convention question is explicable by reference to the White Paper which intends that, by enactment of the Human Rights Act 1998, 'the [Convention] rights will be brought much more fully into the jurisprudence of the courts throughout the United Kingdom and their interpretation . . . far more subtly and powerfully woven into our law'.

3.2.7   The interplay of sections 2 and 3

Sections 2 and 3 of the Act taken together are likely to have two principal effects. First, because the Convention must be given effect wherever possible, and because Strasbourg case law must be taken into account, the Strasbourg method of judicial reasoning will gradually enter English legal practice. This involves an explicit balancing of the rights of individuals against the rights and freedoms of others and the general public interest. Judges and legal representatives will have to begin to structure their arguments in the systematic way that this is done in Strasbourg, namely, to identify the broad prima facie right which may have been infringed, and then to consider limitations to it. Where there is potentially a Convention question in play, the domestic court or tribunal will first have to identify the right in question, including the positive aspects of the right (i.e., the obligations of the court, as a public body, to take positive steps to protect the right). Then the domestic court or tribunal will have to identify the alleged interference with the right; and look to see whether it is prescribed by law. It will next have to decide what objectives are said to be served by the interference, and then whether the interference is necessary in a democratic society for the purposes of achieving those objectives.

Secondly, ss. 2 and 3 read together will mean that the doctrine of precedent will be abrogated to the extent that is necessary to give effect to Convention rights. Strasbourg case law has consistently held that the Convention is 'a living instrument which . . . must be interpreted in the light of present-day conditions' (*Tyrer* v *United Kingdom* (1978) 2 EHRR 1 at para. 31). The s. 3 rule of construction will apply to past as well as future legislation, and in interpreting legislation:

> . . . the courts will not be bound by previous interpretations. They will be able to build a new body of case law, taking into account Convention rights. (White Paper (Cm 3782), para. 2.8.)

Strasbourg case law (which a domestic court must take into account) requires *effective* protection of the Convention rights: '. . . the Convention is intended to guarantee not rights that are theoretical or illusory but rights that are practical and effective' (*Artico* v *Italy* (1980) 3 EHRR 1, para. 33; *Airey* v *Ireland* (1979) 2 EHRR 305).

Accordingly, when United Kingdom courts comply with their obligation under s. 3(1) of the Act, they will have to interpret statutory provisions so as to give real and effective protection to the rights which the Convention was intended to safeguard. It is for this reason that the views in G. Marshall, 'Interpreting interpretation in the Human Rights Bill' [1998] PL 167 are, in our respectful view, misconceived. That article suggests that the more the courts 'read' statutes so as to be compatible with Convention rights, the less protection is afforded to the individual. The opposite is in fact the case. The courts are not enjoined simply to *say* that an interpretation of a statutory provision complies with the Convention even if it does not. On the contrary, they are required, if possible, to find one of the range of possible interpretations which in fact affords real and effective protection to the Convention right, as it applies in the present state of society.

It is true that, by reason of s. 3(2)(b) and (c), this interpretative obligation does not permit courts to 'strike down' primary legislation if it is simply incapable of interpretation so as to conform with the Convention. But many commentators think that the prospect (in the higher courts) of judges being obliged to consider making 'declarations of incompatibility' in cases where they are unable to interpret legislation consistently with the Convention, coupled (in the case of legislation which post-dates the Act) with ministerial statements of compatibility, will be powerful incentives to judges to find consistent interpretations.

Nonetheless, Strasbourg case law is only relevant (not binding) upon domestic courts. Over time, domestic courts may in some cases develop their own standards of interpretation of the Convention. Since the Convention is a 'living instrument' whose interpretation changes from time to time, earlier decisions on the basis of particular Strasbourg case law may need to be reconsidered if, in the meantime, the Commission or Court has arrived at a different interpretation of a particular provision. The duty is to take the case law into account whenever a Convention issue arises, not to follow it. For example, though Strasbourg has not treated gay relationships as family relationships, in *Fitzpatrick* v *Sterling Housing Association Ltd* [1999] 3 WLR 1113, the House of Lords found that, as a matter of English law, a stable gay relationship is a family one.

3.2.8 Summary of the general effect of the Act on interpretation

To summarise the interpretative obligation: in determining cases between private individuals as well as those between an individual and the state, a United Kingdom court (as a public authority) will be obliged to act in a way which is compatible with the Convention, by interpreting statute and common law consistently with it wherever possible, and by exercising judicial discretion compatibly with it. But the interpretative obligation does not create free-standing new rights. A litigant, A, who wishes to use a Convention argument in a case brought against a private opponent B, will need to find an existing private law argument on which to hang the Convention argument, or focus the action on a public body, C, which has failed to protect A's rights from being violated by B. For example, it may be possible on appropriate facts, for an individual to sue the Press Complaints Commission for failure to provide a proper remedy for breach of Article 8 of the Convention by a newspaper.

However, it can be said with a measure of confidence that, over time, Convention standards will infiltrate, influence and may even create new common law rights. For example, the High Court, in determining whether to require a journalist to disclose his or her sources, or whether to award an injunction to prevent breach of confidence will have to decide these questions of discretion in accordance with Article 10 of the Convention (but see 6.3 on exceptions and special cases). A magistrates' court which has been obliged to convict because of a statutory provision which breaches the Convention will, when it exercises its discretion as to sentence, be obliged to give an absolute discharge so as to act as far as possible in accordance with the Convention.

Whereas once Convention arguments were at best factors in ascertaining the scope of the common law or exercises of judicial discretion, now that the Human Rights Act 1998 is in force, a United Kingdom court will be obliged to give effect to Convention rights when performing its public functions, i.e., trying or administering cases — even cases where both parties are private individuals.

Further, since courts and tribunals are public authorities they must exercise their judicial discretion so as to accord with the Convention whenever it is possible to do so. Their obligation will apply to all cases, whether the court is applying the common law or exercising an inherent judicial discretion (i.e., in 'pure' s. 6(1) cases), or where it is interpreting statutes or exercising its own statutory powers (i.e., under s. 6(1), (2) or 3). The requirement to have regard to Strasbourg case law will fall, as a matter of statutory duty, on every court and tribunal from magistrates' court, social security appeal tribunal or employment tribunal to the House of Lords. It goes far beyond the use of the Convention made by United Kingdom courts in the past when courts were permitted, but not required, to refer to Strasbourg case law, which was (consequently) often ignored. There was a certain logic to this position. In the 'gays in the military' case, *R* v *Ministry of Defence, ex parte Smith* [1996] QB 517, the Divisional Court and the Court of Appeal had regard to Strasbourg principles, but then declined to follow them because they were not part of domestic law. In that case, in the Divisional Court, Curtis J asked rhetorically, 'If it makes no difference, why refer to it?'

After the Human Rights Act, the answer will be because the Court must give effect to the Convention unless prevented from doing so by clear statutory words. As the decision of the European Court of Human Rights in *Smith and Grady* v *United Kingdom* (2000) 29 EHRR 548 made clear, reference to the Convention principles would indeed have made a difference in that case, because it found that the exclusion of gay service personnel contravened Article 8 of the European Convention.

Chapter Four
Using the Convention against Public Authorities

4.1 DIRECT ENFORCEMENT OF CONVENTION RIGHTS

4.1.1 The position of public authorities generally

Public authorities are in a special position under the Human Rights Act 1998, because the Convention rights scheduled to the Act can be directly enforced against them. The reason for this is that s. 6 of the Act creates important new obligations upon public authorities, requiring them to act compatibly with the Convention, and s. 7 creates new causes of actions through which these 'vertically effective' rights can be enforced.

Individuals will be able to rely upon Convention rights against public authorities and indeed any body exercising 'functions of a public nature' in respect of those functions (see s. 6(3)(b) and 6(5) of the Human Rights Act 1998). The difficulties in defining a public authority and public functions are considered at 4.3 below.

Section 6(1) of the Act makes it unlawful for a public authority to act in a way which is incompatible with a Convention right. 'Act' includes failure to act: see s. 6(6). This general obligation is very wide, and means that, in the exercise of any power or duty, any public body must act in such a way as to give effect to the Convention.

This means more than avoiding violating Convention rights themselves. Public authorities must also act in a way which gives effect to their positive obligations under the Convention (see 2.6). For example, a local authority faced with a family complaining of racial harassment by gangs of thugs on a council estate must not merely refrain from racially harassing the family itself. In order to comply with its positive obligations under the Convention, the new s. 6(1) duty will mean that the local authority may have to take such positive steps as are necessary to protect the family's right to respect for their private or family life and home without discrimination on grounds of race (under Articles 8 and 14 of the Convention).

Section 6(1) is limited only insofar as is necessary to preserve the concept of Parliamentary sovereignty. First, s. 6(2)(a) provides that s. 6(1) does not apply if the public authority *could not* have acted differently as a result of one or more provisions of primary legislation. Section 6(2)(b) provides that s. 6(1) does not apply if the authority was acting to give effect to or to enforce one or more provisions made under primary legislation which (itself) cannot be read or given effect in a way which is compatible with the Convention rights.

However, s. 6(2) is likely to be of rare application. Most powers or duties *can* be read in a way which is compatible with the Convention: and if public authorities do not themselves comply with s. 6(1) by reading their powers and duties in a Convention-compliant way, the courts (as public authorities themselves) are under their own duties to find a reading of the legislation which permits the public authority to comply with the Convention if at all possible (ss. 3 and 6(1) of the Act — see chapter 3).

The second limit on the effect of s. 6(1) is that Parliament in its legislative capacity is not a 'public authority' (s. 6(3)), and so is not bound by s. 6(1). Though the 'act' of a public authority which can be challenged includes an omission, it does not include a failure to introduce proposals for legislation or a remedial order (s. 6(6)). This means that it will not be possible for an individual to sue the executive for failing to introduce legislation which is necessary to give effect to a Convention right, or the legislature for failing to pass it.

If the violation of a Convention right is contained in primary legislation incapable of consistent interpretation, the only remedy will be to seek a declaration of incompatibility or to take the case to Strasbourg.

In the majority of cases, however, a violation of the Convention by a public authority will contravene s. 6 of the Act.

4.1.2   Ways of using section 6(1) against a public authority

Section 6(1) can be enforced under s. 7 of the Act. Section 7(1) provides that a person who is or would be a victim of an act unlawful by virtue of s. 6(1) can rely on Convention rights:

    (a)   to bring proceedings against the authority under the Human Rights Act 'in the appropriate court or tribunal'; or
    (b)   to rely upon the Convention right or rights concerned 'in any legal proceedings'.

This means that the Human Rights Act creates:

    (a)   a new cause of action for breach of statutory duty;
    (b)   a new head of illegality in judicial review proceedings;
    (c)   a defence in any proceedings which a public authority might itself bring against an individual.

For example, a person might argue that a social services authority has violated Article 8 of the Convention by failing to give access to his or her file, and so is in breach of statutory duty (*Gaskin* v *UK* (1989) 12 EHRR 36). Or it might be said that a decision to refuse to allow a journalist access to a prisoner was *ultra vires* because rules contravened Article 10 of the Convention and the primary legislation did not require them to be read or given effect in that form, so founding a judicial review (*R* v *Secretary of State for the Home Department, ex parte Simms* [1999] 3 WLR 328, HL). Or a defendant in criminal proceedings might raise a violation of the Convention by the prosecution in his or her defence (e.g., *R* v *DPP, ex parte Kebilene* [1999] 3 WLR 972).

A further important point concerning s. 6(1) of the Act is that it will only create new *positive* causes of action for acts or omissions which take place on or after 2 October 2000, but it can provide a defence to proceedings brought by the public authority *whenever* the act or omission complained of took place. So, for example, a prosecution which relies on evidence gathered in violation of Article 8 in 1997 could be challenged by a defendant on that basis at a trial or appeal. But a decision taken on 1 October 2000 by a public authority cannot be challenged by way of judicial review or on the basis that it was a breach of statutory duty under s. 6(1).

The reason for this curious feature is that s. 22(4) of the Act (which came into force well before 2 October 2000) provides that s. 7(1)(b) (reliance on the Convention in legal proceedings) applies to proceedings *brought by or at the instigation of a public authority* whenever the act in question took place, but otherwise only to acts taking place after the coming into force of that section.

4.1.3 Procedural issues

The procedures for raising s. 6 points in legal proceedings are not straightforward. One issue is the question of limitation periods for bringing proceedings directly under s. 7(1)(a) (which are contained in s. 7(5) of the Act), and the way in which these interact with other relevant limitation periods. Another is the bodies which count as 'public authorities' for the purposes of the direct application of the Act, and in respect of which functions. The question of standing and third party interventions are very important, in particular to the evolution of 'public interest' litigation, because s. 7(7) requires English courts to apply Strasbourg case law on who is a victim, not simply to 'have regard' to it. Finally, there are jurisdictional questions as to where proceedings involving s. 6(1) should be brought. These are considered in the remaining sections of this chapter. For an excellent analysis of some of the practical considerations involved in using the Human Rights Act in judicial review proceedings, see Karen Steyn and David Wolfe 'Judicial Review and the Human Rights Act: Some Practical Considerations' [1999] EHRLR 614.

4.2   LIMITATION PERIODS

Originally, the Human Rights Bill did not mention limitation periods in relation to s. 6 cases against public authorities. However, during the course of the Parliamentary debates, a limitation period was introduced and has been enacted as s. 7(5).

This creates a primary limitation period for cases against public bodies alleging a breach of a Convention right of one year beginning with the date that the act complained of took place. This can be extended where the court considers it equitable in all the circumstances, and it is likely that case law from the field of discrimination law about when it is 'equitable' to extend time will be used by analogy. However, this normal limitation period is subject to any rule which imposes a stricter time limit in relation to the proceeding in question (for example, the three-month time limit for bringing proceedings by way of judicial review).

The one-year time limit only applies to claims which directly allege breach of the Convention by a public authority i.e., only where there is a cause of action created by s. 7(1)(a) of the Act. There is no limit to the interpretative obligation in s. 7(1)(b). This may cause difficulties in cases where proceedings under the Act overlap with other proceedings with a longer limitation period. For example, it may prove difficult to bring a case alleging cruel and inhuman treatment under Article 3 against the police within the relevant time limit if other criminal or police complaints proceedings are in force, although this concern is probably met by the extension provisions in s. 7(5)(b).

Section 7(5) will mean that although litigation involving property, such as trespass to land, can be taken up to six years (or in some cases 12 years) after the event, there will be no remedy for violations of a fundamental human right after one year. The difference appears without objective basis and, limiting as it does the right of access to the court (in Article 6 of the Convention), may constitute a violation of Article 14, the anti-discrimination provision in the Convention, but see *Stubbings* v *United Kingdom* (1996) 23 EHRR 213.

4.3   WHEN IS A BODY A 'PUBLIC AUTHORITY' FOR THE PURPOSES OF THE ACT?

For the purposes of the Human Rights Act 1998 it is very important to determine whether a person involved in a breach of Convention rights is a 'public authority', and in respect of which of its functions. If a body is a public authority then it is a body against which the Act creates new *direct* remedies for breach of s. 6(1) of the Act, either by judicial review or for breach of the statutory duty created by s. 6 of the Act to act in conformity with the Convention (unless there is a statutory excuse).

It is also important to draw a distinction between 'pure' public authorities and quasi-public bodies of the kind identified in s. 6(3)(b), because pure public bodies are under a duty to act in conformity with the Convention whether exercising functions governed by public law (e.g., assessment to tax) or functions governed by private law (e.g., making employment contracts); whereas quasi-public authorities will have to comply with s. 6(1) (which requires them to act in conformity with the Convention) in relation to their public functions, not their private law relationships (s. 6(5)). The effect of this is that there will be a direct cause of action available against quasi-public bodies for acting in breach of the Convention, and hence unlawfully when the act under challenge is of a public nature, but not when they are acting within the scope of their *private* law activities.

Thus, the first issue is whether a body is a pure public authority, a quasi-public authority of a s. 6(3)(b) kind, or a private body. Where a body is only a quasi-public authority the second issue is whether the particular action complained of is public or private.

The term 'public authority' is not defined positively in the Act save to say that the term *includes* a court or tribunal (s. 6(3)(a)) and any person certain of whose functions are functions of a public nature (s. 6(3)(b)), but does not include either House of Parliament (save the House of Lords when acting in a judicial capacity), or a person exercising functions in connection with proceedings in Parliament (s. 6(3) and (4)).

Though there may be difficult cases, it is clear that the concept of a public authority will include all bodies which are obviously public in nature, such as government departments, local authorities, police officers and immigration officials. Subject to the qualification in s. 6(2), all of these bodies will act unlawfully if they act inconsistently with the Convention, and this will be the case whether such bodies are acting in a public or a private capacity.

However, as has been observed in the case law concerning judicial review (e.g., *R v Panel on Take-overs and Mergers, ex parte Datafin plc* [1987] QB 815), it is not always easy to categorise a body as either 'public' or 'private'. Section 6(3)(b) includes within the definition of 'public authority' any person 'certain of whose functions are functions of a public nature', but this is limited by s. 6(5) which provides that:

In relation to a particular act, a person is not a public authority by virtue only of subsection (3)(b) if the nature of the act is private.

During the Parliamentary debates, the Lord Chancellor gave, as an example of a s. 6(3)(b) body, Railtrack, which (he said) is a public authority when it exercises public functions in its role of safety regulator, but acts privately in its role as property developer. Doctors would be public authorities in relation to their NHS functions, but not in relation to their private patients, and so on. This would appear to mean that the new cause of action for acting in breach of the Convention could only arise in relation to a quasi-public body in contexts where its functions would be amenable to judicial review and not, for example, in private-law-type employment cases.

The reach of the Human Rights Act 1998 will depend very much on how widely the courts interpret the concept of a public function. As the law stands, the statutory source of the power to undertake a function is an important indicator, as well as the nature of the function. So, to take the example given by the Lord Chancellor, it is debatable whether Railtrack does act in a purely private capacity when it acts as a property developer, since it is a statutory undertaker for the purposes of planning legislation and hence has certain permitted development rights not afforded to ordinary private bodies.

This functional way of determining when a public authority is not a public authority for the purposes of the Act will probably give rise to much uncertainty and to litigation. For example, in general, employment law questions are questions of private law (*R* v *East Berkshire Health Authority, ex parte Walsh* [1985] QB 152). However, they may be questions of public law if they relate to policy questions (*R* v *Crown Prosecution Service, ex parte Hogg* [1994] COD 237). Thus, an employee of a quasi-public body will probably not be able to claim breach of s. 6 of the Act in an 'ordinary' employment situation, because that would be private law, and the decisions which the quasi-public body took as an employer would be taken in its private capacity. But the situation might be different if the issue related to some question relating to public functions, for example, being disciplined for whistle-blowing in relation to Railtrack's activities as a public authority. In such a case, it could be argued that Railtrack would be under a s. 6(1) duty. However, the case law on the 'public/private divide' has been much criticised and is likely to evolve in response to some of the difficulties thrown up by the Human Rights Act.

4.4   STANDING AND INTERVENTIONS: WHO MAY BRING PROCEEDINGS USING THE ACT?

Even before the Human Rights Act 1998 came into effect, all litigants could use Convention arguments in some, albeit limited, contexts (see 1.1). Any legal or natural person could use the Act (this includes companies). Earlier proposals to restrict the benefit of the Act to natural persons would probably themselves have infringed the provisions of Articles 6 and 14 read together (right to a fair trial in respect of civil rights and obligations and right not to be discriminated against in application of the Convention rights).

By virtue of s. 7(1) and (3) of the Act, however, the Act can only be used to bring proceedings by a person who is, or would be, a victim of the violation, even if they would otherwise have standing to be a party to judicial review proceedings on the broader test of 'standing' employed under the old RSC Ord. 53 (now revoked and replaced by Part 54 of the Civil Procedure Rules).

This curious position is likely to lead to many technical debates in court. During the Parliamentary and extra-Parliamentary debates which accompanied the passage of the Human Rights Bill, the restrictive provisions on standing to challenge breaches of Convention rights were one of its most criticised features. In support of the restriction it was argued that, for any violation with real effects, a public interest group would be able to find a 'victim' to act as applicant, so that the standing provision would avoid challenges which were purely academic. It was also said that the courts would be likely to accept '*amicus*' briefs from interested groups as in fact occurred in *R* v *Khan* [1997] AC 558 when the House of Lords considered a written submission on the wider implications of the case prepared by Liberty and in the recent Pinochet extradition proceedings. Nevertheless, the 'victim' provision means that it will be necessary to decide whether a particular litigant is a 'victim' in order to decide whether they can use the Human Rights

Act, and if the litigant is *not* a victim, but still has standing, the Court will have to decide the extent to which the litigant can nevertheless raise Convention arguments under the pre-Act conditions. It seems likely that, applying this test of who is a 'victim', local authorities will probably not be able to use the Human Rights Act (*Austria Municipalities* v *Austria* (1974) 17 YB 338).

The position may be mitigated somewhat by the relaxed rule on third party interventions and '*amicus*' briefs which have already evolved (see *R* v *Department of Health, ex parte Source Informatics* [2000] 2 WLR 940, in which there were four intervenors raising human rights arguments) and are likely to evolve further.

4.4.1 What is a victim?

The concept of victim, in s. 7(7) of the Act, is taken from Article 34 of the Convention as amended by Protocol 11. (Before the amendment the provision was in Article 25, to which the earlier case law refers.) Only a person who would have standing as a victim to bring proceedings in the European Court of Human Rights is counted as a victim for the purposes of s. 7. Section 7(7) requires domestic courts to give effect to Strasbourg case law on who is a 'victim'.

The Court and Commission insist that a person has standing as a victim only if actually and directly affected by the act or the omission that is the subject of the complaint. There is no role for individual 'public defenders' of human rights to be recognised (see *Klass* v *Germany* (1978) 2 EHRR 214, para. 33).

However, in Strasbourg case law it is not necessary for standing that the applicant has actually suffered the consequences of the alleged breach, provided there is a risk of their being directly affected by it (*Klass* v *Germany*, para. 33; *Marckx* v *Belgium* (1979) 2 EHRR 330, para. 27). One example was a gay man living in Northern Ireland who was allowed to complain (successfully) about the criminalisation of all homosexual conduct in private between consenting males, even though he had not yet been prosecuted under the law (*Dudgeon* v *United Kingdom* (1984) Series B 40; and *Norris* v *Ireland* (1988) 13 EHRR 186). But the risk of being affected must be a real threat, not a theoretical possibility (see *Campbell* v *United Kingdom* (1982) 4 EHRR 293). Other examples are cases in which challenges were made to legislation discriminating against children born out of wedlock who were held to be victims of that legislation (*Marckx* v *Belgium*) and a case where a litigant successfully persuaded the Court that she was a victim of the ban on divorce in Ireland because of the consequences for certain family relationships (*Johnston* v *Ireland* (1986) 9 EHRR 203).

The most liberal interpretation of 'victim' was in *Open Door and Dublin Well Woman* v *Ireland* (1992) 15 EHRR 244 where it was held that two abortion advice centres and two counsellors which *offered* abortion advice and two women wishing to *receive* it all had standing to challenge an injunction which was held to breach Article 10.

On the other hand, the Commission refused to consider an applicant a victim because he was not directly affected by the alleged breach in *Leigh* v *United*

Kingdom (1984) 38 DR 74. In that case, three applicants, a journalist and two newspapers, complained that there had been a violation of their right under Article 10 to receive and impart information. This arose out of *Home Office* v *Harman* [1983] 1 AC 280, in which the House of Lords had held that a lawyer had acted in contempt of court when she allowed the first applicant to inspect confidential documents disclosed on discovery after they had been read out in court. The applicants each claimed to be a victim, arguing that their sources of information for journalistic coverage had been adversely affected by the decision. The Commission said that these applicants were interpreting the concept of 'victim' so broadly that it could encompass every newspaper or journalist in the United Kingdom who might conceivably be affected by the decision of the House of Lords. It held that, to be a victim, the form of detriment must be of a less indirect and remote nature.

4.4.2   What are the problems with the provisions on standing?

In many — perhaps most — cases there will be no problem for a litigant in establishing standing to use the Human Rights Act. There could be no doubt, for example, that a person who wants to use Article 5 of the Convention in the context of a refusal of bail in a criminal trial is a victim of the alleged contravention.

But the victim provisions will undoubtedly cause serious problems in the context of judicial review proceedings. Section 7(3) of the Act explicitly applies the 'victim' requirement to standing in such cases. Judicial review proceedings do not just involve the two parties before the court: they relate to a public concern about the decisions of public authorities. In recent years, the High Court has taken a realistic approach to this, and permitted 'public interest' organisations, perhaps not themselves 'suffering' from an unlawful or unreasonable action, to bring proceedings in appropriate cases (e.g., *R* v *Sefton Metropolitan Borough Council, ex parte Help the Aged* [1997] 4 All ER 532; *R* v *Lord Chancellor, ex parte Child Poverty Action Group* [1998] 2 All ER 755). This has been particularly important where the general public interest is involved, as it undoubtedly will be where Human Rights Act arguments are in play.

The provision in s. 7(3) of the Act that, in cases under the Act, an applicant is to be taken to have a sufficient interest to challenge an allegedly unlawful act by way of judicial review only if the applicant is, or would be, a victim of it constitutes a very signficant restriction on the way in which the judges have interpreted the concept of standing in recent years (see, for example, *R* v *Secretary of State for Social Security, ex parte Joint Council for the Welfare of Immigrants* [1997] 1 WLR 275).

The distinction between victims and bodies with standing is likely to lead to conceptual and practical difficulties, first in deciding whether the public interest group is itself a victim or group of victims and secondly in deciding what human rights arguments the group can advance if it is not. The consequence of this unattractive distinction will be that courts have to grapple with two definitions of 'sufficient interest' in judicial review proceedings: one (as defined in the general case law under the old RSC Ord. 53, now replaced by Part 54 of the CPR) for the purposes of deciding whether to grant leave, and another (as statutorily defined in s. 7(3)) for determining whether the Human Rights Act 1998 can be used.

Two types of public-interest litigator have been recognised in recent years (see P. Cane, 'Standing up for the public' [1995] PL 276). In some cases a public-interest group is really an association of interested individuals and may be regarded as a group of persons each of whom may be regarded as a victim. (An example of such a group which might have associational standing to challenge a provision under the Human Rights Act 1998 would be Stonewall, a gay rights group; another is the National Federation of the Self-employed). It remains to be seen whether courts will interpret s. 7(3) as preventing such a group from asserting 'sufficient interest' to bring a human rights challenge. There seems to be no logical reason why it should, particularly in light of s. 11 which preserves existing rights.

The other sort of public-interest group which has standing to bring judicial review is a 'representative' group which may have special expertise. Examples would be Amnesty International or the Joint Council for the Welfare of Immigrants. These groups consist of people who may not themselves suffer in consequence of an allegedly illegal act, but who act on behalf of those who do. They are often well-placed to identify and to bring the proceedings in the public interest, because of particular expertise in a field. Sometimes — like Amnesty International — they may raise arguments for people who would not otherwise be able to challenge a decision because they are not in the jurisdiction; or bring actions where no individual could get legal aid because no individual would suffer a sufficiently large loss to pass the legal aid test or could be expected to bring the case personally (see, e.g., *R* v *Secretary of State for Social Services, ex parte Child Poverty Action Group* [1990] 2 QB 540 at pp. 546–7). This sort of 'representative' body seems to be plainly prevented from arguing Convention points in a judicial review by the terms of s. 7(3), save in so far as it could do so irrespective of the Human Rights Act 1998.

It may be difficult to determine whether a public-interest group is a group of persons who are victims under s. 7(3), or a representative association. For example, what is an expert environmental group which also has members affected by environmental decisions, such as Greenpeace or Friends of the Earth: is it an associational group of victims or a representative body? In *R* v *Inspectorate of Pollution, ex parte Greenpeace Ltd (No. 2)* [1994] 4 All ER 329 the applicant convinced the court that it was a proper person to be heard using both types of standing.

If a public-interest group is considered to be a representative group, and so not a victim, it will have standing to challenge actions by way of judicial review under the common law of human rights if it would have been considered to have sufficient interest before the passing of the Human Rights Act 1998. The Act is not intended to remove existing rights, and we think it unlikely that the judges of the Crown Court list will use the s. 7(3) definition of 'sufficient interest' to draw back from the liberal approach they have adopted to standing in general (see s. 11).

By the same token, it is unlikely that the judges will interpret s. 7(3) so as to prevent an applicant which is a public interest group from arguing Convention points if they do so on the basis of the common law and doctrines which are already available in English law (s. 11). Few commentators think the courts will interpret s. 7(3) so as to reduce their existing power to interpret the common law consistently with the Convention where it is ambiguous to do so. For example, Grosz, Beatson and Duffy argue in *Human Rights: the 1998 Act and the European Convention* (London: Sweet & Maxwell, 2000) at 4.44 that s. 7(3) should not prevent a public interest group from arguing that secondary legislation is *ultra vires* by virtue of s. 3 of the Act or public law principles. But a public interest group which cannot claim to be a victim will not easily be able to found a claim or application for judicial review on ss. 7(1)(a) and 6(1) of the Act.

The consequence of s. 7(3) may be that important breaches of Convention rights may go unremedied because it is not possible to find a nominal applicant.

It is regrettable that the government did not heed the voices of experts such as Lord Lester of Herne Hill, who warned of the difficulties which might arise during the course of the Parliamentary debates on this contentious section of the Act.

4.4.3   Third party interventions

The restrictive provisions of s. 7(3) and 7(7) may be mitigated by public interest groups supporting individuals who can establish their claim to be victims.

In the debates in the House of Lords, the Lord Chancellor expressly stated that 'there is nothing in our Bill which would prevent pressure groups — interest groups — from assisting and providing representation for victims who wish to bring cases forward' and 'interest groups will plainly be able to provide assistance to victims who bring cases under the Bill, including, as I mentioned in Committee, the filing of *amicus* briefs' (Hansard, HL Deb, 5 February 1998, col. 810). He also said that s. 7(3) 'would not prevent the acceptance by the courts in this country of non-governmental organisational briefs here any more than it does in Strasbourg' and that 'as regards oral interventions by a third party, I dare say that the courts will be equally hospitable to oral interventions provided that they are brief' (Hansard, HL Deb, 27 November 1997, cols 832–834).

Third party interventions can provide considerable benefits to courts and litigants. They can draw to the court's attention the wider significance of a point in a way which an individual litigant may be unable to do. They may provide supporting statistical or other evidence. They can help the court to determine whether an interference with a Convention right is 'necessary in a democratic society' or 'proportionate' by drawing to the court's attention the wider social significance or effects of a particular outcome. An example of the European Court of Human Rights permitting such an intervention was in *Young, James & Webster* v *United Kingdom* (1981) 4 EHRR 38, in which the Trades Union Congress was permitted to intervene to file representations as to why the closed shop was necessary in a democratic society.

A particularly effective way in which a third party can intervene is to place a written submission or a witness statement before the court. This technique was adopted, to good effect, in the case of *R* v *Lord Chancellor, ex parte Witham* [1998] QB 575, in which the court used affidavit evidence filed by the Public Law Project to establish that Article 3 of the Supreme Court Fees (Amendment) Order 1996 had the effect of denying the constitutional right of access to the courts to people on low incomes in a variety of categories, without Parliamentary authority, and was accordingly *ultra vires*.

The Human Rights Act 1998 does not give an express right to intervene, except to the Crown, but the House of Lords and the Court of Appeal have shown themselves increasingly willing to allow third party interventions (see Practice Directions and Standing Orders Applicable to Civil Appeals, House of Lords, January 1996, Direction 34.1). Recent examples of such interventions include *R* v *Khan* [1997] AC 558 (in which Liberty intervened); *R* v *Secretary of State for the Home Department, ex parte Thompson and Venables* [1998] AC 407 (in which Justice made submissions, which Lord Browne-Wilkinson relied upon); *R* v *Bow Street Stipendary Magistrate, ex parte Pinochet Ugarte* [1999] 2 WLR 827 (Amnesty International intervened); and *Lubbe* v *Cape plc* [2000] 4 All ER 268 (in which the government of the Republic of South Africa intervened). There are also examples of multiple interventions, for example, *R* v *Department of Health, ex parte Source Informatics plc* [2000] 2 WLR 940.

Third parties are extremely unlikely to be asked to contribute to the costs of proceedings if they intervene in writing, or briefly and orally.

Interventions will only assist, however, if the parties which may have an interest in intervening know that proceedings in their area of interest are happening at all. The Public Law Project has recently monitored cases going through the Crown Office List identifying those which may raise issues of general public importance. However, lawyers representing a client in a case which might benefit from a third party intervention may need to contact potential intervenors themselves to let them know about the existence of the litigation.

4.5 WHICH COURT IS THE APPROPRIATE ONE IN WHICH TO RAISE ARGUMENTS UNDER THE ACT?

According to the White Paper, the Human Rights Act 1998 is intended to 'bring rights home', so that whatever remedy can be secured in Strasbourg should be available in national courts. The Act is intended to achieve this objective by enabling the domestic courts, at all levels, to award the remedies which could be awarded by the European Court of Human Rights in any proceedings. It aims to achieve this by ensuring that the Convention is an intrinsic part of all aspects of the legal system. Thus the Act provides that all courts and tribunals will be able to consider arguments brought under the Convention. It also aims to minimise disruption to existing court and tribunal procedures, and to retain Parliamentary sovereignty. How far all these objectives are achievable and compatible remains to be seen.

Sensibly, the Act does not provide any sort of reference procedure whereby an argument about a Convention point must be sent to a special court for adjudication. Convention arguments will be available in every public forum in which legal rights are determined, from the magistrates' court to the House of Lords. Section 7 of the Act refers to bringing proceedings against a public authority 'in the appropriate court or tribunal' (s. 7(1)(a)) and to relying on Convention rights 'in any legal proceedings' (s. 7(1)(b)) including as a defence.

The ambit of the phrase 'legal proceedings' is not clear; and there may be litigation in future about what constitutes a 'legal proceeding'. For example, is a complaint to a statutory ombudsman a legal proceeding? In most cases, the debate will not be important because the body conducting the proceeding will itself be a public authority and so under a duty to interpret the law in line with the Convention. But questions may arise in relation to non-statutory self-regulatory organisations, especially those apparently subject to contract rather than judicial review, such as the insurance ombudsman or the Jockey Club (see *R* v *Disciplinary Committee of the Jockey Club, ex parte Aga Khan* [1993] 1 WLR 909, CA).

The 'appropriate court or tribunal' will be determined by rules (s. 7(2) and (9)) (see Appendix 2). Claims will go to the court or tribunal most accustomed to dealing with claims analogous to the subject matter in question. There are a number of divisions of judicial labour that would appear to be straightforward. For example, juvenile cases will go to the juvenile court, county court or High Court as before; tax cases to the Special Commissioners. Convention arguments used in criminal proceedings will obviously go to the Crown Court or the magistrates' court.

Some examples are as follows. In a false imprisonment action, a person who wishes to claim damages for breach of Article 3 (freedom from torture or inhuman or degrading treatment) or Article 5 (the right to liberty and security of the person) could bring an action for breach of statutory duty under s. 6(1) of the Human Rights Act 1998 in the High Court or a county court; or the breach could be the basis for a habeas corpus or judicial review application. Article 5 arguments might also be used, for example, to argue for the release of a person before the Mental Health Review Tribunal. A taxpayer who wished to contend that a tax demand based on withdrawal of an extra-statutory concession is insufficiently precise and hence contrary to Protocol 1, Article 1, might be heard before the Special Commissioners of the Inland Revenue. A demonstrator who is prosecuted for obstruction of the highway or obstruction of a police officer may be able to invoke the right to peaceful assembly in Article 11 as a defence in the Crown Court or a magistrates' court.

There will also be many cases where the choice of forum will not be straightforward. One example of the type of case where there might be difficulty would be a challenge to the overall policy of banning gay people from the military, which is arguably contrary to Articles 8 and 14 of the Convention. The fastest and most logical way to get practical relief would be to seek a declaration by way of judicial review — which was unsuccessfully attempted in *R* v *Ministry of Defence, ex parte Smith* [1996] QB 517 before the Act was passed. But it has been held that employment law questions are generally not apt to proceed by way of judicial review (*R* v *East Berkshire Health Authority, ex parte Walsh* [1985] QB 152; *R* v *Secretary of State for Employment, ex parte Equal Opportunities Commission* [1993] ICR 251, reversed on other grounds by the House of Lords [1995] 1 AC 1). Unless the rules are explicit, such a service person could not bring his or her case in an employment tribunal (since service personnel have no right to allege unfair dismissal) so he or she might end up bringing the claim in the High Court or county court for breach of statutory duty, or inviting the Divisional Court not to follow *Walsh* so as to comply with its own s. 6 duty to give effect to the Convention. However, a public-interest group such as Stonewall might not have standing to advance this action by way of judicial review either, because of the narrowness of the 'victim' requirement in s. 7; though it might be able to do so if it could convince the court that it had associational rather than representative standing.

Another example of the type of case where choice of forum arguments may prove complex would be a claim that denial of a social security benefit is a breach of Protocol 1, Article 1 (the right to property), read together with Article 14 of the Convention (the non-discrimination provision). (Two examples are English cases, referred to Strasbourg, in which widowed mothers, but not widowed fathers received a particular allowance.) This would appear to be the type of claim which should properly be brought before the social security commissioners, to ask them to interpret the relevant legislation purposively so as to give effect to the Convention. But if the rule in question is contained in a piece of primary legislation, which is incapable of non-discriminatory interpretation, the only appropriate remedy would seem to be to go to the High Court (perhaps by way of judicial review) to seek a declaration of incompatibility. In practice, this might result either in duplication of proceedings or (particularly in this context, where no legal aid is available for proceedings before the commissioners) a legal wrong going uncorrected.

Another problem relates to bodies such as employment tribunals whose jurisdiction is limited by statute. Clear statutory rules would be needed to confer jurisdiction on such statutory tribunals to hear cases which raise causes of action brought purely under the Human Rights Act 1998 even though they will be able to use the 'interpretative' obligation in ss. 3 and 7(1)(b) in any event, if they do not involve other questions within their jurisdiction. The draft rules available at the time of going to press did not confer jurisdiction on employment tribunals in cases brought under s. 7(1)(a) of the Act, which may cause expense and duplication where, for example, both race and religious discrimination are alleged against a public authority. Unless such rules are made, it is likely that the courts will follow an approach similar to that of the Court of Appeal in *Biggs* v *Somerset County Council* [1996] ICR 364, which dealt with the jurisdiction of employment tribunals (then called industrial tribunals) in relation to 'free-standing' claims under Article 141 of the EC Treaty. This would mean that, unless the litigant could found their cause of action on an *existing* right which *is* within the tribunal's jurisdiction, the law would require claims for breach of statutory duty under the Human Rights Act 1998 to be brought in the High Court or a county court irrespective of the underlying subject matter of the claim. Such duplication will be stressful and expensive for litigants.

Where these complicated jurisdictional questions arise, particularly in statutory tribunals where no legal aid is available, cases may occur in which there is a denial of real and effective access to the court. In certain circumstances, this might constitute a breach of Article 6 of the Convention.

These jurisdictional questions are likely to cause litigation of a rather arid kind in the early years of the Human Rights Act 1998 (see, for example, the debate in *O'Reilly* v *Mackman* [1983] 2 AC 237). It may also result in claims arising out of one factual situation having to be litigated before more than one court or to appeal level in order to achieve a remedy for a breach of the Convention. Such cases might have been avoided if the government had adopted a 'residual reference' procedure for cases where an inferior court or tribunal dealing with a Human Rights Act 1998 question in a case within its jurisdiction considered that there might be a case for a declaration of incompatibility which would be beyond its jurisdiction to award. Under such a procedure the declaration could have been made by the High Court but as part of the main proceedings.

Chapter Five
Remedies

5.1 BREACH OF CONVENTION RIGHTS BY PUBLIC AUTHORITIES

Section 8(1) of the Human Rights Act 1998 authorises a court which has found that an act or proposed act of a public authority is unlawful to grant 'such relief or remedy, or make such order, within its powers as it considers just and appropriate'. The language which s. 8(1) uses is similar to s. 6 of the Hong Kong Bill of Rights Ordinance 1991, which itself is an expanded version of s. 24(1) of the Canadian Charter of Fundamental Rights and Freedoms 1982. This means that the case law from those and other jurisdictions is likely to be taken into account by English courts in developing the principles as to what remedies should be afforded in respect of particular breaches (or acts which constitute proposed breaches) of the Convention.

Since the Act maintains all such remedies as fall within the jurisdiction of the relevant court, the remedies which can be awarded under s. 8(1) will be familiar, i.e., damages, declarations, injunctions, and/or relief available on a prerogative writ brought by way of judicial review: certiorari, mandamus, prohibition.

The Act does not incorporate Article 13 of the Convention — i.e., the duty to afford a real and effective remedy for a Convention right. The rationale seemed to be that the Act itself constituted compliance with Article 13, and perhaps a nervousness about excessive judicial creative zeal. However, s. 2 may incorporate Article 13 in an interpretative context at least, by requiring a court considering any question arising 'in connection with' a Convention right to take into account Convention jurisprudence, in which Article 13 has a significant place.

Courts and tribunals of limited jurisdiction will not be able to award a remedy if it is outside their statutory power to do so. For example, an employment tribunal will not be able to order an injunction to prevent a discriminatory dismissal going ahead (because it has no statutory power to do so), even though this might be necessary to afford just satisfaction of a Convention right. Unless some collateral procedure is developed in the High Court, and in the absence of an incorporated duty to provide an effective remedy for breaches of the Convention, it may be that these jurisdictional restrictions themselves become the subject of Strasbourg challenges, even following incorporation.

In one respect, however, the Act does create new remedies. Section 8(2) permits a court to make an award of damages under the Act where it has the power to award compensation (even if it is not otherwise called damages). This would in principle include statutory tribunals such as employment tribunals. It is possible that in this way employment tribunals would be given power to consider whether, in effect, to override statutory caps on damages for unfair dismissal.

The principles on which damages in respect of a breach of a Convention right may be awarded are set out in s. 8(3) and (4). Section 8(3) provides that damages are only to be awarded where they are necessary to afford 'just satisfaction' to the victim, taking account of all the circumstances of the case, including any other remedy granted by the court or any other court, and the consequences of any decision (of that or any other court) in respect of the breach.

Section 8(4) provides that a court or tribunal deciding whether to award damages and how much to award must take into account the principles applied by the European Court of Human Rights in relation to the award of compensation under Article 41 of the Convention. This means that awards of damages under the Act are likely to be quite low. The quantum of awards granted by the Strasbourg court is cautious, particularly for 'non-pecuniary' damage, e.g., in cases of unlawful detention. A likely range of damages in a non-pecuniary case is between £10,000 and £15,000. See, for example, *Johnson* v *United Kingdom*, Application No. 22520/93, 24 October 1997, in which damages of £10,000 were awarded for unlawful detention of a mental patient. The level of awards under s. 8 of the Human Rights Act 1998 should not be used to detract from the level of damages which an applicant would have obtained in a like action before the enactment of the Convention, such as for false imprisonment. Section 11 of the Act provides that a person may rely on a Convention right without prejudice to any other right or freedom conferred on him or her by or under any (other) law having effect in the United Kingdom.

In general, it is not possible to make a claim for damages against a court which has breached the Convention, even though it is a public authority. Where a first instance court acts unlawfully, s. 9 of the Act requires proceedings in respect of its decision to be brought on appeal from the decision or by way of judicial review. This prevents collateral claims for damages against, for example, a court which it is argued has breached Article 8 of the Convention in determining a family law claim. However, there is provision in s. 9(3) and (4) of the Act for awards of damages against the Crown where any judicial body has been guilty of a breach of Article 5 (e.g., false imprisonment following a bail application), though to claim this remedy, the 'appropriate person', if not already a party to the proceedings, must be joined. The appropriate person (defined in s. 9(5) of the Act) is the minister responsible for the court concerned, or a person or government department nominated by him or her.

There is no remedy in damages where the breach of the Convention is caused by an Act of Parliament. It is still not clear how the Human Rights Act 1998 intends 'just satisfaction' to be afforded in cases where the breach of the Convention is a consequence of a statutory provision, and where a court has made a declaration of incompatibility under s. 4, given the failure to incorporate Article 13.

The question of how costs will be awarded in such cases is a serious issue. We think it would be unacceptable for a litigant who has lost a case because of a statute which breached his or her Convention rights to have to pay the costs of the litigation. This would be a serious deterrent to bringing such actions. Even if costs follow the declaration (i.e., are awarded against the government), this may leave the person who has had property rights violated, and incurred financial loss, or who is left in prison, or with a criminal record, without an effective remedy. In such cases, unless the government takes steps to act in compliance with the declaration of incompatibility, the applicant may be compelled to go to Strasbourg to obtain an effective remedy.

5.2 DECLARATIONS OF INCOMPATIBILITY AND THE 'FAST-TRACK' PROCEDURE

If a court cannot interpret primary legislation in such a way as is compatible with the Convention, then, although it must give primacy to the statute, the higher courts also have the further option of making a 'declaration of incompatibility' (Human Rights Act 1998, s. 4(2)). Thus if a court is unable to construe a statute in a way which is compatible with the Convention, the Act gives it the power to expose the problem by making a declaration that there has been a violation of Convention Rights. This is an improvement over the New Zealand Bill of Rights which simply prevents the courts from declaring legislation invalid if it conflicts with the Bill of Rights but provides power for the court to make a declaration of incompatibility.

5.2.1 The effect of declarations of incompatibility

A declaration of incompatibility will have two effects. First, making a declaration may create public interest and so put pressure on the government to change the law. Secondly, the courts are unlikely to want to make such declarations, which will ensure that they strive to find meanings for statutory provisions which conform with the Convention.

In 'Towards a Constitutional Bill of Rights' [1997] EHRLR 124 Lord Lester of Herne Hill has argued, at p. 127, that:

A Human Rights Act would not be like ordinary legislation of private law. Even though it would not be entrenched, it would be a constitutional measure (what would be described by the Supreme Court of Israel as an 'organic' or 'basic' law), designed to make Convention rights part of the fundamental law of the

United Kingdom. Our courts would therefore adopt the purposive approach taken by the Privy Council, when interpreting similar guarantees of human rights and fundamental freedoms.

Although this article was written before the Human Rights Bill was published, Lord Lester's view was based on a number of Privy Council cases, in particular *Minister of Home Affairs* v *Fisher* [1980] AC 319 at p. 328. He argued that the courts:

> would treat Convention rights as having special constitutional status and weight, and would wherever possible seek to save apparently inconsistent legislation from being construed in a manner which would breach Convention rights, and which would result in unnecessary recourse to the European Court of Human Rights.

The power to make declarations of incompatibility is only available in the higher courts. Although the Convention can be argued in the lower courts because of the effect of ss. 3, 6 and 7, and the lower courts must interpret primary legislation, as far as possible, to make it compatible with the Convention, declarations of incompatibility are *not* available in county courts, tribunals, the Crown Court or magistrates' courts.

If a lower court cannot interpret legislation in a way which conforms with the Convention, then it must follow the legislation and not the Convention. However, to arrive at that point the court would have to come to a view of the effect of the Convention in the instant case. In the reasons for its decision (e.g., a case stated by magistrates for the purposes of an appeal) it will logically, nevertheless, have to set out its view that the legislation is incompatible with the Convention in order for the litigant to make sense of the decision. The lower court's opinion that the provision does not comply with the Convention will not trigger the 'remedial order' provisions in s. 10, but could create the pressure for action to remedy the law.

Although a higher court can make a declaration of incompatibility it will not be able to set aside a statute, because of s. 3(2)(c). However, s. 10 provides a 'fast-track' procedure for the amendment of legislation which has been declared incompatible to bring it in line with human rights principles.

As it was envisaged in the original draft of the Act, the fast-track procedure would have made it easy for the executive to correct breaches of human rights and could have made it politically embarrassing not to do so.

However, late on in the Parliamentary debates, s. 10 was amended. This came about as a result of pressure from MPs concerned about excessive use of 'Henry VIII' clauses, i.e., provisions empowering the executive to legislate without reference to Parliament, like a statute of the reign of Henry VIII which gave the Crown power to repeal Acts of Parliament. In consequence, remedial orders can only be made where there are 'compelling reasons' to do so, and normally by positive resolution procedure (sch. 2).

The consequence of this unfortunate amendment could be that a breach of human rights may go uncorrected for want of Parliamentary time or because it relates to an unpopular group or a controversial cause. But it is precisely this domination of majority over minority interests which human rights law is designed to prevent. The amendment therefore had the unfortunate effect of weakening the structure of the Act: it makes it far less likely that people will litigate with a view to seeking declarations of incompatibility.

There may also be some practical difficulties with using the declaratory procedure. In a civil case, if Convention rights have been violated but it is clear that this was authorised by statute then few litigants will wish to take a case which they are likely to lose unless there is a real prospect of benefit to them such as a retrospective change in the law. It is also to be hoped that where a declaration of incompatibility is made by the court that costs are not awarded against the unsuccessful litigant.

The Act states that a declaration of incompatibility 'is not binding on the parties to the proceedings in which it is made, (s. 4(6)(b)). It is understood that this provision is designed to allow the government to take a different position from that of the court should the case be argued in the European Court of Human Rights.

Of course it is already implicit that the consequences of a declaration of incompatibility do not result in the conclusion of the proceedings being resolved in favour of the litigant whose rights were violated.

5.2.2 Notice provisions

In any case where a court is considering whether to make a declaration of incompatibility, the Crown is entitled to notice of this in accordance with rules of court (s. 5). In some cases the parties will be aware in advance that this is likely and notice can be given in advance. In other cases the Crown will already be a party. However, sometimes the conflict between the Convention and statute will arise in the context of the proceedings themselves. In such circumstances the case will need to be adjourned for notice to be given. The procedure is set out in the Rules. The Practice Direction to Part 19 of the CPR deals with this aspect of human rights litigation and gives full directions as to the procedure to be followed.

Once notice has been given, a minister of the Crown, or a person nominated by the minister, has a right to be joined as a party to the proceedings. The Crown is also given a particular right of appeal, with leave, to the House of Lords against any declaration of incompatibility made in criminal proceedings (s. 5(4)).

It is not clear whether the parties will have to bear the increased costs in such cases. At committee stage in the House of Lords an amendment to ensure that the Crown at least bore its own expenses was debated. The government rejected the proposal preferring to allow the courts to use their current discretion as to how costs are dealt with. It was suggested that factors for the court to consider included whether the case put forward by the person seeking the declaration had merit and whether or not there was any wider public interest in the matter. Also relevant were the means of the parties and of course the outcome of the application for a declaration.

5.2.3   Remedial action following a declaration of incompatibility

The fast-track procedure in s. 10 and sch. 2 for amending legislation which is found to be incompatible with the Convention can be started either following a declaration of incompatibility made under s. 4, or where it appears to the government following a decision of the European Court of Human Rights that a provision of legislation is incompatible with a Convention right. The European Court's decision has to be in a case against the United Kingdom: ministers could start the procedure following a Court decision concerning another country. It is not necessary that the judgment of the Court is in favour of the applicant.

Section 10 empowers a minister to make an order (called a 'remedial order'), which must be embodied in a statutory instrument (s. 20(1)), amending legislation so as to remove its incompatibility with the Convention. The Act provides two procedures for making a remedial order: a standard procedure in sch. 2, para. 2(a), and an emergency procedure in sch. 2, para. 2(b).

The standard procedure of sch. 2, para. 2(a) is a 'positive resolution procedure'. The minister must first, by sch. 2, para. 3, lay before Parliament a document containing a draft of the proposed order together with what is called the 'required information', which is (sch. 2, para. 5):

(a)   an explanation of the incompatibility which the proposed order seeks to remove, including particulars of the court declaration, finding or order which caused the minister to propose a remedial order; and

(b)   a statement of the reasons for proceeding under s. 10 and for making an order in the terms proposed.

This document must be before Parliament for at least 60 days, during which representations about the draft order may be made to the minister, either by Parliament in the form of a report or resolution, or by any other person. The minister can amend the draft in the light of these representations. Whether or not the draft is amended, it must be laid before Parliament again, this time accompanied by a summary of any representations that have been made and details of any changes made as a result. The order does not come into effect unless it is approved by a resolution of each House within 60 days after it is laid for the second time.

Under the emergency procedure of sch. 2, para. 2(b), the minister may make the order before laying it before Parliament, but must state in the order that it appears to him or her that, because of the urgency of the matter, it is necessary to make it without prior Parliamentary approval. However, after making an order under this emergency procedure the minister must, under sch. 2, para. 4, lay the order before Parliament, with the required information, for 60 days, during which representations may be made, as under the standard procedure. The minister can amend the order in the light of the representations, but, whether it is amended or not, the order must be laid before Parliament again, with a summary of representations and details of amendments, and it will cease to have effect 120 days after it was made unless it is approved by a resolution of each House.

The power given by s. 10 to amend legislation applies to both primary and second legislation. This provision will allow campaigners, lobbyists and lawyers to make representations to government to amend primary legislation following any case in the Court in Strasbourg that raises questions about legislation.

The government is not of course bound to act either by way of primary or secondary legislation even following a declaration of incompatibility, though if it did not do so, it would seem to be a virtual certainty that the victim could then seek just satisfaction in the European Court of Human Rights, which would then impose an obligation on the government as a matter of international law to remedy its violation.

A remedial order can be fairly wide in scope and can have a retrospective effect and can 'make different provision for different cases'. This retrospective effect is limited by sch. 2, para. 1(3) which states that, 'No person is to be guilty of an offence solely as a result of the retrospective effect of a remedial order'.

It must be assumed that the power to change the law retrospectively could be used to backdate a change to the date of the domestic court's decision on incompatibility or the judgment of the European Court of Human Rights.

Chapter Six
Exceptions and Special Cases: Article 13 and Freedom of Expression and Religion

The scheme of the Act is to have a consistent group of rules which apply Convention concepts to all litigation. However, there are some minor anomalies.

6.1   ARTICLE 13

The government decided not to incorporate Article 13 of the Convention. Article 13 is the 'remedies' provision. It provides:

> Everyone whose rights and freedoms as set forth in this Convention are violated shall have an effective remedy before a national authority notwithstanding that the violation has been committed by persons acting in an official capacity.

Many informed commentators pressed for the inclusion of Article 13, in order to ensure that effective protection would be given to rights. The government argued in Parliament that the inclusion of Article 13 was unnecessary as the Bill itself provided sufficient procedures and remedies to ensure that the other rights in the Convention could be enforced (see Appendix 4, pp. 205–207). It was also clear that the government was of the opinion that the inclusion of Article 13 might be something of a 'wild card' in the hands of the judiciary. This debate continued in the House of Commons committee stage (see the views of Conservative Attorney-General Sir Nicholas Lyell, Hansard HC, 20 May 1998, col. 976). The Home Secretary explained that the inclusion of Article 13 'would either cause confusion or prompt the courts to act in ways not intended by the Bill — for example, by creating remedies beyond those available in cl. 8. Whatever the outcome, the result would be undesirable.' He continued, 'In considering Article 13, the courts could decide to grant damages in more circumstances than we had envisaged' (20 May 1998, col. 979).

Where Article 13 plays a part in the Strasbourg jurisprudence, courts will be obliged by s. 2 to have regard to it when a question arises under the Act 'in connection with' a Convention right. It is therefore clear that the courts will be able to have regard to Article 13 and the jurisprudence founded on it (see the Lord Chancellor's response to Lord Lester of Herne Hill, Hansard HL, 18 November 1997, col. 477). Whether this will allow the courts to consider this as part of the intention behind the Act under *Pepper* v *Hart* [1993] AC 593 was debated in the House of Commons: Hansard HC 20 May 1998, col. 980.

This may be important in certain cases. For example, in *Chahal* v *United Kingdom* (1996) 23 EHRR 413 the right to an effective remedy was crucial to the judgment of the Court. This was a case involving the detention and threatened deportation of a Sikh activist who the government said was a terrorist. The key question in the case was whether, given that the government claimed that the details of the case against him could not be disclosed to protect national security, the courts could provide an effective remedy. It was decided that there was no effective remedy and as a result of that case the government enacted the Special Immigration Appeals Commission Act 1998, which creates a new special right of appeal in such cases.

6.2   THE CHURCHES AND THE PRESS

The churches and the press were particularly vociferous during the passage of the Bill which became the Human Rights Act 1998. They wished to ensure that particular liberties which they perceived as important would still be protected.

Fears were expressed on behalf of the Church of England, for example, that the Act might lead to questions about whether they could refuse to marry gay couples, or could dismiss teachers who had lost their faith. Sections of the press were concerned that the judiciary might interpret Article 8 of the Convention (right to respect for private and family life) in a way which unacceptably limited the freedom of the press.

After lengthy debates, ss. 12 and 13 of the Act were added as late amendments to meet these concerns.

6.3   FREEDOM OF EXPRESSION

Elements of the press expressed concern that the right to respect for private and family life in Article 8 of the Convention would endanger freedom of the press, because the judges could use it to create a 'right to privacy'.

This is obviously an area in which the judiciary may develop the law over time. One possibility is that the Press Complaints Commission, which is a public authority, could be subject to litigation under s. 6 of the Act if it fails properly to protect Article 8 rights. If a complaint to the PCC were to fail, the complainant might seek to challenge the decision by way of judicial review in the High Court, invoking Article 8 in such proceedings (on the basis of the failure of the Commission and government to protect the complainant's right to privacy). Another possibility, suggested by the Lord Chief Justice, Lord Bingham of Cornhill during the Parliamentary debates, is that the Act will have the effect of binding the *courts* (as public bodies) to create a common law right to privacy, even in the context of disputes between private individuals and organisations. Also, the courts might seek to develop an existing tort such as breach of confidence and expand it to include wider issues of privacy. In a number of cases, the courts have already found the Convention to be relevant in cases concerning private parties. One such case was *Rantzen* v *Mirror Group Newspapers (1986) Ltd* [1994] QB 670, in which the Court of Appeal affirmed that the Convention could be deployed to resolve an ambiguity in primary or subordinate legislation or when a court is considering how a judicial discretion is to be exercised.

Whether the courts do develop the law in this way remains to be seen. It is important to remember that the Strasbourg institutions regard the right to freedom of expression, protected by Article 10, as a particularly important right.

The object of s. 12 is to emphasise that, whatever directions the law takes, the courts must pay due regard to Article 10 and the right to freedom of expression.

Section 12 has a number of components. First, it prevents 'gagging injunctions' being granted *ex parte* except in the rarest of circumstances. It provides that if a court is considering whether to grant any relief which might affect the exercise of the Convention right to freedom of expression, there is a presumption against the grant of such relief. 'No such relief is to be granted' unless the court is satisfied that the person seeking the relief has taken all practicable steps to notify the respondent or there are compelling reasons why the respondent should not be notified (s. 12(1) and (2)). Secondly, the merits of the applicant's case must be tested before any such restraint is made. Section 12(3) provides that no relief is to be granted so as to restrain publication before trial unless the court is satisfied that the applicant is likely to establish that publication should not be allowed.

Thirdly, s. 12(4) provides that the court must have 'particular regard' to the right to freedom of expression, and that where the proceedings relate to material which the respondent claims, or which appears to the court, to be journalistic, literary or artistic material, the court must have regard to the extent to which the material has, or is about to, become available to the public or it is, or would be, in the public interest for the material to be published. It must also have regard to any relevant privacy code, which would clearly encompass the code issued by the Press Complaints Commission.

It is difficult to see quite what effect this will have. Article 10 in itself will require 'particular regard' to be given to the right to freedom of expression; but the court will have to take acount of Strasbourg principles when reaching its decisions, and form its own view on the difficult balance between Article 8 and Article 10 on the facts of a particular case. Strasbourg jurisprudence is very strongly in favour of freedom of expression. There is little authority on how conflicts between privacy and freedom of expression should be resolved (see *Winer* v *United Kingdom* (1986) 48 DR 154 at p. 170). Nevertheless, the state cannot use s. 12 so as to *disregard* the right to privacy. The court, as a public authority, would be in breach of Article 8 if it failed to provide a remedy for violations of privacy which were not justified by Article 8(2).

It is unlikely that this section adds a great deal to the generality of the Act.

6.4 RELIGION

In the same way as s. 12, s. 13 is unlikely to alter much in legal terms. Section 13 provides that if the court's determination of any question under the Act might affect the exercise by a religious organisation, whether as an organisation, or by its members collectively, of the Convention right to freedom of thought, conscience and religion, it must have particular regard to the importance of that right.

This is something which is inherent in the structure of Article 9 of the Convention, which is where that guarantee is to be found. Since the whole scheme of the Convention is to give particular regard to a prima facie right, permitting derogations from it only if they are necessary, proportionate etc., the effect of this section is really to add political comfort to religious interests rather than to add anything in terms of practical effect.

Chapter Seven
Using the Convention as Part of European Union Law

7.1 THE DEVELOPING DOCTRINE OF FUNDAMENTAL RIGHTS IN EU LAW

The European Union is not itself a signatory to the Convention, not being a state (see Opinion 2/94 [1996] ECR 1759). However, there is a developing doctrine of 'fundamental rights' in EU law. They have been important in the EU legal order for some time, and their importance can only develop following the Treaty of Amsterdam. This may have important consequences for using the Convention within the scope of EU law, which are considered below.

The European Court of Justice (ECJ), to which the EC Treaty gave the task of ensuring that 'the law is observed' (Article 220), has said that there are fundamental human rights enshrined in the general principles of EU law, and 'inspired by the constitutional traditions common to the member states' including the European Convention on Human Rights (see *Nold* [1974] ECR 491; *Stauder* v *City of Ulm* [1969] ECR 419). It has gone further, and also recognised the 'special significance' of the Convention as a source of principles of EU law (see *Rutili* v *Ministre de l'Intérieur* [1975] ECR 1219 and *Elliniki Radiophonia Tileorassi AE* v *Dimotiki Etairai Pliroforissi* [1991] ECR I-2925). It has also held that not only the EU institutions but also member states must act in accordance with the Convention in relation to every matter which falls within the scope of EU law (see *Commission* v *Germany* [1989] ECR 1263, para. 10). In his opinion in *Konstantinidis* v *Stadt Altensteig-Standesamt* [1993] ECR I-1191 Advocate General Jacobs said that an EU national could 'oppose any violation of his fundamental rights' when exercising EU free movement rights in another member state (see also *P* v *S* [1996] ECR I-2143, especially the opinion of Advocate General Tesauro and paras 17–22 of the judgment). However, this approach received a setback in *Grant* v *South-West Trains Ltd* [1998] ICR 428 when the European Court of Justice declined to follow the approach of Advocate General Elmer who had advocated using the fundamental rights approach so as to extend the scope of Article 141 of the EC Treaty (concerning equal pay for equal work without sex discrimination) so as to outlaw discrimination on grounds of sexual orientation.

The 'fundamental rights' in the founding treaty (non-discrimination on grounds of sex and nationality) and free movement rights were adopted mainly for economic reasons. However, human rights have undoubtedly gained in importance, particularly since the Treaty of Amsterdam, which creates the competence for the EU to legislate in a number of other anti-discrimination fields (such as race, age, sexuality and disability). There is also discussion of creating an EU Charter of Fundamental Rights.

Also, Article 6(2) of the Treaty on European Union provides:

The Union shall respect fundamental rights, as guaranteed by [the Convention] and as they result from the constitutional traditions common to the member states, as general principles of Community law.

Following the Treaty of Amsterdam, this provision is justiciable for the first time.

It remains the case that EU fundamental rights and Convention rights may not be identical (see paras 34 and 35 of Opinion 2/94). It is unclear whether the ECJ regards the standard in the Convention as mandatory or merely as 'inspiration' or 'guidelines' (*National Panasonic (United Kingdom) Ltd* v *Commission* [1980] ECR 2033; *Commission* v *Germany* [1989] ECR 1263; *Elliniki Radiophonia Tileorassi AE* v *Dimotiki Etairai Pliroforissis*; *P* v *S* [1996] ECR I-2143; *Kremzow* v *Austria* [1997] ECR I-2629; *Martinez Sala* [1998] ECR I-2691; *Bickel & Franz* (case C–274/96) [1998] ECR I-7637.

Convention standards are nonetheless an important aspect of European Union law, and their importance in national law in this context is likely to develop, both as a result of political changes at EU level and because of a heightened awareness of them in the United Kingdom after the Human Rights Act 1998 is brought into force.

7.2 WHY IT MAY BE USEFUL TO USE THE CONVENTION THROUGH EU LAW

European Union law only has an impact on domestic law in fields of EU competence, whereas now the Human Rights Act 1998 is in force, it can be used directly to challenge government action which has an impact on Convention rights. However, 'respect for fundamental rights' is a principle of the law of the European Union too and even after the incorporation of the European Convention on Human Rights into domestic law, there may be cases in areas covered by EU law rights in which the Convention will be more effective if it is used in conjunction with EU law than on its own through the Human Rights Act 1998:

(a) where the violation is contained in a statute, in the sphere of EU competence;

(b)   to broaden the 'victim' provisions;

(c)   to interpret the concept of a 'public authority';

(d)   as a route to a remedy.

The European Communities Act 1972 affords European Union law supremacy over other provisions of domestic law — it can override even statutory provisions where it is directly effective. This makes it in some respects more powerful than the Human Rights Act 1998, which explicitly prevents the courts from using the Convention to 'strike down' incompatible primary legislation (contrast *Marshall* v *Southampton and South West Hampshire Area Health Authority (Teaching)* (case 152/84) [1986] QB 401 and the European Communities Act 1972, s. 2, with the Human Rights Act 1998, s. 3(2)(b) and (c)).

In spheres of European Union law competence, it may therefore be more beneficial to use the Convention through EU law rather than through the Human Rights Act 1998 alone where the challenge is to primary legislation. The Act alone will provide no immediate remedy: it only permits a court to declare the domestic legislation incompatible with the Convention (see s. 4). By contrast, if primary domestic legislation contravenes directly effective EU legislation, the national court is required to disapply the primary domestic legislation (see EC Treaty, Article 10, European Communities Act 1972, s. 2, and *R* v *Secretary of State for Employment, ex parte Equal Opportunities Commission* [1995] 1 AC 1).

Where a court or tribunal can be persuaded that a provision of European Union law must be interpreted in accordance with the Convention, and where EU law is directly effective, the Convention standard will become part of domestic law even to the extent of overriding inconsistent domestic provisions (e.g., *Marshall* v *Southampton and South West Hampshire Area Health Authority (Teaching) (No. 2)* (case C-271/91) [1993] ICR 893).

Secondly, because s. 7 gives only 'victims' of acts standing to sue (see 4.4) the Convention may be more effectively used through EU law if the applicant seeks to remedy a breach of the Convention in a representative capacity. In ordinary judicial review proceedings, a trade organisation or pressure group can bring proceedings in a representative capacity. In domestic law cases, the Human Rights Act 1998 takes a very narrow approach to standing. However, in domestic cases relating to EU law, the Courts have adopted a far wider approach to standing: see, for example, *R* v *Secretary of State for the Environment, ex parte Friends of the Earth* (1995) *The Times*, 8 June. So, in cases engaging EU law, it is arguable that this restrictive approach to standing would not apply, and so an applicant may be able to argue Convention points which would not be available under the Human Rights Act 1998.

Thirdly, EU law may be directly effective against more public bodies than the Human Rights Act 1998 seems to be. So directly effective EU law provisions may help to enforce the Convention against more public bodies than the Act would. As to distinguishing between public and private bodies, there may (or may not) be a difference between:

(a) the test used in judicial review proceedings (see, e.g., *R* v *Panel on Take-overs and Mergers, ex parte Datafin plc* [1987] QB 815), in which questions as to the *sources* of power as well as the functions are potentially relevant;

(b) the test used in EU law, in which a body is held to be an emanation of the state, regardless of its legal form, if it has been made responsible pursuant to a measure adopted by the state for providing a public service, or where it has been given special powers (see *Foster* v *British Gas plc* (case C-188/89) [1990] ECR I-3313); and

(c) the definition of 'public authority' in the Human Rights Act 1998, s. 6 (see 4.3).

There may also be areas in which EU law offers more beneficial remedies than the Human Rights Act 1998. EU law requires, as an aspect of the principle of 'effectiveness', that national law provide an effective remedy for its breach. In particular, it offers the possibility of claims for damages if the government has failed properly to give effect to EU law (*Francovich* v *Italy* (cases C-6 & 9/90) [1991] ECR I-5357), whereas the Human Rights Act 1998 expressly excludes the possibility of damages for failure to legislate (see 4.1).

7.3 THE SITUATIONS IN WHICH THE CONVENTION MAY BE USED THROUGH EU LAW

Section 2 of the European Communities Act 1972 and Article 10 of the EC Treaty require English courts to give EU law rights effect in the United Kingdom without further enactment both through the principle of direct effect and the interpretative *Marleasing* principle (see 3.2 and *Collins* v *Imtrat Handelsgesellschaft mbH* (cases C-92 & 326/92) [1993] ECR I-5145). However, the English judges have not always interpreted the principle consistently as to the 'scope' of EU competence (compare *R* v *Ministry of Agriculture, Fisheries and Food, ex parte Hamble Fisheries (Offshore) Ltd* [1995] 1 CMLR 553 (Sedley J) and *R* v *Ministry of Agriculture, Fisheries and Food, ex parte First City Trading Ltd* [1997] 1 CMLR 250 (Laws J)).

7.4 THE POTENTIAL EFFECT OF THE CONVENTION IN DOMESTIC LAW IF USED VIA EU LAW

European Union law requires that member states must comply with the Convention when transposing EU law into national law (see *Rutili* v *Ministre de l'Intérieur* (case 36/75) [1975] ECR 1219; *Commission* v *Germany* (case 249/86) [1989] ECR 1263). English law which is intended to transpose European Union law into domestic law should therefore also accord with the Convention, as a matter of European *Union* law. Where Convention principles are part of EU law, United Kingdom legislation which purports to implement the EU provision but which contravenes the Convention has been found unlawful, and so been disapplied (see, for example, *Johnston* v *Chief Constable of the Royal Ulster Constabulary* (case 222/84) [1986] ECR 1651; *R* v *Kent Kirk* (case 63/83) [1984] ECR 2689).

The interpretative *Marleasing* principle can be used, not just to challenge actions of EU institutions but also in relation to domestic public bodies when they are acting within the scope of the EU competence. For example, in the *Collins* case, the ECJ found a breach of Article 12 of the EC Treaty because the decision of a German body relating to copyright law discriminated on the grounds of nationality. Though copyright is not in itself a matter covered by EU law, it does relate to rights with economic characteristics within the scope of copyright law.

Where provisions of EU law leave member states with a discretion as to the implementation, EU law requires them to exercise that discretion in accordance with the Convention (*Wachauf* v *Germany* (case 5/88) [1989] ECR 2609). This has been applied in the Scottish courts in *Booker Aquaculture Ltd* v *Secretary of State for Scotland* (1998) *The Times*, 24 September.

Derogations from EU law must be applied in accordance with Convention principles (*Elliniki Radiophonia Tileorassi AE* v *Dimotiki Etairai Pliroforissis* (case C-260/89) [1991] ECR I-2925). For example, Convention principles must be applied in applying the exceptions to the EC Treaty, Article 28 (free movement of goods), Articles 43 and 49 (freedom of establishment, freedom to provide services) and Article 39 (free movement of persons).

Curiously, in areas of EU competence, the ECJ, rather than (or as well as) the European Court of Human Rights, may provide guidance to the interpretation of relevant Convention provisions. In the case of *R* v *Hertfordshire County Council, ex parte Green Environmental Industries Ltd and another* [2000] All ER 773, the question arose whether a local authority could require a company to give answers to requests for information under s. 71(2) of the Environmental Protection Act 1990 (EPA) without giving an undertaking that the information gathered would not be used to prosecute. The EPA was passed to give effect to the European Waste Framework Directive, Council Directive 91/156/EEC, a measure of EU law. The company argued that s. 71(2), EPA must be interpreted in accordance with EU law, including general principles of human rights, and this included the privilege against self-incrimination contained in Article 6(1) of the Convention as an aspect of EU law. The House of Lords felt able to resolve the case before it without dealing with Article 6(1), because the question before it did not involve a trial. However, Lord Cooke observed (at 784E–F) that had it been necessary to determine whether Article 6(1) would have ruled out the admission of prosecution evidence obtained in consequence of the answers given, a reference to the ECJ may have been appropriate.

Chapter Eight
Convention Rights

8.1 INTRODUCTION

This chapter summarises the rights protected under the Convention. It is intended as an introduction to the substantive rights which the Convention protects. We have given some (non-exhaustive) examples of ways in which particular rights may be used in future cases. These are necessarily speculative: the effect of the Convention in domestic law after the Human Rights Act 1998 will depend on the inventiveness of lawyers and the attitude of the judiciary.

Article 1 is simply the duty on the states that have ratified the Convention to 'secure to everyone within their jurisdiction the rights and freedoms' protected by the Convention.

We have included a discussion of Article 13, although it has not been incorporated into English law, because of the important place it has in Convention case law, and the effect it is likely to have on the way other rights under the Convention fall to be interpreted. As part of the duty under s. 2 of the Act to take Convention jurisprudence into account in determining questions that have arisen 'in connection with' Convention rights, the parts of those cases which consider Article 13 in connection with other Convention rights will have to be considered.

When inviting a court to consider Convention jurisprudence under s. 2 it is important to be aware that the decisions are context specific. For example, cases concerning Article 3 in the context of medical treatment may require different policy judgments to those which the Court and Commission have reached in difficult cases involving terrorists.

In this chapter, unless otherwise specified, 'Court' means the European Court of Human Rights and 'Commission' means the European Commission of Human Rights.

8.2 ARTICLE 2: RIGHT TO LIFE

1. *Everyone's right to life shall be protected by law. No one shall be deprived of his life intentionally save in the execution of a sentence of a court following his conviction of a crime for which this penalty is provided by law.*

2.   *Deprivation of life shall not be regarded as inflicted in contravention of this article when it results from the use of force which is no more than absolutely necessary:*

(a)   *in defence of any person from unlawful violence;*

(b)   *in order to effect a lawful arrest or to prevent the escape of a person lawfully detained;*

(c)   *in action lawfully taken for the purpose of quelling a riot or insurrection.*

Article 2 has, not surprisingly, been described by the Court as 'one of the most fundamental provisions in the Convention' (*McCann* v *United Kingdom* (1995) 21 EHRR 97 at para. 197). With very limited exceptions, this right cannot be subject to derogation under Article 15. This Article does not prohibit the use of a death penalty which has been properly authorised, but Protocol 6 has required abolition of the death penalty.

Article 2 is relevant to many aspects of state power including the use of lethal force by the state through the police and armed forces to combat terrorism, fight crime and quell civil unrest. In keeping with the importance of this provision [the right to life] in a democratic society, the Court must, in making its assessment, subject deprivations of life to the most careful scrutiny (*McCann* v *United Kingdom* (1995) 21 EHRR 97 at para. 150).

8.2.1   Positive obligations

Article 2 both prohibits the state from taking life and places on it a positive duty to protect life. The Commission established that the state must 'not only refrain from taking life "intentionally" but, further, take appropriate steps to safeguard life' (*X* v *United Kingdom* (1978) 14 DR 31). States are under a positive obligation to legislate to criminalise private killing. However, Article 2 does not extend to a positive obligation on the state to protect the right to life regardless of the circumstances: *Osman* v *United Kingdom* (2000) 29 EHRR 245. In that case the applicants claimed a violation of Article 2 on the basis that the police failed to protect their relative Ahmed Osman after his teacher had formed a disturbing attachment to him. The police had been warned of the danger but failed to take action despite a number of incidents and reports indicating the likelihood of this happening. The Court found that none of the incidents leading up to the murder of the victim in themselves presented a life-threatening situation, and thus in these circumstances there was no infringement of Article 2. However, the Court did examine the scope of the right to life in cases involving the positive obligation on the state to protect life. It stated, at para. 116:

not every claimed risk to life can entail for the authorities a Convention requirement to take operational measures to prevent that risk from materialising. Another relevant consideration is the need to ensure that the police exercise their powers to control and prevent crime in a manner which fully respects the due process and other guarantees which legitimately place restraints on the scope of their action to investigate crime and bring offenders to justice, including the guarantees contained in Articles 5 and 8 of the Convention.

The duty to enforce the law to protect life also requires the proper investigation of all suspicious deaths. In *McCann* v *United Kingdom* the Commission stated that the obligation to protect life included a 'procedural aspect' which included 'the minimum requirement of a mechanism whereby the circumstances of a deprivation of life by the agents of a state may receive public and independent scrutiny'.

In *Yasa* v *Turkey* (1999) 28 EHRR 408 the applicant and his uncle, both of whom were involved in the sale and distribution of a Kurdish newspaper, had been subject to gun attacks in which the uncle was killed. The applicant claimed that the failure of the authorities properly to investigate the attacks and apprehend the suspects violated his right to life under Article 2 and his right to a judicial remedy under Article 13. The Court held that there had indeed been a violation of Articles 2 and 13 and thus indicated that failure to provide an opportunity for effective investigations into individuals' deaths amounts in itself to a breach of Article 2.

8.2.2 Exceptions to the right to life

The second paragraph of the Article details the exceptions to the right to life. All these situations involve curbing violence or the control of prisoners or criminals — generally, maintaining law and order. 'No more force than is absolutely necessary' is the crucial test for these exceptions. The Commission examined the phrase 'absolutely necessary' in *Stewart* v *United Kingdom* (1984) 38 DR 162. In this case a 13-year-old boy was accidentally killed by a plastic bullet fired into a crowd by the army while trying to quell a riot. The Commission held that this was not a violation of Article 2 as the force fell within the category of 'absolutely necessary'. It stated that force is 'absolutely necessary' if it is 'strictly proportionate to the achievement of the permitted purpose'. The Commission explained further:

In assessing whether the use of force is strictly proportionate, regard must be had to the nature of the aim pursued, the dangers to life and limb inherent in the situation and the degree of risk that the force employed might result in the loss of life. The Commission's examination must have due regard to all the relevant circumstances.

The Commission found that the exceptions included in Article 2(2) indicate that this provision extends to, but is not concerned exclusively with, intentional killing. It stated that Article 2, when read as a whole, indicates that para. 2:

does not primarily define situations where it is permitted intentionally to kill an individual, but defines the situations where it is permitted to 'use force' which may result, as an unintended outcome of the use of force, in the deprivation of life.

The leading case on the use of lethal force is *McCann* v *United Kingdom* (1995) 21 EHRR 97 in which three Provisional IRA members were shot and killed by Special Air Service soldiers in Gibraltar in 1988. The Court held, by a slim 10 to 9 vote, that there had been a violation of Article 2. In making its decision the Court will take into consideration 'not only the actions of the organs of the state who actually administer the force but also the surrounding circumstances including such matters as the planning and control of the actions under examination'. This idea of 'planning and control' is important. The Court held that the state must give appropriate training, instructions and briefing to its agents who are faced with a situation where the use of lethal force is possible. The state must also exercise 'strict control' over any operations that may involve use of lethal force.

A contrasting case to *McCann* is *Andronicou* v *Cyprus* (1997) 25 EHRR 491. This involved a hostage situation where the police mistakenly believed that a gunman had more ammunition and weapons than he actually possessed. The gunman and his hostage were killed by shots fired by the police. The Court sought to determine whether the force administered in this situation was 'strictly proportionate' to the achievement of the aims set out in Article 2(a), (b) and (c). It decided that the degree of force used was proportionate to the dangerous hostage situation. As in *McCann* v *United Kingdom*, the Court looked also to the planning and control of the actions under examination. It found that the police actions were designed and carried out to minimise the risk to the lives of the gunman and his hostage. Even though the police were mistaken about the gunman's weapons, the Court ruled that they had good reason to believe as they did, and were pursuing the legitimate aims of Article 2(2). Therefore, no violation of Article 2 was found in this case.

The Commission also considered the right to life in *Paton* v *United Kingdom* (1980) 19 DR 244. A husband tried to prevent his wife, who was now living separately, from having an abortion. The Commission concluded that the term 'everyone' in the Convention generally applied only post-natally and the life of the foetus was intimately 'connected with, and . . . cannot be regarded in isolation of, the life of the pregnant woman'. However, although the case was declared inadmissible, it concerned the abortion of a foetus of less than 10 weeks, that is, one that had no viable life outside the mother.

8.2.3 Potential issues

Issues that might be raised in domestic courts in relation to Article 2 include whether the planning surrounding the use of lethal force eradicates as far as possible the chances of loss of life; whether the training of police and prison officers to recognise and deal with life-threatening situations is adequate; and whether training in safe ways of restraining violent prisoners complies with the Convention standard.

The standard that applies in England and Wales allows the use of lethal force where such force is reasonable (Criminal Law Act 1967, s. 3). The reasonableness of the *use of force* has to be decided on the basis of the facts which the user of the force honestly believed to exist — a subjective test. The test in Article 2 is different and imposes a higher standard. The standard in the Convention is whether the use of the force was 'absolutely necessary'. On the basis of that test, the determination of whether *the force used* was reasonable must be objectively assessed by deciding whether the force used was disproportionate to the apparent threat that it was intended to prevent. This discrepancy may lead to cases testing the lower domestic standard against the newly incorporated Convention standard of 'absolutely necessary'.

Issues may also arise in medical law, in particular, whether adequate medical assistance has been provided, especially in an emergency. This is the sort of case which will raise difficult questions about the extent of a court's capacity to review the rationale for decisions taken in the exercise of professional judgment or where public authorities have to make difficult decisions about those on life-support systems. The requirement of public authorities to comply with the Convention wherever possible (Human Rights Act 1998, s. 6) may also affect the standard of scrutiny which is used by the courts in determining whether withholding potentially life-saving treatment is reasonable and lawful. See, for example, the difference in view between Laws J at first instance and the Court of Appeal in *R* v *Cambridgeshire District Health Authority, ex parte B* [1995] 1 FLR 1055.

Following *Osman* v *United Kingdom* (2000) 29 EHRR 245 and *Yasa* v *Turkey* (1999) 28 EHRR 408 the need for proper scrutiny under Article 2 is likely to give rise to issues in conjunction with Article 6 and perhaps Article 13 of the Convention (though Article 13 is not specifically incorporated into United Kingdom law). For example in the case of *Keenan* v *UK*, Application No. 27229/95, 22 May 1998, the Commission found a breach of Article 13 in favour of the mother of a prisoner who committed suicide in HMP Exeter. In some cases the culpability of the state for a death will be decided by actions for assault or negligence in the civil courts, where legal aid, disclosure and the usual rules of fairness ordinarily apply. However, many of those who die in police custody or in prison do not have relatives who are financially dependent on them, and so they may not have a cause of action for compensation. Thus, an inquest is the only real remedy. Convention issues which may arise in the investigative process could include the difficulties for relatives given the absence of legal aid, the absence of a duty on the authorities to disclose material and other procedural hurdles in the inquest system. Consideration would need to be given to the adequacy of investigation by the police, of the police and the supervision by the Police Complaints Authority.

Despite the ruling in *Taylor* v *United Kingdom* (1994) 79-A DR 127, where the applicants were unsuccessful when they claimed that the state's failure to set up a public inquiry into killings by a hospital nurse had breached the procedural requirements of Article 2, the domestic courts are showing some sympathy to the imposition of positive obligations in this area, particularly where prisoners are

involved. For example, in *Reeves* v *Commissioner of Police* [1999] 3 WLR 363 it
was held that the police were liable under the Fatal Accidents Act 1976 for the
suicide of a prisoner. The Court of Appeal held that the breach of duty by the
police which facilitated the suicide — leaving the hatch open in the cell door
through which the deceased threaded his belt — led to the death.

8.3   ARTICLE 3: PROHIBITION OF TORTURE

No one shall be subjected to torture or to inhuman or degrading treatment or
punishment.

Article 3 concerns freedom from torture, inhuman treatment, degrading treatment,
inhuman punishment and degrading punishment. The protections of Article 3
cannot be derogated from in any circumstances, even during war or public
emergency (Article 15). This article places a negative duty on the state not to inflict
this suffering on human beings, as well as a positive duty to see that these forms
of suffering are not carried out within its borders.

In *Ireland* v *United Kingdom* (1978) 2 EHRR 25, the Court, at para. 167,
characterised the activities prohibited by Article 3 as:

(a)   Torture: deliberate inhuman treatment causing very serious and cruel
suffering.

(b)   Inhuman treatment: treatment that causes intense physical and mental
suffering.

(c)   Degrading treatment: treatment that arouses in the victim a feeling of fear,
anguish and inferiority capable of humiliating and debasing the victim and possibly
breaking his or her physical or moral resistance.

In *Ireland* v *United Kingdom* the Court examined five techniques used by the
British government to interrogate prisoners allegedly involved in terrorism. These
techniques included forcing them to stand against a wall in an uncomfortable
position, hooding, subjecting them to loud continuous noise, and depriving them
of food, drinks and sleep. Although not rising to the level of torture, the Court
determined that these practices constituted degrading treatment and, therefore,
violated Article 3 (2 EHRR 25 at paras 167–8). In reaching its decision, the Court
held that the treatment by the state 'must attain a minimum level of severity' if it
is to fall within the ambit of Article 3. It described the determination of this
'minimum level' as 'relative' and set out some criteria such as the duration of the
treatment, its physical or mental effects and, in some circumstances, the sex, age
and state of health of the victim (para. 162). These factors are relevant in two
contexts: when determining whether the suffering caused is sufficient to amount to
inhuman or degrading treatment or punishment and when distinguishing between
these lesser kinds of ill-treatment and torture.

There are no exceptions to Article 3, regardless of the conduct of an applicant. For example, in *Chahal* v *United Kingdom* (1996) 23 EHRR 413, a Sikh, believed by the UK government to have engaged in terrorist activities in the UK aimed at undermining the government in India, was subject to a deportation order. He challenged the order under Article 3 of the Convention, arguing that if he were forcibly returned to India there was a real danger of persecution. The Strasbourg Court upheld this claim and observed that there could be no qualification of the protection offered by Article 3, even in the case of individuals representing a threat to public order.

Race discrimination may constitute degrading treatment. In *East African Asians* v *United Kingdom* (1973) 3 EHRR 76 the applicants were British passport holders and had been refused permission to take up residence in the United Kingdom. The Commission considered that:

> the racial discrimination, to which the applicants have been publicly subjected by the application of . . . immigration legislation, constitutes an interference with their human dignity which . . . amounted to 'degrading treatment' in the sense of Article 3 of the Convention.

In *Denmark* v *Greece* (1969) 12 YB Special Vol., the Commission held that torture had occurred. The Commission's finding was confirmed by the Committee of Ministers. The Athens security police were found to have used a system of torture and ill-treatment against political detainees. The Commission referred to non-physical as well as physical torture, describing 'the infliction of mental suffering by creating a state of anguish and stress by means other than bodily assault'. From this and the judgment in *Ireland* v *United Kingdom* (1978) 2 EHRR 25 commentators have surmised that mental anguish alone may constitute torture if it reaches a certain level of severity. The Commission has mentioned mock executions, threats of death and threats of reprisal against a detainee's family as evidence of non-physical torture without concluding that any of these equalled torture in fact.

The Commission has ruled that the state is responsible for the actions of its agents under Article 3. In *Cyprus* v *Turkey* (1976) 4 EHRR 482 the Commission found the state responsible for rapes committed by its soldiers. It held that satisfactory actions had not been taken to prevent these attacks and that disciplinary measures after the conduct were insufficient. In *Ribitsch* v *Austria* (1995) 21 EHRR 573, the Court determined that the physical abuse suffered by the applicant at the hands of the Vienna Federal Police Authority amounted to inhuman and degrading treatment. The applicant claimed that he received punches to the head, kidneys and right arm and kicks to the upper leg and kidneys. He was allegedly pulled to the ground by his hair and his head was banged against the floor. Upon release he suffered from a cervical syndrome, vomiting, diarrhoea and a violent headache.

As well as refraining from inflicting torture, Article 3 places states under a positive obligation to prevent torture. In *Chahal* v *United Kingdom* (1997) 23

EHRR 413, the Court held that a deportation of a person to a country where there was a real risk that he could be tortured could offend Article 3, because of the positive obligation within the Article to prevent torture. The Court made the same ruling in *D* v *United Kingdom* (1997) 24 EHRR 423, although the reasoning was based on the lack of treatment the receiving country would have for the applicant, who had contracted AIDS and had no family in the receiving state. In *Soering* v *United Kingdom* (1989) 11 EHRR 439 the Court took the view that extradition to the United States to face a trial for murder would mean that the applicant would be held on death row pending execution for long periods. This treatment, it was held, would violate Article 3, and so to permit Mr Soering to be extradited to America would constitute a violation of that Article by the United Kingdom.

Other actions which have come within the ambit of Article 3 include rape in custody and corporal punishment. In *Aydin* v *Turkey* (1997) 25 EHRR 251, the applicant was detained by the Turkish security forces and, while in custody, was raped and subjected to various forms of ill-treatment. The Court decided that torture had occurred in contravention of Article 3.

Another case involving the state's positive obligations was *A* v *United Kingdom* (1999) 27 EHRR 611 in which A had been hit by his stepfather with a stick. The stepfather was charged with assault occasioning actual bodily harm. The stepfather contended that the assault amounted to reasonable punishment, which is a defence to a charge of assault by a parent of a child, and he was acquitted. The Court decided there was a violation of Article 3 because the law failed to give adequate safeguards in insufficiently defining what constituted 'reasonable punishment' (see also *Tyrer* v *United Kingdom* (1978) 2 EHRR 1; *Campbell* v *United Kingdom* (1982) 4 EHRR 293; *Costello-Roberts* v *United Kingdom* (1993) 19 EHRR 112).

8.3.1 Potential issues

Article 3 is likely to feature in many asylum and deportation cases because many possible violations of the Article may result from deportation and exclusion.

Another obvious area where Article 3 might have an impact on domestic litigation is the conditions of detention for those held in institutions. However, recent cases suggest that the standard of poor conditions to be met before a violation of Article 3 can be considered is considerable. In *Delazarus* v *United Kingdom*, Application No. 17525/90, 16 February 1993, a prisoner was segregated for over four months as a result of a disciplinary charge. During this time he was not allowed to communicate or associate with other prisoners and was locked in a cell for 23 hours a day with two 30-minute exercise breaks in an individual pen the size of a tennis court. He was able to leave his cell three times a day to empty his chamber pot. The unit was infested with cockroaches and he complained that the cell was cold. He also complained about the racist attitude of the staff. He was, however, able to go to religious services and have visits from relatives and medical and prison staff. The conditions in the prison during this time were criticised by the Chief Inspector of Prisons and the European Committee for the Prevention of

Torture and Inhuman and Degrading Treatment or Punishment. The Commission declared the application inadmissible. The Commission took a similar view in *Windsor* v *United Kingdom*, Application No. 18942/91, 6 April 1993. However, different considerations may apply to such cases as those involving women prisoners giving birth in handcuffs.

Another issue that might arise is the use of CS spray and new-style batons by police officers. Provided the responsibility of the state in such circumstances was clear, cases may also be brought in relation to the government's failure to protect sex offenders who have been released from prison from actions by vigilantes.

Article 3 may also play a role in cases concerning school discipline (even though corporal punishment is unlawful, other forms of punishment may be degrading). Schools may also have positive obligations to protect pupils from bullying by other pupils. Article 3 may also have some application in cases concerning rationing of health care, if palliative treatment is withheld. We are aware of at least one judicial review initiated against a London health care trust in which Article 3 was invoked to challenge the refusal to supply pain-relieving therapy to a severely mentally handicapped woman. The case settled. Arguably Article 3 could even be relevant to the issue of whether the state should permit euthanasia.

8.4 ARTICLE 4: PROHIBITION OF SLAVERY AND FORCED LABOUR

1. No one shall be held in slavery or servitude.

2. No one shall be required to perform forced or compulsory labour.

3. For the purpose of this Article the term 'forced or compulsory labour' shall not include:

   (a) any work required to be done in the ordinary course of detention imposed according to the provisions of Article 5 of this Convention or during conditional release from such detention;

   (b) any service of a military character or, in case of conscientious objectors in countries where they are recognised, service exacted instead of compulsory military service;

   (c) any service exacted in case of an emergency or calamity threatening the life or well-being of the community;

   (d) any work or service which forms part of normal civic obligations.

The prohibition of slavery and servitude is another of the rights from which no derogation is allowed under Article 15. Relatively few Article 4 complaints have been heard by the Court or Commission and none has been upheld.

Slavery has not been defined, but servitude has been held to differ from slavery in that no ownership of the person is claimed. Forced labour differs from servitude in that 'the concept of servitude includes obligation on the part of the "serf" to live on another's property and the impossibility of changing his condition' (D.J.

Harris, M. O'Boyle and C. Warbrick, *Law of the European Convention on Human Rights* (London: Butterworths, 1995), p. 91). There are two elements in the definition of forced labour derived from the International Labour Organisation Convention of 1930 (incorporated into Convention jurisprudence in *X* v *Federal Republic of Germany* (1974) 17 YB 148):

1.   The work must be performed involuntarily.
2.   The requirement to do the work must be unjust or oppressive or the work itself involve avoidable hardship.

The complaints deemed admissible have usually fallen into the categories of (a) treatment of prisoners, (b) professionals being compelled to provide their services free to the community.

In *Van Droogenbroeck* v *Belgium* (1982) 4 EHRR 443, the Court found that a prisoner's sentence did not violate the principles of Article 4. The applicant was sentenced to two years in prison followed by 10 years 'at the government's disposal'. The Court held that this did not amount to 'that particularly serious form of deprivation of liberty' that constitutes servitude (paras 58–9). It went on to rule that this sentence 'did not go beyond what is "ordinary" in this context since it was calculated to assist him in reintegrating himself into society'.

In *Van der Mussele* v *Belgium* (1983) 6 EHRR 163, a barrister tried to extend the boundaries of Article 4 when he claimed that being made to do pro bono legal work for indigent defendants violated the Article 4 prohibition of forced labour. The key question became whether the applicant had 'offered himself voluntarily' when he was taken on as a pupil. The Court asked whether the labour imposed 'a burden which was so excessive or disproportionate to the advantages attached to the future exercise of the profession that the service could not be treated as having been voluntarily accepted'. Ruling against the barrister, the Court relied on the fact that he had entered the profession of his own will, knowing that pro bono work was expected of him. Mr Van der Mussele's case that he was discriminated against in comparison with trainees in other professions, contrary to Article 14, was also dismissed on the basis that they were not in an analogous situation.

8.4.1 Potential issues

It has been argued that Community Service Orders (CSOs) imposed by the criminal courts may violate Article 4, particularly now that the court does not have to obtain the consent of the defendant before imposing such an order. Community service which is imposed 'during conditional release from such detention' is not a violation of the Article. Although the court imposes a CSO instead of a prison sentence, this is not the same as conditional release. However, a challenge may be problematic if a CSO is seen as an alternative to a prison sentence.

8.5 ARTICLE 5: RIGHT TO LIBERTY AND SECURITY

1. Everyone has the right to liberty and security of person. No one shall be deprived of his liberty save in the following cases and in accordance with a procedure prescribed by law:

(a) the lawful detention of a person after conviction by a competent court;

(b) the lawful arrest or detention of a person for non-compliance with the lawful order of a court or in order to secure the fulfilment of any obligation prescribed by law;

(c) the lawful arrest or detention of a person effected for the purpose of bringing him before the competent legal authority on a reasonable suspicion of having committed an offence or when it is reasonably considered necessary to prevent his committing an offence or fleeing after having done so;

(d) the detention of a minor by lawful order for the purpose of educational supervision or his lawful detention for the purpose of bringing him before the competent legal authority;

(e) the lawful detention of persons for the prevention of the spreading of infectious diseases, of persons of unsound mind, alcoholics or drug addicts or vagrants;

(f) the lawful arrest or detention of a person to prevent his effecting an unauthorised entry into the country or of a person against whom action is being taken with a view to deportation or extradition.

2. Everyone who is arrested shall be informed promptly, in a language which he understands, of the reasons for his arrest and of any charge against him.

3. Everyone arrested or detained in accordance with the provisions of paragraph 1(c) of this Article shall be brought promptly before a judge or other officer authorised by law to exercise judicial power and shall be entitled to trial within a reasonable time or to release pending trial. Release may be conditioned by guarantees to appear for trial.

4. Everyone who is deprived of his liberty by arrest or detention shall be entitled to take proceedings by which the lawfulness of his detention shall be decided speedily by a court and his release ordered if the detention is not lawful.

5. Everyone who has been the victim of arrest or detention in contravention of the provisions of this Article shall have an enforceable right to compensation.

Article 5 protects the 'right to liberty and security of person'. This right is not absolute and can be derogated from under Article 15 in times of emergency. The overall purpose of this article has been described by Strasbourg as ensuring that no one is deprived of his or her liberty in an 'arbitrary fashion' (see, e.g., *Engel* v *Netherlands* (1976) 1 EHRR 647 at para. 58). The right to 'security of person' has not been given a separate meaning from the 'right to liberty', and the phrase should be read as a whole so 'security of person' is to be understood in the context of physical liberty (*East African Asians* v *United Kingdom* (1973) 3 EHRR 76). These protections are based on four important principles:

(a)   No one can be deprived of his or her liberty except in accordance with a procedure prescribed by law (Article 5(1)).

(b)   The only grounds upon which a person may be deprived of his or her liberty are set out in Article 5(1)(a) to (f) and this list is exhaustive.

(c)   Any person subject to detention must be able to challenge the legality of that detention (Article 5(4)).

(d)   If it is determined that a person has been detained in violation of this Article, that person has an enforceable right to compensation (Article 5(5)).

8.5.1   Procedure prescribed by law

The rule that a person cannot be deprived of his or her liberty except in accordance with a procedure 'prescribed by law' (Article 5(1)) is designed to prevent arbitrary confinement. This rule has two prongs: first, the procedures created by domestic law must have been complied with fully, and second the domestic law must be formulated clearly to enable ordinary citizens to be able to foresee the circumstances likely to lead them into detention.

If loss of liberty is initiated by arrest then further rights are activated. Arrest is only lawful if it is based on a reasonable suspicion of having committed an offence or when it is reasonably considered necessary to prevent the arrested person from committing an offence or fleeing after commission (Article 5(1)(c)). The arrest is only lawful if the purpose is to bring that person before a competent legal authority (*ibid.*). Anyone detained, not just subject to arrest, must be informed, in a language that he or she understands, of the reasons for the arrest and of any charges against him or her (Article 5(2)). An arrested person shall be brought promptly before a judge or other officer authorised to exercise judicial power (Article 5(3)). Any trial shall take place within a reasonable period (*ibid.*). The arrested person shall be entitled to release pending trial. That release may be conditioned by guarantees to appear for trial (*ibid.*).

8.5.2   Grounds of exception

The list of exceptions to the rights to liberty and security of person in sub-paras (a) to (f) of Article 5(1) is exhaustive and is to be given a 'narrow interpretation' (*Winterwerp* v *Netherlands* (1979) 2 EHRR 387).

Article 5(1)(a)
Article 5(1)(a) permits 'the lawful detention of a person after conviction by a competent court'. A competent court under this Article is one with jurisdiction to try the case and, presumably one that complies with the provisions of Article 6 (*X* v *Austria* (1987) 11 EHRR 112). This Article is concerned only with the fact of detention and not with the conditions of the detention. In order for a detention to be 'lawful' there must be a court judgment that justifies the confinement, as well as lawful procedures followed to effect the detention. Strasbourg has held that Article 5(1)(a) does not permit the Court to review convictions or sentences

imposed by a domestic court — though any such decision would have to comply with Article 6.

Article 5(1)(b)

Article 5(1)(b) sanctions the detention of a person who has failed to observe a court order or obligation. This includes failure to pay a court fine and refusal to submit to a court-ordered medical examination. The obligations may include military service or the filing of tax returns. The Court has held that the order or obligation must be clear, the person detained must usually be given an opportunity to comply with the order or obligation and the detention must be the only reasonable way to secure the fulfilment of the order or obligation.

In *McVeigh v United Kingdom* (1981) 25 DR 15 the obligation was to submit to 'further examination' upon entering Great Britain. Three men were detained for 45 hours under suspicion of terrorist activities but were released and not charged with any crimes. The Commission ruled that in 'limited circumstances of a pressing nature' Article 5(1)(b) could be extended to cover periods of detention necessary to fulfil an obligation. It went on to state, at p. 42:

> In considering whether such circumstances exist, account must be taken . . . of the nature of the obligation. It is necessary to consider whether its fulfilment is [a] matter of immediate necessity and whether the circumstances are such that no other means of securing fulfilment is reasonably practicable. A balance must be drawn between the importance in a democratic society of securing the immediate fulfilment of the obligation in question, and the importance of the right to liberty. The duration of the period of detention is also a relevant factor in drawing such a balance.

Article 5(1)(c)

Article 5(1)(c) concerns the arrest or detention of suspects while involved in the administration of criminal justice. Arrest is only lawful if it is based on a reasonable suspicion that a person has committed a crime, or when it is reasonably considered necessary to prevent a person from committing a crime or from fleeing after committing one. The test of reasonable suspicion is an objective one. In *Fox v United Kingdom* (1990) 13 EHRR 157 the applicants had been arrested under the Northern Ireland (Emergency Provisions) Act 1978, which, at that time, required only that the arresting official 'genuinely and honestly' suspected the person arrested to be a terrorist. The Court found a violation of Article 5(1)(c) on the basis that 'genuine and honest' suspicion was a lower standard than reasonable suspicion and was, therefore, not acceptable under the Convention. In the Court's view, 'reasonable suspicion supposes the existence of facts or information which would satisfy an objective observer that the person concerned may have committed the offence' (para. 32).

In *Murray v United Kingdom* (1994) 19 EHRR 193, another terrorist case, the Court was less robust in its defence of Article 5(1)(c) but the principles in the case are context-specific and may not apply in non-terrorist cases.

An arrest is legal under Article 5(1)(c) only if the purpose is to bring the detainee before a competent legal authority. The fact that the suspect may not ultimately be brought before a court or charged with a crime does not undermine the arrest since 'the existence of such a purpose must be considered independently of its achievement' (*Brogan* v *United Kingdom* (1988) 11 EHRR 117). Internment, such as the type used in Northern Ireland, is at odds with Article 5 (*Lawless* v *Ireland* (1961) 1 EHRR 1).

Article 5(1)(d)

Article 5(1)(d) covers the detention of minors. Below the age of 18 is the accepted European standard for a minor.

Article 5(1)(e)

Article 5(1)(e) permits the detention of those with infectious diseases, persons of unsound mind, alcoholics, drug addicts and vagrants. These people are mentioned because 'they have to be considered as occasionally dangerous for public safety' and 'their own interests may necessitate their detention' (*Guzzardi* v *Italy* (1980) 3 EHRR 333). In our view, a high standard of justification would be necessary to render such detention proportionate. The mere fact of being, for example, a drug addict will be unlikely to justify detention without some other factor (such as objective reason to believe that the person in question would harm himself or herself or others) under Article 5(1)(e).

The combination of the requirement of 'lawfulness' under Article 5(1)(e) and the obligation on the state to allow judicial review of detention under Article 5(4) has led to a number of decisions against measures in states such as the United Kingdom relating to the detention of psychiatric patients (see the discussion later in this section). The validity of continued detention under Article 5(1)(e) depends upon the persistence of the mental disorder: any period of detention beyond this will be in breach of Article 5(1), no matter how compelling the reasons for continuing to detain the patient: *Stanley Johnson* v *United Kingdom* (1999) 27 EHRR 296.

In that case the applicant was a patient at Rampton mental hospital who was found by the Mental Health Tribunal to be no longer suffering from a mental disorder. He was conditionally discharged but no hostel accommodation could be found for him and he had to remain at Rampton. The Strasbourg Court upheld his claim. There were three constituent elements under Article 5(1)(e) which justified the detention of persons of unsound mind:

(a)   the individual must be reliably shown to be of unsound mind;

(b)   the mental disorder must be of a kind or degree warranting compulsory confinement;

(c)   the validity of the continued detention depends upon the persistence of the mental disorder.

Once it was shown that the preconditions justifying the applicant's detention had ceased to exist, the Court accepted that there might be a delay in allowing the unconditional discharge of the patient into the community. However, the Court also stressed that appropriate safeguards should be in place so as to ensure that any deferment of discharge was not unreasonably delayed. It therefore found that the interference with the applicant's right to liberty under Article 5(1) could not be justified by the exception in relation to persons of unsound mind under Article 5(1)(e).

Article 5(1)(f)

Article 5(1)(f) is rather wide. In *Zamir* v *United Kingdom* (1983) 40 DR 42 it was held that the lawfulness of the detention depends only on whether the intention behind the detention was the deportation of the detainee. Where the lawfulness of detention was dependent on domestic laws concerning the legality of deportation, 'the scope of the Commission's review is limited to examining whether there is a legal basis for the detention and whether the decision of the courts on the question of lawfulness could be described as arbitrary in light of the facts of the case'. However, the Commission held in *Lynas* v *Switzerland* (1976) 6 DR 141 that detention can cease to be lawful if the extradition or deportation proceedings are not carried out diligently or amount to an abuse of power (see also *Chahal* v *United Kingdom* (1997) 23 EHRR 413).

8.5.3 Procedural safeguards

Article 5(2)

Under Article 5(2), everyone arrested has the right to be informed in a language which he or she understands of the reasons for the arrest and of any charge against him or her. The purpose of this obligation is to enable the arrested person to challenge the lawfulness of the detention (*X* v *United Kingdom* (1982) 4 EHRR 188). Reasons need not be in writing and formal notification may not be necessary if the reasons are made clear during the arrest. However, in *Ireland* v *United Kingdom* (1978) 2 EHRR 28 the Court held that it was not enough to tell an arrested person that he or she was being held pursuant to the provisions of emergency legislation.

Article 5(3)

Article 5(3) requires that anyone arrested shall be brought promptly before a judge or other officer authorised by law to exercise judicial power. In *Brogan* v *United Kingdom* (1988) 11 EHRR 117, detention for four days and six hours before reaching a court was held to be a violation of Article 5(3). The aim of Article 5(3) is to impose a limit on the length of detention authorised by Article 5(1)(c) by ensuring that the prosecuting authorities do not unreasonably prolong detention. What is intended is that the 'provisional detention of the accused person must not be prolonged beyond a reasonable time' (*Wemhoff* v *Germany* (1968) 1 EHRR 25). The Court in *Neumeister* v *Austria* (1968) 1 EHRR 91 stated, at para. 4:

the reasonableness of the time spent by an accused person in detention up to the beginning of his trial must be assessed in relation to the very fact of his detention. Until conviction he must be presumed innocent, and the purpose of Article 5(3) is essentially to require his provisional release once his continuing detention ceases to be reasonable.

The presumption is that bail should be granted and denial of bail must be justified by relevant and sufficient reasons. Reasons that are justified include:

(a)   a risk that the accused will fail to appear at the trial (*Stögmüller* v *Austria* (1969) 1 EHRR 155);
(b)   a risk that the accused may interfere with the course of justice (*Wemhoff* v *Germany* (1968) 1 EHRR 25);
(c)   a risk of further offences (*Toth* v *Austria* (1991) 14 EHRR 551); and
(d)   for the preservation of public order (*Letellier* v *France* (1991) 14 EHRR 83).

In any of these cases the reason advanced must be justified by the facts in the particular case. In the recent case of *Cabellero* v *United Kingdom* (2000) *The Times*, 29 February, the denial of bail under s. 25 of the Criminal Justice and Public Order Act 1994 was held to be a breach of Article 5(3). This section has now been amended to be Convention and Human Rights Act compliant.

Determining the reasonableness of a period of detention is a matter of fact and degree. In *Wemhoff* v *Germany* the Court developed a two-part test. First, the Court will review whether the reasons advanced by the state for continued detention are relevant and sufficient, that is, whether the domestic determination that the public interest outweighs the right to liberty in any given case can be sustained. Applying this part of the test, the Court has recognised that the argument that a suspect might flee loses practicality as time passes, since it is likely that periods in detention on remand would be deducted from any period of imprisonment imposed on conviction (*Neumeister* v *Austria* (1968) 1 EHRR 91 at para. 6). Second, even if the first limb is satisfied, the Commission and Court will go on to consider whether the proceedings have been unduly prolonged by avoidable delay.

Article 5(4)
Under Article 5(4), anyone under any form of detention must be able to challenge the lawfulness of that detention. However, there are restrictions in relation to convicted persons. Review must be by a court and must be 'speedy'. In *Zamir* v *United Kingdom* (1983) 40 DR 42 the Commission held that seven weeks between applying for habeas corpus and a hearing violated Article 5(4). Where detention is prolonged, this Article requires the availability of a process to enable the lawfulness of the detention to be reviewed at reasonable intervals (*Bezicheri* v *Italy* (1989) 12 EHRR 210).

There has been a series of key cases where the Court has held that Article 5(4) requires a regular review of the lawfulness of continuing detention where the circumstances of the detention change over time. Thus, the lawfulness of detention in psychatric hospitals (*X* v *United Kingdom* (1980) Series B 41); during the discretionary period of discretionary life sentences (*Weeks* v *United Kingdom* (1987) 10 EHRR 293; *Thynne* v *United Kingdom* (1990) 13 EHRR 666); and of young people convicted of murder and detained (*Hussain* v *United Kingdom* (1996) 22 EHRR 1 and *T and V* v *United Kingdom*, 16 December 1999) have been challenged successfully. The recent case of *Curley* v *United Kingdom* (2000) *The Times*, 5 April further clarified the requirements of the Article when it was held that the detention of a prisoner for 10 years after the expiry of tariff without a speedy and effective review by a body capable of ordering his release was a violation. It also held that the Parole Board, even under the new interim arrangements following the case of *Hussain* v *United Kingdom*, was not such a body. These cases have had at their core the fact that the legality of the detention in each case was based on the extent to which the person would be dangerous if released. The assessment of this changed over time and thus so did the justification and therefore legality of the detention. Such a review might also be necessary for lengthy periods on remand regardless of whether there are 'new circumstances'.

The Court held in *Winterwerp* v *Netherlands* (1979) 2 EHRR 387 that the judicial proceedings referred to in Article 5(4) need not always be attended by the same guarantees as those required by Article 6(1) for civil or criminal litigation. Nonetheless, it is essential for the person detained to have access to the Court and the opportunity to be heard in person, or, where necessary, through some form of representation.

8.5.4 Right to compensation

Article 5(5)
Article 5(5) guarantees a right to compensation if a person has been detained in violation of Article 5. This provision requires a binding award of compensation that can be enforced by the courts (see, e.g., *Brogan* v *United Kingdom* (1988) 11 EHRR 117; *Fox* v *United Kingdom* (1990) 13 EHRR 157 and most recently *Cabellero* v *United Kingdom* (2000) *The Times*, 29 February and *Curley* v *United Kingdom* (2000) *The Times*, 5 April).

After the requirements of this provision were brought to the government's attention, it amended the Human Rights Bill so as to make an exception to the general rule that damages could not be obtained against a court, so that damages can be obtained where a court has permitted an unlawful detention (Human Rights Act 1998, s. 9(3) to (5)).

8.5.5 Potential issues

Some stop-and-search provisions in domestic law do not require reasonable suspicion before they can be used to detain people. These include ss. 13A and 13B of the Prevention of Terrorism (Temporary Provisions) Act 1989 and s. 60 of the

Criminal Justice and Public Order Act 1994 and they would, it is argued, fall foul of Article 5(1)(c).

There remains a question of whether the detention of asylum seekers can be justified in the absence of authorisation from a court. The right to be brought before a court may arise within a short period of detention. It is also not sufficient for this issue to be resolved once and for all. There will also need to be a regular review of the justification for the detention (*Amuur* v *France* (1996) 22 EHRR 5323).

Issues relating to the detention of prisoners will be raised. In the light of *Curley* v *United Kingdom* (2000) *The Times*, 5 April, it will be necessary for the government to examine the detention review arrangements of the Parole Board to avoid further successful cases being brought. Also, despite the case of *Wynne* v *United Kingdom* (1994) 19 EHRR 333, the domestic courts in a different case might take the view that the veto by the Home Secretary of the release of mandatory life-sentence prisoners violates Article 5(4) (see, for instance, *Hussain* v *United Kingdom* (1996) 22 EHRR 1). In *T and V* v *United Kingdom* (2000) 30 EHRR 121 the Strasbourg Court held that the continued detention of the Bulger killers without an opportunity for judicial review of the legality of the detention was a breach of Article 5(4). In the light of this, cases of prisoners such as Myra Hindley are likely to raise complicated issues relating to this provision.

Other detention provisions, particularly for patients in psychiatric hospitals might be subject to challenge in the light of *Stanley Johnson* v *United Kingdom* (1999) 27 EHRR 296. For instance, in *R* v *Bournewood Community and Mental Health NHS Trust, ex parte L* [1998] 3 WLR 107 the House of Lords took the view that patients without the ability to consent to admission in hospital could be detained under the common law. However, it is doubtful that they would be able to take the same view having regard to their duties under the Human Rights Act 1998, ss. 2 and 7. Further, the government's proposals relating to the detention of those with so-called Severe Personality Disorders (SPD) without the individuals necessarily having committed an offence may fall foul of the Convention provisions.

8.6   ARTICLE 6: RIGHT TO A FAIR TRIAL

1.   In the determination of his civil rights and obligations or of any criminal charge against him, everyone is entitled to a fair and public hearing within a reasonable time by an independent and impartial tribunal established by law. Judgment shall be pronounced publicly but the press and public may be excluded from all or part of the trial in the interests of morals, public order or national security in a democratic society, where the interests of juveniles or the protection of the private life of the parties so require, or to the extent strictly necessary in the opinion of the court in special circumstances where publicity would prejudice the interests of justice.

2.   Everyone charged with a criminal offence shall be presumed innocent until proved guilty according to law.

3. Everyone charged with a criminal offence has the following minimum rights:

(a) to be informed promptly, in a language which he understands and in detail, of the nature and cause of the accusation against him;

(b) to have adequate time and facilities for the preparation of his defence;

(c) to defend himself in person or through legal assistance of his own choosing or, if he has not sufficient means to pay for legal assistance, to be given it free when the interests of justice so require;

(d) to examine or have examined witnesses against him and to obtain the attendance and examination of witnesses on his behalf under the same conditions as witnesses against him;

(e) to have the free assistance of an interpreter if he cannot understand or speak the language used in court.

Article 6 concerns the right to a fair trial. This right has 'a position of pre-eminence in the Convention' (Harris, O'Boyle and Warbrick, *Law of the European Convention on Human Rights*, p. 164). The Court has stated that there can be no justification for interpreting Article 6(1) of the Convention restrictively (*Moreira de Azevedo* v *Portugal* (1990) 13 EHRR 721). There have been more applications to Strasbourg concerning Article 6 than any other article in the Convention.

Article 6(1) is complex and contains several different elements. The first important issue is its sphere of application. Although there are specific guarantees in relation to those charged with criminal offences, in Article 6(3), these do not necessarily preclude the like guarantees for civil trials, if they are necessary incidents of a 'fair and public hearing'. However, the phrase 'civil right' does not cover all matters which English lawyers would think of as 'civil matters', and so it is important to analyse the scope of a civil right too.

8.6.1 Criminal charge

The Commission and Court have developed criteria for deciding whether an act is a criminal offence for the purposes of the Convention. The primary criteria are: domestic classification, nature of the offence, and severity of the penalty incurred (*Engel* v *Netherlands* (1976) 1 EHRR 647). If a national court classifies an act as a criminal offence, the Court and Commission will not challenge this determination; but if an act is classified as non-criminal in domestic law, this fact is relevant although not definitive. Even loss of liberty as a punishment is not conclusive. In *Engel* v *Netherlands* the fact that Engel faced a penalty of two days' 'strict arrest', for offences against military discipline, was not enough to categorise the offence as criminal. Deciding which side of the line a case will fall is not always easy. In *McFeeley* v *United Kingdom* (1981) 3 EHRR 161 the Commission considered whether Article 6 applied to decisions by prison governors dealing with disciplinary adjudications and concluded that although the results imposed could be severe, the process had not reached the required level to make it a trial of a criminal offence.

8.6.2 Civil right

The right to a fair trial also applies to an individual in the determination of his civil rights and obligations. In many respects, this is a wide phrase: issues arising in contract, commercial law, insurance law, succession, family law and real and personal property are generally regarded as matters to which Article 6 applies. Even a pending negligence claim can be a possession for the purposes of Protocol 1, Article 1, and hence is likely to amount to a civil right for the purposes of Article 6 (*Pressos Compania Naviera SA* v *Belgium* (1995) 21 EHRR 301, though the Court declared it unnecessary to deal with the Article 6 issue in that case).

Article 6(1) guarantees do not apply to proceedings unless they are determinative of a civil right or obligation, as opposed to constituting merely a preliminary investigative stage (see *Fayed* v *United Kingdom* (1994) 18 EHRR 393).

However, it is sometimes difficult to decide whether a case concerns what the Strasbourg institutions would regard as a 'civil right'. The concept is an autonomous one: the classification is not necessarily the same as that in the domestic law of the country concerned (e.g., *James* v *United Kingdom* (1986) 8 EHRR 123).

'Pure' public law rights are generally not regarded as 'civil rights'. This means that, for example, the 'due process' guarantees in Article 6 do not apply to such issues as the categorisation of prisoners (*Brady* v *United Kingdom* (1979) 3 EHRR 297) or decisions involving the entry or removal of immigrants (*Uppal* v *United Kingdom* (1980) 3 EHRR 391). Nor, it would appear, is the right to discretionary benefits a civil right. However, the limitation has been much reduced in recent years, with the Strasbourg institutions increasingly willing to find a 'civil right' within, or alongside a public law right. So, for example, in *Gaygasuz* v *Austria* (1996) 23 EHRR 365 an emergency assistance benefit with contributory elements was property within the scope of Protocol 1, Article 1, and therefore was a 'civil right' for the purposes of considering a breach of Article 14. Planning determinations also affect property rights. Education decisions will affect civil rights under Protocol 1, Article 2. Thus, cases which English lawyers might think of as 'public law' cases may yet involve determinations of civil rights.

Another distinction peculiar to English lawyers' eyes is that matters concerning public employment are not generally considered to concern 'civil rights' by the Strasbourg institutions (see *Koseck* v *Germany* (1986) 9 EHRR 328 and *Neigel* v *France* [1997] EHRLR 424). This leads to results such as in *Balfour* v *United Kingdom* [1997] EHRLR 665, in which a former diplomat was unable to use Article 6 to challenge the use of public interest immunity certificates to exclude evidence from his case alleging unfair dismissal. See also *Huber* v *France* (1998) 26 EHRR 457, which suggested in blanket terms that rights relating to a civil service pension were not 'civil' even though they also had a pecuniary element. In *Pellegrin* v *France*, Application No. 28541/95, 8 December 1999, the Court appeared to suggest that decisions concerning those with functions relating to the 'specific activities' of the public service would be outside the protection provided by Article 6:

the only disputes excluded from the scope of Article 6(1) of the Convention are those which are raised by public servants whose duties typify the specific activities of the public service in so far as the latter is acting as the depositary of public authority responsible for protecting the general interests of the State or other public authorities.

However, it is unclear how this sits with the court's earlier decision in *Vogt* v *Germany* (1995) 21 EHRR 205 where it was held that a civil servant's complaint relating to dismissal from civil service employment *could* amount to a civil right, in the context of freedom of expression. The difference may be whether the public servant is in a 'policy' job, and the extent to which special 'public service' circumstances apply to the case in question.

Disciplinary proceedings which determine a right to practise a profession do concern civil rights and so must conform to Article 6(1) of the Convention (see *König* v *Germany* (1978) 2 EHRR 170; *Wickramsinghe* v *United Kingdom* [1998] EHRLR 338 (General Medical Council disciplinary hearing) and *X* v *United Kingdom* [1998] EHRLR 480).

8.6.3 Fair hearing

Article 6(1) applies to both civil and criminal proceedings. It sets the overall standard to be applied in determining whether a trial has been fair. The more detailed provisions in Article 6(2) and (3) apply only to criminal charges, but the right to a fair hearing has been widely interpreted to give a broad and purposive interpretation, and even guarantees which are specifically protected in relation to criminal trials under Article 6(3) (such as legal aid) may be implied in relation to civil trials also, if they constitute a necessary part of the general right to a fair hearing (*Airey* v *Ireland* (1979) 2 EHRR 305). The Court has held that: 'In a democratic society . . . the right to a fair administration of justice holds such a prominent place that the restrictive interpretation of Article 6(1) [advanced by the state in that case] would not correspond to the aim and purpose of that provision' (*Delcourt* v *Belgium* (1970) 1 EHRR 355, para. 25).

All the detailed provisions of Article 6 are aspects of the overriding obligation to ensure that the proceedings are fair and that the submissions, arguments and evidence have been properly examined (*Kraska* v *Switzerland* (1993) 18 EHRR 188). The right to a fair hearing requires, among other things, that a litigant: (a) has real and effective access to a court, (b) has notice of the time and place of the proceedings, (c) has a real opportunity to present the case sought to be made, and (d) is given a reasoned decision.

In *Neumeister* v *Austria* (1968) 1 EHRR 91 the concept of 'equality of arms' was introduced. This requires that there be a fair balance between the opportunities afforded the parties involved in litigation. A defence witness should be examined under the same conditions as a witness for the prosecution. Each party should be afforded the opportunity to cross-examine the other's evidence and findings. Both parties should certainly have the right to be represented by counsel as well as the right to appear in person. In *Dombo Beheer BV* v *Netherlands* (1993) 18 EHRR 213 the Court stated, at para. 33:

> The Court agrees with the Commission that as regards [civil] litigation involving opposing private interests, 'equality of arms' implies that each party must be afforded a reasonable opportunity to present his case — including his evidence — under conditions that do not place him at a substantial disadvantage vis-à-vis his opponent.

Issues of evidence are obviously crucial to the concept of a fair trial. The Court has taken the view that decisions about evidence are largely a matter for the domestic courts but in *Edwards* v *United Kingdom* (1992) 15 EHRR 417, for instance, disclosure by the prosecution was seen as a crucial precondition of a fair trial. The European Court remains concerned about the extent to which the rules of evidence affect the right to a fair trial. This was particularly evident in the judgment in *McGinley and Egan* v *United Kingdom* (1999) 27 EHRR 1. In that case the applicants, who had been present during nuclear weapons tests on Christmas Island during 1957, claimed that they had been deprived of the right to a fair hearing when they sought to challenge a decision that their leukaemia was not due to exposure to radiation. They were unable to prove this because state documents which may have shown a link between their health problems and exposure to radiation were withheld. The Court held that in these particular circumstances they had failed to avail themselves of the relevant rules in Scottish civil procedure to apply for disclosure of relevant documents. However, on the general point it held that if the government had prevented the applicants from gaining access to documents in its possession, which would have helped them to ground a case, it would have denied them a fair hearing in contravention of Article 6(1).

In *Rowe and Davis* v *United Kingdom* (2000) 30 EHRR 1 the Court found a violation of Article 6(1) where the prosecution failed to place relevant documents before the trial judge or invite him to rule on disclosure. However, in *Jasper* v *United Kingdom* and *Fitt* v *United Kingdom* (2000) 30 EHRR 1 it was held by a 9 to 8 majority that there was no breach of Article 6(1) where Public Interest Immunity (PII) procedures were adopted. The Court ruled that the entitlement to disclosure of relevant evidence is not an absolute right and that competing interests of national security, protecting witnesses at risk of reprisal, and preserving the secrecy of police methods of investigating crime have to be balanced against the accused's rights. Given the narrow majority of this view and the ruling in *Rowe and Davis* v *United Kingdom*, it is likely that this position will be reargued now in the domestic courts.

8.6.4   Public hearings

Although Article 6(1) requires a public hearing, it provides for circumstances where the press and public may be excluded from the proceedings. These include situations where the interests of morals, public order or national security may be compromised; where the interests of juveniles or the protection of the private life of the parties requires; or in situations where publicity could prejudice the interests of justice. In *Diennet* v *France* (1995) 21 EHRR 554 the Court held that the right of a public hearing extended to the disciplinary hearing of a doctor before the French Medical Association.

The judgment is also to be pronounced publicly. Unlike the limitations that apply to a public trial, the right to public pronouncement of the judgment is unqualified. This right has been held not to require the judgment being read in open court provided the outcome is publicly availability (*Pretto* v *Italy* (1983) 6 EHRR 182).

8.6.5 Trial within a reasonable time

Article 6(1) calls for the hearing to be held within a 'reasonable time'. Unlike Article 5(3), which applies only to individuals under arrest, this provision applies to civil and criminal cases and whether an accused is being held or is on bail. What constitutes a reasonable time will depend on the circumstances. In the criminal context the Commission has stated that the relevant point is that 'at which the situation of the person concerned has been substantially affected as a result of a suspicion against him' (*X* v *Austria* (1967) 24 CD 8 at p. 18). This approach has been adopted by the Court and applies even if no charges have been levelled at that point (*Eckle* v *Germany* (1982) 5 EHRR 1). In *Neumeister* v *Austria* (1968) 1 EHRR 91 the accused was investigated on 21 January 1960, charged on 23 February 1961, and indicted on 17 March 1964. The Court chose the date he was charged as the starting point for the period covered by Article 6(1). On the other hand, in a judgment handed down by the Court on the same day, *Wemhoff* v *Germany* (1968) 1 EHRR 55, the accused was determined to have been 'substantially affected' only when he was arrested.

In civil cases the factors to be taken into account are different. In *Darnell* v *United Kingdom* (1993) 18 EHRR 205 the applicant was dismissed from his post with an area health authority in 1984. There then followed several judicial review applications, an industrial tribunal hearing and an Employment Appeal Tribunal appeal, which was finally dismissed in 1993. The Court and Commission found that the total period taken for the trial of the matter to be concluded was unreasonable. This case also illustrates the Court's approach when dealing with the period taken up by appeals, which is to include all the time taken to resolve the matter, including appeals.

8.6.6 Impartiality

Article 6(1) requires an 'independent and impartial tribunal established by law'. The Court has been as concerned with actual impartiality as it has been with the appearance that a tribunal is impartial. For instance, in *Langborger* v *Sweden*

(1989) 12 EHRR 416 the court ruled that Article 6(1) was violated by the membership of a housing tribunal that had the 'possible appearance of lacking impartiality'. In *McGonnell* v *United Kingdom* (2000) 8 BHRC 56, it was held that there was a breach of Article 6(1) where the Bailiff, who presided over the Royal Court of Guernsey in legal proceedings concerning the applicant's planning appeal, had also sat as the Deputy Bailiff over the States of Deliberation when the earlier, detailed development plan had been adopted. However, in this case the Court did not go as far as fully endorsing the doctrine of separation of powers.

Similar issues have been raised in cases concerning disciplinary proceedings — in particular those of court martial procedures. In *Hood* v *United Kingdom* (2000) 29 EHRR 365 the applicant was tried and convicted under the Army Act 1955 by court martial on charges of absence without leave and desertion. Under the provisions of the Act, the convening officer was responsible for convening the court martial and appointing its members and the prosecuting officer. Applying *Findlay* v *United Kingdom* (1997) 24 EHRR 221, the Court observed that a court martial convened pursuant to the Act did not meet the requirements of independence and impartiality set by Article 6, particularly in view of the central part played in the prosecution by the convening officer, who was closely linked to the prosecuting authorities, was superior in rank to members of the court martial and had the power to dissolve the court martial and refuse to confirm its decision. This ruling has been affirmed in the recent case of *Jordan* v *United Kingdom* (2000) *The Times*, 17 March.

In *Pullar* v *United Kingdom* (1996) 22 EHRR 391 the Court found that there was no violation of the applicant's right to a fair trial when the jury which convicted him included an employee of a key prosecution witness. The Court held that the appeal court's reliance on the juror's unchallenged written statement of his impartiality was sufficient for the purposes of Article 6(1).

In the recent case of *Sander* v *United Kingdom* (2000) *The Times*, 12 May, the Court held that there had been a violation of Article 6. In the applicant's domestic case, issues of racial prejudice were raised after a letter was received by the judge from a jury member complaining that two fellow jurors were making racist remarks and jokes. A second letter from the whole jury refuting the allegations in the first was received and finally a third, from one of the alleged jokers, was received denying any racial bias. The Strasbourg Court held that racial bias does not disappear overnight and that as a result the jury should have been discharged. They ruled that the judge's redirection of the jury to stress the importance of avoiding racial prejudice was inadequate.

8.6.7   Access to justice   ✗

The right to real and effective access to a court is a fundamental aspect of Article 6, though it is not without limitations: it is a crucial but not absolute right. In *Golder* v *United Kingdom* (1975) 1 EHRR 524, Article 6 was violated when a prisoner was denied access to a lawyer whom he wished to consult for the purpose of bringing defamation proceedings against a prison warder. But in *Ashingdane* v *United Kingdom* (1985) 7 EHRR 528 the Court found that the restriction in the Mental Health Act 1959 on the right of a psychiatric patient to sue the hospital which cared for him was not absolute and was justified. See also *Stubbings* v *United Kingdom* (1996) 23 EHRR 213, in which it was held that a statutory limitation period for bringing an action did not breach Article 6 or Article 14. There is no right to bring private prosecutions unless a successful subsequent civil action is closely linked to the private prosecution (*Helmers* v *Sweden* (1991) Series A 212-A).

An illustration of the type of limitation which may be placed on access to a court is the case of *Fayed* v *United Kingdom* (1994) 18 EHRR 393, which was an application made by the Fayed brothers arising out of an investigation of their affairs by inspectors appointed by the Department of Trade and Industry. One of their complaints was that, in breach of Article 6(1) of the Convention, English law denied them access to a court to have determined whether there was any justification for the attack on their reputations contained in the inspectors' report. It was accepted that any defamation proceedings would have been met by a successful defence of privilege. The Court concluded that the system of investigation and reporting under the Companies Act 1985 pursued the public interest in the proper conduct of the affairs of public companies whose owners benefit from limited liability, and the objective of according the inspectors freedom to report 'with courage and frankness' was legitimate and proportionate.

Article 6(1) has also been used to challenge prosecutorial prohibitions. For example, in *Osman* v *United Kingdom* (2000) 29 EHRR 245, the applicants claimed that the English rule of immunity that prevented them from pursuing a negligence action against the police breached their right of access to the courts under Article 6. Their claim was upheld with the majority of the Court of the opinion that Article 6(1) was applicable to the case on the basis that the exclusionary rule against actions in negligence against the police did not work as a blanket ban; that the courts could conduct their assessment as to the applicability of the rule in *Hill* v *Chief Constable of West Yorkshire Police* [1989] AC 53 on a case-by-case basis. Therefore the applicants had been denied access to the court for the assertion of their 'civil rights' under Article 6(1). Judge Jambrek urged the Court to take on a more extensive interpretation of 'civil rights and obligations': the Court should only need to be satisfied that a right existed under the domestic law — in this case, a right derived from the general tort of negligence or the duty of care owed by the police to the plaintiff. The only condition for the Court's recognition of a right as a 'civil right', thereby guaranteeing an applicant the right of access to a domestic court, would be that the right at issue is recognised in the national legal system as an individual right within the sphere of general individual freedom.

Article 6(1) concerns the right to access to justice in a purely civil context. In *Airey* v *Ireland* (1979) 2 EHRR 305 the Court considered whether the right of access to domestic courts included the existence of civil legal aid. The Court stated:

To hold that so far-reaching an obligation exists would . . . sit ill with the facts that the Convention contains no provision on legal aid for those disputes. . . . However, despite the absence of . . . a clause for civil litigation, Article 6(1) may sometimes compel the state to provide for the assistance of a lawyer when such assistance proves indispensable for an effective access to the court, either because legal representation is rendered compulsory, as is done by the domestic law of certain contracting states . . . or by reason of the complexity of the procedure of the case.

On the facts of that case, which concerned an emotionally and legally complex matrimonial dispute, with important issues of child custody at stake, it was held that the guarantee of real and effective access to a court and the concept of 'equality of arms' did require a lawyer to be provided free of charge to Mrs Airey by the Irish state.

The right to be provided with legal representation means the right to be provided with genuine and effective representation, not the mere presence of a lawyer (see *Artico* v *Italy* (1980) 3 EHRR 1).

8.6.8   Presumption of innocence

Article 6(2) provides for the presumption of innocence of the defendant in criminal trials (*Funke* v *France* (1993) 16 EHRR 297). This principle assumes that the prosecution will need to produce evidence of guilt in the trial (*Barberà* v *Spain* (1988) 11 EHRR 360). In *Minelli* v *Switzerland* (1983) 5 EHRR 554 the Court concluded that presumption of innocence means that the defendant has the right to be heard in his or her own defence. However, domestic laws which place the onus on the defendant to prove certain elements of his or her defence do not necessarily violate this provision (*Lingens* v *Austria* (1981) 26 DR 171). Equally the provision does not necessarily prevent presumptions of law or fact from being in favour of the prosecution and against the defendant. However, these presumptions must be 'within reasonable limits' (*Salabiaku* v *France* (1988) 13 EHRR 379).

In *Murray* v *United Kingdom* (1996) 22 EHRR 29 the Court considered whether the drawing of adverse inferences from exercising the right to silence was a violation of Article 6 and held that on the facts of the case the drawing of inferences did not interfere with his right to a fair trial. Murray was arrested under the Prevention of Terrorism (Temporary Provisions) Act 1989 and taken to the police station. While being interviewed he stated repeatedly that he had 'nothing to say'. He was only able to see his solicitor after 48 hours, and in subsequent interviews he stated that he had 'been advised by my solicitor not to answer any of your questions'. During several interviews that lasted for 21 hours and 39 minutes over two days, these statements were the only ones made by the applicant. Murray also refused to give any evidence at trial and no witnesses were called on his behalf. The Court, at para. 45, made it clear that:

there can be no doubt that the right to remain silent under police questioning and the privilege against self-incrimination are generally recognised international standards which lie at the heart of the notion of a fair procedure under Article 6. By providing the accused with protection against improper compulsion by the authorities these immunities contribute to avoiding miscarriages of justice and to securing the aims of Article 6.

The Commission and Court accepted that a jury, which did not have to give reasons, might not be so careful about the weight to be given to the adverse inference. *Murray* was a case where guilt was decided by a judge who had to give reasons.

In the recent case of *Condron* v *United Kingdom* (2000) *The Times*, 9 May, the Strasbourg authorities held that allowing a jury to draw an adverse influence from 'no comment' police interviews after caution was a violation of Article 6. The applicants in this case were heroin addicts charged with supplying heroin. Their solicitor had advised them not to answer police questions as he thought they were unfit to be questioned. At trial both defendants gave evidence and first-time explanations for aspects of the prosecution case. The domestic Court of Appeal held that the summing-up was defective but the conviction was 'safe'. The Strasbourg Court did not agree though and held that the test was 'fairness' not 'safety' and found a violation of Article 6. However, the Court declined to rule on further defence submissions that adverse inferences can only be drawn after proof of a prima facie case and cannot be the main basis for a conviction.

In the first domestic case on the Human Rights Act to reach the House of Lords, *R* v *DPP, ex parte Kebilene* [1999] 3 WLR 972, the substantive point of discussion was whether the reverse onus provisions in the Prevention of Terrorism Act (Temporary Provisions) 1989, ss. 16A and 16B offended against the principle of the presumption of innocence in Article 6(2). The House of Lords did not follow the position taken by the Lord Chief Justice in the Divisional Court. Lord Bingham had decided that these provisions in a 'blatant and obvious way undermined the presumption of innocence'.

In *Saunders* v *United Kingdom* (1996) 23 EHRR 313 the Court found a violation of Article 6(1) when the applicant complained that he was denied a fair hearing because of the use at his criminal trial of statements obtained from him by Department of Trade and Industry inspectors in exercise of their statutory powers under the Companies Act 1985 to compel him to answer questions and provide information. The majority of the Court did not support the dissenting judgment of Judge Marten, who distinguished between serious fraud and ordinary crimes on the basis that in most cases discovery of the crime nearly always precedes the investigation, which aims at identifying the culprit, whereas in fraud cases the investigation generally has as its purpose to ascertain whether or not a crime has been committed at all.

8.6.9 Further specific rights in criminal cases

The Court has clearly stated that the rights in Article 6(3) are only particular examples of the overall right to a fair trial (*Artico* v *Italy* (1980) 3 EHRR 1;

Edwards v *United Kingdom* (1992) 15 EHRR 417). Nevertheless the requirement to afford adequate facilities for the defence in Article 6(3)(b) creates an additional positive obligation. As the Court said in *Can* v *Austria* (1985) 8 EHRR 121:

> the accused must have the opportunity to organise his defence in an appropriate way and without restriction as to the possibility to put all the relevant defence arguments before the trial court and thus to influence the outcome of the proceedings.

Article 6(3) sets forth further safeguards which apply to criminal trials. These are the minimum rights to be afforded a defendant in a criminal trial.

Article 6(3)(a) guarantees prompt, intelligible notification of charges. The right to know the case against the accused is seen as essential to preparing an informed defence. It requires that a defendant is notified in a language that he or she understands (*Brozicek* v *Italy* (1989) 12 EHRR 371).

Article 6(3)(b) requires that the accused be given adequate time and facilities to mount a defence. This principle is obviously relative, but the Commission has created some guidelines in holding it to be 'the right of the accused to have at his disposal, for the purpose of exonerating himself or to obtain a reduction in his sentence, all relevant elements that have been or could be collected by the competent authorities' (*Jespers* v *Belgium* (1981) 27 DR 61).

Article 6(3)(c) gives the right to representation and legal aid. This section gives way to three principles: (a) the right to defend oneself, (b) the right to legal assistance of one's choosing, and (c) the right to free legal assistance if one is indigent and if the interests of justice so require. These principles apply to the pre-trial stages as well as the trial itself.

In *Benham* v *United Kingdom* (1996) 22 EHRR 293 the Court considered whether unavailability of full legal aid for a committal hearing in a poll tax case constituted a violation of Article 6. In answering this question, the Court stated that regard must be had to the severity of the penalty at stake and the complexity of the case. In general, the Court held that, 'Where deprivation of liberty is at stake, the interests of justice in principle call for legal representation'. In the specific case before them, the Court went on to decide, at para. 64, that:

> In view of the severity of the penalty risked by the applicant and the complexity of the applicable law, the Court considers that the interests of justice demand that, in order to receive a fair hearing, the applicant ought to have benefited from free legal representation during the proceedings before the magistrates. In conclusion, there has been a violation of Article 6(1) and (3)(c) of the Convention taken together.

In *Quaranta* v *Switzerland* (1991) Series A 205, the Court held that the article required free legal aid to be provided in connection with the defendant's appearances before an investigating judge in the civil law system. In *Imbrioscia* v

Switzerland (1993) 17 EHRR 441 the Court was asked to consider whether the defendant was entitled to have a lawyer present at pre-trial questioning. Harris, O'Boyle and Warbrick's view of the case (in *The Law of the European Convention on Human Rights*, p. 257) is that:

> What emerges . . . is that Article 6(3)(c) does not require a state to take the initiative to invite an accused's lawyer to be present during questioning in the course of the investigation. However, although the Court does not say this in so many words, it would appear from the tenor of its judgment that if the accused or his lawyer requests the latter's attendance, this must be allowed if, as is likely, there is a risk the information obtained will prejudice the accused person's defence.

In *Murray* v *United Kingdom* (1996) 22 EHRR 29 the Court held that the exclusion of a lawyer from the police station when the individual was being questioned, in the circumstances of the restriction of the right to silence and the threat of an adverse inference being drawn from silence, constituted a violation of Article 6.

In *Granger* v *United Kingdom* (1990) 12 EHRR 469 the Court found that the defendant should have received free legal assistance 'in the interests of justice'. The defendant was denied legal aid during an appeal in respect of a five-year sentence. Granger appeared for himself against a QC and a junior counsel for the Crown. The Court found a violation of Article 6(3)(c), citing the defendant's obvious lack of understanding regarding the intricacies of the law in the face of the professional prosecution.

This right is not restricted of course to the provision of legal aid. In *S* v *Switzerland* (1991) 14 EHRR 670 the police had set up a special unit to investigate a protest group concerned with arms dealing and nuclear power. The police shadowed the members, tapped telephones and regularly emptied their dustbins. One of those subsequently arrested was held in custody and when his lawyer came to see him, the interview was supervised by police officers. In addition, letters written by him to his lawyer were intercepted and later used for graphological reports. The argument that the surveillance of the lawyer was necessary to prevent collusion, and the potential for this was indicated by the fact that all the defence lawyers proposed to coordinate their defence strategy, was rejected by the Court which said: 'Free communication between a lawyer and his detained client is a fundamental right which is essential in a democratic society, above all in the most serious of cases'.

Article 6(3)(d) ensures the right to the attendance of witnesses and their examination. This is in line with the above-mentioned 'equality of arms' principle and applies to both the accusatorial and inquisitorial systems of criminal law.

Article 6(3)(e) guarantees the right to an interpreter in the defendant's native language if he or she does not speak the language of the tribunal. In *Zana* v *Turkey* (1998) 4 BHRC 241, Z refused to answer allegations against him in criminal proceedings in respect of statements he had made supporting an armed group, the Workers' Party of Kurdistan. The reason for his refusal was because he would not speak Turkish and wished to proceed in Kurdish, his mother tongue. The Court held that his subsequent conviction amounted to a breach of his right to a fair trial.

8.6.10   Evidence in criminal proceedings

Evidence is in general a matter for the domestic courts and Article 6 does not require any particular rules of evidence provided the trial as a whole is fair (*Edwards* v *United Kingdom* (1992) 15 EHRR 417). However, the use of particular evidence, such as that obtained by maltreatment, may make the trial unfair. Similarly the use of hearsay evidence without the opportunity of this evidence being tested may also create unfairness (*Kostovski* v *Netherlands* (1989) 12 EHRR 434; *Unterpertinger* v *Austria* (1986) 13 EHRR 175). The Court has also considered the use of evidence from anonymous witnesses (*Kostovski* v *Netherlands* (1989) 12 EHRR 434; *Windisch* v *Austria* (1990) 13 EHRR 281; *Doorson* v *Netherlands* (1996) 22 EHRR 330; *Van Mechelen* v *Netherlands* (1997) 25 EHRR 647); entrapment (*Teixeira de Castro* v *Portugal* (9 June 1998, noted at [1998] Crim LR 751); witnesses giving evidence behind screens (*X* v *United Kingdom* (1992) 15 EHRR CD 113); accomplices (*X* v *United Kingdom* (1976) 4 DR 115); undercover agents (*X* v *Germany* (1987) 11 EHRR 84); undercover police officers (*Van Mechelen* v *Netherlands* (1998) 25 EHRR 647) and pleas of guilt from co-defendants (*MH* v *United Kingdom* [1997] EHRLR 279).

In the light of *Khan* v *United Kingdom* (2000) *The Times*, 23 May and in the context of the Human Rights Act 1998, domestic courts will have to grapple with the admissibility of evidence gathered as a result of a breach of the Convention itself. In a recent House of Lords case, *Morgans* v *DPP* [2000] 2 WLR 386, it was held that information which is produced as a result of unwarranted interceptions should neither be used in evidence, nor disclosed to the defence and stated that 'the prohibitions in section 9(1) are inconsistent with the defendant's right to a fair trial'. In this instance information which had been recorded by an unwarranted telephone call logging device attached to a suspected computer hacker's telephone line was held to be communication and not merely metering information. However, neither Article 6 nor Article 8 was expressly considered in relation to disclosure.

In New Zealand, the slightly weaker Bill of Rights has been interpreted so that evidence obtained in breach, prima facie, not admissible (*R* v *Kirifi* [1992] 2 NZLR 8; *R* v *Butcher* [1992] 2 NZLR 257; *R* v *Goodwin (No. 1)* [1993] 2 NZLR 153; *R* v *Goodwin (No. 2)* [1993] 2 NZLR 390; *R* v *Te Kira* [1993] 3 NZLR 257.

8.6.11   Disclosure in criminal proceedings

It is arguable that the denial of disclosure to the defence of material that the prosecution has in its possession, and which they could use if they chose, inevitably creates unfairness. In *Kaufman* v *Belgium* (1986) 50 DR 98 the Commission decided that:

everyone who is a party to . . . proceedings should have a reasonable opportunity of presenting his case to the court under conditions which do not place him at a substantial disadvantage vis-à-vis his opponent.

Whether there is any actual unfairness and, therefore, whether the Court will find a violation in any particular case, will depend on the importance of the material to the defence. The Commission and the Court have already recognised that the right to a fair trial requires the prosecution to disclose all relevant evidence to the defence (*Jespers v Belgium* (1981) 27 DR 61; *Edwards v United Kingdom* (1992) 15 EHRR 417). In *Bendenoun v France* (1994) 18 EHRR 54 the Court decided that this principle applies whether or not the prosecution intends to rely on the documents and whether or not the defence decides to use them.

A practice that may interfere with the Article 6 right to a fair trial is the restricted disclosure now available from the prosecution in the United Kingdom as a result of the Criminal Procedure and Investigations Act 1996 (see the discussion of *Rowe and Davis v United Kingdom* (2000) 30 EHRR 1 and *McGinley and Egan v United Kingdom* (1999) 27 EHRR 1 at 8.6.3).

In *Jespers v Belgium* (1981) 27 DR 61 the Commission held that the 'equality of arms' principle imposes on prosecution and investigating authorities an obligation to disclose any material in their possession. This also applies to any material to which they *could* gain access which may assist the accused in exonerating himself. Such a duty is necessary to redress the inequality of resources between the prosecution and defence. This principle extends to material that might undermine the credibility of a prosecution witness. In *Jespers v Belgium* the Commission stated, at pp. 87–8:

> . . . the prosecution has at its disposal, to back the accusation, facilities deriving from its powers of investigation supported by judicial and police machinery with considerable technical resources and means of coercion. It is in order to establish equality, as far as possible, between the prosecution and the defence that national legislation in most countries entrusts the preliminary investigation to a member of the judiciary or, if it entrusts the investigation to the public prosecutor's department, instructs the latter to gather evidence in favour of the accused as well as against him.
>
> . . . everyone charged with a criminal offence should enjoy . . . the opportunity to acquaint himself, for the purpose of preparing his defence, with the results of investigations carried out throughout the proceedings. . . . a right to access to the prosecution file . . . can be inferred from Article 6, para. 3(b). . . .
>
> In short, Article 6, para. 3(b), recognises the right of the accused to have at his disposal, for the purposes of exonerating himself or of obtaining a reduction in his sentence, all relevant elements that have been or could be collected by the competent authorities.

Also, in *Edwards v United Kingdom* (1992) 15 EHRR 417 the Court stated, at para. 36, that it:

considers that it is a requirement of fairness under Article 6(1), indeed one which is recognised under English law, that the prosecution authorities disclose to the defence all material evidence for or against the accused and that the failure to do so in the present case gave rise to a defect in the trial process.

Article 6 is at the centre of Strasbourg jurisprudence, but the Commission and the Court tread a fine line in deciding how far to monitor the internal workings of the varying legal systems of the signatory states, including the differences between adversarial and inquisitorial criminal justice systems. They are prepared to intervene where they regard the procedure adopted as violating the essence of a fair trial but they have thus far pursued a policy of not questioning a national court with regard to the merits of a case based on the facts presented.

8.6.12 Potential issues

As already seen in the Scottish Courts, the largest number of issues requiring resolution after the Human Rights Act 1998 comes into force will arise in criminal cases and as a result of Article 6 of the Convention but the Article will also have a significant impact in civil cases.

There have been a proliferation of cases relating to the independence and impartiality of tribunals. In *Starrs and Chalmers* v *Procurator Fiscal* (2000) UKHRR 78 it was held that the appointment of temporary Sheriffs under s. 11(4) of the Sheriff Courts (Scotland) Act 1971 was incompatible with Article 6(1) as they did not constitute an independent and impartial tribunal. The court was particularly concerned that decisions about appointment and tenure were in the hands of the Lord Advocate, who was also head of the prosecution service. This violated the right to a fair trial for similar reasons as in *McGonnell* v *United Kingdom* (2000) 8 BHRC 56. In *Hoekstra and others* v *HM Advocate* (2000) *The Times*, 14 April it was ordered that a continuation of a staged appeal hearing, which was dealing with Convention points as devolution issues, be heard by a new three-judge court. This was because the first three-judge court included Lord McCluskey who had published a newspaper article a month earlier in which he quoted an earlier article he had written about the Canadian Charter (which was based on the Convention) as providing 'a field day for crackpots, a pain in the neck for judges and legislators and a goldmine for lawyers'. The senior members of the Appeal Court of the High Court of Justiciary held that Lord McCluskey was not objectively impartial and should not continue to hear the next stages of the appeal.

In another Scottish case, *Brown* v *Procurator Fiscal, Dunfermline* [2000] UKHRR 239, the Scottish Appeal Court held that the use of evidence obtained as a result of the use of the Road Traffic Act 1988, s. 172 violated the presumption of innocence in Article 6(2). This provision, which applies both North and South of the border, imposes a duty on the keeper of a vehicle to provide information on the identity of the person driving it. Failure to supply this information is a criminal offence in itself. Evidence obtained through the enforcement of this duty can be used against the person who was under a duty to supply it. The use of this evidence obtained under this compulsion in a subsequent substantive criminal trial is a violation of the presumption of innocence. The same issue has already arisen in the English courts in a case before Justice Jackson in Birmingham (unreported).

Article 6 will provide considerable opportunities to consider issues of evidence. In the light of the Strasbourg Court's ruling in *Rowe and Davis* v *United Kingdom* (2000) 30 EHRR 1, the current Public Interest Immunity (PII) regime will probably come under close scrutiny. Whether the regime under the Criminal Procedure and Investigations Act 1996, whereby secondary disclosure is postponed until after a defence statement, is compatible with Strasbourg principles is a question which will have to be considered by the English courts. Further, the broad categories of sensitive material contained in the Attorney-General's Guidelines may come under scrutiny and have to be balanced against the Strasbourg Court's principle of proportionality.

The increase in the use of covert surveillance, entrapment and informers by the police will increase the possibilities not only of issues about disclosure but also about allowing witnesses to be questioned in court behind screens or anonymously. In *Nottingham City Council* v *Amin* [2000] 1 WLR 1071, the Divisional Court demonstrated the approach courts may sometimes take under s. 2 of the Human Rights Act by distinguishing Strasbourg case law on *agents provocateurs*. (Permission was granted, but not pursued, to go to the House of Lords, and the same result may not obtain in a future case in the House of Lords or Strasbourg.)

In criminal cases the test for whether legal aid should be granted is the same as in the Convention (Article 6(3)(c)), that is whether it is necessary 'in the interests of justice'. After the Human Rights Act 1998 comes into force there will be many criminal prosecutions where defendants will raise Convention rights other than the right to a fair trial. In particular, in public order and protest cases, people will want to raise issues of freedom of expression and assembly. Where such substantive Convention rights are raised, criminal legal aid will need to be granted. This will also be the case where, for instance, legal aid ordinarily might not be granted because there is no risk of imprisonment — see for example, the Public Order Act 1986, s. 5.

Saunders v *United Kingdom* (1996) 23 EHRR 313 will have implications for the use of evidence gathered from statutory enquiries in a wide range of cases concerning regulation of financial services and the attempt to stem serious fraud. The provisions of the Companies Act 1985 which were there called into question have analogues in other regulatory acts, such as the Financial Services Act 1986, ss. 177 and 178, the Insolvency Act 1986, ss. 236 and 433 and the Criminal Justice Act 1987, s. 2. The prosecuting authorities and the courts will have to have regard to the Convention case law in determining whether to attempt to adduce, or to admit, evidence garnered as a result of these enquiries. In *R* v *Morrisey* (1997) 2 Cr App R 426 the Court of Appeal held that it was unable to interpret the Police and Criminal Evidence Act 1984, s. 78, so as to exclude evidence gathered under the Financial Services Act 1986, s. 177, and so it could not give effect to the

Saunders judgment in domestic law. It is doubtful whether a court having full regard to its interpretative obligation under the Human Rights Act 1998, s. 2, would take the same view; or if it did, it might feel itself compelled to issue a statement of incompatibility. In fact, the Attorney-General has issued guidance to prosecutors which ensures such evidence is not used. The DTI has adopted a practice of not using admissions made under compulsion to inspectors as evidence in criminal prosecutions (*R* v *Secretary of State for Trade and Industry, ex parte McCormick* [1998] BCC 379 at 383).

Journalists may seek to challenge courts that refuse to allow them to be present or to report parts of trials or the details of those giving evidence. On the other hand, there are also likely to be proceedings where parties seek to use Article 6, perhaps in conjunction with Article 8, to seek to restrict the reporting of particularly sensitive trials.

Even some of the powers of Parliament itself may not comply with the Convention. In *Demicoli* v *Malta* (1991) 14 EHRR 47 the Court decided that actions taken, against a publisher for contempt of Parliament, by Parliament itself by summoning the individual for examination did not comply with Article 6.

The question of the availability or non-availability of legal aid in civil cases will also raise issues under Article 6. For example, the absence of legal aid for a complex social security matter before the Social Security Commissioner, or in relation to a legally complex and emotionally distressing sexual harassment case before an employment tribunal could both raise the question of whether the access to court in each case was 'real and effective'. So too could the absence of a right to a translator for a non-English speaking or hearing-impaired litigant in civil trials (the fixed daily translation rate of £30 will not purchase a translator's time, and particularly not that of two sign language interpreters, and some tribunals have taken to providing, for example, speech-to-text registers for deaf litigants at their own expense, even where legal aid is not available).

It is true that legal aid in civil cases is treated differently from the requirement in criminal cases in Article 6 (*Airey* v *Ireland* (1979) 2 EHRR 305), nevertheless the Legal Services Commission will also have to ensure that legal aid is available for cases where there is no effective access to the court (see *Aerts* v *Belgium* (2000) 29 EHRR 50).

It is not clear at the time of writing how the Legal Services Commission will deal with cases which might lead to a declaration of incompatibility but no other remedy for the applicant.

The limits on the reach of particular causes of action could be seen as constituting a violation of Article 6 (see *Osman* v *United Kingdom* (2000) 29 EHRR 245). This judgment could lead to the reopening of other cases limiting the right to claim in negligence against particular categories of persons for public policy reasons, such as social workers or psychiatrists employed to report to public authorities (see *X (Minors)* v *Bedfordshire County Council* [1995] 2 AC 633). For example, the House of Lords held in *Phelps* v *Hillingdon London Borough Council* (2000) *The Times*, 28 July that a local education authority could be vicariously liable for breaches by those whom it employed, including educational psychologists and teachers, of their duties of care towards pupils. Breaches could include failure to diagnose dyslexic pupils and to provide appropriate education for pupils with special educational needs.

It is also possible that some dispute resolution procedures which adjudicate and award compensation, like procedures adopted by some ombudsmen, may potentially violate the Convention because of the absence of 'public hearings'. It is probable that notionally 'internal' disciplinary procedures such as those held by self-regulating organisations or the professions will be held to fall within the scope of 'proceedings' governed by Article 6 where they affect the rights of individuals (*Wickramsinghe* v *United Kingdom* [1998] EHRLR 338). In the light of recent cases ruling that the court martial procedures provided for under the Army Act breach Article 6 rights (see *Hood* v *United Kingdom* (2000) 29 EHRR 365 and *Jordan* v *United Kingdom* (2000) *The Times*, 17 March), there will most likely be an examination of the composition of disciplinary panels and the procedures adopted by such bodies.

Finally, in the context of trials, it will be important for lawyers to consider whether other articles of the Convention can be used (e.g., the right to freedom of expression as a defence in a public order offence).

8.7 ARTICLE 7: NO PUNISHMENT WITHOUT LAWFUL AUTHORITY

1. No one shall be held guilty of any criminal offence on account of any act or omission which did not constitute a criminal offence under national or international law at the time when it was committed. Nor shall a heavier penalty be imposed than the one that was applicable at the time the criminal offence was committed.

2. This Article shall not prejudice the trial and punishment of any person for any act or omission which, at the time when it was committed, was criminal according to the general principles of law recognised by civilised nations.

Article 7 guards against retrospective criminal laws. It prohibits the conviction of a defendant in a criminal case for an action that was not illegal when it was carried out. This Article also forbids a heavier criminal sentence being imposed than that which was in effect at the time of the commission of the crime. The principles of Article 7 apply to both national legislation and the actions of criminal courts. Paragraph 2 of the Article provides for a narrow exception to the principles detailed in para. 1.

Article 7 embodies the principle of legal certainty, requiring that criminal laws be framed in sufficiently clear terms so as to enable the persons to whom they are addressed to distinguish between permissible and prohibited behaviour.

In *Welch* v *United Kingdom* (1995) 20 EHRR 247, the applicant was arrested on drug charges in November 1986. In January 1987, a law concerning the seizure of any proceeds gained as a result of the drug trade came into effect. The applicant argued that, if this new law was applied to him, it would constitute retrospective criminal legislation and offend Article 7. On the other hand, the United Kingdom argued that the confiscation of these proceeds, as well as imprisonment as punishment for their non-payment, did not constitute penalties for the purpose of Article 7. The Court disagreed with the United Kingdom and ruled that the retrospective application of the confiscation order was a penalty and offended Article 7. It found (at para. 34) that Welch faced more 'far-reaching detriment' as a result of the government seizure than he would have at the time he perpetrated the crimes.

However, in the case of *SW* v *United Kingdom* (1995) 21 EHRR 363 it was held that the change in the direction of the common law with regard to rape within marriage was sufficiently foreseeable to mean that Article 7 was not violated when a man was convicted for raping his wife.

8.7.1 Potential issues

It is unlikely that many issues will arise under Article 7 because it is unusual for Parliament to impose retrospective penalties. However, current examples might include legislation directed at sex offenders. The Criminal Evidence (Amendment) Act 1997 allows the police to take samples for DNA profiling purposes of those convicted of offences before that Act came into force but it is not clear whether this would be a 'penalty'. There is also considerable pressure on the government to change the law so that sex offenders who have been given determinate sentences may be kept under supervision on release and recalled to prison if they are likely to re-offend. It may be assumed, at least prima facie, that any such proposals would violate Article 7.

8.8   ARTICLE 8: RIGHT TO RESPECT FOR PRIVATE AND FAMILY LIFE

1.   Everyone has the right to respect for his private and family life, his home and his correspondence.
2.   There shall be no interference by a public authority with the exercise of this right except such as is in accordance with the law and is necessary in a democratic society in the interests of national security, public safety or the economic well-being of the country, for the prevention of disorder or crime, for the protection of health or morals, or for the protection of the rights and freedoms of others.

Article 8 protects the right to respect for a person's private and family life, home and correspondence. The majority of the case law is concerned with defining 'private life', 'family life', 'home' and 'correspondence'. Article 8 has been used in a wide range of contexts: from phone tapping to the use of medical records in court; from the rights of children whose parents are deported to the right to have records altered, to the rights of transsexuals to have their status recognised on official records; from the right to protection from aircraft noise to the right to practise one's sexuality. The Court has held that the essential object of Article 8 is to protect the individual against arbitrary action by the public authorities (*Kroon* v *Netherlands* (1994) 19 EHRR 263).

The Court has also held that the right to respect for private life contains both positive and negative aspects — not just that the state should refrain from interference but also that it has an obligation to provide for an effective respect for private life. The Court stated in *Stjerna* v *Finland* (1994) 24 EHRR 194 that:

> the boundaries between the State's positive and negative obligations under Article 8 do not lend themselves to precise definition. . . . In both contexts regard must be had to the fair balance that has to be struck between the competing interests of the individual and of the community as a whole (*Stjerna* v *Finland* (1994) 24 EHRR 194).

8.8.1   The scope of Article 8(2)

Article 8(2) does not mean that *any* interference with a person's privacy which is intended for one of the specified purposes can be justified. Interference by the state with a person's private and family life, home or correspondence must be justified by one of the exceptions detailed in Article 8(2) and must be the minimum necessary to obtain the legitimate aims. Only these exceptions, along with the restrictions in Article 17, are allowed. These limitations may only be justified if they are 'in accordance with the law' and in all cases, 'necessary in a democratic society'. These phrases, as discussed in chapter 3, have a distinct meaning. Briefly, 'in accordance with the law' entails three things:

(a)   There must be a specific legal rule or regime which authorises the interference.

(b)   The citizen must have adequate access to the law in question (*Sunday Times* v *United Kingdom* (1979) 2 EHRR 245).

(c)   The law must be formulated with sufficient precision to enable the citizen to foresee the circumstances in which the law would or might be applied (*Malone* v *United Kingdom* (1984) 7 EHRR 14).

Even if a measure has been taken in pursuit of one of the legitimate interests listed in the second paragraph of Article 8, the measure must be tested to determine whether it is 'necessary in a democratic society'. The Court has held that the notion of necessity implies two things:

(a)   that an interference corresponds to a pressing social need (*Sunday Times* v *United Kingdom*);

(b)   that it is proportionate to the legitimate aim pursued.

This test of 'proportionality' means that if a measure has been adopted which infringes an individual's convention right in some way, it will not be considered disproportionate if it is restricted in its application and effect, and is duly attended by safeguards in national law so that the individual is not subject to arbitrary treatment (*MS* v *Sweden* (1999) 28 EHRR 313). Conversely the state must not act disproportionately to achieve a legitimate aim (*McLeod* v *United Kingdom* (1999) 27 EHRR 493) or 'use a sledgehammer to crack a nut'.

8.8.2   Private life

In *Niemietz* v *Germany* (1992) 16 EHRR 97 the concept of private life was held to cover the right to develop one's own personality as well as one's right to create relationships with others. The Court held, at para. 29, that, in defining 'private life' for the purposes of Article 8:

> . . . it would be too restrictive to limit the notion to an 'inner circle' in which the individual may live his own personal life as he chooses and to exclude therefrom entirely the outside world not encompassed within that circle. Respect for private life must also comprise to a certain degree the right to establish and develop relationships with human beings.

In *X* v *Netherlands* (1985) 8 EHRR 235 the Court found that the sexual assault of a young mentally handicapped woman obviously offended the concept of private life for the purposes of Article 8. On the other hand, in *Costello-Roberts* v *United Kingdom* (1993) 19 EHRR 112 the Court looked at corporal punishment inflicted on a private school pupil by a teacher and found that this action did not violate the Article. The Court will seemingly look to the seriousness of the invasion in its decision, as it said that the pupil's complaint, 'did not entail adverse effects for his physical or moral integrity sufficient to bring it within the scope of the prohibition contained in Article 8' (at para. 36).

Article 8 may also cover intrusions into the public sphere through environmental damage. There are a number of cases in which this has been accepted. In *Rayner* v *United Kingdom* (1986) 47 DR 5, for example, the Commission considered the application of a man complaining about the amount of air traffic over his home. He argued that the aircraft noise interfered with his rights to respect for his private life and his home. The Commission agreed that this complaint fell within the ambit of Article 8 and held that it included 'indirect intrusions which are unavoidable consequences of measures not directed against private individuals'. However, the Commission decided that the interference with the right was justified under Article 8(2). See also *López Ostra* v *Spain* (1994) 20 EHRR 277, para. 51, in which it was held that permitting a waste treatment plant to operate in breach of a licence condition may affect the right of enjoyment of people's homes and so affect their right to private and family life even if it did not adversely affect their health. However, it would seem that on the present state of the law, Article 8 may not require the government to take positive steps to allow private life to take place in public spaces: see *Botta* v *Italy* (1998) 26 EHRR 241 where it was held that Articles 8 and 14 did not require the state to make access to a beach available to disabled persons. The situation may be different if the space is owned by a public authority. See also *Guerra* v *Italy* (1998) 26 EHRR 357.

Article 8 also concerns sexual activities as an element of private life. In *Dudgeon* v *United Kingdom* (1981) 4 EHRR 149 the Court considered a person's sexual life to be 'a most intimate aspect' of his or her private life. In that case the applicant complained of the criminalisation of all homosexual behaviour in Northern Ireland. The Court found this legislation to be in violation of Article 8 because it was too far-reaching and not proportionate to any possible legitimate governmental aims (at para. 61). In *S* v *United Kingdom* (1986) 47 DR 274, the Commission held that the relationship between a homosexual couple is within the notion of private life. See also *X* v *United Kingdom* (1997) 24 EHRR 143.

Recently the Court held in *Smith and Grady* v *United Kingdom* (2000) 29 EHRR 548 that investigations conducted by the Ministry of Defence into the sexual orientation of members of the services, together with their consequent discharge from the armed forces, constituted 'especially grave' interferences with their private lives. The Court rejected the government's argument that such a policy was justified to preserve the morale of the fighting forces, saying that the Ministry of Defence could not ignore widespread and developing views in other contracting states in favour of the admission of homosexuals into the armed forces of those states.

In *Sutherland* v *United Kingdom* [1998] EHRLR 117 the Commission took the view that the different ages of consent between heterosexuals and homosexuals was a violation of Article 8, in combination with Article 14. On the other hand, in *Laskey* v *United Kingdom* (1997) 24 EHRR 39 the Court found no violation of Article 8 where the applicants were imprisoned as a result of sadomasochistic activities captured on videotape. In that case, the police came into possession of video films depicting sadomasochistic encounters between the applicants and 44 other homosexual men. Although the activity was all consensual, the men were charged with offences including assault and wounding. All applicants were sentenced to imprisonment and, while their sentences were reduced, their convictions were upheld on appeal. The Court found unanimously that this action did not unjustifiably interfere with their right to respect for their private life.

Article 8 has been held to protect the right of a transsexual to have his or her changed sex recognised by the state. In *B* v *France* (1992) 16 EHRR 1 the Court held that the French government violated the article when it refused to allow a change to the applicant's birth certificate. The Court has taken a different view in applications against the United Kingdom in *Rees* v *United Kingdom* (1986) 9 EHRR 56, *Cossey* v *United Kingdom* (1990) 13 EHRR 622 and *Sheffield* v *United Kingdom* (1999) 27 EHRR 163.

The right to a private life under Article 8 also includes the right not to have private information disclosed to third parties. This includes the unnecessary disclosure of confidential medical data in legal proceedings (*Z* v *Finland* (1998) 25 EHRR 371) and the unauthorised passing on of medical information from a hospital to authorities in the process of verifying a claim for social insurance and disability benefit (*MS* v *Sweden* (1999) 28 EHRR 313). In both cases a breach of Article 8 was found to have taken place but in each case the breach was held to be justified on the particular facts of the case. In slightly different circumstances a violation could be found.

'Private life' can extend to the office context, for example, in *Halford* v *United Kingdom* (1997) 24 EHRR 523 it was held that the bugging of private telephone calls made to an office telephone could constitute a violation of the right to respect for private life (see also *Niemietz* v *Germany* (1992) 16 EHRR 97).

8.8.3   Family life

With regard to family life, Article 8 case law has seen an evolution in what is considered 'family' (see J. Liddy, 'The concept of family life under the European Convention on Human Rights' [1998] EHRLR 15). Family life is now considered to extend beyond formal relationships and legitimate arrangements. In *Marckx* v *Belgium* (1979) 2 EHRR 330 the Court found legislation that discriminated against children born outside of wedlock to be in violation of Article 8. Indeed, the Court has held that 'the mutual enjoyment by parent and child of each other's company constitutes a fundamental element of family life' (*B* v *United Kingdom* (1988) 10 EHRR 87).

In *K* v *United Kingdom* (1986) 50 DR 199 the Commission interpreted the notion of family life when it stated, 'The question of the existence or non-existence of "family life" is essentially a question of fact depending upon the real existence in practice of close personal ties'. In *Kroon* v *Netherlands* (1994) 19 EHRR 263 the Court determined that, as a rule, living together may be a requirement for a relationship under Article 8, but exceptionally other factors may also serve to demonstrate that a relationship has sufficient constancy to create de facto 'family ties'. Generally, the Court and Commission consider a family to be a male and female and their children. Homosexual and transsexual unions are not protected under the Article's family life principle, although those relationships may be protected under the private life principle (*S* v *United Kingdom* (1986) 47 DR 274 and *X* v *United Kingdom* (1997) 24 EHRR 143). In *X* v *United Kingdom* (1997) 24 EHRR 143 it was held that the right to a family life did not protect life with a transsexual partner. It was held that the failure to register a female-to-male transsexual as the father of his female partner's child did not constitute a breach of Article 8.

Article 8 covers more than negative obligations of non-interference, but also creates positive obligations. In *Kroon* v *Netherlands* (1994) 19 EHRR 263 the Court recognised, at para. 31, that there are 'positive obligations inherent in the "effective" respect for family life'. For instance, in *Airey* v *Ireland* (1979) 2 EHRR 305 the Court found an Irish law which prohibited a woman from separating from an abusive spouse to be in violation of Article 8.

The right to family life is likely to be disrupted by immigration controls and procedures. This may have major implications for immigration lawyers. See further N. Mole, 'Constructive Deportation' [1995] EHRLR 63; C. Warbrick, 'The Structure of Article 8' [1998] EHRLR 32; M. Hunt and R. Singh, *A Practitioner's Guide to the Impact of the Human Rights Act 1998* (Oxford: Hart, 2000); H. Storey, 'Implications of incorporation of the ECHR in the immigration and asylum context' [1998] EHRLR 452. However, the Strasbourg institutions have taken the view that if the family can go elsewhere to re-establish itself then the immigration procedures do not violate that right (*X* v *United Kingdom*, Application No. 3325/67). Similarly, there will be no violation where the disruption has been caused by the applicant's own making because he has breached immigration controls (*X* v *United Kingdom* (1987) 11 EHRR 48).

The rights of parents to a private family life may be infringed if they are not allowed sufficient involvement in decisions taken by public authorities in fostering arrangements, taking children into care, or denying parents access to their children once in care. In *W, B* v *United Kingdom* (1987) 10 EHRR 29 and *R* v *United Kingdom* (1988) 10 EHRR 74 the Court found a violation of Article 8 because parents were denied proper access to their children held in care and insufficient involvement in the local authority's decision-making process. Likewise, when the state intervenes by removing children into care, Article 8 requires that the natural parents be properly involved in the decision-making process, and that full account is taken of their views and wishes (see *Johansen* v *Norway* (1996) 23 EHRR 33).

8.8.4 Home

In *Gillow* v *United Kingdom* (1986) 11 EHRR 335, the Court held that the notion of 'home' could extend to the place where one intends to live. The applicants in this case were absent from their house in Guernsey for 18 years because the husband's job caused him to travel. The government refused the couple a new residence permit when they finally returned, arguing that this was not their home. The Commission and Court held that, in this case, there was a right to 're-establish home life'. In *Buckley* v *United Kingdom* (1996) 23 EHRR 101 the Court defined 'home' as a continuous residence with no intention to establish home elsewhere.

The concepts of home life and private life may overlap. In *Niemietz* v *Germany* (1992) 16 EHRR 97 the Court extended the notion of 'privacy' to include some places of work. The case involved a search by the police of a lawyer's office. The Court held that the Article protected his office space. The lawyer's office was protected because the Court accepted that one's private life was carried on both at 'home' and, at time, elsewhere, including the office.

In *McLeod* v *United Kingdom* (1999) 27 EHRR 493 the Court held that the common law and statutory powers of the police to enter private premises to prevent a breach of the peace had an adequate legal basis 'in accordance with the law' for the purposes of Article 8(2) and that the aim pursued, the prevention of crime, was legitimate. However, on the facts of this case the Court found that the police action, though justified, had been disproportionate. The applicant was a woman whose estranged husband had arrived with the police to collect property from the former matrimonial home, apparently pursuant to a court order (which did not in fact authorise entry). The Court considered that the police had violated her right to respect for privacy and home life by entering the house as there had been little or no risk of disorder and therefore their action was found to be disproportionate. Thus, in operational terms, an action of a public authority may not survive European Court scrutiny even though the policy satisfies the legitimate aim test. Civil search powers in the course of executing an Anton Piller order (now search order) have also been held to be justified under the 'rights of others' and 'economic well-being of the country' exceptions to Article 8(2) (see *Chappel* v *United Kingdom* (1990) 12 EHRR 1).

So far, however, the article's notion of respect for home has not been extended to the right to have a home (see *Buckley* v *United Kingdom* (1994) 18 EHRR CD 123).

8.8.5   Correspondence

The right to respect for one's correspondence is a right to uninterrupted and uncensored communication with others. In the telephone-tapping case, *Malone* v *United Kingdom* (1984) 7 EHRR 14, the Court found that the British government violated Article 8 when it intercepted the phone calls of the applicant, an antique dealer convicted of receiving stolen goods. The Court reasoned that, because the government did not have statutory procedures for monitoring the phone calls of private citizens, it was not acting in accordance with the law. The Court said, at para. 79:

> In view of the attendant obscurity and uncertainty as to the state of the law in this essential respect, . . . the law of England and Wales does not indicate with reasonable clarity the scope and manner of exercise of the relevant discretion conferred on the public authorities. To that extent, the minimum degree of legal protection to which citizens are entitled under the rule of law in a democratic society is lacking.

The Court considered the same issue in *Halford* v *United Kingdom* (1997) 24 EHRR 523, where the applicant, a former Assistant Chief Constable, complained that calls which she had made from her office and home telephones were intercepted by the police in order to gather information for use against her in sex discrimination proceedings. The Commission found no proof that the applicant's home telephone was being monitored, but the Court held that Article 8 was violated with respect to the calls made from the applicant's office because there was no legal regulation of it.

Some considerable case law is dedicated to prisoners' rights under Article 8. The Court and Commission recognise that the restrictions inherent in imprisonment violate the rights under Article 8(1), but that these restrictions can sometimes be justified under Article 8(2).

As concerns prisoner correspondence, the Court has held that a prisoner has the right to communicate with his or her lawyer with almost no interference. In *Golder* v *United Kingdom* (1975) 1 EHRR 524 the Court held that there was no justification in restricting the applicant's correspondence with his lawyer. While the prison may interfere with non-legal correspondence, the Court in *Silver* v *United Kingdom* (1983) 5 EHRR 347 stated that Strasbourg will investigate these interferences to make sure that they are justified under Article 8(2).

8.8.6 Potential issues

Article 8 is likely to provide fertile ground for imaginative litigation. This is partly because the right to privacy is not reflected to any great extent in domestic common law or in statute and partly because Article 8 can have an effect in diverse fields such as environmental and immigration law. Further, the scope of Article 8(2) and the interplay between Articles 8(1), 8(2) (privacy and its intentions) and 10(1) and 10(2) (freedom of expression and its limitations) are some of the most fundamental questions in a democratic society, particularly one with a powerful press. Thus, the question of how courts can give full effect, by s. 12 of the Human Rights Act 1998, to Article 8 whilst respecting the particular importance accorded to Article 10 will be an important issue. The following developments may create challenges because of the absence of comprehensive and adequate regulation:

(a) Listening devices, telephone taps, electronic monitoring of the Internet and e-mails, and covert surveillance. The Police Act 1997 and the Regulation of Investigatory Powers Act 2000 are attempts by the government to ensure that interference by the police and others with privacy is 'in accordance with the law'. However, there are serious questions about whether this new regime is compliant with the Human Rights Act.

(b) Closed-circuit television surveillance. The domestic challenge to the lack of regulation in *R* v *Brentwood Borough Council, ex parte Peck* (1997) *The Times*, 18 December has been submitted to the Commission.

Respect for private life is likely to raise new issues in a variety of circumstances. Until the Regulation of Investigatory Powers Act 2000 came into force, there was very little regulation of the privacy of employees (see *Halford* v *United Kingdom* (1997) 24 EHRR 523). Employees of public authorities will have a new right to respect for their privacy (under s. 6 of the Human Rights Act, read with Article 8) save where interference is justified. Article 8 will be a factor to be taken into account in certain cases in determining whether a dismissal is fair or unfair under the Employment Rights Act 1996. Article 8 will also be relevant in determining the scope of the contractual duty of mutual trust and confidence implied into an employment contract, so as, for example, to challenge random drug tests at work. The common law of confidence and legislation concerning access to records, such as the Data Protection Act 1998, will have to be read so as to conform with Article 8 of the Convention.

The right to respect for family life may also be helpful to those wishing to challenge the ways that courts and local authorities deal with divorce, care proceedings, adoption, the rights of other relatives to access to the child (and vice versa). It will also be important for those wishing to challenge decisions by the immigration authorities which are likely to lead to disruption of their family life.

Over time the courts may be able to expand the concept of family life to include gay and lesbian relationships — see J. Liddy, 'The concept of family life under the European Convention on Human Rights' [1981] EHRLR 15 and the decision of the House of Lords in *Fitzpatrick* v *Sterling Housing Association Ltd* [1999] 3 WLR 1113.

8.9   ARTICLE 9: FREEDOM OF THOUGHT, CONSCIENCE AND RELIGION

1.   Everyone has the right to freedom of thought, conscience and religion; this right includes freedom to change his religion or belief and freedom, either alone or in community with others and in public or private, to manifest his religion or belief, in worship, teaching, practice and observance.

2.   Freedom to manifest one's religion or beliefs shall be subject only to such limitations as are prescribed by law and are necessary in a democratic society in the interests of public safety, for the protection of public order, health or morals, or for the protection of the rights and freedoms of others.

Article 9 protects the rights to hold religious beliefs, to change one's beliefs and the right to manifest them in 'worship, teaching, practice and observance', whether alone or with others, in public or in private. The right to hold religious beliefs is absolute, whereas the right to manifest them can be limited under Article 9(2) (*Church of X* v *United Kingdom* (1968) 12 YB 306).

Cases in Strasbourg concerning Article 9 deal with issues such as the practice of religion, conscientious objection and pacifism, and prisoners' rights.

However, the Strasbourg case law places considerable weight on Article 9(2), and is relatively narrow when it seeks to balance the right to religious expression and the contractual rights of others, specifically employers. In cases in which discrimination because of the consequences of a religious belief have been alleged, the Strasbourg jurisprudence is extremely restrictive.

In *X* v *United Kingdom* (1981) 22 DR 27 (which arose from *Ahmed* v *Inner London Education Authority* [1978] QB 36) the Commission held that the decision of the ILEA not to release a Muslim schoolteacher to attend mosque on Friday afternoons was not a breach of Article 9, because he had not disclosed this need at interview or during the first six years of employment. The Commission accepted that the education authority had reached a fair balance between the applicant's religious requirements and its own need to organise the school timetable efficiently. Therefore the United Kingdom's failure to provide a remedy for his dismissal fell within Article 9(2). More recently, in *Stedman* v *United Kingdom* [1997] EHRLR 545 the Commission dismissed an application which complained that a requirement that a Christian employee should work on Sundays breached her Article 9 rights. Although the Commission agreed that the United Kingdom could be required to protect Ms Stedman from the actions of a private company, it held that there was no requirement to do so in this case because 'Ms Stedman was dismissed for failing to agree to work certain hours rather than for her religious beliefs, as such, and was free to resign'.

These two cases illustrate, first, the broad scope which the European Court of Human Rights has given to Article 9(2), emphasising the primacy of contractual obligations which employees have undertaken over prima facie rights, and, secondly, the undeveloped nature of the concept of indirect discrimination — at least with respect to Article 9.

However, some cases have succeeded under Article 9. For example, in *Kokkinakis* v *Greece* (1993) 17 EHRR 397 the Court considered the actions of two Jehovah's Witnesses who engaged in door-to-door evangelism. The couple were convicted of the crime of proselytism and fined. The Court recognised that attempting to convert others was a manifestation of belief capable of protection under Article 9(1). It decided that the limitation on this right was prescribed by law, and that the law itself had a legitimate aim, namely the protection of the rights and freedoms of others. However, it held that the decision to prosecute was 'not justified by a pressing need' because no regard had been given to whether the couple had used improper means to evangelise; hence there was a violation of Article 9.

Cases involving conscientious objection have also been raised under Article 9, in conjunction with Article 4(3)(b), which excludes compulsory service for conscientious objectors from the definition of 'forced or compulsory labour' for the purpose of Article 4. Reading the two articles together, Strasbourg has adopted the policy that under Article 9 no one is entitled to exemption on the grounds of conscience from either military service or substitute service (*Autio* v *Finland* (1991) 72 DR 245).

Issues of prisoners' rights have raised Article 9. Most deal with prisoners who allege that they are unable satisfactorily to practise their religions in prison. In *X* v *United Kingdom* (1976) 5 DR 100 the Commission considered the application of a prisoner who had been refused permission to keep a religious book in his cell. The *T'ai Chi Ch'uan and I Ching* contained an illustrated section on martial arts which the prison authorities considered to be dangerous to the general population. The Commission held that this action did violate Article 9(1) but was justified by Article 9(2), and therefore declared the application inadmissible.

8.9.1 Potential issues

Article 9 may benefit minority religious groups in particular contexts: for example, a local authority wishing to oppose the building of a temple would have to show that it had regard to the right to respect for manifestation of religious beliefs, and that any restriction was both prescribed by law, met a legitimate aim and was proportionate.

It is somewhat more doubtful whether Article 9 will have a significant effect in relation to employment law.

One argument is that courts and tribunals could use Article 9 to extend the scope of the Race Relations Act 1976. But in relation to direct discrimination law, the language of the 1976 Act cannot stretch so far — 'racial group' and 'discrimination on racial grounds' mean discrimination on the grounds of colour, race, nationality or ethnic origins, and have been comprehensively defined. Some religious groups will fall within that definition, such as Jews and Sikhs. Others, such as Christians and Muslims, who have more heterogeneous national, ethnic and racial origins, will not. For example, in *Mandla* v *Dowell Lee* [1983] 2 AC 548 the House of Lords held that Sikhs do constitute a 'racial group' in a broad historical and ethnic sense, having regard to their long shared history, cultural traditions, common geographical or ancestral origin, common language and literature, common religion and membership of a minority. It overturned the Court of Appeal, which had held that discrimination against wearers of turbans might be religious discrimination but was not racial discrimination. Equally, discrimination against Jews can be race discrimination (*Seide* v *Gillette Industries Ltd* [1980] IRLR 427 (by reason of ties of blood)). But Rastafarians have been held not to fall within the definition of a separate ethnic or racial group (*Crown Suppliers (Property Services Agency)* v *Dawkins* [1993] ICR 517), as have Muslims (*J.H. Walker Ltd* v *Hussain* [1996] IRLR 11).

In so far as discrimination on the grounds of religious belief or practice may have a disparate adverse impact on a particular racial group and so constitute indirect *race* discrimination, it is already prohibited as a result of domestic law: see, for example, *Walker (J.H.) Ltd* v *Hussain* [1996] IRLR 11. Discrimination against a Muslim or a Hindu is likely to constitute indirect discrimination on grounds of race because any condition applied which a Muslim or Hindu is less likely than others to be able to meet would be such that the proportion of persons from the Indian subcontinent who would comply would be significantly smaller than the proportion of persons not from the Indian subcontinent who could comply. Although the question of what is 'justifiable' for the purposes of the Race Relations Act 1976, s. 1(1)(b), may be investigated within the framework of Article 9, the jurisprudence of the European Court does not suggest that tribunals will have to depart significantly from their current approach. However, a court which did not provide a remedy against an employer who permitted employees to observe one particular day of worship (e.g., Sunday) but not another (e.g., Friday) might be in breach of Articles 9 and 14 read together. It would probably be necessary to apply to the Strasbourg Court claiming that the government had breached Articles 9 and 14 by failing to extend the protection contained in the Employment Rights Act 1996, ss. 36–43, for those who do not wish to work on a Sunday, to those who do not wish to work on any other religious day of worship.

During the Parliamentary debates on the Human Rights Bill, members of certain churches became concerned that the effect of Article 9 of the Convention would be to prevent them from selecting employees in a manner consistent with the ethos and beliefs of their organisation. The solution adopted by the government is contained in s. 13 of the Act. This section provides that if the court's determination of any question under the Act might affect the exercise by a religious organisation (whether as an organisation, or by its members collectively) of the Convention right to freedom of thought, conscience and religion, the court must have 'particular regard' to the importance of that right.

Section 13 is really no more than an exhortation to apply the balance inherent in Article 9 properly. It might, however, affect the outcome in a case about discrimination with respect to dismissal, such as *O'Neill* v *Governors of St Thomas More Roman Catholic Voluntarily Aided Upper School* [1997] ICR 33, where it was held that to dismiss a teacher in a Catholic school by reason of pregnancy was sex discrimination. The governors argued that it was not the fact of pregnancy *per se* which caused the dismissal, but other issues surrounding the pregnancy (i.e., the mother being unmarried and the father of the child being the local Catholic priest) and which affected the religious character of the school, that caused the dismissal. It was held that these factors could not be separated from the fact of the pregnancy

Following the coming into force of the Human Rights Act 1998, this case might be decided differently.

8.10   ARTICLE 10: FREEDOM OF EXPRESSION

1.   Everyone has the right to freedom of expression. This right shall include freedom to hold opinions and to receive and impart information and ideas without interference by public authority and regardless of frontiers. This Article shall not prevent States from requiring the licensing of broadcasting, television or cinema enterprises.

2.   The exercise of these freedoms, since it carries with it duties and responsibilities, may be subject to such formalities, conditions, restrictions or penalties as are prescribed by law and are necessary in a democratic society, in the interests of national security, territorial integrity or public safety, for the prevention of disorder or crime, for the protection of health or morals, for the protection of the reputation or rights of others, for preventing the disclosure of information received in confidence, or for maintaining the authority and impartiality of the judiciary.

Article 10 guarantees the 'freedom to hold opinions and to receive and impart information and ideas without interference by public authority and regardless of frontiers'. In *Handyside* v *United Kingdom* (1976) 1 EHRR 737 at para. 49 the Court sought to define the meaning of freedom of expression for the purposes of Article 10:

Freedom of expression constitutes one of the essential foundations of . . . a [democratic] society, one of the basic conditions for its progress and for the development of every man. Subject to para. 2 of Article 10, it is applicable not

only to 'information' or 'ideas' that are favourably received or regarded as
inoffensive or as a matter of indifference, but also to those that offend, shock or
disturb the state or any sector of the population. Such are the demands of that
pluralism, tolerance and broadmindedness without which there is no 'democratic
society'.

The right concerns the freedom to hold ideas, and to receive options and
information, as well as the right to express them. The concept of 'expression'
covers words, pictures, images and actions intended to express an idea or to present
information (*Stevens* v *United Kingdom* (1986) 46 DR 245). It may also help
someone who is prevented from receiving information (*Autronic AG* v *Switzerland*
(1990) 12 EHRR 485), though it does not create a general right to 'freedom of
information' (*Leander* v *Sweden* (1987) 9 EHRR 433). But a requirement to hand
over information may be a consequent requirement of protecting another right
(*Gaskin* v *United Kingdom* (1989) 12 EHRR 36 (right to social services file central
to right to respect for family life under Article 8 for a person brought up in social
services' care)).

Article 10 protects a wide range of types of expression, including:

(a)   political (such as distribution of political leaflets before an election
(*Bowman* v *United Kingdom* (1998) 26 EHRR 1);
(b)   journalistic (such as refusal to disclose journalistic sources (*Goodwin* v
United Kingdom (1996) 22 EHRR 123));
(c)   artistic (e.g., *Müller* v *Switzerland* (1988) 13 EHRR 212; *Wingrove* v
United Kingdom (1996) 24 EHRR 1); and
(d)   commercial (e.g., *Barthold* v *Germany* (1985) 7 EHRR 383 (vets' advertising); *Colman* v *United Kingdom* (1993) 18 EHRR 119 (doctors' advertising)).

Convention jurisprudence also gives different weight to different kinds of
expression. The most important expression — political speech — therefore is likely
to be protected to a much larger extent by the Court than the least important —
commercial speech.

Article 10 also protects the right to be provided with information (see *Open
Door and Dublin Well Woman* v *Ireland* (1992) 15 EHRR 244).

In practice, the Court gives rather stronger protection to political and journalistic
expression than to other forms of expression, though the Court has expressly
disavowed any theoretical basis for this distinction (*Thorgeirson* v *Iceland* (1992)
14 EHRR 843 at para. 64). Though the Court has never gone so far as the US
Supreme Court in *New York Times* v *Sullivan* (1964) 376 US 254, which requires
proof of malice in defamation cases brought by public figures, it affords considerable protection to those who criticise politicians and other public figures, such as
judges, whether or not the views they express are facts or based on opinion, and
whether or not they are politely or elegantly expressed, unless they are 'gratuitous
personal attacks' (*Oberschlick* v *Austria* (1997) 25 EHRR 357; *De Haes* v *Belgium*

(1997) 25 EHRR 1). The Court is interested in protecting the elements of a free press — such as the rights of journalists to protect their sources as well as the actual expression of view (*Goodwin* v *United Kingdom* (1996) 22 EHRR 123).

However, in other areas, the Court is more likely to give greater weight to the rights and freedoms of others. For example, in *Otto-Preminger Institute* v *Austria* (1994) 19 EHRR 34 the Court decided that it was within the State's margin of appreciation to decide to forfeit a film which satirised God, Jesus and Mary in a predominantly Catholic country, because it could be said to be 'necessary in a democratic society'. A similar conclusion was recently reached in *Wingrove* v *United Kingdom* (1996) 24 EHRR 1, in which the British Board of Film Classification refused a certificate for a video called *Visions of Ecstasy*.

The balance between the importance of the right to freedom of expression to a democratic system overall and the rights and the freedoms of others has caused the Court great difficulty. This is partly because the right to freedom of expression can often conflict with competing social interests such as the right to a fair trial (*Sunday Times* v *United Kingdom* (1979) 2 EHRR 245), the protection of the democratic process (e.g., *Bowman* v *United Kingdom* (1998) 26 EHRR 1), the privacy of others (e.g., *Lingens* v *Austria* (1986) 8 EHRR 103), and the right to respect for thought, conscience and religion (e.g., *Otto-Preminger Institute* v *Austria* (1994) 19 EHRR 34).

Article 10(1) specifically states that it does not prevent states from requiring the licensing of broadcasting, television or cinema enterprises, and the list of exceptions in Article 10(2) is longer and more specific than in relation to other articles. Article 10(2) specifically states that the exercises of the freedoms in Article 10(1) 'carries with it duties and responsibilities'.

Nevertheless it is clear from the case law that the Court will require a strong justification for interfering with the right to freedom of expression. It will ask whether the restriction is 'prescribed by law' and whether a pressing 'social need' is 'convincingly established' (*Handyside* v *United Kingdom* (1976) 1 EHRR 737; *Sunday Times* v *United Kingdom* (1979) 2 EHRR 245; *Weber* v *Switzerland* (1990) 12 EHRR 508). Although the common law is sufficient to constitute 'law' for these purposes if it is 'adequately accessible' and 'formulated with sufficient precision' (see *Sunday Times* v *United Kingdom*). In the case of *Steel* v *United Kingdom* (1999) 28 EHRR 603 the Court held that protesters handing out leaflets at a conference protesting at the sale of weapons had been conducting a peaceful protest and their detention for offences against the Public Order Act 1986 and their subsequent bind-over was an interference with their right to freedom of expression. In a similar case, *Hashman and Harrup* v *United Kingdom* (2000) 8 BHRC 104, the Court decided that the imposition of binding-over orders on hunt saboteurs for behaviour that was not unlawful but *contra bonos mores* was insufficiently precise to be justified as a limitation on the applicants' right to protest against hunting with hounds. Both these cases also engage Article 11 issues.

When considering its judgment the Court will also examine whether the restriction can be 'justified as being necessary in a democratic society'. This involves it in considering the facts and circumstances prevailing before it. So, for example, it has upheld injunctions to restrain the publication of Peter Wright's *Spycatcher* before it was published in other countries, and held that risk of material prejudicial to MI5 justified the injunctions (*Observer* v *United Kingdom* (1991) 14 EHRR 153), whereas it took a different view after the book was available in other jurisdictions, and the justification no longer stood. See also *Goodwin* v *United Kingdom* (1996) 22 EHRR 123, in which the Court recognised that fining a journalist who refused to disclose his sources for contempt of court was 'prescribed by law' and 'pursued a legitimate aim', but was nonetheless disproportionate in the circumstances, and *Tolstoy Miloslavsky* v *United Kingdom* (1995) 20 EHRR 442, in which a level of libel damages which at the time was not open to review by the Court of Appeal and, at £1.5 million, was so high as to stifle freedom of speech, was not necessary in a democratic society and hence breached Article 10.

However, in other cases concerning freedom of expression, the Court felt it appropriate to draw back from pronouncing on the proportionality issue, holding that the decision reached by the national court has been within its 'margin of appreciation' (e.g., *Handyside* v *United Kingdom* (1976) 1 EHRR 737).

8.10.1 Potential issues

The House of Lords has said that the right to freedom of expression in the United Kingdom already broadly reflects the jurisprudence of Article 10 of the Convention (*R* v *Secretary of State for the Home Department, ex parte Brind* [1991] 1 AC 696), and in *Camelot Group plc* v *Centaur Communications Ltd* [1998] 2 WLR 379 it was held that the provisions in the Contempt of Court Act 1981 sufficiently protected Article 10 rights.

Nevertheless, it is likely that careful consideration of the case law in individual cases will have an effect on a wide variety of exercises of judicial discretion. Although courts have sometimes been prepared to have regard to the terms of Article 10 in determining whether to prevent a political demonstration or industrial action taking place (*Middlebrook Mushrooms Ltd* v *Transport and General Workers' Union* [1993] IRLR 232), now that the Human Rights Act 1998 is in force, courts will have to exercise any judicial discretion they have so as to accord with Article 10, having regard to the case law (ss. 2, 3 and 6 of the Act). For example, in *Steel* v *United Kingdom* (1999) 28 EHRR 603, the applicants had been involved in a number of different protests and had been arrested for causing a breach of the peace and were detained. In some of the cases the magistrates subsequently asked the applicants to accept bind-overs but they refused and they were imprisoned as a result. They argued that their detentions violated Article 5(1) and Articles 6, 10 and 13. The argument succeeded under Article 10 and this will also have an effect on cases concerning attempts to restrain breaches of confidence or libels.

The position of the media and others involved in publication will probably be considerably enhanced by Article 10 read with s. 12 of the Act, which will make it significantly more difficult to obtain a pre-trial injunction. An example of the possible broad scope of Article 10 was recently illustrated by the House of Lords when they applied Article 10 to find prison rules, which prevented prisoners from speaking to journalists in the absence of undertakings from the journalists not to publish the results of conversations, disproportionate and *ultra vires*: *R* v *Secretary of State for the Home Department, ex parte Simms* [1999] 3 WLR 328.

In the field of employment law, Article 10 may make an impact on, for example, dismissals based on whistle-blowing (although this is now subject to separate statutory regulation), and dismissal or discrimination cases based on failure to obey dress codes. For example, cases such as *Burrett* v *West Birmingham Health Authority* [1994] IRLR 7 (requirement for female but not male nurse to wear a cap, admitted to serve no practical purpose, was justified) and *Smith* v *Safeway plc* [1996] ICR 868 (ban on long hair for men but not women was justified) may need to be revisited, in the light of Article 10 read with Article 14.

Article 10 may offer new defences in certain criminal trials, such as those under the Official Secrets Act (where at present even the most trivial disclosure can justify prosecution, without any need for proportionality), or in trials involving alleged obscenity or indecency. In many public order cases, particularly those that have arisen from marches, demonstrations and protests, defendants are likely to want to argue that their right to freedom of expression, assembly or privacy will be violated by the conviction.

8.11 ARTICLE 11: FREEDOM OF ASSEMBLY AND ASSOCIATION

1. Everyone has the right to freedom of peaceful assembly and to freedom of association with others, including the right to form and to join trade unions for the protection of his interests.

2. No restrictions shall be placed upon the exercise of these rights other than such as are prescribed by law and are necessary in a democratic society in the interests of national security or public safety, for the prevention of disorder or crime, for the protection of health or morals or for the protection of the rights and freedoms of others. This Article shall not prevent the imposition of lawful restrictions on the exercise of these rights by members of the armed forces, of the police or of the administration of the state.

Article 11 protects the right to freedom of peaceful assembly and to freedom of association with others. It includes the right to form and to join trade unions for the protection of a person's interests. Rights under Article 11 are qualified in two ways: first, because a court or tribunal will often be required to balance competing rights under Article 11 with rights under other articles of the Convention and, secondly, because of the qualifications in Article 11(2).

Article 11 contains a positive obligation for authorities to protect the exercise of the rights contained in it. In *Plattform 'Ärzte für das Leben'* v *Austria* (1988) 13 EHRR 204 it was held that the state had a duty to protect the participants in a

peaceful demonstration from disruption by a violent counter-demonstration. The
Court held, at para. 32, that:

> Genuine, effective freedom of peaceful assembly cannot . . . be reduced to a
> mere duty on the part of the state not to interfere: a purely negative conception
> would not be compatible with the object and purpose of Article 11. . . . Article
> 11 sometimes requires positive measures to be taken, even in the sphere of
> relations between individuals, if need be.

In the context of freedom of association, the Court held that the Convention
safeguards upon the freedom for individual trade unionists to protect their interests
by trade union action were rights which the state must 'both permit and make
possible' (*National Union of Belgian Police* v *Belgium* (1975) 1 EHRR 578, para.
39). Trade unions may themselves sometimes count as victims in the context of
violations of Article 11 (*ibid.*, *Schmidt* v *Sweden* (1976) 1 EHRR 632).

The right to freedom of association protects the right to join or form other
'associations' (such as political parties) as well as the right to join trade unions.
Professional regulatory bodies set up by a state to regulate a profession, with
compulsory membership within a profession, do not fall within this definition of
an association (*Le Compte* v *Belgium* (1981) 4 EHRR 1). A bar association and an
architects' association are not within the definition; but a taxi drivers' association
has been held to fall within it (*Sigurdur A. Sigurjónsson* v *Iceland* (1993) 16 EHRR
462).

The 'closed shop' is not always a violation of Article 11. In *Young* v *United
Kingdom* (1981) 4 EHRR 38 it was held that a closed shop was a violation of
Article 11, because the refusal to join a union led to 'a threat of dismissal involving
loss of livelihood' which was 'a most serious form of compulsion' and as such
struck 'at the very substance of the freedom guaranteed by Article 11'. However,
in *Sibson* v *United Kingdom* (1993) 17 EHRR 193 an employer exercised his
contractual right to transfer an employee to a different depot after he resigned from
one union to join another, and others refused to work with him. The Court held
that moving him to a different depot did not 'strike at the very substance of the
freedom of association guaranteed by Article 11' because there was no question of
him losing his job.

Article 11 does not create a right to membership of a particular association in
all circumstances. In *Cheall* v *United Kingdom* (1985) 42 DR 178, the Commission
decided that generally an individual had no right to belong to a particular trade
union. The decision to expel Mr Cheall was analysed as the decision of a private
body exercising its rights under Article 11 not to associate with him. However, the
Commission made the point that the right of the trade union to choose its members
is not absolute:

> . . . for the right to join a union to be effective the state must protect the
> individual against any abuse of a dominant position by trade unions. . . . Such

abuse might occur, for example, where exclusion or expulsion was not in accordance with union rules or where the rules were wholly unreasonable or arbitrary or where the consequences of exclusion or expulsion resulted in exceptional hardship such as job loss because of a closed shop.

Article 11 may also protect a right to strike. In *Schmidt* v *Sweden* (1976) 1 EHRR 632 the Court described such a right as 'without any doubt one of the most important' of the means by which Article 11 rights are protected, but did not consider that the right to strike was 'indispensable for the effective enjoyment of trade union freedom' and therefore always protected by Article 11.

In relation to freedom of assembly, Article 11 only applies to peaceful gatherings and does not encompass 'a demonstration where the organisers and participants have violent intentions which result in public disorder' (*G* v *Germany* (1989) 60 DR 256). However, a just balance must be achieved. In *Ezelin* v *France* (1991) 14 EHRR 362 a demonstrator who was a lawyer by profession refused to leave when a march disintegrated into violence, and refused to answer questions at a subsequent inquiry. The French Court of Appeal, exercising its disciplinary function over lawyers, reprimanded him for 'breach of discretion', though his actions were not unlawful. The Court regarded this as disproportionate to the state's need to prevent disorder. It held that a 'just balance' must not discourage people from making their beliefs known in a peaceful way.

The Convention permits states to place limitations on the exercise of these rights by members of the armed forces, police or members of the administration of the state. In *Council of Civil Service Unions* v *United Kingdom* (1987) 50 DR 228 (the GCHQ case) the Commission took the view that that staff at GCHQ were 'members of the administration of the State' and that therefore there was no breach of the Convention in the decision of the British government to prohibit them from membership of trade unions. By contrast, in *Vogt* v *Germany* (1995) 21 EHRR 205 the Commission said that German schoolteachers were not 'members of the administration of the State', and the Court held that this part of Article 11(2) 'should be interpreted narrowly in the light of the post held by the official concerned'.

8.11.1 Potential issues

In the recent admissibility decision in *NATFHE* v *United Kingdom* (1998) 25 EHRR 122 it was held that the requirements, contained in the Trade Union and Labour Relations (Consolidation) Act 1992, ss. 226A and 234A, that a trade union must notify an employer of, *inter alia*, those who will be taking part in industrial action, do not violate Article 11 in the context of other statutory protections against discrimination on grounds of trade union membership.

Article 11 arguments may be of some use in other areas of trade union law. For example, the law on picketing contained in s. 220 of the 1992 Act and the Code on Picketing, which are generally interpreted so as to limit the number of pickets to six at 'or near' the place of work, will have to be interpreted consistently with the balance in Article 11; and Article 11 may be in play when courts consider the scope of the common law of trespass.

It could be argued that, in interpreting what constitutes 'unjustified' discipline and expulsion from a union under the Trade Union and Labour Relations (Consolidation) Act 1992, ss. 64 to 67 and 174 to 178, courts will have to have regard to Strasbourg jurisprudence such as *Cheall* v *United Kingdom* (1985) 42 DR 178, and the right of the majority of members of a trade union not to associate with another member. However, this might require a declaration of incompatibility in relation to the 'automatically unfair' categories in s. 65(2) of the Act, which are clear and explicit on the fact of the statute.

Another issue which has been debated in the European Court is the extent to which Article 11 will be interpreted so as to give a right to representation of an employee by a trade union 'for the protection of his interests' (*Swedish Engine Drivers' Union* v *Sweden* (1976) 1 EHRR 617). This is the argument in *Wilson* v *United Kingdom*, Application No. 30668/96, 16 September 1997, which arose from *Newspapers Associated Ltd* v *Wilson* [1995] 2 AC 454 and which the Commission has now referred to the Court.

In the context of public order, the right to assemble for political purposes may be improved. For example, arrests for behaviour likely to cause a breach of the peace or convictions for public order offences may violate Article 11 if the law is not sufficiently clear (*Steel* v *United Kingdom* (1999) 28 EHRR 603), or if the restrictions imposed are not proportionate or necessary in a democratic society (*Ezelin* v *France* (1991) 14 EHRR 362).

8.12   ARTICLE 12: RIGHT TO MARRY

Men and women of marriageable age have the right to marry and to found a family, according to the national laws governing the exercise of this right.

The first thing one realises about Article 12 is its brevity. The Article carries no exception clause and gives the state wide berth to regulate the exercise of the rights.

Article 12 is a limited right and therefore is much narrower in scope than 'family life' in Article 8. The article is focused on procreation within the traditional family unit. For instance, in *Rees* v *United Kingdom* (1986) 9 EHRR 56 the Court was unwilling to recognise that the Article 12 right to found a family can exist outside of a marriage.

An example of the wide powers given to the state is shown in *Johnston* v *Ireland* (1986) 9 EHRR 203, in which the Court held that there is no violation of the Article if a state prohibits a divorced person from remarrying.

So far Article 12 only applies to biologically opposite sexes. Prohibition of homosexual and transsexual marriage will not violate the Article. In *Cossey* v *United Kingdom* (1990) 13 EHRR 622 the Court upheld a law that denied a post-operative male-to-female transsexual the right to marry a male partner. The Court in *Rees* v *United Kingdom* (1986) 9 EHRR 56, which also denied a transsexual the right to marry, held, at para. 49, that:

> . . . the right to marry guaranteed by Article 12 refers to the traditional marriage between persons of opposite biological sex. This appears also from the wording of the Article which makes it clear that Article 12 is mainly concerned to protect marriage as the basis of the family.

In *Hamer* v *United Kingdom* (1979) 24 DR 5 and *Draper* v *United Kingdom* (1980) 24 DR 72 the Commission ruled that prohibiting prisoners from marrying interfered with their Article 12 rights and served no legitimate state objective.

8.12.1   Potential issues

The jurisprudence under Article 12 does not yet allow members of the same sex to marry each other and the restriction of the right by the use of the phrase 'according to national laws' makes the provision less useful to applicants than it might otherwise be.

The right to found a family has been used on behalf of prisoners serving long sentences to have children using artificial insemination although conjugal visits may not be required (*GS; RS* v *United Kingdom*, Application No. 17142/90, European Commission of Human Rights, 10 July 1991).

When Diane Blood sought to use her dead husband's sperm to conceive a child she only succeeded on the basis of European Community free movement law. Had the Human Rights Act 1998 been in force she may have succeeded more easily by invoking Articles 12 and 8.

8.13   ARTICLE 13: RIGHT TO AN EFFECTIVE REMEDY

Everyone whose rights and freedoms as set forth in this Convention are violated shall have an effective remedy before a national authority notwithstanding that the violation has been committed by persons acting in an official capacity.

This Article is not directly incorporated by the Human Rights Act 1998 into domestic law, but is likely to play an important role in the interpretative obligation in s. 3 of the Act because it is so often referred to in Strasbourg cases, which will have to be considered by virtue of s. 2.

Article 13 requires member states to provide a real and effective remedy in a domestic court for violations of the substantive rights enumerated in the Convention.

This means that there must be domestic procedures for deciding 'arguable claims', not just a remedy in relation to actual breaches of the Convention. The remedy claimed must 'involve the determination of the claim as well as the possibility of redress', and may be determined by the court on a complaint filed by the applicant or of its own motion (*Klass* v *Germany* (1978) 2 EHRR 214).

The question will often be whether all the procedures, in the lower tribunals and the courts, taken together, amount to an 'effective remedy'. For example *Silver* v *United Kingdom* (1983) 5 EHRR 347 concerned a claim by a prisoner that his correspondence had been interfered with contrary to Article 8. The Court took the view that neither the prison board of visitors, the Parliamentary Commissioner for Administration, the Home Secretary nor subsequent judicial review of the Home Secretary's decisions was a sufficiently effective remedy to comply with Article 13.

Equally, in *Govell* v *United Kingdom* (Application No. 27237/95, European Commission of Human Rights, 26 February 1997) it was held that the police complaints procedure is an inadequate remedy for the purposes of Article 13. This position was re-affirmed in the recent case of *Khan* v *United Kingdom* (2000) *The Times*, 23 May, where it was held that there was a violation of Article 13 (in conjunction with Article 8) on the basis that the Police Complaints Authority was not a sufficiently independent body to protect individuals from abuse of authority.

Much of the United Kingdom case law is concerned with the extent to which judicial review proceedings, in which issues of fact can rarely be considered, can be treated as an effective remedy. The Court's case law in this respect is variable.

In *Soering* v *United Kingdom* (1989) 11 EHRR 439 the Court found judicial review to be an effective remedy for the purposes of Article 13. The applicant was threatened with extradition to the United States of America to face a charge of murder. The Court held that the 'death-row phenomenon' (being kept on death row for long periods of time before a final decision is pronounced on execution) constituted torture or inhuman and degrading treatment. The fact that a United Kingdom court would have jurisdiction to set aside a decision for this reason convinced the Court that this review constituted an effective remedy.

This meant that in *Vilvarajah* v *United Kingdom* (1991) 14 EHRR 248, in which the Commission had decided that an appeal on the merits *after* an applicant had left the United Kingdom is not an effective remedy for potential breaches of Article 3, the Court declined to address the point because it had already decided that judicial review was an adequate remedy, and an individual would not be removed from the jurisdiction during that process.

However, in *Chahal* v *United Kingdom* (1997) 23 EHRR 413 the Court held unanimously that there had been a violation of Article 13 in conjunction with Article 3. A Sikh separatist leader was detained in custody for deportation purposes in response to the Home Secretary's determination that he was a threat to national security. The Court found that this deportation would be a violation of Article 3, as the applicant would face a real risk of being subjected to ill-treatment in the receiving country. Because neither the advisory panel nor the courts could review the Home Secretary's decision to deport the applicant, the Court found that there were no effective remedies available to the applicant.

It seems, however, that *Chahal* may be confined to cases where national security issues have been invoked. In *D* v *United Kingdom* (1997) 24 EHRR 423 the applicant sought to rely on the decision in *Chahal* to persuade the Court not to follow its conclusion in *Soering* and *Vilvarajah* that judicial review proceedings were an effective remedy in complaints raised under Article 3 in the context of deportation and extradition. D, who was dying of AIDS, challenged the Chief Immigration Officer's decision not to let him stay on compassionate grounds. He argued that judicial review proceedings were an insufficient remedy because the Court of Appeal did not seek to ask itself whether Article 3 would be breached by the deportation, but merely asked whether the decision-maker had taken the matter into account. The Court, however, held that there was no reason to depart from the two earlier cases, because the Court afforded 'anxious scrutiny' in cases involving a risk to life expectancy. This approach has been criticised (N. Blake, 'Judicial review of discretion in human rights cases' [1997] EHRLR 391).

The Court has regarded judicial review and/or appeal from a tribunal of fact on a point of law as constituting an adequate remedy in other contexts too (*Bryan* v *United Kingdom* (1995) 21 EHRR 342). However, where there is no system of regulating interferences with rights by private bodies, there will be a breach of Article 13 (*Halford* v *United Kingdom* (1997) 24 EHRR 523).

Recently in *Smith and Grady* v *United Kingdom* (2000) 29 EHRR 548, the Court took the very clear position that, in the circumstances of that case, judicial review was not an effective remedy for the purposes of Article 13. However, the domestic courts themselves stated as much when they were dealing with the case on judicial review. If the case had been taken after October 2000 the result might have been very different, thus perhaps reducing the importance of the case for assessing judicial review.

8.13.1 Potential issues

Although Article 13 is not itself incorporated into United Kingdom law, it has been considered by the Strasbourg institutions in connection with other Convention rights.

Since, by virtue of s. 2 of the Human Rights Act 1998, the Strasbourg case law must be taken into account when a United Kingdom court is considering a case 'in connection with' a right which has been incorporated, it will be interesting to see the extent to which Article 13 will affect the decisions of the English courts as a side effect of their s. 2 duty to have regard to Strasbourg case law.

Article 13 could be used in conjunction with Article 2 (see the earlier discussion at 8.2.3) to give the family of those who die in suspicious circumstances (from the use of force in custody) a judicial remedy. In connection with this point see the recent case of *Keenan* v *United Kingdom*, Application No. 27229/95, 22 May 1998. Article 13 could also be used in connection with Article 6 to challenge the standard of review to be applied to self-regulating bodies in judicial review proceedings, on the basis of the case law that says that, since they make up their own rules, they are to be left 'pretty much to get on with it' (see *R* v *Panel on Take-overs and Mergers, ex parte Datafin plc* [1987] QB 815).

8.14   ARTICLE 14: PROHIBITION ON DISCRIMINATION

The enjoyment of the rights and freedoms set forth in this Convention shall be secured without discrimination on any ground such as sex, race, colour, language, religion, political or other opinion, national or social origin, association with a national minority, property, birth or other status.

Article 14 is not a general 'equal treatment' guarantee. Unlike other human rights instruments such as Article 26 of the International Covenant on Civil and Political Rights of 1966, the Convention contains no free-standing prohibition of discrimination. It only requires access to other Convention rights to be equal: in effect it is a guarantee of equality before the law of the Convention. This means that it can only operate within the ambit of another Convention right. It has been described as 'a parasitic provision and not a general proscription against every kind of discrimination' (D.J. Harris, M. O'Boyle and C. Warbrick, *Law of the European Convention on Human Rights*, p. 463).

The Council of Europe has now drawn up a new protocol, Protocol 12, which would give a general prohibition on discrimination and promote equality. The Protocol is open for signature on 4 November 2000, but it is unlikely that the United Kingdom government will incorporate the new Protocol in the immediate future.

Although it is not a freestanding provision, Article 14 is wider than some other human rights equality guarantees because the grounds on which discrimination is prohibited are very wide. The particular grounds of prohibited discrimination specified in Article 14 are only examples and the phrase 'or other status' has been broadly interpreted.

Article 14 is a qualified right in the sense that not all differences in treatment are contrary to Article 14. Differences of treatment of people in like situations within the sphere of another Convention right will contravene Article 14 unless they can be shown to be justified and proportionate. Justification for discrimination, however, generally requires particularly strict justification.

Grounds of discrimination identified by the Court and Commission have included sex, marital status, sexual orientation, birth inside or outside marriage, being a particular business singled out from others, trade union status, military status, conscientious objection, poverty and imprisonment, and these categories are not closed.

A claim falls 'within the ambit' of a Convention right if it concerns the subject matter protected by that article of the Convention. However, there does *not* need to be an actual violation of that other Convention right in order to establish a violation of Article 14. In practice, however, the applicant will usually wish to establish a violation of both the substantive right and Article 14. In many cases the Court, once it has found a breach of the substantive right, has often held that it is unnecessary to go on to consider whether there has also been a breach of Article 14. For example, in *Dudgeon* v *United Kingdom* (1981) 4 EHRR 149, which concerned the criminalisation of all homosexual activity in Northern Ireland, the claim was brought under Article 8 (right to respect for private and family life) and Article 14; but having found a breach of Article 8, the Court found it unnecessary to consider whether there was also discrimination on grounds of sexual orientation. In *Smith and Grady* v *United Kingdom* (2000) 29 EHRR 548 a violation of Articles 8 and 14 were claimed following the applicants' discharge from the armed services on the grounds of their homosexuality. The Court upheld the complaints under Article 8 and concluded that the claim under Article 14 had been subsumed under that finding of a violation.

In the *Belgian Linguistic Case (No. 2)* (1968) 1 EHRR 252 the Court held that a failure to maintain a particular type of school was not itself a violation of Article 14, but a state which had set up such an establishment could not operate discriminatory entrance requirements for it, because this would violate Article 14. Another example of the scope of Article 14 given in that case is access to a court. Article 6 does not require a right of appeal but, if one exists, it would violate Article 6 read with Article 14 if certain people were barred from appealing without a legitimate reason while others with the same cause of action could appeal. See also *Inze* v *Austria* (1987) 10 EHRR 394; *Abdulaziz* v *United Kingdom* (1985) 7 EHRR 471, paras 65, 71 and 72. In *National Union of Belgian Police* v *Belgium* (1975) 1 EHRR 578 the Court said, 'It is as though Article 14 formed an integral part of each of the articles laying down rights and freedoms whatever their nature.'

Not all forms of differentiation amount to discrimination in Convention terms; it is only different treatment of people 'placed in analogous situations' which falls within the scope of Article 14 (*Lithgow* v *United Kingdom* (1986) 8 EHRR 329).

The person asserting the violation must establish that their situation can be considered similar to those who have been treated differently (*Fredin* v *Sweden* (1991) 13 EHRR 784, para. 60). The Court has often decided cases alleging discriminatory treatment by determining that no Article 14 question is raised because the comparison is not truly with a person in an analogous situation. In *Van der Mussele* v *Belgium* (1983) 6 EHRR 163 the Court held that trainee barristers could not legitimately be compared with trainees in other professions because the differences between their situations were too great.

This approach means that Article 14 is not as strong as it could be for protecting the right to respect for difference. For example, the Court has held that differential treatment of gay and heterosexual relationships is not discriminatory (see *Kerkhoven* v *Netherlands*, Application No. 15666/89, European Commission of Human Rights, 19 May 1992, though this was a case under Article 8 relating to the sharing of the parental role) and *X* v *United Kingdom* (1997) 24 EHRR 143).

Where people in factually similar circumstances are treated dissimilarly, there will be discrimination if a measure creates differential treatment which does not pursue a legitimate aim, or if it is disproportionate to the aim pursued. In the *Belgian Linguistic Case (No. 2)* (1968) 1 EHRR 252 the Court said, at para. 10:

The existence of such a justification must be assessed in relation to the aims and effects of the measure under consideration, regard being had to the principles which normally prevail in democratic societies. A difference of treatment in the exercise of a right laid down in the Convention must not only pursue a legitimate aim: Article 14 is likewise violated when it is clearly established that there is no reasonable relationship of proportionality between the means employed and the aim sought to be realised.

See also *Rasmussen* v *Denmark* (1984) 7 EHRR 371. The concepts of whether there has been different treatment of people in analogous situations, and whether discrimination is justified, have often been blurred in the Strasbourg case law.

In determining what is a 'legitimate aim', the Court has sometimes employed the 'margin of appreciation' doctrine (e.g., *Inze* v *Austria* (1987) 10 EHRR 394 and *Gillow* v *United Kingdom* (1986) 11 EHRR 335), though administrative convenience may not amount to a legitimate aim of social policy (see *Darby* v *Sweden* (1990) 13 EHRR 774 at para. 33). There are some grounds for distinguishing how people are treated, such as race or gender, or legitimacy, which the Court will not normally accept. In such cases, 'very weighty reasons' would be needed to justify discrimination. In *Schmidt* v *Germany* (1994) 18 EHRR 513 the Court said, at para. 24, 'Very weighty reasons would have to be put forward before the Court could regard a difference of treatment based exclusively on the ground of sex as compatible with the Convention.' See also *Inze* v *Austria* (1987) 10 EHRR 394 and, more recently, *Van Raalte* v *Netherlands* (1997) 24 EHRR 503.

The concept of indirect discrimination is relatively undeveloped in the Strasbourg case law. The *Belgian Linguistics* decision implies that the Convention is capable of covering both direct and indirect discrimination. The Court in that case suggested that justification of a measure would be required where the 'aims *and effects*' were discriminatory and there was no reasonable relationship of proportionality between the means employed and the aim sought to be realised. However, the idea has not been developed in the Convention case law. In *Abdulaziz* v *United Kingdom* (1985) 7 EHRR 471, Immigration Rules disqualified people who had never met their intended partners from entering the country for the purposes of marriage. This had a far greater impact on would-be entrants from the Indian subcontinent, where arranged marriages are traditional, than those from elsewhere. Although a minority of the Commission had concluded that the 'practical effect' of the rule was race discrimination, the Court did not properly analyse the indirect discrimination question, running it together with the question of the good faith and justifiability of the government's explanation for the Rules.

8.14.1 Potential issues

The incorporation of Article 14 into United Kingdom law is, in itself, unlikely to add much to existing anti-discrimination legislation — such as the Sex Discrimination Act 1975 and the Race Relations Act 1976 — in fields where it applies. However, there are many fields (such as public/immigration law decisions) to which the Race Relations Act 1976 did not apply, and in such contexts, Article 14, particularly read together with the Race Relations (Amendment) Act 2000, and other rights such as Article 8 (right to respect for private and family life), might have a significant effect.

Article 14 could also be used to challenge a police force which exercises stop-and-search powers in a way which disproportionately affects people from ethnic minorities: this could constitute a breach of Article 5 and/or Article 8 coupled with Article 14.

Article 14 has been used in the past, and may be used in the future, to test different treatment of different groups under tax and/or benefit regimes in combination with Article 1 of Protocol 1. See the discussion of *MacGregor* v *United Kingdom* [1998] EHRLR 354 (in relation to tax allowances) and *Cornwell* v *United Kingdom* (2000) *The Times*, 10 May (in relation to social security benefits) at 18.9.1.

The Human Rights Act 1998 might also be used in developing protection from indirect discrimination in the application of Convention principles in the future, but only if domestic courts are willing to fuse concepts learned from domestic and European Community law with the protection on grounds of other statuses afforded by Article 14. This is possible even in relation to Convention questions because s. 2 of the Human Rights Act 1998 permits United Kingdom courts to go beyond the case law of the European Court of Human Rights, because it does not bind domestic courts to follow that case law, but only to take it into account. If Protocol 12 becomes part of our law, this will create a very significant equality guarantee.

8.15   ARTICLE 15: EXCEPTION IN TIME OF WAR

1.   In time of war or other public emergency threatening the life of the nation any High Contracting Party may take measures derogating from its obligations under this Convention to the extent strictly required by the exigencies of the situation, provided that such measures are not inconsistent with its other obligations under international law.

2.   No derogation from Article 2, except in respect of deaths resulting from lawful acts of war, or from Articles 3, 4 (para. 1) and 7 shall be made under this provision.

3.   Any High Contracting Party availing itself of this right of derogation shall keep the Secretary General of the Council of Europe fully informed of the measures which it has taken and the reasons therefor. It shall also inform the Secretary General of the Council of Europe when such measures have ceased to operate and the provisions of the Convention are again being fully executed.

Article 15 allows a government to derogate from its obligations under the Convention during 'war or other public emergency threatening the life of the nation', but only 'to the extent strictly required by the exigencies of the situation'. This enables a state to restrict the exercise of some of the rights and freedoms, but only in so far as is necessary to deal with the emergency.

The United Kingdom has used this provision several times in relation to the conflict in Northern Ireland. There is only one derogation currently in place (see 9.1) and that also relates to that conflict and the Prevention of Terrorism (Temporary Provisions) Act 1989. The derogation in force allows the police to detain people under this law for up to seven days despite the previous judgment of the European Court of Human Rights that this was a breach of Article 5(3) of the Convention (*Brogan* v *United Kingdom* (1988) 11 EHRR 117). In *Brannigan* v *United Kingdom* (1993) 17 EHRR 539 the Court held that this derogation satisfied Article 15 and that therefore the applicants could not validly complain of a violation of Article 5(3). The Court accepted the view of the United Kingdom government that there was an emergency threatening the life of the nation and that the provision allowing detentions for seven days without access to the court was necessary. For both tests the Court allowed the United Kingdom a wide margin of appreciation.

The ceasefire and political agreement have reduced the conflict considerably in Northern Ireland and the number of terrorist incidents has reduced very considerably since the circumstances described in *Brannigan* v *United Kingdom*. It is therefore submitted that detentions for longer than four days, which are contrary to Article 5(3), are not protected by Article 15 and the derogation is unlawful despite the margin of appreciation that might ordinarily be granted. However, as the derogation is set out in the Act any such challenge would have to be made in Strasbourg rather than in the domestic courts.

The government has determined that this derogation from Article 5(3) will expire five years after the Human Rights Act 1998 comes into force unless both Houses of Parliament agree that it should be renewed, and similarly thereafter (White Paper, *Rights Brought Home: The Human Rights Bill* (Cm 3782), para. 4.4). The Terrorism Act 2000 creates a new procedure for the detention and interrogation of suspects and involves access to a court within four days. Now this provision is in place the derogation will no longer be necessary.

8.16   ARTICLE 16: RESTRICTIONS ON POLITICAL ACTIVITY OF ALIENS

Nothing in Articles 10, 11 and 14 shall be regarded as preventing the High Contracting Parties from imposing restrictions on the political activities of aliens.

Article 16 allows states a considerable latitude to interfere with the political rights of aliens. In *Piermont* v *France* (1995) 20 EHRR 301, the Commission recognised that this provision was outdated. It stated, '. . . those who drafted [Article 16] were subscribing to a concept that was then prevalent in international law, under which a general, unlimited restriction of the political activities of aliens was thought legitimate'. Although the Court decided on the facts of the case that Article 16 need not be specifically considered, some consideration was given to the Article by four judges who gave a dissenting opinion. They stated that:

we would accept that the object and purpose of Article 16 should . . . be examined in the context of paragraph 2 of Article 10. In particular, when the proportionality of the interference with Mrs Piermont's freedom of expression is under consideration, account should be taken of the principle embodied in Article 16.

Given the importance of the rights contained in Article 10, the limitation contained in Article 16 is likely to be of little importance.

It also seems clear from this case that Members of the European Parliament cannot be regarded as aliens within any jurisdiction in the European Union and as a result of the rights of citizenship created by the Maastricht Treaty this must be extended to all citizens of the EU.

It has been suggested by D.J. Harris, M. O'Boyle and C. Warbrick, at p. 510, that the expression 'political activities' might only apply narrowly to the setting up and operation of political parties, expressions of opinion in connection with these parties and voting in elections.

Certainly Article 16 has little support and the Parliamentary Assembly of the Council of Europe recommended its removal on 25 January 1977.

8.17   ARTICLE 17

Nothing in this Convention may be interpreted as implying for any State, group or person any right to engage in any activity or perform any act aimed at the destruction of any of the rights and freedoms set forth herein or at their limitation to a greater extent than is provided for in the Convention.

The primary purpose of Article 17 is to safeguard the provisions of the Convention from abuse at the hands of extremists. It may be invoked by persons against a government or be used by a government to defend its actions against persons. It may not, however, be used to deny the rights and freedoms of people considered extremists by the state. For instance, in *Lawless v Ireland* (1961) 1 EHRR 1, the Court held that Article 17 could not be used to deny IRA members the right to liberty or a fair trial.

8.18   ARTICLE 18

The restrictions permitted under this Convention to the said rights and freedoms shall not be applied for any purpose other than those for which they have been prescribed.

Aimed primarily at the ulterior motive, Article 18 is a parasitic provision. In *Kamma v Netherlands* (1974) 1 DR 4, the Commission described the Article thus: 'Article 18, like Article 14 of the Convention, does not have an autonomous role. It can only be applied in conjunction with other Articles of the Convention. There may, however, be a violation of Article 18 in connection with another Article, although there is no violation of that Article taken alone.'

8.19   PROTOCOL 1, ARTICLE 1: PROTECTION OF PROPERTY

Every natural or legal person is entitled to the peaceful enjoyment of his possessions. No one shall be deprived of his possessions except in the public interest and subject to the conditions provided for by law and by the general principles of international law.

The preceding provisions shall not, however, in any way impair the right of a State to enforce such laws as it deems necessary to control the use of property in accordance with the general interest or to secure the payment of taxes or other contributions or penalties.

The right to property proved to be one of the most controversial issues to confront the drafters of the Convention, because certain states (principally the United Kingdom and Sweden) did not wish to divest themselves of the power to acquire property for the purposes of nationalisation and other socio-economic programmes. Some states argued that property is an economic, rather than a civil, right and that a human rights convention was an inappropriate way to protect it (see J. Kingston, 'Rich people have rights too? The status of property as a fundamental right' in L. Heffernan (ed.), *Human Rights: A European Perspective*, Dublin: Round Hall Press, 1994). Consequently the right to property conferred by, Protocol 1, Article 1 is highly qualified and has been interpreted by the Court so as to give the state a wide margin of appreciation when interfering with that right.

In *Sporrong* v *Sweden* (1982) 5 EHRR 35 the Court analysed Protocol 1, Article 1 and broke it down into its component parts. The Court gave, at para. 61, an interpretation of Protocol 1, Article 1 which it has approved in subsequent cases, such as *Lithgow* v *United Kingdom* (1986) 8 EHRR 329, para. 106.

In order to show that Protocol 1, Article 1, has been violated, it must be shown that:

(a)   the peaceful enjoyment of the applicant's possessions has been interfered with by the state (rule 1), or

(b)   the applicant has been deprived of possessions by the state (rule 2), or

(c)   the applicant's possessions have been subjected to control by the state (rule 3).

But interference, deprivation or control will not violate Protocol 1, Article 1 if done 'in the public interest' or 'to enforce such laws [as the state] deems necessary to control the use of property in accordance with the general interest'.

In determining the level of permissible interference with peaceful enjoyment of possessions the Court applies the 'fair balance' test. Any interference must achieve a fair balance between the demands of the general interests of the community and the protection of the fundamental rights of individuals. There must be a reasonable relationship of proportionality between the means employed and the aim pursued. The availability of an effective remedy and compensation is relevant in assessing whether a fair balance has been struck.

Sporrong v *Sweden* (1982) 5 EHRR 35 related to town planning in the city of Stockholm. The applicants owned properties that were subject to lengthy expropriation permits and prohibitions on construction. The Court held that there had been an interference with the applicants' rights of property by rendering the substance of ownership 'precarious and defeasible'. The prohibitions on construction were characterised as a 'control on the use' of the property within the third rule, while the expropriation permits were an interference within the first rule. The fair balance between the protection of the right of property and the requirements of the general interest had been upset by the prolonged extension of the permits and prohibitions. As the domestic law did not provide a means for the applicants to seek a reduction in the time limits for expropriation or to claim compensation, they had unnecessarily borne an individual and excessive burden. A violation of Protocol 1, Article 1 had thus occurred. For a case concerning environmental laws, see *Matos e Silva Lda* v *Portugal* [1997] EHRLR 109.

The issue of deprivation of property was also raised in *Holy Monasteries* v *Greece* (1994) 20 EHRR 1. Greece passed laws that created a presumption in favour of state ownership of disputed monastic land. In assessing whether the fair balance test was satisfied, the Court considered that the compensation terms in the legislation were relevant to ensure that the monasteries did not bear a disproportionate burden. The Court held, at para. 71:

> In this connection, the taking of property without payment of an amount reasonably related to its value will normally constitute a disproportionate interference and a total lack of compensation can be considered justifiable under Protocol 1, Article 1 only in exceptional circumstances. Article 1 does not, however, guarantee a right to full compensation in all circumstances, since legitimate objectives of 'public interest' may call for reimbursement of less than the full market value.

The Court held that the lack of compensation provided to the Greek Monasteries meant that the deprivation did not comply with the fair balance test, and accordingly there was held to have been a violation of Protocol 1, Article 1.

Previously, however, in *Lithgow* v *United Kingdom* (1986) 8 EHRR 329 the Court held that inadequate compensation may be justified where the public interest is great. The case concerned the nationalisation of the applicants' property under the Aircraft and Shipbuilding Industries Act 1977. While not contesting the principle of nationalisation as such, they claimed that the compensation offered by the state was grossly inadequate and thus Protocol 1, Article 1 had been violated. The Court rejected this claim and stated, at para. 122:

Compensation must normally be reasonably related to the value of the property taken, but Protocol 1, Article 1, does not guarantee full compensation in all cases. Legitimate objectives of public interest may justify reimbursement at less than the full market value; the nature of the property taken and the circumstances of the taking may be taken into account in holding the balance between public and private interests. The standard of compensation for a whole industry may therefore differ from the standard required in other cases. The Court will respect the national legislature's judgment in this respect unless manifestly without reasonable foundation.

The Court held that the government's method of valuation (which based the amount of compensation on the value of shares, rather than the value of assets, at a point in time before the decision to nationalise was announced) was not inconsistent with Protocol 1, Article 1, and no violation had occurred.

In deciding whether a deprivation is in the public interest the Court affords the state a wide margin of appreciation in deciding what public interest demands. The characterisation of an objective of deprivation as being in the public interest is a question left almost exclusively to the determination of the state.

James v *United Kingdom* (1986) 8 EHRR 123 concerned the compulsory transfer of ownership of residential properties in central London to the tenants of those properties pursuant to the Leasehold Reform Act 1967, which was designed to protect long-term tenants' moral entitlement to their properties at the end of their leases. The property owners complained that the compulsory nature of, and the calculation of the price of, the transfers violated Protocol 1, Article 1. The Court was unanimous in holding that compulsory transfer from one individual to another may be a legitimate means of promoting the public interest, even where the community at large has no direct enjoyment of the property taken. The objective of eliminating social injustice by leasehold reform is within the state's margin of appreciation. The means chosen to regulate the injustice was not proportionate, nor was it unreasonable to restrict the right of enfranchisement to less valuable houses since they were perceived as cases of greatest hardship.

The deprivation of property must be 'subject to the conditions provided for by law'. This means that there must exist a basis for the deprivation in domestic law which must be accessible and sufficiently certain, and which protects against arbitrariness (*Sunday Times* v *United Kingdom* (1979) 2 EHRR 245). In *James* v *United Kingdom* the Court (at para. 67) held that the Leasehold Reform Act 1967 was not arbitrary simply because it provided compensation at less than full market value. In *Hentrich* v *France* (1994) 18 EHRR 440, however, a law creating a right of pre-emption over land to enable the Commissioner of Revenue to collect tax was held to violate Protocol 1, Article 1 because it 'operated arbitrarily and selectively and was scarcely foreseeable, and it was not attended by the basic procedural safeguards'. Other methods were available to the state to prevent tax evasion which were adequate.

The third rule contained in Protocol 1, Article 1 recognises that states are entitled to control the use of property where it is considered to be in the general interest to do so or to secure the payment of taxes or other contributions or penalties.

Controls on the use of property have included laws requiring positive action by property owners, as in *Denev v Sweden* (1989) 59 DR 127 where environmental laws obliged a landowner to plant trees, as well as restrictions on their activities, such as planning controls, seizure of property for legal proceedings and inheritance laws.

In a number of cases the Court has considered housing laws that suspended or staggered the enforcement of eviction orders by residential property owners against their tenants. These laws have been held to constitute 'controls on the use of property'. The Court stated in *Mellacher v Austria* (1989) 12 EHRR 391:

> The second paragraph reserves to states the right to enact such laws as they deem necessary to control the use of property in accordance with the general interest.
>
> Such laws are especially common in the field of housing, which in our modern societies is a central concern of social and economic policies.
>
> In order to implement such policies, the legislature must have a wide margin of appreciation both with regard to the existence of a problem of public concern warranting measures of control and as to the choice of the detailed rules for the implementation of such measures.

The need to strike a fair balance between the general interest and the rights of individual property owners pervades the whole of Protocol 1, Article 1, including its second paragraph. Thus in *Spadea v Italy* (1995) 21 EHRR 482 it was held that the applicants had been treated fairly by the laws suspending a tenant eviction order, whereas the applicant in *Scollo v Italy* (1995) 22 EHRR 514 had not. In both cases the suspensions of the eviction orders had the reasonable aim of preventing a large number of people all becoming homeless at the same time. The facts of each case meant that the application of the fair balance test produced different results.

Another example of laws that have been characterised as a 'control on the use of the property' are forfeiture laws. In *Handyside v United Kingdom* (1976) 1 EHRR 737 the Court found no violation where books that had been held to have been obscene were destroyed by the state. Customs seizure of gold bullion owned by the applicants, which a third party had attempted to import illegally, was a permissible control on the use of property (*Allgemeine Gold- und Silberscheidean-stalt v United Kingdom* (1986) 9 EHRR 1). *Air Canada v United Kingdom* (1995) 20 EHRR 150 concerned seizure by Customs authorities of the applicant's aircraft, in which a third party had smuggled cannabis, and which the applicant company had to pay £50,000 to retrieve. In all these cases the Court applied the fair balance test, and in all of the cases the laws were considered proportional.

The ability of the state to levy tax is specifically preserved in the second paragraph. The fair balance test generally applies to this control on the use of property only in so far as it will require procedural guarantees to establish the applicant's liability to make payments — the state can decide for itself as to levels of tax, and the means of assessment and collection.

In *Gasus Dosier- und Fördertechnik GmbH* v *Netherlands* (1995) 20 EHRR 403 the Court said it 'will respect the legislature's assessment in [enforcing tax obligations] unless it is devoid of reasonable foundation'. In *National and Provincial Building Society* v *United Kingdom* (1997) 25 EHRR 127 the court upheld retrospective legislation designed to frustrate a claim that the applicants may have made to recover tax they had already paid. This was characterised as a control on the use of property, and was held to have been justified to prevent the applicants from exploiting a technical defect in laws that sought to change the method by which tax was assessed. By adopting retrospective measures to reaffirm their intention to collect the tax (after legislation had been invalidated by the domestic courts on technical grounds) the legislature 'did not upset the fair balance between the demands of the general interests of the community and the protection of the fundamental rights of the applicant society' (at p. 170).

The Court has interpreted the concept of 'possessions' broadly. It includes land, contractual rights and leases, shares, patents and debts. The goodwill of a business and liquor licences have been held to fall within the scope of Protocol 1, Article 1 (see, for example, *Tre Traktörer AB* v *Sweden* (1989) 13 EHRR 309). In the case of *Pressos Compania Naviera SA* v *Belgium* (1995) 21 EHRR 301 the Court considered that the concept extended to a claim for compensation in tort.

However, the position is rather more equivocal in relation to pecuniary rights gained by virtue of public law. In such cases the Court will consider whether the right is nevertheless in the nature of a possession. The question of whether a pension or social security entitlement is a possession was considered by the Commission in early cases (*X* v *Netherlands* (1971) 38 CD 9; *Muller* v *Austria* (1975) 3 DR 25), which created a distinction between contributory and non-contributory schemes. A contributory scheme creates an individual share in the fund, and a claim to this type of benefit is a possession. In a non-contributory scheme the relation between the payment of contributions through the general tax system and the latter benefit is much less obvious, and creates merely an expectation of a benefit, the amount of which depends upon regulations and conditions prevailing at the time of claim. Thus Protocol 1, Article 1 does not create a general right to a social security. As Harris, O'Boyle and Warbrick point out, an applicant seeking to use Protocol 1, Article 1 to establish a right to a pension must 'demonstrate that he has a legal right to some benefit if he satisfies certain conditions, rather than that he seeks to ensure that a discretion is exercised in his favour' (*Law of the European Convention on Human Rights*, p. 518). For a recent case in which discrimination on the grounds of nationality in relation to a contributory social security benefit was held to be a violation, see *Gaygusuz* v *Austria* (1996) 23 EHRR 365.

8.19.1   Potential issues

Arguments in relation to Protocol 1, Article 1 are likely to be combined with arguments under Article 14.

Social security and taxation laws which discriminate on the grounds of sex have been challenged in the cases of *MacGregor* v *United Kingdom* [1998] EHRLR 354 and *Cornwell* v *United Kingdom* (2000) *The Times*, 10 May. In the first case the Commission held admissible a complaint that the applicant was a victim of a violation of Article 14 in conjunction with Protocol 1, Article 1 in relation to laws which allowed an exemption from tax for women caring for their disabled husbands, but not for men caring for disabled wives. In the second case a widower who was not entitled to the same benefits that a bereaved widow would have had under current social security legislation alleged discrimination. The Commission declared the case admissible and a friendly settlement was reached on the basis that the applicant widower was paid the same amount that a widow in the same situation would have received.

The business community is likely to raise Protocol 1, Article 1 in the domestic courts following incorporation. It has been suggested that laws levying a 'windfall tax' on the excess profits of privatised utilities and laws which impose a three-year statutory limitation on reclaiming overpayments of VAT and excise duty will be the subject of challenges based on this Article though such arguments may founder on the *Lithgow* decision (M. Smyth, 'The United Kingdom's incorporation of the European Convention and its implications for business' [1998] EHRLR 273).

The proposed ban on fox-hunting, where it occurs on private land, may be the subject of a challenge based on Protocol 1, Article 1, and will raise questions of the extent to which the state may control the use of possessions.

Cases involving enforcement of planning laws may also raise issues of whether the interference with property rights concerned are legitimate and proportionate.

8.20   PROTOCOL 1, ARTICLE 2: RIGHT TO EDUCATION

No person shall be denied the right to education. In the exercise of any functions which it assumes in relation to education and to teaching, the State shall respect the right of parents to ensure such education and teaching in conformity with their own religious and philosophical convictions.

This provision caused disagreement among states during its drafting because of fears that the existence of such a right would impose onerous positive obligations upon governments. Thus it appears in the negative ('no person shall be denied the right to education') as opposed to the original positive form ('every person has the right to education'). Several states, including the United Kingdom, have reservations to this Article which reflect this concern. The United Kingdom's reservation reads '. . . the principle affirmed in the second sentence of Protocol 1, Article 2 is accepted by the United Kingdom only so far as it is compatible with the provision of efficient instruction and training and the avoidance of unreasonable public expenditure'.

In the *Belgian Linguistic Case (No. 2)* (1968) 1 EHRR 252, the Court held that despite this negative formulation the first sentence of Protocol 1, Article 2 does enshrine a right. However, the negative formulation indicates that the contracting parties did not recognise such a right as would have required them to establish at their own expense, or to subsidise, education of any particular type or at any particular level. Since all member states at the time of signing the Protocol possessed, and continued to possess, a general and official educational system, there was no question of requiring each state to establish such a system. Implied in such a right was the right to be educated in one of the national languages. Although Protocol 1, Article 2 is potentially wide and protects: the right of access to educational institutions which exist; a right to an effective education; and a right to recognition of studies successfully completed, the negative formulation of the first sentence would be sufficient to defeat a claim alleging violation based on failure to allocate resources to particular educational provisions.

The emphasis is on primary and secondary education. It is recognised that the state may limit tertiary education to those who will benefit from it (*X v United Kingdom* (1980) 23 DR 228; *Glazewska v Sweden* (1985) 45 DR 300). The right is that of the student, which can be exercised by the parents on their behalf when they are young, and by the student personally when they grow older.

The state may require parents to send their children to school or educate them adequately at home (*Family H v United Kingdom* (1984) 37 DR 105). It may allow private education and schools, but is under no obligation to fund or subsidise these arrangements.

The second sentence of Protocol 1, Article 2 seeks to prevent the state from indulging in indoctrination of children through the education system by providing to parents the right to have their religious and philosophical convictions respected. This applies to all educational systems, be they public or private, and to all functions the state exercises with respect to education, be they academic or administrative.

In *Campbell v United Kingdom* (1982) 4 EHRR 293 two parents challenged the existence of corporal punishment in state schools, on the basis that it was contrary to their philosophical beliefs. The Court upheld their complaint. It held that the obligation to respect religious and philosophical convictions is not confined to the content of educational instruction, but includes the organisation and financing of public education, the supervision of the educational system in general and questions of discipline.

The extent to which the religious and philosophical convictions of parents can influence the provision of education is limited, however, in a number of ways. First the conviction itself must come within the limited definition set out in *Campbell v United Kingdom*. The parents must also show that the holding of the belief is the reason for their objection to what the state is doing, and that they have brought the reason for their objection to the attention of the authorities. Finally the state will not contravene Protocol 1, Article 2 if the education system conveys religious or philosophical knowledge in an objective, critical and pluralistic manner.

In *Kjeldsen v Denmark* (1976) 1 EHRR 711 parents challenged a law which made sex education a compulsory component of the curriculum of state primary schools. The Court held:

The State was forbidden to pursue an aim of indoctrination that might be considered as not respecting parents' religious and philosophical convictions: this was the limit that could not be exceeded.

The Court looked at the nature of the sex education and concluded that it did not overstep the bounds of what a democratic state might regard as being in the public interest. The instruction was a way of objectively conveying information, with no attempt to indoctrinate towards a particular moral view. The law did not therefore offend the parents' religious and philosophical convictions to the extent forbidden by Protocol 1, Article 2. The Court further held that if the parents wished to disassociate their children from the sex education programme, the alternatives of a highly subsidised private school system, where the law did not apply as strictly, or home education existed.

In the case of *Valsamis* v *Greece* (1996) 24 EHRR 294 the Court applied the principles developed in *Kjeldsen* v *Denmark* and *Campbell* v *United Kingdom* to a challenge to Greek law which caused the one-day suspension of children of Jehovah's Witnesses for refusing to take part in a nationalistic military parade. The Court found that no violation of Protocol 1, Article 2 arose.

Where a conflict arises between the child's right to education and respect for a parent's convictions, the former will prevail. Allowing parents the options of sending their child to a private school or educating them at home is sufficient to deal with the conflicts. As noted previously, there is no obligation on the state to subsidise the alternatives.

Protocol 1, Article 2 is subject to the prohibition on discrimination found in Article 14 of the Convention. This issue was raised in the *Belgian Linguistic Case (No. 2)* (1968) 1 EHRR 252, which concerned legislation that dictated the language of education in certain areas of Belgium. A school which failed to comply with the language rules could suffer penalties which included denial of public support and non-recognition. The parents, who were French-speaking, argued that their children's right to education, their right to respect for their family life (Article 8) and the protection from discrimination had all been violated. The Court ruled against them. Language was not within the concept of 'philosophical convictions' for the purposes of Protocol 1, Article 2. In relation to discrimination it held that Article 14 did not prohibit all difference in treatment, but that the principle of equality of treatment was only violated if the distinction had no objective and reasonable justification. Article 14 of the Convention and Protocol 1, Article 2 ensure that the right to education is secured without discrimination, and in the absence of any express terms the two provisions do not guarantee to everyone the right to be educated in the language of their choice. For a further discussion on discrimination and state grants to schools, see Harris, O'Boyle and Warbrick, *Law of the European Convention on Human Rights*, pp. 548–9.

8.20.1 Potential issues

Protocol 1, Article 2 is likely to be used (in combination with Article 14) in challenges to circumstances in which the religious and cultural needs of one ethnic, religious or political group are given greater provision than those of another (see the *Belgian Linguistic Case (No. 2)* (1968) 1 EHRR 252).

The expulsion of disruptive children from schools may also be an area in which the right to education is raised, particularly if inadequate resources are made available for home education and other alternatives.

Since part of the right to education is 'the right to develop a personality in conjunction with others' the Human Rights Act 1998 may assist in argument with local education authorities or the Special Education Needs Tribunal concerning the provision necessary to meet special educational needs in connection with emotional and behavioural difficulties or disorders on the autistic continuum. However, the scope of the reservations means that the Convention is unlikely to enable parents to claim specific special educational provision (*Simpson* v *United Kingdom* (1989) 64 DR 188; *Ford* v *United Kingdom* [1996] EHRLR 534).

Since the School Standards and Framework Act 1998 now outlaws corporal punishment in *all* schools, not just state schools, the Convention is unlikely to extend the law far in the light of *Campbell* v *United Kingdom* (1982) 4 EHRR 293 and *A* v *United Kingdom* (1999) 27 EHRR 611.

8.21   PROTOCOL 1, ARTICLE 3: RIGHT TO FREE ELECTIONS

The High Contracting Parties undertake to hold free elections at reasonable intervals by secret ballot, under conditions which will ensure the free expression of the opinion of the people in the choice of the legislature.

By Protocol 1, Article 3, states which have ratified the Protocol undertake to hold free elections. It was held in *Mathieu-Mohin* v *Belgium* (1987) 10 EHRR 1 that Protocol 1, Article 3 does give rise to an individual right and can be the object of a complaint.

Mathieu-Mohin v *Belgium* is the central case to have been decided by the Court regarding this provision, and concerned the rather complex electoral laws existing in Belgium. Several general principles relating to Protocol 1, Article 3 were established.

The Court approved of the Commission's broad interpretation that the scope of Protocol 1, Article 3 extended to the concept of subjective rights of participation — the right to vote and the right to stand for election to the legislature. However, it went on to state that the rights are not absolute. Conditions placed by the state on the right to vote and stand for election are not in principle precluded by Protocol 1, Article 3, and the states enjoy a wide margin of appreciation in this sphere, for example, in relation to the disenfranchisement of convicted prisoners (*H* v *Netherlands* (1983) 33 DR 242) or citizens resident abroad (*X* v *United Kingdom* (1979) 15 DR 137), and language requirements (*Frysky Nasjonale Partij* v *Netherlands* (1985) 45 DR 240), provided that the conditions are imposed in pursuit of a legitimate aim, that the means employed are not disproportionate and that they do not thwart the free expression of the opinion of the people in the choice of the legislature.

Protocol 1, Article 3 only applies to the legislature, or at least one chamber if there are two or more. It does not necessarily mean the national parliament. In *Mathieu-Mohin* v *Belgium* regional councils were held to be constituent parts of the legislature. The Commission has decided that other elected bodies, such as the former metropolitan county councils in England, are not 'legislatures' for the purpose of Protocol 1, Article 3 (*Booth-Clibborn* v *United Kingdom* (1985) 43 DR 236). The Commission has ruled that referenda are not subject to Protocol 1, Article 3 (*X* v *Germany* (1975) 3 DR 98; *X* v *United Kingdom* (1975) 3 DR 165).

There is no obligation to introduce a specific system of voting, such as proportional representation. The state again has a wide margin of appreciation. It does not have to introduce a system of voting which ensures that all votes have equal weight as regards the outcome of the election or that all candidates have equal chances of victory. In *Liberal Party* v *United Kingdom* (1980) 21 DR 211 a challenge was made to the system of 'first past the post' elections in the United Kingdom, which inevitably disadvantaged smaller political parties. The Commisson found the complaint inadmissible stating that the United Kingdom system was a fair one overall and that it did not become unfair because of the results that flowed from it.

The Court in *Mathieu-Mohin* v *Belgium* observed that for the purpose of Protocol 1, Article 3 any electoral system must be assessed in the light of the political evolution of the country concerned. Features that would be unacceptable in the context of one system may be justified in another, as long as the chosen system provides for conditions which will ensure the 'free expression of the opinion of the people in the choice of the legislature'. The same position was taken by the Court, departing from the view of the Commission, in *Gitonas* v *Greece*, 1 July 1997.

In the case of *Bowman* v *United Kingdom* (1998) 26 EHRR 1 the Court examined the relationship of Article 3 of Protocol 1 to Article 10 of the Convention (freedom of expression) in the context of electoral laws that limited the amount of money spent by unauthorised persons on publications during an election period, and found the limits to be a disproportionate infringement to the right of free speech, not outweighed by the need to hold free elections.

8.21.1 Potential issues

Laws which have the practical effect of disenfranchising groups of people may contravene Protocol 1, Article 3. For example, an inadequate system of postal voting might prevent disabled or ill people from exercising their right to vote. Residential requirements that are not flexible enough to recognise the situation of homeless people may also run contrary to this right. The proposals in the Representation of the People Bill may go some way to addressing these concerns.

It is arguable that Protocol 1, Article 3, could have an effect on restrictions upon the way parties select candidates for Parliament. Restrictions on selection by parties is allowed, but only if it does not constitute a disproportionate limit to freedom of political expression (see *W* v *Belgium* (1975) 2 DR 110 at p. 116). For example, the Sex Discrimination Act 1975, s. 13, which relates to selection of candidates for jobs or posts, has been held by an industrial tribunal to prevent the Labour Party from having women-only shortlists (*Jepson* v *Labour Party* [1996] IRLR 116). It is arguable that by applying the law on 'jobs' to selections of the legislature, the tribunal restricted the expression of political views disproportionately, so in contravention of Protocol 1, Article 3. If taken to its logical conclusion, this would prevent (for example) a 'black power' party from fielding only black candidates because of the like provision in the Race Relations Act 1976. The tribunal's view was never tested in a higher court, and is contrary to the two opinions received (before and after the tribunal's decision) by the Equal Opportunities Commission (see *Equality in the 21st Century: A New Approach* (EOC, 1998)).

Protocol 1, Article 3 stipulates that elections be held by secret ballot. United Kingdom electoral practice arguably breaches this requirement by allowing 'vote tracing' to occur. The system is designed to prevent fraudulent persons from impersonating voters by recording each voter's electoral roll number on the counterfoil of his or her ballot paper. Anyone with access to election papers after an election can simply match the numbers up to establish who voted for whom. There have been concerns expressed that state security agencies have indulged in this practice to establish who supported parties with controversial and non-mainstream policies (see *Ballot Secrecy* (Liberty and the Electoral Reform Society)).

8.22   PROTOCOL 4 — INTRODUCTION

Protocol 4 was opened for signature in September 1963, but it has not been ratified by the United Kingdom. The principal reason for this is that the British Nationality Act 1981, which denies the right of entry to some classes of United Kingdom nationals (British Dependent Territories citizens, British Overseas citizens, British Subjects and British Nationals (Overseas)), conflicts with Article 3 of the Protocol. The government at present has no intention of ratifying this Protocol

8.23   PROTOCOL 4, ARTICLE 1

No one shall be deprived of his liberty merely on the ground of inability to fulfil a contractual obligation.

This provision is almost identical to Article 11 of the United Nations' International Covenant on Civil and Political Rights, to which the United Kingdom is subject, and it is impossible to find an example of a United Kingdom law that would breach it. It applies only to contractual obligations, and does not affect imprisonment for breach of a court order, such as inability to pay a fine. It is limited to an 'inability to fulfil a contractual obligation', thus excluding from its application a refusal to fulfil such an obligation by someone with the means to fulfil it. The word 'merely' excludes cases in which the defaulter acts fraudulently or maliciously. Thus in *X* v *Germany* (1971) 14 YB 692 this Article did not protect a person who was detained for refusing to execute an affidavit in respect of his property at the request of his creditor.

8.24   PROTOCOL 4, ARTICLE 2

1.   Everyone lawfully within the territory of a state shall, within that territory, have the right to liberty of movement and freedom to choose his residence.

2.   Everyone shall be free to leave any country, including his own.

3.   No restrictions shall be placed on the exercise of these rights other than such as are in accordance with law and are necessary in a democratic society in the interests of national security or public safety, for the maintenance of order public, for the prevention of crime, for the protection of health or morals, or for the protection of the rights and freedoms of others.

4.   The rights set forth in paragraph 1 may also be subject, in particular areas, to restrictions imposed in accordance with law and justified by the public interest in a democratic society.

Freedom of movement within a territory applies to 'everyone', including aliens 'lawfully' in a territory. The power of a state to control the entry of non-nationals is preserved by the inclusion of the word 'lawfully'.

This right of free movement is limited by the restrictions found in Protocol 4, Article 2(3) and (4). The first are the usual ones, concerned with national security or public safety, the maintenance of public order, the prevention of crime, for the protection of health or morals, or for the protection of the rights and freedoms of others. The restriction is subject to the requirement that it be necessary in a democratic society. These restrictions are similar in content to those found in Articles 8–11 of the Convention. Protocol 4, Article 2(4) creates a further restriction not found elsewhere, that of the 'public interest'. This formulation was preferred by the Committee of Experts, a majority of whom rejected a reference to 'economic welfare' being included. However, commentators have suggested that the term 'public interest' is broad enough to include consideration of the economic welfare of society (Harris, O'Boyle and Warbrick, *Law of the European Convention on Human Rights*, pp. 560–1; P. van Dijk and F. van Hoof (eds), *Theory and Practice of the European Convention on Human Rights*, 2nd ed. (Kluwer, 1990), p. 492). All restrictions on freedom of movement are subject to the principle of proportionality, the doctrine of the margin of appreciation, and must be in accordance with law. For examples of cases concerning Protocol 4, Article 2, see *X* v *Belgium* (1981) 24 DR 198; *Schmid* v *Austria* (1985) 44 DR 195; *Raimondo* v *Italy* (1994) 18 EHRR 237.

The freedom to leave a state applies to nationals and aliens alike, and is subject to the same restrictions that apply to freedom of movement within a state (see

X v *Germany* (1997) 9 DR 190; *M* v *Germany* (1984) 37 DR 113; *Piermont* v *France* (1995) 20 EHRR 301).

Protocol 4, Article 5, which applies to the Protocol as a whole, provides that if a state which ratifies the Protocol declares that it also applies to an external territory, that external territory is to be treated as separate from the state's metropolitan territory for the purposes of Protocol 4, Articles 2 and 3.

8.25   PROTOCOL 4, ARTICLE 3

1.   No one shall be expelled, by means either of an individual or of a collective measure, from the territory of the state of which he is a national.

2.   No one shall be deprived of the right to enter the territory of the state of which he is a national.

Protocol 4, Article 3(1) prohibits the expulsion of nationals from the territory of their own state, and Protocol 4, Article 3(2) guarantees the right of a national to enter the territory of his or her state.

An expulsion occurs when 'a person is obliged permanently to leave the territory of the state . . . without being left the possibility of returning later' (*X* v *Austria* (1974) 46 CD 214). Extradition is not within this definition and is outside the scope of this Article (*Bruckmann* v *Germany* (1974) 17 YB 458).

Protocol 4, Article 5 applies (see 8.24), so that a state's external territories declared subject to the Article are considered separate from the metropolitan territory. This would have allowed the United Kingdom to distinguish between nationals denied entry under the British Nationality Act 1981.

8.26   PROTOCOL 4, ARTICLE 4

Collective expulsion of aliens is prohibited.

This Article refers to expulsion by a collective measure, as opposed to an expulsion following an individual decision about a particular person. In *A* v *Netherlands* (1988) 59 DR 274 it was held that it was not a collective expulsion where a number of asylum seekers from the same country had been expelled for similar reasons as each had received an individual reasoned decision. 'Expulsion' in this context has the same meaning as in Protocol 4, Article 3. In such a case the issue of discriminatory treatment may of course arise.

8.27   PROTOCOL 6

Article 1
The death penalty shall be abolished. No person shall be condemned to such penalty or executed.

Article 2
A State may make provision in its law for the death penalty in respect of acts committed in time of war or of imminent threat of war; such penalty shall be applied only in the instances laid down in the law and in accordance with its provisions. The state shall communicate to the Secretary General of the Council of Europe the relevant provisions of that law.

Article 3
No derogation from the provisions of this Protocol shall be made under Article 15 of the Convention.

Article 4
No reservation may be made under Article 64 of the Convention in respect of the provisions of this Protocol.

This Protocol extends the protection of life provided by Article 2 of the Convention by expressly abolishing the death penalty in peacetime, and by creating an enforceable personal right not to be condemned to death or executed. Protocol 6, Articles 3 and 4 disallow any derogations or reservations.

The Protocol was opened to signature in April 1983, came into force in March 1985 and has so far been ratified by 28 states, not including the United Kingdom. The death penalty was suspended for the offence of murder in 1959 and abolished in 1965 by domestic United Kingdom law, but remained in relation to treason, piracy and a number of offences under military law. The Crime and Disorder Act abolishes the death penalty for these offences.

The Court considered the relationship between Protocol 6 and Articles 2 and 3 of the Convention in *Soering* v *United Kingdom* (1989) 11 EHRR 439, at paras 101–4, in response to an argument advanced by Amnesty International that capital punishment should now be considered inhuman and degrading within the meaning of Article 3 of the Convention in light of evolving standards with regard to the existence and use of such punishment in Western Europe. The Court rejected this submission, pointing to the facts that Protocol 6 had been introduced to create a new obligation to abolish the death penalty, optional for each state, and that Article 2 of the Convention, concerning the right to life, expressly preserved the option of the death penalty.

8.28 PROTOCOL 7 — INTRODUCTION

Following the adoption by the General Assembly of the United Nations of the International Covenant on Civil and Political Rights in 1966, the Council of Europe commissioned its Committee of Experts to investigate any problems that may have arisen from the coexistence of the Covenant and the European Convention. That report was the basis of further work in 1976 aimed at extending the human and political rights and freedoms set forth in the Convention. Protocol 7, which was opened for signature in 1984, seeks to bring the Convention in line with the International Covenant. The United Kingdom is not as yet a signatory. It is likely, however, that this Protocol will be ratified in the near future, after the amendment of anachronistic laws which created inequality between spouses.

There have been no Court decisions concerning any of the articles in Protocol 7, and few Commission decisions. The Council of Europe has published an explanatory memorandum, *Text of Protocol No. 7 and Explanatory Memorandum*, CE Doc H (84) 5 (Strasbourg: Council of Europe, 1984), which, although not binding upon either the Court or the Commission, will serve as an aid to interpretation in the future.

8.29   PROTOCOL 7, ARTICLE 1

1.   An alien lawfully resident in the territory of a state shall not be expelled therefrom except in pursuance of a decision reached in accordance with law and shall be allowed:

a.   to submit reasons against his expulsion;

b.   to have his case reviewed, and

c.   to be represented for these purposes before the competent authority or a person or persons designated by that authority.

2.   An alien may be expelled before the exercise of his rights under paragraph 1. a, b and c of this article, when such expulsion is necessary in the interests of public order or is grounded on reasons of national security.

This provision affords a minimum guarantee that the procedural rights specified are complied with by a state seeking to expel a lawfully resident alien.

It is a precondition that the person is 'lawfully resident'. The Article does not therefore apply to an alien who has arrived but not yet passed through immigration control, a person in transit or admitted for a limited period for a non-residential purpose, or those awaiting a decision on a residence application (*Explanatory Memorandum*, para. 9).

The term 'lawfully' refers to domestic law, and it is for that law to determine the conditions under which the person's presence is lawful. The provision applies to aliens who enter unlawfully but who have regularised their position, but not to those whose permit has expired, who are in breach of conditions or who entered unlawfully and remain so (*ibid.*).

Expulsion means any measure compelling the departure of an alien from the territory, except extradition, and is a concept independent of any national law definition. A decision to expel must be made in 'accordance with law' (see 2.2). The subparagraphs then set out three guarantees, namely that the person concerned may submit reasons against his or her expulsion, have the case reviewed and be represented before the relevant authority. In exceptional cases, which involve the interests of public order or reasons of national security, an alien may be expelled before the exercise of his or her rights. The principles of proportionality should be taken into account in this regard, and the rights to review are to be available after expulsion (see *Chahal* v *United Kingdom* (1997) 23 EHRR 413).

The *Explanatory Memorandum* explains the right to have the case reviewed further. It does not require a two-stage process before different authorities, only that the 'competent authorities' should review the case in the light of the reasons against expulsion. The competent authority does not have to afford the alien an oral hearing — a written procedure will suffice. It does not need to be the authority upon whom the final decision to expel rests, but may only have power of recommendation to the body that does make the final decision. This Article does not relate to the appeal against review procedures that some states have. It is further noted in the *Memorandum* that a decision to deport does not involve a determination of the person's civil rights or of a criminal charge within the meaning of Article 6 of the Convention, and accordingly Protocol 7, Article 1 does not affect the interpretation of Article 6. The competent authority does not have to comply with the Article 6 characteristics of a judicial body. As Harris, O'Boyle and Warbrick observe (*Law of the European Convention on Human Rights*, p. 566), this interpretation of Protocol 7, Article 1 merely requires that the executive take into account the arguments of an alien against his or her expulsion, and 'offers only a modest guarantee of procedural due process'.

8.30   PROTOCOL 7, ARTICLE 2

1.   Everyone convicted of a criminal offence by a tribunal shall have the right to have his conviction or sentence reviewed by a higher tribunal. The exercise of this right, including the grounds on which it may be exercised, shall be governed by law.

2.   This right may be subject to exceptions in regard to offences of a minor character, as prescribed by law, or in cases in which the person concerned was tried in the first instance by the highest tribunal or was convicted following an appeal against acquittal.

Protocol 7, Article 2 extends the general right to a fair trial provided by Article 6 of the Convention. While the latter Article has been interpreted to control any right to an appeal that the state, in its discretion, provides, it does not require that there be such a right. Protocol 7, Article 2 establishes such a right.

The right is restricted to offences which are tried by bodies that are 'tribunals' for the purpose of Article 6 of the Convention. This would exclude cases of a disciplinary nature. Other limits are found in para. 2 — offences of a 'minor character' are excluded, as are cases where the person was convicted by the highest tribunal or following an appeal against acquittal. Where a person has pleaded guilty, the right to appeal may be limited to one against sentence only, and may be satisfied by leave to appeal proceedings where leave is not granted. The appeal may be limited to law, or may include questions of fact also — 'the modalities for the exercise of the right and the grounds on which it may be exercised' are matters to be determined by domestic law (*Explanatory Memorandum*, para. 18).

8.31 PROTOCOL 7, ARTICLE 3

When a person has by a final decision been convicted of a criminal offence and when subsequently his conviction has been reversed, or he has been pardoned, on the ground that a new or newly discovered fact shows conclusively that there has been a miscarriage of justice, the person who has suffered punishment as a result of such conviction shall be compensated according to the law or the practice of the state concerned, unless it is proved that the non-disclosure of the unknown fact in time is wholly or partly attributable to him.

A right to compensation for miscarriages of justice is thus established, subject to conditions. The person must have been convicted of a criminal offence by a final decision, and suffered punishment as a result. The *Explanatory Memorandum* quotes another Council of Europe memorandum relating to the validity of criminal judgments, which defines a final decision as one which has acquired the force of *res judicata*. A decision is final where it is irrevocable in that no further ordinary remedies are available, the parties have exhausted such remedies or have allowed the time limit to expire without availing themselves of the remedy. Thus Protocol 7, Article 3 does not apply in cases where a conviction is overturned on an ordinary appeal, or when charges are dismissed in the trial court.

The right to compensation only arises, the *Explanatory Memorandum* states, 'where the person's conviction has been reversed or he has been pardoned, in either case on the grounds that a new or newly discovered fact shows conclusively that there has been a miscarriage of justice — that is, some serious failure in the judicial process involving grave prejudice to the convicted person' (para. 32).

There will be no right to compensation if it is shown that the non-disclosure of the unknown fact in time was wholly or partly attributable to the convicted person.

The nature of the procedures to establish a miscarriage of justice is a matter of domestic law or practice for the state. In the United Kingdom the relevant provision is s. 133 of the Criminal Justice Act 1988. Once established, the intention of the Article is that compensation should be paid by the state. If it is not, presumably a violation of this Article will have occurred.

8.32 PROTOCOL 7, ARTICLE 4

1. No one shall be liable to be tried or punished again in criminal proceedings under the jurisdiction of the same state for an offence of which he has already been finally acquitted or convicted in accordance with the law and penal procedure of that state.

2. The provisions of the preceding paragraph shall not prevent the reopening of the case in accordance with the law and penal procedure of the state concerned, if there is evidence of new or newly discovered facts, or if there has been a fundamental defect in the previous proceedings, which could affect the outcome of the case.

3. No derogation from this Article shall be made under Article 15 of the Convention.

Article 4 incorporates the protection against double jeopardy into the Convention. It is limited to the same national jurisdiction, so that it remains possible to be convicted of the same offence in different jurisdictions. It only applies to criminal proceedings. A 'final' conviction must have been recorded, the meaning of which, the *Explanatory Memorandum* suggests (para. 29), will be the same as that suggested for Protocol 7, Article 3 (see 8.31).

Paragraph 2 allows the reopening of a case in exceptional circumstances, where there is evidence of new or newly discovered facts, or where there has been a fundamental defect in the previous proceedings. The *Macpherson Report on the Stephen Lawrence Inquiry* recommended a review of the current protection against double jeopardy and the Law Commission recently published a consultation paper on the subject. It is likely that any moves by the government to legislate in this direction would fall foul of Convention provisions.

8.33   PROTOCOL 7, ARTICLE 5

Spouses shall enjoy equality of rights and responsiblities of a private law character between them, and in their relations with their children, as to marriage, during marriage and in the event of its dissolution. This Article shall not prevent states from taking such measures as are necessary in the interest of the children.

This Article places an obligation on the state to provide a system of laws by which spouses have equal rights and responsibilities concerning matters of private law, such as property rights and their relations with their children. It does not apply to areas of law external to the relationship of marriage, such as administrative, fiscal, criminal, social, ecclesiastical or labour laws.

It is only concerned with spouses, and specifically precludes the period before marriage. The Article is not meant in any way to prevent the state from taking such measures as are necessary in the interests of children. Nor is it to prevent the state taking due account of all relevant factors when reaching decisions about the distribution of property upon the dissolution of marriage. There is no obligation imposed on states to provide for dissolution of marriage (*Explanatory Memorandum*, para. 35).

8.34   PROTOCOL 12

1. The enjoyment of any right set forth by law shall be secured without discrimination on any ground such as sex, race, colour, language, religion, political or other opinion, national or social origin, association with a national minority, property, birth or other status.

*2. No one shall be discriminated against by any public authority on any
ground such as those mentioned in paragraph 1.*

Protocol 12 is not yet part of the European Convention on Human Rights.
However, it is now open for signature, and may be adopted by the signatory states
in due course. Protocol 12 provides a substantive right to equality of treatment in
like situations. It does not need to be tied to an existing Convention right, as does
Article 14, which is sometimes criticised by commentators for its limited scope. If
it were to be adopted as part of the Convention and scheduled to the Human Rights
Act, it would bring the Convention into line with Article 26 of the United Nations'
International Convenant on Civil and Political Rights. It would be of great
importance to English discrimination law, significantly broadening the bases for
discrimination in relation to fields in which it could operate.

Chapter Nine
Derogations and Reservations

9.1 DEROGATIONS

Section 1(2) of the Human Rights Act 1998 allows the government to avoid the incorporation of the Convention to the extent that it has lodged a 'derogation' with the Council of Europe, as defined in s. 14. Article 15 of the Convention states:

> In time of war or other public emergency threatening the life of the nation any High Contracting Party may take measures derogating from its obligations under this Convention to the extent strictly required by the exigencies of the situation.

Thus, as a matter of international law, the government, by lodging a derogation in Strasbourg, can, to the extent that the derogation is lawful under Article 15, avoid a particular obligation in particular circumstances. See, for instance, S.R. Chowdhury, *Rule of Law in a State of Emergency* (London: Pinter, 1989). Article 15 does *not* allow derogations from Articles 2 (the right to life), 3 (freedom from torture), 4(1) (slavery and servitude) and 7 (retrospective criminal penalties).

The United Kingdom has, in the past, used Article 15 in relation to Northern Ireland. It currently has a derogation in force which allows the police to detain people under the Prevention of Terrorism (Temporary Provisions) Act 1989 for up to seven days. In *Brogan* v *United Kingdom* (1988) 11 EHRR 117 the Court in Strasbourg decided that periods of longer than four days' detention for interrogation without access to a judge violated the requirement to bring the suspect before a judge 'promptly' as set out in Article 5(3). Instead of changing the law to comply, the government entered a derogation pursuant to Article 15 with the Council of Europe. This derogation argued that the conflict in Northern Ireland was an emergency threatening the life of the nation and the provisions of the 1989 Act were necessary. The lawfulness of this derogation was then subject to an unsuccessful challenge (*Brannigan* v *United Kingdom* (1993) 17 EHRR 539).

Section 14 of the Act identifies 'designated derogations', which, under s. 16, are permitted to continue for up to five years. At present the only designated derogation is the derogation from Article 5(3) of the Convention in relation to the Prevention of Terrorism (Temporary Provisions) Act 1989 which is set out in Part I of sch. 3 to the 1998 Act. Section 14(5) allows the Secretary of State to amend sch. 3 to the Act to enable the continuation of the current derogation and to add any future derogations. The Act does not permit the United Kingdom to make a 'designated derogation' for the purposes of domestic law unless it reflects an actual derogation lodged with the Council of Europe. The effect of making a designated derogation is to exclude the article in question from being a 'Convention right' for the purposes identified in that derogation (see s. 1(2)). However, as can be seen from the text of the derogation presently contained in sch. 3 to the Act, derogations are likely to be specific and to refer to particular statutory powers. So, notwithstanding the derogation with respect to the Prevention of Terrorism Act 1989, Article 5(3) is not excluded from English law overall, and continues to apply in all other circumstances. The Terrorism Act 2000 creates a new procedure for the detention and interrogation of suspects and involves access to a court within four days. Once this provision is in place the derogation will no longer be necessary.

9.2   RESERVATIONS

The Human Rights Act 1998 also creates the concept of 'designated reservations' (s. 15). A reservation to an international treaty is a device used by a signatory state to reserve particular policies or law in order to exempt them from challenge under the instrument. Reservations can only be made at the time of ratification, though amendments to the Convention by a new protocol might allow a new reservation. There is currently one reservation by the United Kingdom: the second sentence of Article 2 of Protocol 1 (which requires education to be provided in conformity with parents' religious and philosophical convictions) has been accepted only so far as it is compatible with the provision of efficient instruction and training and the avoidance of unreasonable public expenditure. The reservation is set out in Part II of sch. 3 to the Act.

Chapter Ten
Institutional Framework

10.1 A HUMAN RIGHTS COMMITTEE IN PARLIAMENT

The government have proposed that Parliament should set up a Human Rights Committee or Committees of each House. In the Labour Party consultation paper *Bringing Rights Home* it was stated that 'Parliament itself should play a leading role in protecting the rights which are at the heart of a parliamentary democracy' and this was repeated in the White Paper, *Rights Brought Home* (Appendix 3). This idea seems to have originated in Francesca Klug, *A People's Charter: Liberty's Bill of Rights* (1991) and was adopted by the Labour Party in 1993 to resurface in *Bringing Rights Home* and finally in the White Paper. It was suggested that the new committee might conduct enquiries on a range of human rights issues relating to the Convention and produce reports to assist the government and Parliament in deciding what action to take. It might also want to range more widely and examine issues relating to the other international obligations of the United Kingdom such as proposals to accept new rights under other human rights treaties. It was also suggested that one of the committee's main tasks might be to conduct an inquiry into whether a Human Rights Commission is needed and how it should operate.

A possible model for a joint committee of the Lords and the Commons has been produced by the pressure groups Charter 88, Justice, the Institute of Public Policy Research, the King's College Human Rights Incorporation Project, Liberty and the 1990 Trust. The former Leader of the House of Commons, Ann Taylor, considered these ideas and on 14 December 1998 the new Leader of the Commons, Mrs Margaret Beckett, said:

> I am pleased to announce today that both Houses will be asked to appoint a Joint Committee on human rights. It is intended to set up that Committee before the Human Rights Act 1998 comes fully into force so that it will have time to prepare its work.
>
> We envisage that the Joint Committee's terms of reference will include the conduct of inquiries into general human rights issues in the United Kingdom,

the scrutiny of remedial orders, the examination of draft legislation where there is doubt about compatibility with the ECHR, and the issue of whether there is a need for a human rights commission to monitor the operation of the Human Rights Act.' (House of Commons, Hansard col. 604.)

Professor David Feldman has been appointed as Legal Adviser to the Committee, which is likely to start its work in October 2000.

10.2   A HUMAN RIGHTS COMMISSION

One of the aspects of the Human Rights Act 1998 which was most criticised during its passage through Parliament was the decision not to set up a Human Rights Commission at the same time. The White Paper, *Rights Brought Home*, states that more consideration would have to be given to the relationship of a new Commission to the existing bodies set up to promote anti-discrimination legislation like the Equal Opportunities Commission and the Commission for Racial Equality. Clearly financial constraints were also a factor. The option of setting up a Human Rights Commission in future has not been ruled out.

Chapter Eleven
When Rights Have Not Been Brought Home: Taking a Case to Strasbourg

11.1 INTRODUCTION

Since the Human Rights Act 1998 maintains Parlimentary sovereignty, it is likely there will be cases in which breaches of Convention rights will still arise which cannot be rectified in domestic courts. These situations are likely to arise where the breach in question arises by statute, or by a failure to legislate which cannot be rectified by the common law or statutory interpretation. Finally, the domestic courts may not be as robust in their protection of human rights as the Court in Strasbourg. In such circumstances the Strasbourg Court will be available for litigants who consider that the domestic courts have failed to remedy a Convention violation.

The requirement to exhaust all alternative remedies first will be even more crucial now that the Convention is part of domestic law. In particular cases, the litigant may be required to seek a declaration of incompatibility before seeking to go to Strasbourg, although it is likely that the procedure for seeking declarations of incompatibility (see 5.2) will be insufficient to afford an effective remedy under Article 13, and so the Court in Strasbourg may not require the applicant to seek such a declaration in order to exhaust domestic remedies.

Greater interest in and understanding of the Convention will probably lead to more rather than fewer cases being taken to the Court. Even after the Act is brought into force, practitioners will need to understand Strasbourg procedure.

This chapter outlines the procedure for making applications to the European Court in Strasbourg. It is included to ensure that those who have exhausted their domestic remedies in the United Kingdom have information on how to proceed further. The system for dealing with applications changed on 1 November 1998 and this chapter refers to the new procedure. The rules of the new Court are reproduced in Appendix 2. For further information on the procedure see P. Leach,

Taking a Case to the European Court of Human Rights (London: Blackstone Press, 2000).

The European Commission of Human Rights continued to exist only until November 1999 to deal with outstanding applications and individuals will now have direct access to the Court. The Court consists of one person nominated by each of the countries belonging to the Council of Europe (Article 20). These persons act in their individual capacity and cannot be government officials (though they can be ex-government lawyers). For the vast majority of cases the Court will sit in Chambers of seven judges (Convention, Article 27(1)).

There are two ways in which alleged breaches of the Convention's provisions by the United Kingdom can be brought to the attention of the Court. The first is through a complaint made by one of the other countries which are also bound by the Convention (Article 33). It was as a result of a complaint by the Republic of Ireland that certain interrogation practices used in Northern Ireland were held to amount to inhuman and degrading treatment (*Ireland* v *United Kingdom* (1978) 2 EHRR 25). Countries are, however, reluctant to bring cases against each other and will only do so in the most extreme cases or where their own interests are affected.

The second method of complaint — by the person whose rights have been infringed — is used much more frequently and with greater effect. Any person, non-governmental organisation or group of individuals (whatever their nationality) can complain about a country bound by the Convention (Article 34). The United Kingdom has allowed complaints by individuals (the individual right of petition) since 1966. The complaints can be about the law or acts of public bodies or the decisions of courts.

The procedure for making a complaint is relatively straightforward. It is not, however, a speedy process and the delays are undoubtedly exacerbated by the many complaints that do not fall within the ambit of the Convention or do not comply with its requirements and which are rejected at the early stages. In fact over 95 per cent of cases never make it to a hearing. It is crucially important, therefore, to ensure that an application complies with the admissibility requirements set out below and contains all of the facts and arguments of law.

Unlike cases in the courts of the United Kingdom the decision to allow a case to continue is made on the basis of the papers alone and if a case is declared inadmissible at an early stage there are no further steps that can be taken and no further applications can be made concerning the same facts. It is therefore not sufficient merely to complete the application form. To have a real chance of success it will be necessary to set out separately the facts, the relevant domestic law and detailed submissions on Convention law.

One of the best ways of setting out the application itself is to model it on a decision of the Court. These are often models of clarity and any application so constructed will help to reduce the workload of those in the Court secretariat, and give the best chance of success.

11.2   LEGAL AID

11.2.1   Domestic legal aid for Strasbourg cases

The United Kingdom's legal aid scheme has not in the past covered complaints to the Court. Even though the Human Rights Act 1998 has come into force, legal aid is probably still not available.

The Access to Justice Act 1999 provides in s. 19 that the Legal Services Commission 'may not fund as part of the Community Legal Service or Criminal Defence services relating to any law other than that of England and Wales, unless any such law is relevant for determining any issue relating to the law of England and Wales'. The same section gives the Lord Chancellor a discretion (by order) to extend the coverage of legal help.

The structure of the Human Rights Act 1998 does not make the Convention part of the law of England and Wales directly. It appears to remain 'law other than that of England and Wales'. However, Convention law may be 'relevant for determining any issue relating to the law of England and Wales'. On the basis of this argument, if a judgment of the European Court of Human Rights was necessary for determining the interpretation of English law, then domestic legal aid would be available. The difficulty for any applicant will be that the need to exhaust domestic remedies before launching proceedings in Strasbourg will mean that the issue of English law is likely to have been determined already. The Strasbourg Court, unlike the European Court of Justice, does not allow interlocutory references to resolve the interpretation of Convention law.

There may, however, be circumstances in which domestic legal aid would be available. An example might be a case where the domestic courts had not found a violation of the Convention, but the alleged violation of the Convention was a continuing one (say the retention of information by a public authority allegedly contrary to Article 8). If it were arguable that the Strasbourg Court might take a different view and as a result the applicant could then take new domestic proceedings, the Strasbourg proceedings would be 'relevant for determining any issue relating to the law of England and Wales'.

The case would therefore be capable of being funded under the Access to Justice Act 1999. But the Funding Code Criteria, according to which the Commission determines applications for funding, permit the Legal Services Commission to refuse an application for legal representation or support funding if 'alternative funding is available to the client . . . or if there are other persons or bodies, including those who might benefit from the proceedings, who might reasonably be expected to . . . fund the case' (Funding Code Standard Criteria for Legal Representation and Support Funding, para. 5.4.2). The European Court of Human Rights has its own legal aid system. It is very limited, but the Legal Services Commission may regard it as 'alternative funding available to the client'.

11.2.2   Strasbourg legal aid

The Court itself may provide legal aid, but only towards the end of the examination of a complaint's admissibility and not before it is lodged. Furthermore, legal costs are recoverable where a complaint is successful (r. 91 of the Rules of the European Court of Human Rights). There are no fees payable to the Court and there is no liability to meet the costs of the government in any event.

Once communication (see below) has occurred, legal aid will be available for those who would qualify on income and capital grounds for civil legal aid in this country. Legal aid is available from Strasbourg, although the assessment of the legal aid is carried out by the civil legal aid authorities in this country. Legal aid once granted will pay a standard amount for the preparation of the original application (approximately 2000 francs) and for the drafting of the reply to the government's response to the application. If the case is never communicated, no legal aid is available.

A further payment can be made to cover representation by one lawyer at any hearing and the travel and accommodation costs of the lawyer and the applicant. In certain circumstances Strasbourg legal aid will stretch to two lawyers.

11.3   MAKING A COMPLAINT

A complaint does not have to be made initially on any special application form although it will be necessary to complete one eventually. Complaints should be directed to:

Secretary of the European Court of Human Rights
Council of Europe
F-67075 Strasbourg-Cedex
France

Tel: 00 33 88 41 2018
Fax: 00 33 03 41 27 30

The following information will be required and should, therefore, be provided in the letter to the Court (r. 47):

(a)   The applicant's name, age, address and occupation.
(b)   The name, address and occupation of anyone acting as the representative.
(c)   The respondent country.
(d)   A clear and concise statement of the facts, including of course the exact dates.
(e)   The relevant domestic law.
(f)   The provisions of the Convention on which it is relied with any relevant case law.

(g) The object of the application (for example, the repeal or amendment of certain legislation or the reversal of a decision and compensation).

(h) The details of all remedies (including any appeal) which have been pursued within the country concerned and, where appropriate, an explanation of why any available remedies have not been pursued.

(i) The judgments, decisions and any other documents relating to the complaint.

11.4 ADMISSIBILITY

Applications made will be allocated to a chamber of the Court (r. 52). The Court's first task is to decide whether the application is admissible (i.e., falls within its terms of reference) (Article 35). Inadmissible and unmeritorious applications will be sifted out by committees of three judges (Article 35 and r. 53).

The application will be first referred to a member of the Court — the rapporteur — who may ask for further information from the applicant or the government before reporting on the case to the chamber or referring the case to a committee (rr. 49 and 54). A case can be declared inadmissible at this early stage by a Committee without calling on the government to reply formally to the application. If the committee does not declare the application inadmissible it will be sent on to the Chamber of Seven Judges. They too can declare the application inadmissible, request further information from the parties or give notice to the respondent state (r. 54). In 1995 only 40 of the nearly 1,000 applications reached the stage where the Commission requested the government's response, that is, to use the Strasbourg jargon, where the case was 'communicated' (r. 46(2)(b)).

If the case is communicated, the applicant will be sent a copy of the government's observations and can in turn make observations in reply. The Court will impose time limits for these observations (r. 54(5)). Again, as the case can be ended without any hearing at this stage, any reply must be comprehensive and well argued.

The overwhelming majority (95 per cent) of applications were found to be inadmissible by the Commission in the past. This is likely to continue under the new system. This underlines the importance of a thorough evaluation of the case and the best possible original application. There is no appeal against a decision that a case is inadmissible. Moreover, a case that has been admitted can, on further examination by the Court, be rejected as inadmissible. The Chamber can decide, either itself or as a result of a request by one of the parties, to hold a hearing on admissibility. In those circumstances the chamber is also likely to ask the parties to deal with the merits of the case at the same time.

A complaint will be ruled inadmissible in the following circumstances (Article 35).

(a) It is anonymous.

(b) It was not made within six months of the violation or the final decision relating to the alleged violation of the Convention. Very little flexibility for cases brought outside this time limit is permitted although the lack of knowledge of the violation may make a later application possible. See, for instance, *Hilton* v *United Kingdom* (1998) 57 DR 108, in which a journalist was refused a job with the BBC but only discovered that this was a result of a secret vetting process nine years later. Of course some violations are of a continuing nature. For example, in *Norris* v *Ireland* (1988) 13 EHRR 186, the applicant was concerned about the criminal-isation of homosexual acts.

(c)   The applicant is not a victim for the purposes of Article 34. Someone who runs the risk of being directly affected by a future act may be a victim. See *Norris* v *Ireland* or *Campbell* v *United Kingdom* (1982) 4 EHRR 293, in which a child ran the risk of being subjected to corporal punishment although he had not yet been affected. The victim must, for instance, show that he or she is personally affected and, if claiming a violation on the basis of national law or policy, that he or she is affected to a greater extent than others.

(d)   It concerns a matter already dealt with by the Court or some other international process. As the United Kingdom does not at present allow the right of petition to the United Nations Human Rights Committee or other similar bodies this is rarely a problem for complaints against the United Kingdom.

(e)   It is incompatible with the Convention, i.e., it concerns a country, period in time or territory to which the Convention does not apply, or a right not guaranteed by it.

(f)   The domestic remedies have not been exhausted. This means that the applicant has failed to pursue any judicial or administrative procedure that can lead to a binding decision and so would not include any discretionary or political remedies, such as a complaint to the ombudsman (*Montion* v *France* (1987) 52 DR 227) or the Police Complaints Authority (*Govell* v *United Kingdom*, Application No. 27237/95, European Commission of Human Rights, 26 February 1997). This does not mean that hopeless domestic cases must be pursued or appealed. Furthermore only 'effective' remedies need to be pursued. However, the failure to use an obvious remedy which might succeed would create problems and, unless appeals are hopeless, failing to appeal is likely to lead to a decision that the application is inadmissible (see, for example, *De Wilde* v *Belgium* (1971) 1 EHRR 432). Obtaining competent counsel's opinion may be sufficient to demonstrate that it is pointless to appeal.

(g)   The claim is 'manifestly ill-founded' (i.e., the facts do not disclose any prima facie violation of the Convention). See below.

(h)   It is an abuse of the right of petition (for example, the primary aim is political, the Court is being misled, or insulting or threatening languarge was used before the Court or the government).

The most difficult criterion to assess is that an application is 'manifestly ill-founded'. This is really a merits test and cases which are arguable are excluded on this criterion. It represents a fairly high leave requirement and ensures that cases that reach the Court are very likely to be successful. For instance, up to 1988, just over a half of cases taken against the United Kingdom that were argued in the Court were successful.

It is likely to take several months and possibly longer before the Court decides on the admissibility of a case but it will give priority to urgent cases (i.e., those where a person's life or well-being is immediately threatened by the action being complained about) (rr. 40–41). In such cases, the Court should be contacted by telephone, telex or fax. The Court may then ask the government to refrain from acting until the application has been considered. Although not bound to do so, the government is likely to accede to such a request.

The Court will give its decision on admissibility in writing (r. 56).

11.5   THE SECOND STAGE

The Court then considers the merits of the application. In parallel, once the Court decides that the application is admissible, it will try to reach a 'friendly settlement' (i.e., a negotiated agreement) between the applicant and the government (Article 38; r. 62).

The settlement may simply involve the payment of compensation or the making of a decision (for example, the revocation of a deportation order) but it may also require a change in the law or administrative practice which gave rise to the complaint. The Court has to be satisfied that any settlement takes account of the general interest (for example, where a complaint arose from the application of the rules restricting access by prisoners to legal advice, the settlement would require the reform of those rules as well as the payment of compensation).

If there is no settlement there will then be further written and oral submissions by the government and the applicant, who may be represented by a lawyer for this purpose (r. 36). It is also possible for the Court to allow any person, organisation or government to make submissions relevant to the case (Article 36 and r. 61). Liberty for instance has put in submissions in the past, including *McCann* v *United Kingdom* (1995) 21 EHRR 97: *Brannigan* v *United Kingdom* (1993) 17 EHRR 539; *Murray* v *United Kingdom* (1994) 19 EHRR 193; *Saunders* v *United Kingdom* (1994) 18 EHRR CD 23; *Chahal* v *United Kingdom* (1997) 23 EHRR 413; *Halford* v *United Kingdom* (1997) 24 EHRR 523; *Sheffield* v *United Kingdom* (1999) 27 EHRR 163.

The oral hearing itself is very short. (Under the old procedure, a party was given only 30 minutes to put its case and 15 minutes to reply to the other party. It was rare for questions to be asked.) Speeches must be written in advance to ensure that they can be translated simultaneously and smoothly.

In exceptional cases the chamber will relinquish jurisdiction in favour of a grand chamber of 17 judges, which will decide the more important issues (Article 30 and r. 72). All the parties will have to consent to this process.

The judge of the respondent state will sit *ex officio* as part of the chamber or grand chamber (Article 27(2)).

Where the Court considers that there has been a violation, it may also (in the same or a later judgment) award 'just satisfaction' (i.e., damages and reimbursement of legal costs) (Article 41 and r. 60). The Court's judgment is not automatically binding on the government as a result of the Human Rights Act 1998, s. 2 (which requires United Kingdom courts to take into account Strasbourg jurisprudence when deciding cases under the Act). It has very strong — almost overriding — pervasive legal effect within the United Kingdom (but does not automatically overturn the legislation or decision). The government must, however, as a matter of international law take the necessary steps to implement the judgment and the Committee of Ministers is responsible for ensuring that this is done.

One new right created by Protocol 11 is the right of appeal from a judgment of a chamber to the grand chamber (Article 43 and r. 73). The parties have three months to seek leave for a referral to the grand chamber. Leave will be decided by a panel of five judges who 'shall accept the request if the case raises a serious question affecting the interpretation or application of the Convention or the protocols thereto, or a serious issue of general importance'. This new right of appeal will not be available to those whose cases have been declared inadmissible.

Appendix One
Text of the Human Rights Act 1998

CHAPTER 42

ARRANGEMENT OF SECTIONS

Human Rights Act 1998

1998 CHAPTER 42

An Act to give further effect to rights and freedoms guaranteed under the European Convention on Human Rights; to make provision with respect to holders of certain judicial offices who become judges of the European Court of Human Rights; and for connected purposes. [9th November 1998]

BE IT ENACTED by the Queen's most Excellent Majesty, by and with the advice and consent of the Lords Spiritual and Temporal, and Commons, in this present Parliament assembled, and by the authority of the same, as follows:—

Introduction

1. The Convention Rights

(1) In this Act 'the Convention rights' means the rights and fundamental freedoms set out in—

  (a) Articles 2 to 12 and 14 of the Convention,

  (b) Articles 1 to 3 of the First Protocol, and

  (c) Articles 1 and 2 of the Sixth Protocol,

as read with Articles 16 to 18 of the Convention.

(2) Those Articles are to have effect for the purposes of this Act subject to any designated derogation or reservation (as to which see sections 14 and 15).

(3) The Articles are set out in Schedule 1.

(4) The Secretary of State may by order make such amendments to this Act as he considers appropriate to reflect the effect, in relation to the United Kingdom, of a protocol.

(5) In subsection (4) 'protocol' means a protocol to the Convention—

  (a) which the United Kingdom has ratified; or

  (b) which the United Kingdom has signed with a view to ratification.

(6) No amendment may be made by an order under subsection (4) so as to come into force before the protocol concerned is in force in relation to the United Kingdom.

2. Interpretation of Convention rights

(1) A court or tribunal determining a question which has arisen in connection with a Convention right must take into account any—

(a) judgment, decision, declaration or advisory opinion of the European Court of Human Rights,

(b) opinion of the Commission given in a report adopted under Article 31 of the Convention,

(c) decision of the Commission in connection with Article 26 or 27(2) of the Convention, or

(d) decision of the Committee of Ministers taken under Article 46 of the Convention,

whenever made or given, so far as, in the opinion of the court or tribunal, it is relevant to the proceedings in which that question has arisen.

(2) Evidence of any judgment, decision, declaration or opinion of which account may have to be taken under this section is to be given in proceedings before any court or tribunal in such manner as may be provided by rules.

(3) In this section 'rules' means rules of court or, in the case of proceedings before a tribunal, rules made for the purposes of this section—

(a) by the Lord Chancellor or the Secretary of State, in relation to any proceedings outside Scotland;

(b) by the Secretary of State, in relation to proceedings in Scotland; or

(c) by a Northern Ireland department, in relation to proceedings before a tribunal in Northern Ireland—

(i) which deals with transferred matters; and

(ii) for which no rules made under paragraph (a) are in force.

Legislation

3. Interpretation of legislation

(1) So far as it is possible to do so, primary legislation and subordinate legislation must be read and given effect in a way which is compatible with the Convention rights.

(2) This section—

(a) applies to primary legislation and subordinate legislation whenever enacted;

(b) does not affect the validity, continuing operation or enforcement of any incompatible primary legislation; and

(c) does not affect the validity, continuing operation or enforcement of any incompatible subordinate legislation if (disregarding any possibility of revocation) primary legislation prevents removal of the incompatibility.

4. Declaration of incompatibility

(1) Subsection (2) applies in any proceedings in which a court determines whether a provision of primary legislation is compatible with a Convention right.

(2) If the court is satisfied that the provision is incompatible with a Convention right, it may make a declaration of that incompatibility.

(3)   Subsection (4) applies in any proceedings in which a court determines whether a provision of subordinate legislation, made in the exercise of a power conferred by primary legislation, is compatible with a Convention right.

(4)   If the court is satisfied—

    (a)   that the provision is incompatible with a Convention right, and

    (b)   that (disregarding any possibility of revocation) the primary legislation concerned prevents removal of the incompatibility,

it may make a declaration of that incompatibility.

(5)   In this section 'court' means—

    (a)   the House of Lords;

    (b)   the Judicial Committee of the Privy Council;

    (c)   the Courts-Martial Appeal Court;

    (d)   in Scotland, the High Court of Justiciary sitting otherwise than as a trial court or the Court of Session;

    (e)   in England and Wales or Northern Ireland, the High Court or the Court of Appeal.

(6)   A declaration under this section ('a declaration of incompatibility')—

    (a)   does not affect the validity, continuing operation or enforcement of the provision in respect of which it is given; and

    (b)   is not binding on the parties to the proceedings in which it is made.

5.   Right of Crown to intervene

(1)   Where a court is considering whether to make a declaration of incompatibility, the Crown is entitled to notice in accordance with rules of court.

(2)   In any case to which subsection (1) applies—

    (a)   a Minister of the Crown (or a person nominated by him),

    (b)   a member of the Scottish Executive,

    (c)   a Northern Ireland Minister,

    (d)   a Northern Ireland department,

is entitled, on giving notice in accordance with rules of court, to be joined as a party to the proceedings.

(3)   Notice under subsection (2) may be given at any time during the proceedings.

(4)   A person who has been made a party to criminal proceedings (other than in Scotland) as the result of a notice under subsection (2) may, with leave, appeal to the House of Lords against any declaration of incompatibility made in the proceedings.

(5)   In subsection (4)—

'criminal proceedings' includes all proceedings before the Courts-Martial Appeal Court; and

'leave' means leave granted by the court making the declaration of incompatibility or by the House of Lords.

Public authorities

6.   Acts of public authorities

(1)   It is unlawful for a public authority to act in a way which is incompatible with a Convention right.

(2)   Subsection (1) does not apply to an act if—

   (a)   as the result of one or more provisions of primary legislation, the authority could not have acted differently; or

   (b)   in the case of one or more provisions of, or made under, primary legislation which cannot be read or given effect in a way which is compatible with the Convention rights, the authority was acting so as to give effect to or enforce those provisions.

(3)   In this section 'public authority' includes—

   (a)   a court or tribunal, and

   (b)   any person certain of whose functions are functions of a public nature,

but does not include either House of Parliament or a person exercising functions in connection with proceedings in Parliament.

(4)   In subsection (3) 'Parliament' does not include the House of Lords in its judicial capacity.

(5)   In relation to a particular act, a person is not a public authority by virtue only of subsection (3)(b) if the nature of the act is private.

(6)   'An act' includes a failure to act but does not include a failure to—

   (a)   introduce in, or lay before, Parliament a proposal for legislation; or

   (b)   make any primary legislation or remedial order.

7.   Proceedings

(1)   A person who claims that a public authority has acted (or proposes to act) in a way which is made unlawful by section 6(1) may—

   (a)   bring proceedings against the authority under this Act in the appropriate court or tribunal, or

   (b)   rely on the Convention right or rights concerned in any legal proceedings,

but only if he is (or would be) a victim of the unlawful act.

(2)   In subsection (1)(a) 'appropriate court or tribunal' means such court or tribunal as may be determined in accordance with rules; and proceedings against an authority include a counterclaim or similar proceeding.

(3)   If the proceedings are brought on an application for judicial review, the applicant is to be taken to have a sufficient interest in relation to the unlawful act only if he is, or would be, a victim of that act.

(4)   If the proceedings are made by way of a petition for judicial review in Scotland, the applicant shall be taken to have title and interest to sue in relation to the unlawful act only if he is, or would be, a victim of that act.

(5)   Proceedings under subsection (1)(a) must be brought before the end of—

   (a)   the period of one year beginning with the date on which the act complained of took place; or

   (b)   such longer period as the court or tribunal considers equitable having regard to all the circumstances,

but that is subject to any rule imposing a stricter time limit in relation to the procedure in question.

(6) In subsection (1)(b) 'legal proceedings' includes—

(a) proceedings brought by or at the instigation of a public authority; and

(b) an appeal against the decision of a court or tribunal.

(7) For the purposes of this section, a person is a victim of an unlawful act only if he would be a victim for the purposes of Article 34 of the Convention if proceedings were brought in the European Court of Human Rights in respect of that act.

(8) Nothing in this Act creates a criminal offence.

(9) In this section 'rules' means—

(a) in relation to proceedings before a court or tribunal outside Scotland, rules made by the Lord Chancellor or the Secretary of State for the purposes of this section or rules of court,

(b) in relation to proceedings before a court or tribunal in Scotland, rules made by the Secretary of State for those purposes,

(c) in relation to proceedings before a tribunal in Northern Ireland—

(i) which deals with transferred matters; and

(ii) for which no rules made under paragraph (a) are in force,

rules made by a Northern Ireland department for those purposes,
and includes provision made by order under section 1 of the Courts and Legal Services Act 1990.

(10) In making rules, regard must be had to section 9.

(11) The Minister who has power to make rules in relation to a particular tribunal may, to the extent he considers it necessary to ensure that the tribunal can provide an appropriate remedy in relation to an act (or proposed act) of a public authority which is (or would be) unlawful as a result of section 6(1), by order add to—

(a) the relief or remedies which the tribunal may grant; or

(b) the grounds on which it may grant any of them.

(12) An order made under subsection (11) may contain such incidental, supplemental, consequential or transitional provision as the Minister making it considers appropriate.

(13) 'The Minister' includes the Northern Ireland department concerned.

8. Judicial remedies

(1) In relation to any act (or proposed act) of a public authority which the court finds is (or would be) unlawful, it may grant such relief or remedy, or make such order, within its powers as it considers just and appropriate.

(2) But damages may be awarded only by a court which has power to award damages, or to order the payment of compensation, in civil proceedings.

(3) No award of damages is to be made unless, taking account of all the circumstances of the case, including—

(a) any other relief or remedy granted, or order made, in relation to the act in question (by that or any other court), and

(b) the consequences of any decision (of that or any other court) in respect of that act, the court is satisfied that the award is necessary to afford just satisfaction to the person in whose favour it is made.

(4)   In determining—

(a)   whether to award damages, or

(b)   the amount of an award,

the court must take into account the principles applied by the European Court of Human Rights in relation to the award of compensation under Article 41 of the Convention.

(5)   A public authority against which damages are awarded is to be treated—

(a)   in Scotland, for the purposes of section 3 of the Law Reform (Miscellaneous Provisions) (Scotland) Act 1940 as if the award were made in an action of damages in which the authority has been found liable in respect of loss or damage to the person to whom the award is made;

(b)   for the purposes of the Civil Liability (Contribution) Act 1978 as liable in respect of damage suffered by the person to whom the award is made.

(6)   In this section—

'court' includes a tribunal;

'damages' means damages for an unlawful act of a public authority; and

'unlawful' means unlawful under section 6(1).

9.   Judicial acts

(1)   Proceedings under section 7(1)(a) in respect of a judicial act may be brought only—

(a)   by exercising a right of appeal;

(b)   on an application (in Scotland a petition) for judicial review; or

(c)   in such other forum as may be prescribed by rules.

(2)   That does not affect any rule of law which prevents a court from being the subject of judicial review.

(3)   In proceedings under this Act in respect of a judicial act done in good faith, damages may not be awarded otherwise than to compensate a person to the extent required by Article 5(5) of the Convention.

(4)   An award of damages permitted by subsection (3) is to be made against the Crown; but no award may be made unless the appropriate person, if not a party to the proceedings, is joined.

(5)   In this section—

'appropriate person' means the Minister responsible for the court concerned, or a person or government department nominated by him;

'court' includes a tribunal;

'judge' includes a member of a tribunal, a justice of the peace and a clerk or other officer entitled to exercise the jurisdiction of a court;

'judicial act' means a judicial act of a court and includes an act done on the instructions, or on behalf, of a judge; and

'rules' has the same meaning as in section 7(9).

Remedial action

10. Power to take remedial action

(1) This section applies if—

(a) a provision of legislation has been declared under section 4 to be incompatible with a Convention right and, if an appeal lies—

(i) all persons who may appeal have stated in writing that they do not intend to do so;

(ii) the time for bringing an appeal has expired and no appeal has been brought within that time; or

(iii) an appeal brought within that time has been determined or abandoned; or

(b) it appears to a Minister of the Crown or Her Majesty in Council that, having regard to a finding of the European Court of Human Rights made after the coming into force of this section in proceedings against the United Kingdom, a provision of legislation is incompatible with an obligation of the United Kingdom arising from the Convention.

(2) If a Minister of the Crown considers that there are compelling reasons for proceeding under this section, he may by order make such amendments to the legislation as he considers necessary to remove the incompatibility.

(3) If, in the case of subordinate legislation, a Minister of the Crown considers—

(a) that it is necessary to amend the primary legislation under which the subordinate legislation in question was made, in order to enable the incompatibility to be removed, and

(b) that there are compelling reasons for proceeding under this section, he may by order make such amendments to the primary legislation as he considers necessary.

(4) This section also applies where the provision in question is in subordinate legislation and has been quashed, or declared invalid, by reason of incompatibility with a Convention right and the Minister proposes to proceed under paragraph 2(b) of Schedule 2.

(5) If the legislation is an Order in Council, the power conferred by subsection (2) or (3) is exercisable by Her Majesty in Council.

(6) In this section 'legislation' does not include a Measure of the Church Assembly or of the General Synod of the Church of England.

(7) Schedule 2 makes further provision about remedial orders.

Other rights and proceedings

11. Safeguard for existing human rights

A person's reliance on a Convention right does not restrict—

(a) any other right or freedom conferred on him by or under any law having effect in any part of the United Kingdom; or

(b) his right to make any claim or bring any proceedings which he could make or bring apart from sections 7 to 9.

12.　Freedom of expression

(1)　This section applies if a court is considering whether to grant any relief which, if granted, might affect the exercise of the Convention right to freedom of expression.

(2)　If the person against whom the application for relief is made ('the respondent') is neither present nor represented, no such relief is to be granted unless the court is satisfied—

(a)　that the applicant has taken all practicable steps to notify the respondent; or

(b)　that there are compelling reasons why the respondent should not be notified.

(3)　No such relief is to be granted so as to restrain publication before trial unless the court is satisfied that the applicant is likely to establish that publication should not be allowed.

(4)　The court must have particular regard to the importance of the Convention right to freedom of expression and, where the proceedings relate to material which the respondent claims, or which appears to the court, to be journalistic, literary or artistic material (or to conduct connected with such material), to—

(a)　the extent to which—

(i)　the material has, or is about to, become available to the public; or

(ii)　it is, or would be, in the public interest for the material to be published;

(b)　any relevant privacy code.

(5)　In this section—

'court' includes a tribunal; and

'relief' includes any remedy or order (other than in criminal proceedings).

13.　Freedom of thought, conscience and religion

(1)　If a court's determination of any question arising under this Act might affect the exercise by a religious organisation (itself or its members collectively) of the Convention right to freedom of thought, conscience and religion, it must have particular regard to the importance of that right.

(2)　In this section 'court' includes a tribunal.

Derogations and reservations

14.　Derogations

(1)　In this Act 'designated derogation' means—

(a)　the United Kingdom's derogation from Article 5(3) of the Convention; and

(b)　any derogation by the United Kingdom from an Article of the Convention, or of any protocol to the Convention, which is designated for the purposes of this Act in an order made by the Secretary of State.

(2)　The derogation referred to in subsection (1)(a) is set out in Part I of Schedule 3.

(3)   If a designated derogation is amended or replaced it ceases to be a designated derogation.

(4)   But subsection (3) does not prevent the Secretary of State from exercising his power under subsection (1)(b) to make a fresh designation order in respect of the Article concerned.

(5)   The Secretary of State must by order make such amendments to Schedule 3 as he considers appropriate to reflect—

  (a)   any designation order; or

  (b)   the effect of subsection (3).

(6)   A designation order may be made in anticipation of the making by the United Kingdom of a proposed derogation.

15.   Reservations

(1)   In this Act 'designated reservation' means—

  (a)   the United Kingdom's reservation to Article 2 of the First Protocol to the Convention; and

  (b)   any other reservation by the United Kingdom to an Article of the Convention, or of any protocol to the Convention, which is designated for the purposes of this Act in an order made by the Secretary of State.

(2)   The text of the reservation referred to in subsection (1)(a) is set out in Part 11 of Schedule 3.

(3)   If a designated reservation is withdrawn wholly or in part it ceases to be a designated reservation.

(4)   But subsection (3) does not prevent the Secretary of State from exercising his power under subsection (1)(b) to make a fresh designation order in respect of the Article concerned.

(5)   The Secretary of State must by order make such amendments to this Act as he considers appropriate to reflect—

  (a)   any designation order; or

  (b)   the effect of subsection (3).

16.   Period for which designated derogations have effect

(1)   If it has not already been withdrawn by the United Kingdom, a designated derogation ceases to have effect for the purposes of this Act—

  (a)   in the case of the derogation referred to in section 14(1)(a), at the end of the period of five years beginning with the date on which section 1(2) came into force;

  (b)   in the case of any other derogation, at the end of the period of five years beginning with the date on which the order designating it was made.

(2)   At any time before the period—

  (a)   fixed by subsection (1)(a) or (b), or

  (b)   extended by an order under this subsection,

comes to an end, the Secretary of State may by order extend it by a further period of five years.

(3)   An order under section 14(1)(b) ceases to have effect at the end of the period for consideration, unless a resolution has been passed by each House approving the order.

(4)   Subsection (3) does not affect—

(a)   anything done in reliance on the order; or

(b)   the power to make a fresh order under section 14(1)(b).

(5)   In subsection (3) 'period for consideration' means the period of forty days beginning with the day on which the order was made.

(6)   In calculating the period for consideration, no account is to be taken of any time during which—

(a)   Parliament is dissolved or prorogued; or

(b)   both Houses are adjourned for more than four days.

(7)   If a designated derogation is withdrawn by the United Kingdom, the Secretary of State must by order make such amendments to this Act as he considers are required to reflect that withdrawal.

17.   Periodic review of designated reservations

(1)   The appropriate Minister must review the designated reservation referred to in section 15(1)(a)—

(a)   before the end of the period of five years beginning with the date on which section 1(2) came into force; and

(b)   if that designation is still in force, before the end of the period of five years beginning with the date on which the last report relating to it was laid under subsection (3).

(2)   The appropriate Minister must review each of the other designated reservations (if any)—

(a)   before the end of the period of five years beginning with the date on which the order designating the reservation first came into force; and

(b)   if the designation is still in force, before the end of the period of five years beginning with the date on which the last report relating to it was laid under subsection (3).

(3)   The Minister conducting a review under this section must prepare a report on the result of the review and lay a copy of it before each House of Parliament.

Judges of the European Court of Human Rights

18.   Appointment to European Court of Human Rights

(1)   In this section 'judicial office' means the office of—

(a)   Lord Justice of Appeal, Justice of the High Court or Circuit judge, in England and Wales;

(b)   judge of the Court of Session or sheriff, in Scotland;

(c)   Lord Justice of Appeal, judge of the High Court or county court judge, in Northern Ireland.

(2)   The holder of a judicial office may become a judge of the European Court of Human Rights ('the Court') without being required to relinquish his office.

(3) But he is not required to perform the duties of his judicial office while he is a judge of the Court.

(4) In respect of any period during which he is a judge of the Court—

(a) a Lord Justice of Appeal or Justice of the High Court is not to count as a judge of the relevant court for the purposes of section 2(1) or 4(1) of the Supreme Court Act 1981 (maximum number of judges) nor as a judge of the Supreme Court for the purposes of section 12(1) to (6) of that Act (salaries etc.);

(b) a judge of the Court of Session is not to count as a judge of that court for the purposes of section 1(1) of the Court of Session Act 1988 (maximum number of judges) or of section 9(1)(c) of the Administration of Justice Act 1973 ('the 1973 Act') (salaries etc.);

(c) a Lord Justice of Appeal or judge of the High Court in Northern Ireland is not to count as a judge of the relevant court for the purposes of section 2(1) or 3(1) of the Judicature (Northern Ireland) Act 1978 (maximum number of judges) nor as a judge of the Supreme Court of Northern Ireland for the purposes of section 9(1)(d) of the 1973 Act (salaries etc.);

(d) a Circuit judge is not to count as such for the purposes of section 18 of the Courts Act 1971 (salaries etc.);

(e) a sheriff is not to count as such for the purposes of section 14 of the Sheriff Courts (Scotland) Act 1907 (salaries etc.);

(f) a county court judge of Northern Ireland is not to count as such for the purposes of section 106 of the County Courts Act (Northern Ireland) 1959 (salaries etc.).

(5) If a sheriff principal is appointed a judge of the Court, section 11(1) of the Sheriff Courts (Scotland) Act 1971 (temporary appointment of sheriff principal) applies, while he holds that appointment, as if his office is vacant.

(6) Schedule 4 makes provision about judicial pensions in relation to the holder of a judicial office who serves as a judge of the Court.

(7) The Lord Chancellor or the Secretary of State may by order make such transitional provision (including, in particular, provision for a temporary increase in the maximum number of judges) as he considers appropriate in relation to any holder of a judicial office who has completed his service as a judge of the Court.

Parliamentary procedure

19. Statements of compatibility

(1) A Minister of the Crown in charge of a Bill in either House of Parliament must, before Second Reading of the Bill—

(a) make a statement to the effect that in his view the provisions of the Bill are compatible with the Convention rights ('a statement of compatibility'); or

(b) make a statement to the effect that although he is unable to make a statement of compatibility the government nevertheless wishes the House to proceed with the Bill.

(2) The statement must be in writing and be published in such manner as the Minister making it considers appropriate.

Supplemental

20. Orders etc. under this Act

(1) Any power of a Minister of the Crown to make an order under this Act is exercisable by statutory instrument.

(2) The power of the Lord Chancellor or the Secretary of State to make rules (other than rules of court) under section 2(3) or 7(9) is exercisable by statutory instrument.

(3) Any statutory instrument made under section 14, 15 or 16(7) must be laid before Parliament.

(4) No order may be made by the Lord Chancellor or the Secretary of State under section 1(4), 7(11) or 16(2) unless a draft of the order has been laid before, and approved by, each House of Parliament.

(5) Any statutory instrument made under section 18(7) or Schedule 4, or to which subsection (2) applies, shall be subject to annulment in pursuance of a resolution of either House of Parliament.

(6) The power of a Northern Ireland department to make—

    (a)   rules under section 2(3)(c) or 7(9)(c), or

    (b)   an order under section 7(11),

is exercisable by statutory rule for the purposes of the Statutory Rules (Northern Ireland) Order 1979.

(7) Any rules made under section 2(3)(c) or 7(9)(c) shall be subject to negative resolution; and section 41(6) of the Interpretation Act (Northern Ireland) 1954 (meaning of 'subject to negative resolution') shall apply as if the power to make the rules were conferred by an Act of the Northern Ireland Assembly.

(8) No order may be made by a Northern Ireland department under section 7(11) unless a draft of the order has been laid before, and approved by, the Northern Ireland Assembly.

21. Interpretation etc.

(1) In this Act—

'amend' includes repeal and apply (with or without modifications);

'the appropriate Minister' means the Minister of the Crown having charge of the appropriate authorised government department (within the meaning of the Crown Proceedings Act 1947);

'the Commission' means the European Commission of Human Rights;

'the Convention' means the Convention for the Protection of Human Rights and Fundamental Freedoms, agreed by the Council of Europe at Rome on 4th November 1950 as it has effect for the time being in relation to the United Kingdom;

'declaration of incompatibility' means a declaration under section 4;

'Minister of the Crown' has the same meaning as in the Ministers of the Crown Act 1975;

'Northern Ireland Minister' includes the First Minister and the deputy First Minister in Northern Ireland;

'primary legislation' means any—

    (a)   public general Act;

    (b)   local and personal Act;

    (c)   private Act;

    (d)   Measure of the Church Assembly;

    (e)   Measure of the General Synod of the Church of England;

    (f)   Order in Council—

        (i)   made in exercise of Her Majesty's Royal Prerogative;

        (ii)   made under section 38(1)(a) of the Northern Ireland Constitution Act 1973 or the corresponding provision of the Northern Ireland Act 1998; or

        (iii)   amending an Act of a kind mentioned in paragraph (a), (b) or (c);

and includes an order or other instrument made under primary legislation (otherwise than by the National Assembly for Wales, a member of the Scottish Executive, a Northern Ireland Minister or a Northern Ireland department) to the extent to which it operates to bring one or more provisions of that legislation into force or amends any primary legislation;

'the First Protocol' means the protocol to the Convention agreed at Paris on 20th March 1952;

'the Sixth Protocol' means the protocol to the Convention agreed at Strasbourg on 28th April 1983;

'the Eleventh Protocol' means the protocol to the Convention (restructuring the control machinery established by the Convention) agreed at Strasbourg on 11th May 1994;

'remedial order' means an order under section 10;

'subordinate legislation' means any—

    (a)   Order in Council other than one—

        (i)   made in exercise of Her Majesty's Royal Prerogative;

        (ii)   made under section 38(1)(a) of the Northern Ireland Constitution Act 1973 or the corresponding provision of the Northern Ireland Act 1998; or

        (iii)   amending an Act of a kind mentioned in the definition of primary legislation;

    (b)   Act of the Scottish Parliament;

    (c)   Act of the Parliament of Northern Ireland;

    (d)   Measure of the Assembly established under section 1 of the Northern Ireland Assembly Act 1973;

    (e)   Act of the Northern Ireland Assembly;

    (f)   order, rules, regulations, scheme, warrant, byelaw or other instrument made under primary legislation (except to the extent to which it operates to bring one or more provisions of that legislation into force or amends any primary legislation);

    (g)   order, rules, regulations, scheme, warrant, byelaw or other instrument made under legislation mentioned in paragraph (b), (c), (d) or (e) or made under an Order in Council applying only to Northern Ireland;

(h)   order, rules, regulations, scheme, warrant, byelaw or other instrument made by a member of the Scottish Executive, a Northern Ireland Minister or a Northern Ireland department in exercise of prerogative or other executive functions of Her Majesty which are exercisable by such a person on behalf of Her Majesty;

'transferred matters' has the same meaning as in the Northern Ireland Act 1998; and

'tribunal' means any tribunal in which legal proceedings may be brought.

(2)   The references in paragraphs (b) and (c) of section 2(1) to Articles are to Articles of the Convention as they had effect immediately before the coming into force of the Eleventh Protocol.

(3)   The reference in paragraph (d) of section 2(1) to Article 46 includes a reference to Articles 32 and 54 of the Convention as they had effect immediately before the coming into force of the Eleventh Protocol.

(4)   The references in section 2(1) to a report or decision of the Commission or a decision of the Committee of Ministers include references to a report or decision made as provided by paragraphs 3, 4 and 6 of Article 5 of the Eleventh Protocol (transitional provisions).

(5)   Any liability under the Army Act 1955, the Air Force Act 1955 or the Naval Discipline Act 1957 to suffer death for an offence is replaced by a liability to imprisonment for life or any less punishment authorised by those Acts; and those Acts shall accordingly have effect with the necessary modifications.

22.   Short title, commencement, application and extent

(1)   This Act may be cited as the Human Rights Act 1998.

(2)   Sections 18, 20 and 21(5) and this section come into force on the passing of this Act.

(3)   The other provisions of this Act come into force on such day as the Secretary of State may by order appoint; and different days may be appointed for different purposes.

(4)   Paragraph (b) of subsection (1) of section 7 applies to proceedings brought by or at the instigation of a public authority whenever the act in question took place; but otherwise that subsection does not apply to an act taking place before the coming into force of that section.

(5)   This Act binds the Crown.

(6)   This Act extends to Northern Ireland.

(7)   Section 21(5), so far as it relates to any provision contained in the Army Act 1955, the Air Force Act 1955 or the Naval Discipline Act 1957, extends to any place to which that provision extends.

SCHEDULES

Section 1(3)

SCHEDULE 1
THE ARTICLES

PART I
THE CONVENTION

RIGHTS AND FREEDOMS

Article 2
Right to life

1.   Everyone's right to life shall be protected by law. No one shall be deprived of his life intentionally save in the execution of a sentence of a court following his conviction of a crime for which this penalty is provided by law.

2.   Deprivation of life shall not be regarded as inflicted in contravention of this Article when it results from the use of force which is no more than absolutely necessary:

(a)   in defence of any person from unlawful violence;

(b)   in order to effect a lawful arrest or to prevent the escape of a person lawfully detained;

(c)   in action lawfully taken for the purpose of quelling a riot or insurrection.

Article 3
Prohibition of torture

No one shall be subjected to torture or to inhuman or degrading treatment or punishment.

Article 4
Prohibition of slavery and forced labour

1.   No one shall be held in slavery or servitude.

2.   No one shall be required to perform forced or compulsory labour.

3.   For the purpose of this Article the term 'forced or compulsory labour' shall not include:

(a)   any work required to be done in the ordinary course of detention imposed according to the provisions of Article 5 of this Convention or during conditional release from such detention;

(b)   any service of a military character or, in case of conscientious objectors in countries where they are recognised, service exacted instead of compulsory military service;

(c)   any service exacted in case of an emergency or calamity threatening the life or well-being of the community;

(d)   any work or service which forms part of normal civic obligations.

Article 5
Right to liberty and security

1.   Everyone has the right to liberty and security of person. No one shall be deprived of his liberty save in the following cases and in accordance with a procedure prescribed by law:

(a)   the lawful detention of a person after conviction by a competent court;

(b)   the lawful arrest or detention of a person for non-compliance with the lawful order of a court or in order to secure the fulfilment of any obligation prescribed by law;

(c)   the lawful arrest or detention of a person effected for the purpose of bringing him before the competent legal authority on reasonable suspicion of having committed an offence or when it is reasonably considered necessary to prevent his committing an offence or fleeing after having done so;

(d)   the detention of a minor by lawful order for the purpose of educational supervision or his lawful detention for the purpose of bringing him before the competent legal authority;

(e)   the lawful detention of persons for the prevention of the spreading of infectious diseases, of persons of unsound mind, alcoholics or drug addicts or vagrants;

(f)   the lawful arrest or detention of a person to prevent his effecting an unauthorised entry into the country or of a person against whom action is being taken with a view to deportation or extradition.

2.   Everyone who is arrested shall be informed promptly, in a language which he understands, of the reasons for his arrest and of any charge against him.

3.   Everyone arrested or detained in accordance with the provisions of paragraph 1(c) of this Article shall be brought promptly before a judge or other officer authorised by law to exercise judicial power and shall be entitled to trial within a reasonable time or to release pending trial. Release may be conditioned by guarantees to appear for trial.

4.   Everyone who is deprived of his liberty by arrest or detention shall be entitled to take proceedings by which the lawfulness of his detention shall be decided speedily by a court and his release ordered if the detention is not lawful.

5.   Everyone who has been the victim of arrest or detention in contravention of the provisions of this Article shall have an enforceable right to compensation.

Article 6
Right to a fair trial

1.   In the determination of his civil rights and obligations or of any criminal charge against him, everyone is entitled to a fair and public hearing within a reasonable time by an independent and impartial tribunal established by law. Judgment shall be pronounced publicly but the press and public may be excluded from all or part of the trial in the interest of morals, public order or national security in a democratic society, where the interests of juveniles or the protection

of the private life of the parties so require, or to the extent strictly necessary in the opinion of the court in special circumstances where publicity would prejudice the interests of justice.

2.   Everyone charged with a criminal offence shall be presumed innocent until proved guilty according to law.

3.   Everyone charged with a criminal offence has the following minimum rights:

(a)   to be informed promptly, in a language which he understands and in detail, of the nature and cause of the accusation against him;

(b)   to have adequate time and facilities for the preparation of his defence;

(c)   to defend himself in person or through legal assistance of his own choosing or, if he has not sufficient means to pay for legal assistance, to be given it free when the interests of justice so require;

(d)   to examine or have examined witnesses against him and to obtain the attendance and examination of witnesses on his behalf under the same conditions as witnesses against him;

(e)   to have the free assistance of an interpreter if he cannot understand or speak the language used in court.

Article 7
No punishment without law

1.   No one shall be held guilty of any criminal offence on account of any act or omission which did not constitute a criminal offence under national or international law at the time when it was committed. Nor shall a heavier penalty be imposed than the one that was applicable at the time the criminal offence was committed.

2.   This Article shall not prejudice the trial and punishment of any person for any act or omission which, at the time when it was committed, was criminal according to the general principles of law recognised by civilised nations.

Article 8
Right to respect for private and family life

1.   Everyone has the right to respect for his private and family life, his home and his correspondence.

2.   There shall be no interference by a public authority with the exercise of this right except such as is in accordance with the law and is necessary in a democratic society in the interests of national security, public safety or the economic well being of the country, for the prevention of disorder or crime, for the protection of health or morals, or for the protection of the rights and freedoms of others.

Article 9
Freedom of thought, conscience and religion

1.   Everyone has the right to freedom of thought, conscience and religion; this right includes freedom to change his religion or belief and freedom, either alone

or in community with others and in public or private, to manifest his religion or belief, in worship, teaching, practice and observance.

2.   Freedom to manifest one's religion or beliefs shall be subject only to such limitations as are prescribed by law and are necessary in a democratic society in the interests of public safety, for the protection of public order, health or morals, or for the protection of the rights and freedoms of others.

Article 10
Freedom of expression

1.   Everyone has the right to freedom of expression. This right shall include freedom to hold opinions and to receive and impart information and ideas without interference by public authority and regardless of frontiers. This Article shall not prevent States from requiring the licensing of broadcasting, television or cinema enterprises.

2.   The exercise of these freedoms, since it carries with it duties and responsibilities, may be subject to such formalities, conditions, restrictions or penalties as are prescribed by law and are necessary in a democratic society, in the interests of national security, territorial integrity or public safety, for the prevention of disorder or crime, for the protection of health or morals, for the protection of the reputation or rights of others, for preventing the disclosure of information received in confidence, or for maintaining the authority and impartiality of the judiciary.

Article 11
Freedom of assembly and association

1.   Everyone has the right to freedom of peaceful assembly and to freedom of association with others, including the right to form and to join trade unions for the protection of his interests.

2.   No restrictions shall be placed on the exercise of these rights other than such as are prescribed by law and are necessary in a democratic society in the interests of national security or public safety, for the prevention of disorder or crime, for the protection of health or morals or for the protection of the rights and freedoms of others. This Article shall not prevent the imposition of lawful restrictions on the exercise of these rights by members of the armed forces, of the police or of the administration of the State.

Article 12
Right to marry

Men and women of marriageable age have the right to marry and to found a family, according to the national laws governing the exercise of this right.

Article 14
Prohibition of discrimination

The enjoyment of the rights and freedoms set forth in this Convention shall be secured without discrimination on any ground such as sex, race, colour, language, religion, political or other opinion, national or social origin, association with a national minority, property, birth or other status.

Article 16
Restrictions on political activity of aliens

Nothing in Articles 10, 11 and 14 shall be regarded as preventing the High Contracting Parties from imposing restrictions on the political activity of aliens.

Article 17
Prohibition of abuse of rights

Nothing in this Convention may be interpreted as implying for any State, group or person any right to engage in any activity or perform any act aimed at the destruction of any of the rights and freedoms set forth herein or at their limitation to a greater extent than is provided for in the Convention.

Article 18
Limitation on use of restrictions on rights

The restrictions permitted under this Convention to the said rights and freedoms shall not be applied for any purpose other than those for which they have been prescribed.

PART II
THE FIRST PROTOCOL

Article 1
Protection of property

Every natural or legal person is entitled to the peaceful enjoyment of his possessions. No one shall be deprived of his possessions except in the public interest and subject to the conditions provided for by law and by the general principles of international law.

The preceding provisions shall not, however, in any way impair the right of a State to enforce such laws as it deems necessary to control the use of property in accordance with the general interest or to secure the payment of taxes or other contributions or penalties.

Article 2
Right to education

No person shall be denied the right to education. In the exercise of any functions which it assumes in relation to education and to teaching, the State shall respect the right of parents to ensure such education and teaching in conformity with their own religious and philosophical convictions.

Article 3
Right to free elections

The High Contracting Parties undertake to hold free elections at reasonable intervals by secret ballot, under conditions which will ensure the free expression of the opinion of the people in the choice of the legislature.

PART III
THE SIXTH PROTOCOL

Article 1
Abolition of the death penalty

The death penalty shall be abolished. No one shall be condemned to such penalty or executed.

Article 2
Death penalty in time of war

A State may make provision in its law for the death penalty in respect of acts committed in time of war or of imminent threat of war; such penalty shall be applied only in the instances laid down in the law and in accordance with its provisions. The State shall communicate to the Secretary General of the Council of Europe the relevant provisions of that law.

SCHEDULE 2
REMEDIAL ORDERS

Orders

1.—(1)   A remedial order may—

(a)   contain such incidental, supplemental, consequential or transitional provision as the person making it considers appropriate;

(b)   be made so as to have effect from a date earlier than that on which it is made;

(c)   make provision for the delegation of specific functions;

(d)   make different provision for different cases.

(2)   The power conferred by sub-paragraph (1)(a) includes—

(a)   power to amend primary legislation (including primary legislation other than that which contains the incompatible provision); and

(b)   power to amend or revoke subordinate legislation (including subordinate legislation other than that which contains the incompatible provision).

(3)   A remedial order may be made so as to have the same extent as the legislation which it affects.

(4)   No person is to be guilty of an offence solely as a result of the retrospective effect of a remedial order.

Procedure

2.   No remedial order may be made unless—

(a)   a draft of the order has been approved by a resolution of each House of Parliament made after the end of the period of 60 days beginning with the day on which the draft was laid; or

(b)   it is declared in the order that it appears to the person making it that, because of the urgency of the matter, it is necessary to make the order without a draft being so approved.

Orders laid in draft

3.—(1)   No draft may be laid under paragraph 2(a) unless—

(a)   the person proposing to make the order has laid before Parliament a document which contains a draft of the proposed order and the required information; and

(b)   the period of 60 days, beginning with the day on which the document required by this sub-paragraph was laid, has ended.

(2)   If representations have been made during that period, the draft laid under paragraph 2(a) must be accompanied by a statement containing—

(a)   a summary of the representations; and

(b)   if, as a result of the representations, the proposed order has been changed, details of the changes.

Urgent cases

4.—(1)   If a remedial order ('the original order') is made without being approved in draft, the person making it must lay it before Parliament, accompanied by the required information, after it is made.

(2)   If representations have been made during the period of 60 days beginning with the day on which the original order was made, the person making it must (after the end of that period) lay before Parliament a statement containing—

(a)   a summary of the representations; and

(b)   if, as a result of the representations, he considers it appropriate to make changes to the original order, details of the changes.

(3)   If sub-paragraph (2)(b) applies, the person making the statement must—

(a)   make a further remedial order replacing the original order; and

(b)   lay the replacement order before Parliament.

(4)   If, at the end of the period of 120 days beginning with the day on which the original order was made, a resolution has not been passed by each House approving the original or replacement order, the order ceases to have effect (but without that affecting anything previously done under either order or the power to make a fresh remedial order).

Definitions

5.   In this Schedule—

'representations' means representations about a remedial order (or proposed remedial order) made to the person making (or proposing to make) it and includes any relevant Parliamentary report or resolution; and

'required information' means—

(a)   an explanation of the incompatibility which the order (or proposed order) seeks to remove, including particulars of the relevant declaration, finding or order; and

(b)   a statement of the reasons for proceeding under section 10 and for making an order in those terms.

Calculating periods

6.   In calculating any period for the purposes of this Schedule, no account is to be taken of any time during which—
  (a)   Parliament is dissolved or prorogued; or
  (b)   both Houses are adjourned for more than four days.

SCHEDULE 3
DEROGATION AND RESERVATION
PART I
DEROGATION

The 1988 notification

The United Kingdom Permanent Representative to the Council of Europe presents his compliments to the Secretary General of the Council, and has the honour to convey the following information in order to ensure compliance with the obligations of Her Majesty's Government in the United Kingdom under Article 15(3) of the Convention for the Protection of Human Rights and Fundamental Freedoms signed at Rome on 4 November 1950.

There have been in the United Kingdom in recent years campaigns of organised terrorism connected with the affairs of Northern Ireland which have manifested themselves in activities which have included repeated murder, attempted murder, maiming, intimidation and violent civil disturbance and in bombing and fire raising which have resulted in death, injury and widespread destruction of property. As a result, a public emergency within the meaning of Article 15(1) of the Convention exists in the United Kingdom.

The Government found it necessary in 1974 to introduce and since then, in cases concerning persons reasonably suspected of involvement in terrorism connected with the affairs of Northern Ireland, or of certain offences under the legislation, who have been detained for 48 hours, to exercise powers enabling further detention without charge, for periods of up to five days, on the authority of the Secretary of State. These powers are at present to be found in Section 12 of the Prevention of Terrorism (Temporary Provisions) Act 1984, Article 9 of the Prevention of Terrorism (Supplemental Temporary Provisions) Order 1984 and Article 10 of the Prevention of Terrorism (Supplemental Temporary Provisions) (Northern Ireland) Order 1984.

Section 12 of the Prevention of Terrorism (Temporary Provisions) Act 1984 provides for a person whom a constable has arrested on reasonable grounds of suspecting him to be guilty of an offence under Section 1, 9 or 10 of the Act, or to be or to have been involved in terrorism connected with the affairs of Northern Ireland, to be detained in right of the arrest for up to 48 hours and thereafter, where the Secretary of State extends the detention period, for up to a further five days. Section 12 substantially re-enacted Section 12 of the Prevention of Terrorism (Temporary Provisions) Act 1976 which, in turn, substantially re-enacted Section 7 of the Prevention of Terrorism (Temporary Provisions) Act 1974.

Article 10 of the Prevention of Terrorism (Supplemental Temporary Provisions) (Northern Ireland) Order 1984 (SI 1984/417) and Article 9 of the Prevention of Terrorism (Supplemental Temporary Provisions) Order 1984 (SI 1984/418) were both made under Sections 13 and 14 of and Schedule 3 to the 1984 Act and substantially re-enacted powers of detention in Orders made under the 1974 and 1976 Acts. A person who is being examined under Article 4 of either Order on his arrival in, or on seeking to leave, Northern Ireland or Great Britain for the purpose of determining whether he is or has been involved in terrorism connected with the affairs of Northern Ireland, or whether there are grounds for suspecting that he has committed an offence under Section 9 of the 1984 Act, may be detained under Article 9 or 10, as appropriate, pending the conclusion of his examination. The period of this examination may exceed 12 hours if an examining officer has reasonable grounds for suspecting him to be or to have been involved in acts of terrorism connected with the affairs of Northern Ireland.

Where such a person is detained under the said Article 9 or 10 he may be detained for up to 48 hours on the authority of an examining officer and thereafter, where the Secretary of State extends the detention period, for up to a further five days.

In its judgment of 29 November 1988 in the Case of *Brogan and Others*, the European Court of Human Rights held that there had been a violation of Article 5(3) in respect of each of the applicants, all of whom had been detained under Section 12 of the 1984 Act. The Court held that even the shortest of the four periods of detention concerned, namely four days and six hours, fell outside the constraints as to time permitted by the first part of Article 5(3). In addition, the Court held that there had been a violation of Article 5(5) in the case of each applicant.

Following this judgment, the Secretary of State for the Home Department informed Parliament on 6 December 1988 that, against the background of the terrorist campaign, and the over-riding need to bring terrorists to justice, the Government did not believe that the maximum period of detention should be reduced. He informed Parliament that the Government were examining the matter with a view to responding to the judgment. On 22 December 1988, the Secretary of State further informed Parliament that it remained the Government's wish, if it could be achieved, to find a judicial process under which extended detention might be reviewed and where appropriate authorised by a judge or other judicial officer. But a further period of reflection and consultation was necessary before the Government could bring forward a firm and final view.

Since the judgment of 29 November 1988 as well as previously, the Government have found it necessary to continue to exercise, in relation to terrorism connected with the affairs of Northern Ireland, the powers described above enabling further detention without charge for periods of up to 5 days, on the authority of the Secretary of State, to the extent strictly required by the exigencies of the situation to enable necessary enquiries and investigations properly to be completed in order to decide whether criminal proceedings should be instituted. To the extent that the exercise of these powers may be inconsistent with the obligations imposed by the Convention the Government has availed itself of the right of derogation conferred by Article 15(1) of the Convention and will continue to do so until further notice.

Dated 23 December 1988.

The 1989 notification

The United Kingdom Permanent Representative to the Council of Europe presents his compliments to the Secretary General of the Council, and has the honour to convey the following information.

In his communication to the Secretary General of 23 December 1988, reference was made to the introduction and exercise of certain powers under section 12 of the Prevention of Terrorism (Temporary Provisions) Act 1984, Article 9 of the Prevention of Terrorism (Supplemental Temporary Provisions) Order 1984 and Article 10 of the Prevention of Terrorism (Supplemental Temporary Provisions) (Northern Ireland) Order 1984.

These provisions have been replaced by section 14 of and paragraph 6 of Schedule 5 to the Prevention of Terrorism (Temporary Provisions) Act 1989, which make comparable provision. They came into force on 22 March 1989. A copy of these provisions is enclosed.

The United Kingdom Permanent Representative avails himself of this opportunity to renew to the Secretary General the assurance of his highest consideration.

23 March 1989.

PART II
RESERVATION

At the time of signing the present (First) Protocol, I declare that, in view of certain provisions of the Education Acts in the United Kingdom, the principle affirmed in the second sentence of Article 2 is accepted by the United Kingdom only so far as it is compatible with the provision of efficient instruction and training, and the avoidance of unreasonable public expenditure.

Dated 20 March 1952. Made by the United Kingdom Permanent Representative to the Council of Europe.

SCHEDULE 4
JUDICIAL PENSIONS

Duty to make orders about pensions

1.—(1) The appropriate Minister must by order make provision with respect to pensions payable to or in respect of any holder of a judicial office who serves as an ECHR judge.

(2) A pensions order must include such provision as the Minister making it considers is necessary to secure that—

(a)   an ECHR judge who was, immediately before his appointment as an ECHR judge, a member of a judicial pension scheme is entitled to remain as a member of that scheme;

(b)   the terms on which he remains a member of the scheme are those which would have been applicable had he not been appointed as an ECHR judge; and

(c)   entitlement to benefits payable in accordance with the scheme continues to be determined as if, while serving as an ECHR judge, his salary was that which would (but for section 18(4)) have been payable to him in respect of his continuing service as the holder of his judicial office.

Contributions

2.   A pensions order may, in particular, make provision—

(a)   for any contributions which are payable by a person who remains a member of a scheme as a result of the order, and which would otherwise be payable by deduction from his salary, to be made otherwise than by deduction from his salary as an ECHR judge; and

(b)   for such contributions to be collected in such manner as may be determined by the administrators of the scheme.

Amendments of other enactments

3.   A pensions order may amend any provision of, or made under, a pensions Act in such manner and to such extent as the Minister making the order considers necessary or expedient to ensure the proper administration of any scheme to which it relates.

Definitions

4.   In this Schedule—
'appropriate Minister' means—

(a)   in relation to any judicial office whose jurisdiction is exercisable exclusively in relation to Scotland, the Secretary of State; and

(b)   otherwise, the Lord Chancellor;
'ECHR judge' means the holder of a judicial office who is serving as a judge of the Court;
'judicial pension scheme' means a scheme established by and in accordance with a pensions Act;
'pensions Act means—

(a)   the County Courts Act (Northern Ireland) 1959;

(b)   the Sheriffs' Pensions (Scotland) Act 1961;

(c)   the Judicial Pensions Act 1981; or

(d)   the Judicial Pensions and Retirement Act 1993; and
'pensions order' means an order made under paragraph 1.

Appendix Two
Human Rights Act 1998 Rules

CIVIL PROCEDURE (AMENDMENT NO. 4) RULES 2000
(SI 2000, No. 2092) (L. 16)

The Civil Procedure Rule Committee, having power under section 2 of the Civil Procedure Act 1997 to make rules of court under section 1 of that Act, after consulting in accordance with section 2(6)(a) of that Act, make the following Rules—

1.   Citation, commencement and interpretation
These Rules may be cited as the Civil Procedure (Amendment No. 4) Rules 2000 and shall come into force on 2 October 2000.

2.   In these Rules—

(a)   a reference to a Part or rule by number alone means the Part or rule so numbered in the Civil Procedure Rules 1998;

(b)   a reference to an Order by number and prefixed by 'RSC' means the RSC Order so numbered in Schedule 1 to those Rules; and

(c)   a reference to an Order by number and prefixed by 'CCR' means the CCR Order so numbered in Schedule 2 to those Rules.

3.   Amendments to Civil Procedure Rules 1998
For the definition of 'defendant's home court' in rule 2.3(1), substitute—
' "defendant's home court" means—

(a)   if the claim is proceeding in a county court, the county court for the district in which the defendant resides or carries on business; and

(b)   if the claim is proceeding in the High Court, the district registry for the district in which the defendant resides or carries on business or, where there is no such district registry, the Royal Courts of Justice;'.

4.   For paragraphs (1) and (2) of rule 3.7, substitute—
'(1)   This rule applies where—

(a)   an allocation questionnaire or a listing questionnaire is filed without payment of the fee specified by the relevant Fees Order;

(b) the court dispenses with the need for an allocation questionnaire or a listing questionnaire or both;

(c) these Rules do not require an allocation questionnaire or a listing questionnaire to be filed in relation to the claim in question; or

(d) the court has made an order giving permission to proceed with a claim for judicial review.

(Rule 26.3 provides for the court to dispense with the need for an allocation questionnaire and rules 28.5 and 29.6 provide for the court to dispense with the need for a listing questionnaire)

(Rule 54.12 provides for the service of the order giving permission to proceed with a claim for judicial review)

(2) The court will serve a notice on the claimant requiring payment of the fee specified in the relevant Fees Order if, at the time the fee is due, the claimant has not paid it or made an application for exemption or remission.'.

5. After rule 6.5, insert—

'(Rule 42.1 provides that if the business address of his solicitor is given that solicitor will be treated as acting for that party)'.

6. After rule 7.10, insert—

'7.11 Human Rights

(1) A claim under section 7(1)(a) of the Human Rights Act 1998 in respect of a judicial act may be brought only in the High Court.

(2) Any other claim under section 7(1)(a) of that Act may be brought in any court.'.

7. In rule 13.4, omit paragraph (1A).

8. After rule 19.4, insert—

'19.4A Human Rights

Section 4 of the Human Rights Act 1998

(1) The court may not make a declaration of incompatibility in accordance with section 4 of the Human Rights Act 1998 unless 21 days' notice, or such other period of notice as the court directs, has been given to the Crown.

(2) Where notice has been given to the Crown a Minister, or other person permitted by that Act, shall be joined as a party on giving notice to the court.

(Only courts specified in section 4 of the Human Rights Act 1998 can make a declaration of incompatibility)

Section 9 of the Human Rights Act 1998

(3) Where a claim is made under that Act for damages in respect of a judicial act—

(a) that claim must be set out in the statement of case or the appeal notice; and

(b) notice must be given to the Crown.

(4)   Where paragraph (3) applies and the appropriate person has not applied to be joined as a party within 21 days, or such other period as the court directs, after the notice is served, the court may join the appropriate person as a party.

(A practice direction makes provision for these notices)'.

9.   In rule 24.3(2)—

(a)   omit the word 'and' at the end of sub-paragraph (b) and for the semicolon after the word 'rem' substitute a full stop; and

(b)   omit sub-paragraph (c).

10.   After rule 26.10, insert—

'26.11   Trial with a jury

An application for a claim to be tried with a jury must be made within 28 days of service of the defence.

(Section 69 of the Supreme Court Act 1981 and section 66 of the County Courts Act 1984 specify when a claim may be tried with a jury)'.

11.   Rules 27.12 and 27.13 are revoked.

12.   In rule 27.14(2)(c), omit 'under rule 27.12'.

13.   In rule 30.3(2)—

(a)   for the full stop at the end of sub-paragraph (f) substitute a semicolon; and

(b)   after sub-paragraph (f), insert—

'(g)   whether the making of a declaration of incompatibility under section 4 of the Human Rights Act 1998 has arisen or may arise.'.

14.   Rule 30.8 is revoked.

15.   After rule 33.8, insert—

'33.9   Human Rights

(1)   This rule applies where a claim is—

(a)   for a remedy under section 7 of the Human Rights Act 1998 in respect of a judicial act which is alleged to have infringed the claimant's Article 5 Convention rights; and

(b)   based on a finding by a court or tribunal that the claimant's Convention rights have been infringed.

(2)   The court hearing the claim—

(a)   may proceed on the basis of the finding of that other court or tribunal that there has been an infringement but it is not required to do so, and

(b)   may reach its own conclusion in the light of that finding and of the evidence heard by that other court or tribunal.'.

16.   In rule 36.6(5), after 'withdrawn' insert 'or reduced'.

17.   For rule 36.2 1(6), substitute—

'(6)   Where the court awards interest under this rule and also awards interest on the same sum and for the same period under any other power, the total rate of interest may not exceed 10% above base $^{(gl)}$.'.

18.   In rule 39.3(4), omit 'for an order to restore proceedings'.

19.   In rule 47.17(3), after the words 'in accordance with' insert 'community legal service or'.

20.   For rule 52.1(2), substitute—

'(2)   This Part does not apply to an appeal in detailed assessment proceedings against a decision of an authorised court officer.'.

21.   After rule 52.1(2), omit the words from '(Rules 27.12' to 'small claims track))'.

22.   After Part 53, insert Part 54 (judicial review) as set out in the Schedule to these Rules.

23.   RSC Order 53 is revoked.

24.   RSC Order 57 is revoked.

25.   In RSC Order 64, rule 4, paragraph (b) is revoked.

26.   In RSC Order 98, rule 2(3), omit 'in accordance with Order 57, rule 2,'.

27.   CCR Order 49, rule 6 is revoked.

28.   After CCR Order 49, rule 6A(17), insert—

'(17A)   Where the defendant seeks postponement of possession on the ground of exceptional hardship under section 89 of the Housing Act 1980, the judge may direct a hearing of that issue.

(17B)   Where the judge directs a hearing under paragraph (17A) it must be held before the date on which possession is to be given up.

(17C)   Where the judge is satisfied, on a hearing directed under paragraph (17A), that exceptional hardship would be caused by requiring possession to be given up by the date in the order of possession, he may vary the date on which possession must be given up.'.

29.   Transitional provisions
Where a person has, before 2nd October 2000, filed a notice of appeal in a claim allocated to the small claims track—

(a)   Part 52 shall not apply to the appeal to which that notice relates; and

(b)   rules 27.12 and 27.13 shall apply to that appeal as if they had not been revoked.

30.   Where a person has, before 2nd October 2000, filed an application for permission to make an application for judicial review in accordance with RSC Order 53—

(a)   Part 54 shall not apply to that application for permission or the application for judicial review to which it relates; and

(b)   RSC Order 53 shall apply to those applications as if it had not been revoked.

SCHEDULE

Rule 22

PART 54

JUDICIAL REVIEW

Contents of this Part

54.1   Scope and interpretation

(1)   This Part contains rules about judicial review.

(2)   In this Part—

(a)   a 'claim for judicial review' means a claim to review the lawfulness of—

(i)   an enactment; or

(ii)   a decision, action or failure to act in relation to the exercise of a public function.

(b)   an order of mandamus is called a 'mandatory order';

(c)   an order of prohibition is called a 'prohibiting order';

(d)   an order of certiorari is called a 'quashing order';

(e)   'the judicial review procedure' means the Part 8 procedure as modified by this Part;

(f) 'interested party' means any person (other than the claimant and defendant) who is directly affected by the claim; and

(g) 'court' means the High Court, unless otherwise stated.

(Rule 8.1 (6)(b) provides that a rule or practice direction may, in relation to a specified type of proceedings, disapply or modify any of the rules set out in Part 8 as they apply to those proceedings)

54.2 When this Part must be used

The judicial review procedure must be used in a claim for judicial review where the claimant is seeking—

(a) a mandatory order;

(b) a prohibiting order;

(c) a quashing order; or

(d) an injunction under section 30 of the Supreme Court Act 1981 (restraining a person from acting in any office in which he is not entitled to act).

54.3 When this Part may be used

(1) The judicial review procedure may be used in a claim for judicial review where the claimant is seeking—

(a) a declaration; or

(b) an injunction[(g1)].

(Section 31(2) of the Supreme Court Act 1981 sets out the circumstances in which the court may grant a declaration or injunction in a claim for judicial review).

(Where the claimant is seeking a declaration or injunction in addition to one of the remedies listed in rule 54.2, the judicial review procedure must be used).

(2) A claim for judicial review may include a claim for damages but may not seek damages alone.

(Section 31(4) of the Supreme Court Act 1981 sets out the circumstances in which the court may award damages on a claim for judicial review).

54.4 Permission required

The court's permission to proceed is required in a claim for judicial review whether started under this Part or transferred to the Administrative Court.

54.5 Time limit for filing claim form

(1) The claim form must be filed—

(a) promptly; and

(b) in any event not later than 3 months after the grounds to make the claim first arose.

(2) The time limit in this rule may not be extended by agreement between the parties.

(3) This rule does not apply when any other enactment specifies a shorter time limit for making the claim for judicial review.

54.6 Claim form

(1) In addition to the matters set out in rule 8.2 (contents of the claim form) the claimant must also state—

    (a) the name and address of any person he considers to be an interested party;

    (b) that he is requesting permission to proceed with a claim for judicial review; and

    (c) any remedy (including any interim remedy) he is claiming.

(Part 25 sets out how to apply for an interim remedy)

(2) The claim form must be accompanied by the documents required by the relevant practice direction.

54.7 Service of claim form

The claim form must be served on—

    (a) the defendant; and

    (b) unless the court otherwise directs, any person the claimant considers to be an interested party,

within 7 days after the date of issue.

54.8 Acknowledgment of service

(1) Any person served with the claim form who wishes to take part in the judicial review must file an acknowledgment of service in the relevant practice form in accordance with the following provisions of this rule.

(2) Any acknowledgment of service must be—

    (a) filed not more than 21 days after service of the claim form; and

    (b) served on

        (i) the claimant; and

        (ii) subject to any direction under rule 54.7(b), any other person named in the claim form,

as soon as practicable and, in any event, not later than 7 days after it is filed.

(3) The time limits under this rule may not be extended by agreement between the parties.

(4) The acknowledgment of service—

    (a) must—

        (i) where the person filing it intends to contest the claim, set out a summary of his grounds for doing so; and

        (ii) state the name and address of any person the person filing it considers to be an interested party; and

    (b) may include or be accompanied by an application for directions.

(5) Rule 10.3(2) does not apply.

54.9 Failure to file acknowledgment of service

(1) Where a person served with the claim form has failed to file an acknowledgment of service in accordance with rule 54.8, he—

    (a) may not take part in a hearing to decide whether permission should be given unless the court allows him to do so; but

(b)   provided he complies with rule 54.14 or any other direction of the court regarding the filing and service of—

(i)   detailed grounds for contesting the claim or supporting it on additional grounds; and

(ii)   any written evidence,

may take part in the hearing of the judicial review.

(2)   Where that person takes part in the hearing of the judicial review, the court may take his failure to file an acknowledgment of service into account when deciding what order to make about costs.

(3)   Rule 8.4 does not apply.

54.10   Permission given

(1)   Where permission to proceed is given the court may also give directions.

(2)   Directions under paragraph (1) may include a stay$^{(gl)}$ of proceedings to which the claim relates.

(Rule 3.7 provides a sanction for the non-payment of the fee payable when permission to proceed has been given).

54.11   Service of order giving or refusing permission

The court will serve—

(a)   the order giving or refusing permission; and

(b)   any directions,

on—

(i)   the claimant;

(ii)   the defendant; and

(iii)   any other person who filed an acknowledgment of service.

54.12   Permission decision without a hearing

(1)   This rule applies where the court, without a hearing—

(a)   refuses permission to proceed; or

(b)   gives permission to proceed—

(i)   subject to conditions; or

(ii)   on certain grounds only.

(2)   The court will serve its reasons for making the decision when it serves the order giving or refusing permission in accordance with rule 54.11.

(3)   The claimant may not appeal but may request the decision to be reconsidered at a hearing.

(4)   A request under paragraph (3) must be filed within 7 days after service of the reasons under paragraph (2).

(5)   The claimant, defendant and any other person who has filed an acknowledgment of service will be given at least 2 days' notice of the hearing date.

54.13   Defendant etc. may not apply to set aside $^{(gl)}$

Neither the defendant nor any other person served with the claim form may apply to set aside $^{(gl)}$ an order giving permission to proceed.

54.14   Response

(1)   A defendant and any other person saved with the claim form who wishes to contest the claim or support it on additional grounds must file and serve—

(a)   detailed grounds for contesting the claim or supporting it on additional grounds; and

(b)   any written evidence,

within 35 days after service of the order giving permission.

(2)   The following rules do not apply—

(a)   rule 8.5(3) and 8.5(4) (defendant to file and serve written evidence at the same time as acknowledgment of service); and

(b)   rule 8.5(5) and 8.5(6) (claimant to file and serve any reply within 14 days).

54.15   Where claimant seeks to rely on additional grounds

The court's permission is required if a claimant seeks to rely on grounds other than those for which he has been given permission to proceed.

54.16   Evidence

(1)   Rule 8.6 does not apply.

(2)   No written evidence may be relied on unless—

(a)   it has been served in accordance with any—

(i)   rule under this Part; or

(ii)   direction of the court; or

(b)   the court gives permission.

54.17   Court's powers to hear any person

(1)   Any person may apply for permission—

(a)   to file evidence; or

(b)   make representations at the hearing of the judicial review.

(2)   An application under paragraph (1) should be made promptly.

54.18   Judicial review may be decided without a hearing

The court may decide the claim for judicial review without a hearing where all the parties agree.

54.19   Court's powers in respect of quashing orders

(1)   This rule applies where the court makes a quashing order in respect of the decision to which the claim relates.

(2)   The court may—

(a)   remit the matter to the decision-maker; and

(b)   direct it to reconsider the matter and reach a decision in accordance with the judgment of the court.

(3)   Where the court considers that there is no purpose to be served in remitting the matter to the decision-maker it may, subject to any statutory provision, take the decision itself.

(Where a statutory power is given to a tribunal, person or other body it may be the case that the court cannot take the decision itself).

54.20 Transfer

The court may—

(a) order a claim to continue as if it had not been started under this Part; and

(b) where it does so, give directions about the future management of the claim.

(Part 30 (transfer) applies to transfers to and from the Administrative Court)

CRIMINAL APPEAL (AMENDMENT) RULES 2000
(SI 2000, No. 2036)

We, the Crown Court Rule Committee, in exercise of the powers conferred on us by sections 84(1), 84(2) and 86 of the Supreme Court Act 198 and section 5 of the Human Rights Act 1998, hereby makes the following Rules:

1. Citation and commencement

These Rules may be cited as the Criminal Appeal (Amendment) Rules 2000 and shall come into force on 2 October 2000.

2. Amendment of Criminal Appeal Rules 1968

The Criminal Appeal Rules 1968 shall be amended as follows—

(a) in rule 2, after paragraph (2)(a) there shall be inserted—

'(aa) A notice of the grounds of appeal or application set out in Form 3 shall include notice—

(i) of any application to be made to the court for a declaration of incompatibility under section 4 of the Human Rights Act 1998; or

(ii) of any issue for the court to decide which may lead to the court making such a declaration.

(ab) Where the grounds of appeal or application include notice in accordance with paragraph (aa) above, a copy of the notice shall be served on the prosecutor by the appellant.'.

(b) after rule 14 there shall be inserted—

'**14.A Human Rights Act**

(1) The court shall not consider making a declaration of incompatibility under section 4 of the Human Rights Act 1998 unless it has given written notice to the Crown.

(2) Where notice has been given to the Crown, a Minister, or other person entitled under the Human Rights Act 1998 to be joined as a party, shall be so joined on giving written notice to the court.

(3) A notice given under paragraph (1) above shall be given to—

(a) the person named in the list published under section 17(1) of the Crown Proceedings Act 1947; or

(b) in the case of doubt as to whether any and if so which of those departments is appropriate, the Treasury Solicitor.

(4) A notice given under paragraph (1) above, shall provide an outline of the issues in the case and specify—

(a)　the prosecutor and appellant;

(b)　the date, judge and court of the trial in the proceedings from which the appeal lies;

(c)　the provision of primary legislation and the Convention right under question.

(5)　Any consideration of whether a declaration of incompatibility should be made, shall be adjourned for—

(a)　21 days from the date of the notice given under paragraph (1) above; or

(b)　such other period (specified in the notice), as the court shall allow in order that the relevant Minister or other person, may seek to be joined and prepare his case.

(6)　Unless the court otherwise directs, the Minister or other person entitled under the Human Rights Act 1998 to be joined as a party shall, if he is to be joined, give written notice to the court and every other party.

(7)　Where a Minister of the Crown has nominated a person to be joined as a party by virtue of section 5(2)(a) of the Human Rights Act 1998, a notice under paragraph (6) above shall be accompanied by a written nomination signed by or on behalf of the Minister.'

(c)　in rule 15 after paragraph (1)(d) there shall be inserted—

'(e)　in the case of a declaration of incompatibility under section 4 of the Human Rights Act 1998, the declaration shall be served on—

(i)　all of the parties to the proceedings; and

(ii)　where a Minister of the Crown has not been joined as a party, the Crown (in accordance with rule 14A(3) above).'.

A LORD CHANCELLOR'S DEPARTMENT CONSULTATION PAPER

Human Rights Act 1998: Draft Rules & Practice Directions

March 2000

This paper proposes rules and practice directions for the civil and family courts in England and Wales up to and including the Court of Appeal under the Human Rights Act 1998 ('the Act'). They will come into force when the main provisions of the Act are implemented on 2 October 2000. Draft rules and practice directions are at Annex A for civil proceedings and at Annex B for family proceedings.

Introduction

1.　In framing the Human Rights Act, the Government's intention was to avoid having to create new procedures, courts and remedies, wherever possible, in the belief that the scheme of the Act should allow for most situations. The areas where new material is required is therefore limited to the following:

(a)　Section 2: citation of Strasbourg jurisprudence;

(b)   Section 5: notification of the Crown where the Court is considering making a declaration of incompatibility;

(c)   Section 7: procedures for dealing with claims brought under the Human Rights Act alone rather than in existing proceedings;

(d)   Section 9: joining the Crown to proceedings where an award of Article 5 damages is to be made against it, and ensuring that such proceedings are heard in the appropriate court.

Section 2

2.   Section 2(2) of the Act provides that evidence of Strasbourg jurisprudence of which account may have to be taken in proceedings is to be given in such manner as may be provided by rules. This provision is more extensive than was made for EC law and for non-UK decisions in the Competition Act 1998 but as Section 2(2) says 'as may be provided in rules,' rules are not essential. Instead, we believe it would be more appropriate to specify what can be cited as Strasbourg jurisprudence in less formal means such as practice directions or guidance. This will make it quicker to add to the list as and when new law reports are produced, which will certainly be the case in this new area of law. It will also ensure that the procedures that have to be followed when citing Strasbourg authorities are clear and will establish which texts are preferred. Draft paragraphs in practice directions for the courts governed by the Civil Procedure Rules and family proceedings are included in the annexes to this paper and similar material will be drafted for civil proceedings in the magistrates' courts. The Home Office will draft the material required for criminal proceedings.

3.   Strasbourg authorities should be cited from authoritative and complete reports that are readily available. We believe that the reports highlighted in the attached practice direction meet these criteria but would be grateful to be informed of others. Permission from the Court would be required to cite from any other report. We propose that a party wishing to cite Strasbourg jurisprudence should give to the court and any other party a list of the Strasbourg authorities for citation and copies of the reports from which they are to be cited not more than 7 days nor less than three days before the hearing. This follows the procedure in the first practice direction to CPR Part 39.

4.   Many tribunals do not have specific power to make formal practice directions but are governed by rules allowing them to regulate their own proceedings, including the circulation of informal guidance. For the reasons set out in paragraph 2 above, we believe this would be the most appropriate means of specifying what can be cited as Strasbourg jurisprudence. LCD has invited each of the tribunals for which it is responsible to adapt the material produced for the civil courts. This material has been offered to other departments so they can consider how Strasbourg jurisprudence should be cited in their tribunals, depending on the formality of proceedings in each tribunal.

Section 5

5. The Act provides that, so far as it is possible to do so, primary (and subordinate) legislation must be read and given effect in a way that is compatible with the Convention rights. Where, in spite of its efforts to read a provision of primary legislation compatibly, a Court is satisfied that it is incompatible with a Convention right, it may, if it is a court listed in section 4(5), make a declaration of incompatibility. Section 5(1) of the Act then provides that 'where a Court is considering whether to make declaration of incompatibility, the Crown is entitled to notice in accordance with rules of court.' The draft text is intended to give effect to the intention of the legislation that the Crown should be notified at the earliest time, rather than just before a declaration is made. However, we do not propose that notice should be given any earlier; for example, even if a party seeks the remedy in a claim form.

6. This provision gives the Crown the opportunity, if it wishes, to make any relevant arguments to the Court before it decides to make a declaration. While there is a requirement for the Crown to be notified, there is no requirement for the Crown to intervene. This will depend upon the circumstances of the case.

7. Under Section 5(1), we propose that it will be the Court that provides notice to the Crown once it begins to consider making a declaration of incompatibility, rather than the parties. This is because it is the Court that is considering making the declaration and it is the Court that will be best placed to provide useful information to the Crown to enable it to determine whether it wishes to be joined as a party. This approach gives the Court prime responsibility for managing the case, as encouraged in the Civil Procedure Rules.

8. The draft rule and practice direction therefore stipulate that notice is to be given by the Court itself in writing and should be sent to the person named in the list published by HM Treasury under Section 17 of the Crown Proceedings Act 1947. The notice should contain sufficient details to identify the claim, the parties to the claim, the court, the Convention rights under consideration and a short statement of the issues which have led to the Court considering making a declaration of incompatibility.

9. Section 5(3) provides that notice by the Crown under Section 5(2) that it wishes to take up its entitlement to be joined can be given at any time during the proceedings. Once the Court gives notice, however, the Court will need to allow the Crown a minimum period of time to determine whether it wishes to be joined. A balance needs to be struck here between, on the one hand, affording the Crown sufficient time to make a reasoned decision on whether it wishes to be joined and, on the other, not delaying the case. We therefore propose that the Crown should be allowed 21 days in the first instance to state whether it wished to be joined as a party, unless the circumstances of the case mean that the Court orders otherwise. The Crown would, however, be able to apply, if necessary, for an extension of the time limit. We would be grateful for views on whether this proposal strikes the correct balance.

10.   Where the Minister has nominated a person to be joined as a party the notice must be accompanied by the written nomination. Notice should be given to the relevant Government Department (or if none, or if the court is uncertain which is the relevant department, the Attorney General) even where the Crown is already party to the proceedings in some other capacity. This is to ensure that the specific issue of the fact that the Court is considering making a declaration of incompatibility is considered appropriately by the Crown.

11.   The appropriate rules and paragraphs in practice directions for civil and family proceedings are included in the annexes to this paper. The Home Office will draft the material required for criminal proceedings.

Section 7

12.   We propose that a free-standing case under Section 7(1)(a) of the Act should be brought in the following ways—

- using the existing judicial review procedures;
- in the county court or in the High Court where a claim for damages is made (unless this is associated with a claim for judicial review). The normal jurisdictional limits should apply;
- in the county court or in the High Court following a finding of unlawfulness under Section 7(1)(b) in some other court or tribunal which did not have the power to award damages or compensation. This would cover, for example, actions in respect of a claim for damages in a criminal case arising out of a ruling by a Magistrates' Court or the Crown Court that the prosecution had acted unlawfully. The normal criteria for determining whether a civil case should be started in a county court or the High Court should again apply. The person seeking a civil remedy should be able to rely upon the finding of unlawfulness in the other court as prima facie evidence that the defendant authority acted unlawfully. The previous finding of unlawfulness (even if it resulted from a collateral challenge in the earlier proceedings) would be treated, by analogy, in the same way that Section 11 of the Civil Evidence Act 1968 c. 64 treats a conviction for the purpose of civil proceedings. It would be open to the defendant to refute the finding on grounds of fact or law using the authority under paragraph 4 of Schedule 1 to the Civil Procedure Act 1997.

13.   The procedures to allow such claims to be heard are set out in the attached paragraphs of practice directions to the Civil Procedure Rules.

14.   Section 7(11) of the Act enables Ministers to make rules for individual tribunals to ensure that they can provide appropriate relief or remedies in relation to an act of a public authority, which is unlawful under Section 6(1) of the HRA. It was thought that rules would be required in this respect for the Immigration Appellate Authorities but the position has been resolved here by the Immigration and Asylum Act 1999. No other tribunals requiring rules to this effect have yet been identified so there is no intention at this stage to draft rules under Section 7(11).

Section 9

15.   Section 9 applies to proceedings under Section 7(1)(a) in respect of judicial acts. The proposed rules and practice direction apply specifically to proceedings that fall within the exception in Section 9(3), that being where damages are sought in respect of a judicial act that breaches Article 5 of the Convention. The proposals are designed to ensure that:

(a)   Issues of Article 5 unlawful detention and Article 5(5) damages are determined in the appropriate court.

(b)   The Lord Chancellor can be joined to proceedings at a resource efficient stage that is convenient for all the parties involved.

16.   The first proposed rule provision relates to the limited circumstances where a committal order made by a District Judge is appealed on the grounds that it breached Article 5. The provision provides that in such circumstances the matter may be transferred to the Crown Office List. Although there is normally the opportunity to appeal to a Circuit Judge within the County Court, we believe it would be preferable initially to direct such issues to the Divisional Court of the High Court so that the novel and complex issues surrounding Article 5 unlawful detention fall to the senior judiciary to consider. It can therefore play a supervisory role during the early stages of incorporation, thus ensuring that consistent and authoritative principles are established in relation to Article 5 unlawful detention and the quantum of Article 5(5) damages.

17.   Accordingly the rule provision provides a discretionary power to transfer these cases to the Crown Office List. This is complemented by a provision in a proposed accompanying practice direction, which indicates that this should be the normal course of action until further notice. This provides the flexibility that will mean that, once firm Article 5 principles have been established, a transfer to the Crown Office List will no longer be necessary in these circumstances and the matter can be determined by a Circuit Judge in the County Court. This rule provision will be needed for both civil and family proceedings.

18.   The second proposed rule provision concerns proceedings for Article 5(5) damages that have reached the High Court following a finding of a breach in the Crown Court. As a result of Section 8(2) (which provides that damages may only be awarded by a court which has the power to do so in civil proceedings) the Crown Court cannot go on to award damages where it has found a breach of Article 5 (in an appeal from the magistrates' court). In such circumstances the question of damages will be transferred to the High Court. This proposed rule provision provides that the Crown Court's finding will be treated as prima facie evidence of a breach for the High Court damages proceedings, and the High Court may reconsider the finding if the Lord Chancellor chooses to contest it. The proposed provision would ensure that ultimate determination of the meaning of 'unlawful detention' and the quantum of Article 5(5) damages can be focused in the High Court. This is important for the reasons mentioned in paragraph 16 above.

19.   We also propose additions to practice directions applying to civil and family courts, covering the following Section 9 related issues:

(a)   The joining of the Lord Chancellor to Section 9 cases. Section 9(4) requires that, for an award to be made under Section 9(3), the appropriate person must be joined to the proceedings (if not already a party). The practice direction will provide that an applicant must state on the notice of appeal/application for judicial review if (s)he is seeking damages under Article 5(5) in respect of a judicial act. The Lord Chancellor should be notified at this stage (except where the appeal is to the Crown Court in which case the Lord Chancellor will only be notified if and when a breach is found). He then has 21 days to indicate whether he wishes to be joined from the outset, either to contest the substance of the claim, or to make representations on the quantum of damages. Otherwise he will be joined for the purposes of Section 9(4) if and when a finding of a breach is made.

(b)   The need for the court to address specifically whether a detention was ordered in breach of Article 5. Where a claim for Article 5(5) damages has been included on the notice of appeal or application for judicial review, the court considering the appeal must explicitly address whether the detention was unlawful in terms of Article 5. It will therefore be clear whether the applicant is entitled to compensation, or whether their detention was merely quashed on grounds other than Article 5.

(c)   The requirement that, until further notice, appeals against the detention order of a District Judge should be transferred to the Crown Office List. This is designed to operate in conjunction with the discretionary power in the rules to transfer such appeals to the Crown Office List. Its purpose, as explained in paragraph 14 above, is to ensure that in the early stages of implementation, the novel and complex issues surrounding Article 5 are resolved by the senior judiciary. Once firm and consistent principles have been established, it may be indicated that it is no longer necessary for these appeals to be transferred to the Crown Office List as a matter of course.

Appendix Three
The Government's White Paper

RIGHTS BROUGHT HOME: THE HUMAN RIGHTS BILL

Presented to Parliament by the Secretary of State for the Home Department
by Command of Her Majesty
October 1997
(Cm 3782)

PREFACE BY THE PRIME MINISTER

The Government is pledged to modernise British politics. We are committed to a comprehensive programme of constitutional reform. We believe it is right to increase individual rights, to decentralise power, to open up government and to reform Parliament.

The elements are well known:

— a Scottish Parliament and a Welsh Assembly giving the people of Scotland and Wales more control over their own affairs within the United Kingdom;
— new rights, based on bringing the European Convention on Human Rights into United Kingdom law;
— an elected Mayor and new strategic authority for London with more accountability in the regions of England;
— freedom of information;
— a referendum on the voting system for the House of Commons; and
— reform of the House of Lords.

This White Paper explains the proposals contained in the Human Rights Bill which we are introducing into Parliament. The Bill marks a major step forward in the achievement of our programme of reform. It will give people in the United Kingdom opportunities to enforce their rights under the European Convention in

British courts rather than having to incur the cost and delay of taking a case to the European Human Rights Commission and Court in Strasbourg. It will enhance the awareness of human rights in our society. And it stands alongside our decision to put the promotion of human rights at the forefront of our foreign policy.

I warmly commend these proposals to Parliament and to the people of this country.

Tony Blair

INTRODUCTION AND SUMMARY

The Government has a Manifesto commitment to introduce legislation to incorporate the European Convention on Human Rights into United Kingdom law. The Queen's Speech at the opening of the new Parliament announced that the Government would bring forward a Bill for this purpose in the current Session. We are now introducing the Human Rights Bill into Parliament. This White Paper explains what the Bill does, and why.

Before the General Election the Labour Party published a consultation document, *Bringing Rights Home*, setting out in some detail the case for incorporation. and its preliminary proposals for the way this should be done. A number of individuals and organisations responded helpfully with a range of comments on the paper, and have continued to make their knowledge and advice available to the Government. The Government's proposals for the Bill take full account of the responses to *Bringing Rights Home*. Any further comments in response to this White Paper or on the Bill should be sent to:

Human Rights Unit
Home Office
50 Queen Anne's Gate
London SW1H 9AT.

We may make any comments we receive publicly available. Respondents who would prefer their comments to be treated in confidence are invited to indicate this expressly.

Chapter 1 of this White Paper explains the content and status of the European Convention on Human Rights and why the Government considers it desirable to give people in this country easier access to their Convention rights.

The United Kingdom is bound in international law to observe the Convention, which it ratified in 1951, and is answerable for any violation. In some limited circumstances, the United Kingdom courts can already take the Convention into account in domestic proceedings. But public authorities in the United Kingdom are not required as a matter of domestic law to comply with the Convention and, generally speaking, there is no means of having the application of the Convention rights tested in the United Kingdom courts. The Government believes that these arrangements are no longer adequate, given the importance which it attaches to the maintenance of basic human rights in this country, and that the time has come to 'bring rights home'.

Chapter 2 explains the Government's proposals to make the Convention rights enforceable directly in this country. The Bill makes it unlawful for public authorities to act in a way which is incompatible with the Convention rights. This will make it possible for people to invoke their rights in any proceedings — criminal or civil — brought against them by a public authority, or in proceedings which they may bring against a public authority. The Government prefers a system in which Convention rights can be called upon as they arise, in normal court proceedings, rather than confining their consideration to some kind of constitutional court. Courts and tribunals will be able to award whatever remedy, within their normal powers, is appropriate in the circumstances.

Although the courts will not, under the proposals in the Bill be able to set aside Acts of the United Kingdom Parliament, the Bill requires them to interpret legislation as far as possible in accordance with the Convention. If this is not possible, the higher courts will be able to issue a formal declaration to the effect that the legislative provisions in question are incompatible with the Convention rights. It will then be up to the Government and Parliament to put matters right. The Bill makes a 'fast-track' procedure available for the purpose of amending the law so as to bring it into conformity with the Convention.

Chapter 3 sets out the other measures which the Government intends to take to ensure that the Convention rights are taken more fully into account in the development of new policies and of legislation. It also suggests that Parliament should itself establish a new Human Rights Committee. Amongst the matters on which the Government would welcome advice from a Parliamentary Committee is the possible establishment of a Human Rights Commission, but for the time being the Government has concluded that a new Commission should not be set up by means of this Bill.

Chapter 4 reviews the position on the derogation and reservation which the United Kingdom currenty has in place in respect of the Convention and its First Protocol. The Government has concluded that these must remain for the time being, but the Bill requires any derogation to be subject to perodic renewal by Parliament and reservations to be subject to periodic review.

Chapter 4 also reviews the position in respect of those Protocols to the Convention which guarantee other rights (Protocols 4, 6 and 7) and which the United Kingdom has not so far accepted. The Government does not propose that the United Kingdom should ratify at present Protocol 4 or Protocol 6, but it does propose to sign and ratify Protocol 7 once some existing legislation has been amended.

The Annex [which is not reprinted here] sets out the text of the Convention rights themselves.

CHAPTER 1 THE CASE FOR CHANGE

The European Convention on Human Rights

1.1 The European Convention for the Protection of Human Rights and Fundamental Freedoms is a treaty of the Council of Europe. This institution was established at the end of the Second World War, as part of the Allies' programme to reconstruct durable civilisation on the mainland of Europe. The Council was established before the European Union and, although many nations are members of both, the two bodies are quite separate.

1.2 The United Kingdom played a major part in drafting the Convention, and there was a broad agreement between the major political parites about the need for it (one of its draftsmen later became, as Lord Kilmuir, Lord Chancellor in the Conservative Administration from 1954 to 1962). The United Kingdom was among the first group of countries to sign the Convention. It was the very first country to ratify it, in March 1951. In 1966 the United Kingdom accepted that an individual person, and not merely another State, could bring a case against the United Kingdom in Strasbourg (the home of the European Commission of Human Rights and Court of Human Rights, which were established by the Convention). Successive administrations in the United Kingdom have maintained these arrangements.

1.3 The European Convention is not the only international human rights agreement to which the United Kingdom and other like-minded countries are party, but over the years it has become one of the premier agreements defining standards of behaviour across Europe. It was also for many years unique because of the system which it put in place for people from signatory countries to take complaints to Strasbourg and for those complaints to be judicially determined. These arrangements are by now well tried and tested. The rights and freedoms which are guaranteed under the Convention are ones with which the people of this country are plainly comfortable. They therefore afford an excellent basis for the Human Rights Bill which we are now introducing.

1.4 The constitutional arrangements in most continental European countries have meant that their acceptance of the Convention went hand in hand with its incorporation into their domestic law. In this country it was long believed that the rights and freedoms guaranteed by the Convention could be delivered under our common law. In the last two decades, however, there has been a growing awareness that it is not sufficient to rely on the common law and that incorporation is necessary.

1.5 The Liberal Democrat Peer, Lord Lester of Herne Hill QC, recently introduced two Bills on incorporation in the House of Lords (in 1994 and 1996). Before that, the then Conservative MP Sir Edward Gardner QC introduced a private member's Bill on incorporation into the House of Commons in 1987. At the time of introducing his Bill he commented on the language of the articles in the Convention saying: 'It is language which echoes right down the corridors of history. It goes deep into our history and as far back as Magna Carta.' (Hansard

HC, 6 February 1987. col. 1224.) In preparing this White Paper the Government
has paid close attention to earlier debates and proposals for incorporation.

The Convention rights

1.6   The Convention contains articles which guarantee a number of basic
human rights. They deal with the right to life (Article 2): torture or inhuman or
degrading treatment or punishment (Article 3); slavery and forced labour (Article
4); liberty and security of person (Article 5); fair trial (Article 6); retrospective
criminal laws (Article 7): respect for private and family life, home and correspondence (Article 8): freedom of thought, conscience and religion (Article 9); freedom
of expression (Article 10); freedom of peaceful assembly and freedom of association, including the right to join a trade union (Article 11); the right to marry and
to found a family (Article 12); and discrimination in the enjoyment of these rights
and freedoms (Article 14).

1.7   The United Kingdom is also a party to the First Protocol to the Convention,
which guarantees the right to the peaceful enjoyment of possessions (Article 1),
the right to education (Article 2) and the right to free elections (Article 3).

1.8   The rights in the Convention are set out in general terms, and they are
subject in the Convention to a number of qualifications which are also of a general
character. Some of these qualifications are set out in the substantive Articles
themselves (see, for example, Article 10, concerning freedom of expression);
others are set out in Articles 16 to 18 of the Convention. Sometimes too the rights
guaranteed under the Convention need to be balanced against each other (for
example, those guaranteed by Article 8 and Article 10).

Applications under the Convention

1.9   Anyone within the United Kingdom jurisdiction who is aggrieved by an
action of the executive or by the effect of the existing law and who believes it is
contrary to the European Convention can submit a petition to the European
Commission of Human Rights. The Commission will first consider whether the
petition is admissible. One of the conditions of admissibility is that the applicant
must have gone through all the steps available to him or her at home for
challenging the decision which he or she is complaining about. If the Commission
decides that a complaint is admissible and if a friendly settlement cannot be
secured, it will send a confidential report to the Committee of Ministers of the
Council of Europe, stating its opinion on whether there has been a violation. The
matter may end there with a decision by the Committee (which in practice always
adopts the opinion of the Commission), or the case may be referred on to the
European Court of Human Rights[1] for consideration. If the Court finds that there

---

[1] Protocol 11 to the Convention, which will come into force on 1 November 1998, will replace the
existing part-time European Commission and Court of Human Rights with a single full-time Court.

has been a violation it may itself 'afford just satisfaction' to the injured party by an award of damages or an award of costs and expenses. The Court may also find that a formal finding of a violation is sufficient. There is no appeal from the Court.

Effect of a Court judgment

1.10 A finding by the European Court of Human Rights of a violation of a Convention right does not have the effect of automatically changing United Kingdom law and practice: that is a matter for the United Kingdom Government and Parliament. But the United Kingdom, like all other States who are parties to the Convention, has agreed to abide by the decisions of the Court or (where the case has not been referred to the Court) the Committee of Ministers. It follows that, in cases where a violation has been found the State concerned must ensure that any deficiency in its internal laws is rectified so as to bring them into line with the Convention. The State is responsible for deciding what changes are needed, but it must satisfy the Committee of Minister that the steps taken are sufficient. Successive United Kingdom administrations have accepted these obligations in full.

Relationship to current law in the United Kingdom

1.11 When the United Kingdom ratified the Convention the view was taken that the rights and freedoms which the Convention guarantees were already, in substance, fully protected in British law. It was not considered necessary to write the Convention itself into British law, or to introduce any new laws in the United Kingdom in order to be sure of being able to comply with the Convention.

1.12 From the point of view of the *international* obligation which the United Kingdom was undertaking when it signed and ratified the Convention, this was understandable. Moreover, the European Court of Human Rights explicitly confirmed that it was not a necessary part of proper observance of the Convention that it should be incorporated into the laws of the States concerned.

1.13 However, since its drafting nearly 50 years ago, almost all the States which are party to the European Convention on Human Rights have gradually incorporated it into their domestic law in one way or another. Ireland and Norway have not done so, but Ireland has a Bill of Rights which guarantees rights similar to those guaranteed by the Convention and Norway is also in the process of incorporating the Convention. Several other countries with which we have close links and which share the common law tradition, such as Canada and New Zealand, have provided similar protection for human rights in their own legal systems.

The case for incorporation

1.14 The effect of non-incorporation on the British people is a very practical one. The rights, originally developed with major help from the United Kingdom

Government, are no longer actually seen as British rights. And enforcing them takes too long and costs too much. It takes on average five years to get an action into the European Court of Human Rights once all domestic remedies have been exhausted; and it costs an average of £30,000. Bringing these rights home will mean that the British people will be able to argue for their rights in the British courts — without this inordinate delay and cost. It will also mean that the rights will be brought much more fully into the jurisprudence of the courts throughout the United Kingdom and their interpretation will thus be far more subtly and powerfully woven into our law. And there will be another distinct benefit. British judges will be enabled to make a distinctively British contribution to the development of the jurisprudence of human rights in Europe.

1.15   Moreover in the Government's view the approach which the United Kingdom has so far adopted towards the Convention does not sufficiently reflect its importance and has not stood the test of time.

1.16   The most obvious proof of this lies in the number of cases in which the European Commission and Court have found that there have been violations of the Convention rights in the United Kingdom. The causes vary. The Government recognises that interpretations of the rights guaranteed under the Convention have developed over the years reflecting changes in society and attitudes. Sometimes United Kingdom laws have proved to be inherently at odds with the Convention rights. On other occasions, although the law has been satisfactory, something has been done which our courts have held to be lawful by United Kingdom standards but which breaches the Convention. In other cases again, there has simply been no framework within which the compatibility with the Convention rights of an executive act or decision can be tested in the British courts: these courts can of course review the exercise of executive discretion, but they can do so only on the basis of what is lawful or unlawful according to the law in the United Kingdom as it stands. It is plainly unsatisfactory that someone should be the victim of a breach of the Convention standards by the State yet cannot bring any case at all in the British courts, simply because British law does not recognise the right in the same terms as one contained in the Convention.

1.17   For individuals and for those advising them, the road to Strasbourg is long and hard. Even when they get there, the Convention enforcement machinery is subject to long delays. This might be convenient for a government which was half-hearted about the Convention and the right of individuals to apply under it, since it postpones the moment at which changes in domestic law or practice must be made. But it is not in keeping with the importance which this Government attaches to the observance of basic human rights.

Bringing rights home

1.18   We therefore believe that the time has come to enable people to enforce their Convention rights against the State in the British courts, rather than having to incur the delays and expense which are involved in taking a case to the European

Human Rights Commission and Court in Strasbourg and which may altogether deter some people from pursuing their rights. Enabling courts in the United Kingdom to rule on the application of the Convention will also help to influence the development of case law on the Convention by the European Court of Human Rights on the basis of familiarity with our laws and customs and of sensitivity to practices and procedures in the United Kingdom. Our courts decisions will provide the European Court with a useful source of information and reasoning for its own decisions. United Kingdom judges have a very high reputation internationally, but the fact that they do not deal in the same concepts as the European Court of Human Rights limits the extent to which their judgments can be drawn upon and followed. Enabling the convention rights to be judged by British courts will also lead to closer scrutiny of the human rights implications of new legislation and new policies. If legislation is enacted which is incompatible with the Convention a ruling by the domestic courts to that effect will be much more direct and immediate than a ruling from the European Court of Human Rights. The Government of the day and Parliament, will want to minimise the risk of that happening.

1.19   Our aim is a straightforward one. It is to make more directly accessible the rights which the British people already enjoy under the Convention. In other words, to bring those rights home.

CHAPTER 2 THE GOVERNMENT'S PROPOSALS FOR ENFORCING THE CONVENTION RIGHTS

2.1   The essential feature of the Human Rights Bill is that the United Kingdom will not be bound to give effect to the Convention rights merely as a matter of international law, but will also give them further effect directly in our domestic law. But there is more than one way of achieving this. This chapter explains the choices which the Government has made for the Bill.

A new requirement on public authorities

2.2   Although the United Kingdom has an international obligation to comply with the Convention there at present is no requirement in our domestic law on central and local government, or others exercising similar executive powers, to exercise those powers in a way which is compatible with the Convention. This Bill will change that by making it unlawful for public authorities to act in a way which is incompatible with the Convention rights. The definition of what constitutes a public authority is in wide terms. Examples of persons or organisations whose acts or omissions it is intended should be able to be challenged include central government (including executive agencies); local government; the police; immigration officers; prisons; courts and tribunals themselves: and, to the extent that they are exercising public functions, companies responsible for areas of activity which were previously within the public sector, such as the privatised utilities. The actions of Parliament, however, are excluded.

2.3   A person who is aggrieved by an act or omission on the part of a public authority which is incompatible with the Convention rights will be able to challenge the act or omission in the courts. The effects will be wide-ranging. They will extend both to legal actions which a public authority pursues against individuals (for example, where a criminal prosecution is brought or where an administrative decision is being enforced through legal proceedings) and to cases which individuals pursue against a public authority (for example, for judicial review of an executive decision). Convention points will normally be taken in the context of proceedings instituted against individuals or already open to them, but if none is available, it will be possible for people to bring cases on Convention grounds alone. Individuals or organisations seeking judicial review of decisions by public authorities on Convention grounds will need to show thay they have been directly affected as they must if they take a case to Strasbourg.

2.4   It is our intention that people or organisations should be able to argue that their Convention rights have been infringed by a public authority in our courts at any level. This will enable the Convention rights to be applied from the outset against the facts and background of a particular case, and the people concerned to obtain their remedy at the earliest possible moment. We think this is preferable to allowing cases to run their ordinary course but then referring them to some kind of separate constitutional court which, like the European Court of Human Rights, would simply review cases which had already passed through the regular legal machinery. In considering Convention points our courts will be required to take account of relevant decisions of the European Commission and Court of Human Rights (although these will not be binding).

2.5   The convention is often described as a 'living instrument' because it is interpreted by the European Court in the light of present-day conditions and therefore reflects changing social attitudes and the changes in the circumstances of society. In future our judges will be able to contribute to this dynamic and evolving interpretation of the Convention. In particular, our courts will be required to balance the protection of individuals' fundamental rights against the demands of the general interest of the community, particularly in relation to Articles 8–11 where a State may restrict the protected right to the extent that this is 'necessary in a democratic society'.

Remedies for a failure to comply with the Convention

2.6   A public authority which is found to have acted unlawfully by failing to comply with the Convention will not be exposed to criminal penalties. But the court or tribunal will be able to grant the injured person any remedy which is within its normal powers to grant and which it considers appropriate and just in the circumstances. What remedy is appropriate will of course depend both on the facts of the case and on a proper balance between the rights of the individual and the public interest. In some cases, the right course may be for the decision of the public authority in the particular case to be quashed. In other cases, the only appropriate remedy may be an award of damages. The Bill provides that, in considering an award of damages on Convention grounds, the courts are to take into account the principles applied by the European Court of Human Rights in awarding compensation, so that people will be able to receive compensation from a domestic court equivalent to what they would have received in Strasbourg.

Interpretation of legislation

2.7   The Bill provides for legislation — both Acts of Parliament and secondary legislation — to be interpreted so far as possible so as to be compatible with the Convention. This goes far beyond the present rule which enables the courts to take the Convention into account in resolving any ambiguity in a legislative provision. The courts will be required to interpret legislation so as to uphold the Convention rights unless the legislation itself is so clearly incompatible with the Convention that it is impossible to do so.

2.8   This 'rule of construction' is to apply to past as well as to future legislation. To the extent that it affects the meaning of a legislative provision the courts will not be bound by previous interpretations. They will be able to build a new body of case law, taking into account the Convention rights.

A declaration of incompatibility with the Convention rights

2.9   If the courts decide in any case that it is impossible to interpret an Act of Parliament in a way which is compatible with the Convention, the Bill enables a formal declaration to be made that its provisions are incompatible with the Convention. A declaration of incompatibility will be an important statement to make, and the power to make it will be reserved to the higher courts. They will be able to make a declaration in any proceedings before them, whether the case originated with them (as, in the High Court, on judicial review of an executive act) or in considering an appeal from a lower court or tribunal. The Government will have the right to intervene in any proceedings where such a declaration is a possible outcome. A decision by the High Court or Court of Appeal, determining whether or not such a declaration should be made, will itself be appealable.

Effect of court decisions on legislation

2.10   A declaration that legislation is incompatible with the Convention rights will not of itself have the effect of changing the law, which will continue to apply. But it will almost certainly prompt the Government and Parliament to change the law.

2.11   The Government has considered very carefully whether it would be right for the Bill to go further, and give the courts in the United Kingdom the power to set aside an Act of Parliament which they believe is incompatible with the Convention rights. In considering this question we have looked at a number of models. The Canadian Charter of Rights and Freedoms 1982 enables the courts to strike down any legislation which is inconsistent with the Charter, unless the legislation contains an explicit statement that it is to apply 'notwithstanding' the provisions of the Charter. But legislation which has been struck down may be re-enacted with a 'notwithstanding' clause. In New Zealand, on the other hand, although there was an earlier proposal for legislation on lines similar to the Canadian Charter, the human rights legislation which was eventually enacted after wide consultation took a different form. The New Zealand Bill of Rights Act 1990 is an 'interpretative' statute which requires past and future legislation to be interpreted consistently with the rights contained in the Act as far as possible but provides that legislation stands if that is impossible. In Hong Kong, a middle course was adopted. The Hong Kong Bill of Rights Ordinance 1991 distinguishes between legislation enacted before and after the Ordinance took effect: previous legislation is subordinated fto the provisions of the Ordinance, but subsequent legislation takes precedence over it.

2.12   The Government has also considered the European Communities Act 1972 which provides for European law, in cases where that law has 'direct effect', to take precedence over domestic law. There is, however, an essential difference between European Community law and the European Convention on Human Rights, because it is a *requirement* of membership of the European Union that member States give priority to directly effective EC law in their own legal systems. There is no such requirement in the Convention.

2.13   The Government has reached the conclusion that courts should not have the power to set aside primary legislation past or future, on the ground of incompatibility with the Convention. this conclusion arises from the importance which the Government attaches to Parliamentary sovereignty. In this context, Parliamentary sovereignty means that Parliament is competent to make any law on any matter of its choosing and no court may question the validity of any Act that is passes. In enacting legislation, Parliament is making decisions about important matters of public policy. The authority to make those decisions derives from a democratic mandate. Members of Parliament in the House of Commons possess such a mandate because they are elected, accountable and representative. To make provision in the Bill for the courts to set aside Acts of Parliament would confer on the judiciary a general power over the decisions of Parliament which under our present constitutional arrangements they do not possess, and would be likely on occasions to draw the judiciary into serious conflict with Parliament. There is no evidence to suggest that they desire this power, nor that the public wish them to have it. Certainly this Government has no mandate for any such change.

2.14   It has been suggested that the courts should be able to uphold the rights in the Human Rights Bill in preference to any provisions of earlier legislation which are incompatible with those rights. This in on the basis that a later Act of Parliament takes precedence over an earlier Act if there is a conflict. But the Human Rights Bill is intended to provide a new basis for judicial interpretation of all legislation, not a basis for striking down any part of it.

2.15 The courts will, however, be able to strike down or set aside secondary legislation which is incompatible with the Convention, unless the terms of the parent statute make this impossible. The courts can already strke down or set aside secondary legislation when they consider it to be outside the powers conferred by the statute under which it is made, and it is right that they should be able to do so when it is incompatible with the Convention rights and could have been framed differently.

Entrenchment

2.16 On one view, human rights legislation is so important that it should be given added protection from subsequent amendment or repeal. The Constitution of the United States of America, for example, guarantees rights which can be amended or repealed only by securing qualified majorities in both the House of Representatives and the Senate and among the States themselves. But an arrangement of this kind could not be reconciled with our own constitutional traditions, which allow any Act of Parliament to be amended or repealed by a subsequent Act of Parliament. We do not believe that it is necessary or would be desirable to attempt to devise such a special arrangement for this Bill.

Amending legislation

2.17 Although the Bill does not allow the courts to set aside Acts of Parliament, it will nevertheless have a profound impact on the way that legislation is interpreted and applied, and it will have the effect of putting the issues squarely to the Government and Parliament for further consideration. It is important to ensure that the Government and Parliament, for their part, can respond quickly. In the normal way, primary legislation can be amended only by further primary legislation, and this can take a long time. Given the volume of Government business, an early opportunity to legislate may not arise; and the process of legislating is itself protracted. Emergency legislation can be enacted very quickly indeed, but it is introduced only in the most exceptional circumstances.

2.18 The Bill provides for a fast-track procedure for changing legislation in response either to a declaration of incompatibility by our own higher courts or to a finding of a violation of the Convention in Strasbourg. The appropriate Government Minister will be able to amend the legislation by Order so as to make it compatible with the Convention. The Order will be subject to approval by both Houses of Parliament before taking effect, except where the need to amend the legislation is particularly urgent, when the Order will take effect immediately but will expire after a short period if not approved by Parliament.

2.19 There are already precedents for using secondary legislation to amend primary legislation in some circumstances, and we think the use of such procedure is acceptable in this context and would be welcome as a means of improving the observance of human rights. Plainly the Minister would have to exercise this power only in relation to the provisions which contravene the Convention, together with any necessary consequential amendments. In other words, Ministers would not have carte blanche to amend unrelated parts of the Act in which the breach is discovered.

Scotland

2.20 In Scotland, the position with regard to Acts of the Westminster Parliament will be the same as in England and Wales. All courts will be required to interpret the legislation in a way which is compatible with the Convention so far as possible. If a provision is found to be incompatible with the Convention, the Court of Session or the High Court will be able to make a declarator to that effect, but this will not affect the validity or continuing operation of the provision.

2.21 The position will be different, however, in relation to Acts of the Scottish Parliament when it is established. The Government has decided that the Scottish Parliament will have no power to legislate in a way which is incompatible with the Convention; and similarly that the Scottish Executive will have no power to make subordinate legislation or to take executive action which is incompatible with the Convention. It will accordingly be possible to challenge such legislation and actions in the Scottish courts on the ground that the Scottish Parliament or Executive has incorrectly applied its powers. If the challenge is successful then the legislation or action would be held to be unlawful. As with other issues concerning the powers of the Scottish Parliament there will be a procedure for inferior courts to refer such issues to the superior Scottish courts; and those courts in turn will be able to refer the matter to the Judicial Committee of the Privy Council. If such issues are decided by the superior Scottish courts, an appeal from their decision will be to the Judicial Committee. These arrangements are in line with the Government's general approach to devolution.

Wales

2.22 Similarly the Welsh Assembly will not have power to make subordinate legislation or take executive action which is incompatible with the Convention. It will be possible to challenge such legislation and action in the courts and for them to be quashed, on the ground that the Assembly has exceeded its powers.

Northern Ireland

2.23 Acts of the Westminster Parliament will be treated in the same way in Northern Ireland as in the rest of the United Kingdom. But Orders in Council and other related legislation will be treated as subordinate legislation. In other words, they will be struck down by the courts if they are incompatible with the Convention. Most such legislation is a temporary means of enacting legislation which would otherwise be done by measures of a devolved Northern Ireland legislature.

CHAPTER 3 IMPROVING COMPLIANCE WITH THE
CONVENTION RIGHTS

3.1   The enforcement of Convention rights will be a matter for the courts, whilst the Government and Parliament will have the different but equally important responsibility of revising legislation where necessary. But it is also highly desirable for the Government to ensure as far as possible that legislation which it places before Parliament in the normal way is compatible with the Convention rights, and for Parliament to ensure that the human rights implications of legislation are subject to proper consideration before the legislation in enacted.

Government legislation

3.2   The Human Rights Bill introduces a new procedure to make the human rights implications of proposed Government legislation more transparent. The responsible Minister will be required to provide a statement that in his or her view the proposed Bill is compatible with the Convention. The Government intends to include this statement alongside the Explanatory and Financial Memorandum which accompanies a Bill when it is introduced into each House of Parliament.

3.3   There may be occasions where such a statement cannot be provided, for example because it is essential to legislate on a particular issue but the policy in question requires a risk to be taken in relation to the Convention, or because the arguments in relation to the Convention issues raised are not clear-cut. In such cases, the Minister will indicate that he or she cannot provide a positive statement but that the Government nevertheless wishes Parliament to proceed to consider the Bill. Parliament would expect the Minister to explain his or her reasons during the normal course of the proceedings on the Bill. This will ensure that the human rights implications are debated at the earliest opportunity.

Consideration of draft legislation within Government

3.4   The new requirement to make a statement about the compliance of draft legislation with the Convention will have a significant and beneficial impact on the preparation of draft legislation within Government before its introduction into Parliament. It will ensure that all Ministers their departments and officials are fully seised of the gravity of the Convention's obligations in respect of human rights. But we also intend to strengthen collective Government procedures so as to ensure that a proper assessment is made of the human rights implications when collective approval is sought for a new policy, as well as when any draft Bill is considered by Ministers. Revised guidance to Departments on these procedures will, like the existing guidance be publicly available.

3.5   Some central coordination will also be extremely desirable in considering the approach to be taken to Convention points in criminal or civil proceedings or in proceedings for judicial review to which a Government department is a party.

This is likely to require an interdepartmental group of lawyers and administrators meeting on a regular basis to ensure that a consistent approach is taken and to ensure that developments in case law are well understood by all those in Government who are involved in proceeding on Convention points. We do not, however, see any need to make a particular Minister responsible for promoting human rights across Government, or to set up a separate new Unit for this purpose. The responsibility for complying with human rights requirements rests on the Government as a whole.

A Parliamentary Committee on Human Rights

3.6 *Bringing Rights Home* suggested that 'Parliament itself should play a leading role in protecting the rights which are at the heart of a parliamentary democracy'. How this is achieved is a matter for Parliament to decide, but in the Government's view the best course would be to establish a new Parliamentary Committee with functions relating to human rights. This would not require legislation or any change in Parliamentary procedure. There could be a Joint Committee of both Houses of Parliament or each House could have its own Committee; or there could be a Committee which met jointly for some purposes and separately for others.

3.7   The new Committee might conduct enquiries on a range of human rights issues relating to the Convention and produce reports so as to assist the Government and Parliament in deciding what action to take. It might also want to range more widely, and examine issues relating to the other international obligations of the United Kingdom such as proposals to accept new rights under other human rights treaties.

Should there be a Human Rights Commission?

3.8   *Bringing Rights Home* canvassed views on the establishment of a Human Rights Commission, and this possibility has received a good deal of attention. No commitment to establish a Commission was, however, made in the Manifesto on which the Government was elected. The Government's priority is implementation of its Manifesto commitment to give further effect to the Convention rights in domestic law so that people can enforce those rights in United Kingdom courts. Establishment of a new Human Rights Commission is not central to that objective and does not need to form part of the current Bill.

3.9   Moreover, the idea of setting up a new human rights body is not universally acclaimed. Some reservations have been expressed particularly from the point of view of the impact on existing bodies concerned with particular aspects of human rights, such as the Commission for Racial Equality and the Equal Opportunities Commission, whose primary concern is to protect the rights for which they were established. A quinquennial review is currently being conducted of the Equal Opportunities Commission, and the Government has also decided to establish a new Disability Rights Commission.

3.10   The Government's conclusion is that, before a Human Rights Commission could be established by legislation, more consideration needs to be given to how it would work in relation to such bodies, and to the new arrangements to be established for Parliamentary and Government scrutiny of human rights issues. This is necessary not only for the purposes of framing the legislation but also to justify the additional public expenditure needed to establish and run a new Commission. A range of organisational issues need more detailed consideration before the legislative and financial case for a new Commission is made, and there needs to be a greater degree of consensus on an appropriate model among existing human rights bodies.

3.11   However, the Government has not closed its mind to the idea of a new Human Rights Commission at some stage in the future in the light of practical experience of the working of the new legislation. If Parliament establishes a Committee on Human Rights, one of its main tasks might be to conduct an inquiry into whether a Human Rights Commission is needed and how it should operate. The Government would want to give full weight to the Committee's report in considering whether to create a statutory Human Rights Commission in future.

3.12   It has been suggested that a new Commission might be funded from non-Government sources. The Government would not wish to deter a move towards a non-statutory, privately financed body if its role was limited to functions such as public education and advice to individuals. However, a non-statutory body could not absorb any of the functions of the existing statutory bodies concerned with aspects of human rights.

CHAPTER 4 DEROGATIONS, RESERVATIONS AND OTHER PROTOCOLS

Derogations

4.1   Article 15 of the Convention permits a State to derogate from certain Articles of the Convention in time of war or other public emergency threatening the life of the nation. The United Kingdom has one derogation in place, in respect of art. 5(3) of the Convention.

4.2   The derogation arose from a case in 1988 in which the European Court of Human Rights held that the detention of the applicants in the case before it under the Prevention of Terrorism (Temporary Provisions) Act 1984 for more than four days constituted a breach of art. 5(3) of the Convention, because they had not been brought promptly before a judicial authority. The Government of the day entered a derogation following the judgment in order to preserve the Secretary of State's power under the Act to extend the period of detention of persons suspected of terrorism connected with the affairs of Northern Ireland for a total of up to seven days. The validity of the derogation was subsequently upheld by the European Court of Human Rights in another case in 1993.

4.3   We are considering what change might be made to the arrangements under the prevention of terrorism legislation. Substituting judical for executive authority for extensions, which would mean that the derogation could be withdrawn, would require primary legislation. In the meantime, however, the derogation remains necessary. The Bill sets out the text of the derogation, and art. 5(3) will have effect in domestic law for the time being subject to its terms.

4.4 Given our commitment to promoting human rights, however, we would not want the derogation to remain in place indefinitely without good reasons. Accordingly its effect in domestic law will be time-limited. If not withdrawn earlier, it will expire five years after the Bill comes into force unless both Houses of Parliament agree that it should be renewed and similarly thereafter. The Bill contains similar provision in respect of any new derogation which may be entered in future.

Reservations

4.5 Article 64 of the Convention allows a state to enter a reservation when a law in force is not in conformity with a Convention provision. The United Kingdom is a party to the First Protocol to the Convention, but has a reservation in place in respect of Article 2 of the Protocol. Article 2 sets out two principles. The first states that no person shall be denied the right to education. The second is that in exercising any functions in relation to education and teaching, the State shall respect the right of parents to ensure that such education and teaching is in conformity with their own religious and philosophical convictions. The reservation makes it clear that the United Kingdom accepts this second principle only so far as it is compatible with the provision of efficient instruction and training, and the avoidance of unreasonable public expenditure.

4.6 The reservation reflects the fundamental principle originally enacted in the Education Act 1944, and now contained in section 9 of the Education Act 1996, 'that pupils are to be educated in accordance with the wishes of their parents so far as that is compatible with the provision of efficient instruction and training and the avoidance of unreasonable public expenditure'. There is similar provision in Scottish legislation. The reservation does not affect the right to education in Article 2. Nor does it deny parents the right to have account taken of their religious or philosophical convictions. Its purpose is to recognise that in the provision of State-funded education a balance must be struck in some cases between the convictions of parents and what is educationally sound and affordable.

4.7 Having carefully considered this, the Government has concluded that the reservation should be kept in place. Its text is included in the Bill, and Article 2 of the First Protocol will have effect in domestic law subject to its terms.

4.8 Whilst derogations are permitted under the Convention only in times of war or other public emergency, and so are clearly temporary, there is no such limitation in respect of reservations. We do not therefore propose to make the effect of the reservation in domestic law subject to periodic renewal by Parliament, but the Bill requires the Secretary of State (the Secretary of State for Education and

Employment) to review the reservation every five years and to lay a report before Parliament.

Other Protocols

4.9   Protocols 4, 6 and 7 guarantee a number of rights additional to those in the original Convention itself and its First Protocol. These further rights have been added largely to reflect the wider range of rights subsequently included under the International Covenant on Civil and Political Rights. There is no obligation upon States who are party to the original Convention to accept these additional Protocols, but the Government has taken the opportunity to review the position of the United Kingdom on Protocols 4, 6 and 7.

4.10   Protocol 4 contains a prohibition on the deprivation of liberty on grounds of inability to fulfil contractual obligations; a right to liberty of movement; a right to non-expulsion from the home State; a right of entry to the State of which a person is a national; and a prohibition on the collective expulsion of aliens. These provisions largely reflect similar (but not identical) rights provided under the International Covenant on Civil and Political Rights. Protocol 4 was signed by the United Kingdom in 1963 but not subsequently ratified because of concerns about what is the exact extent of the obligation regarding a right of entry.

4.11   These are important rights, and we would like to see them given formal recognition in our law. But we also believe that existing laws in relation to different categories of British nationals must be maintained. It will be possible to ratify Protocol 4 only if the potential conflicts with our domestic laws can be resolved. This remains under consideration but we do not propose to ratify Protocol 4 at present.

4.12   Protocol 6 requires the complete abolition of the death penalty other than in time of war or imminent threat of war. It does not permit any derogation or reservation. The Protocol largely parallels the Second Optional Protocol to the International Covenant on Civil and Political Rights, which the United Kingdom has not accepted.

4.13   The death penalty was abolished as a sentence for murder in 1965 following a free vote in the House of Commons. It remains as a penalty for treason, piracy with violence, and certain armed forces offences. No execution for these offences has taken place since 1946, when the wartime Nazi propagandist William Joyce (known as Lord Haw-Haw) was hanged at Wandsworth prison. The last recorded execution for piracy was in 1830. Thus there might appear to be little difficulty in our ratifying Protocol 6. This would, however, make it impossible for a United Kingdom Parliament to reintroduce the death penalty for murder, short of denouncing the European Convention. The view taken so far is that the issue is not one of basic constitutional principle but is a matter of judgment and conscience to be decided by Members of Parliament as they see fit. For these reasons we do not propose to ratify Protocol 6 at present.

4.14   Protocol 7 contains a prohibition on the expulsion of aliens without a decision in accordance with the law or opportunities for review; a right to a review of conviction or sentence after criminal conviction; a right to compensation following a miscarriage of justice; a prohibition on double jeopardy in criminal cases; and a right to equality between spouses. These rights reflect similar rights protected under the International Covenant on Civil and Political Rights.

4.15   In general the provisions of Protocol 7 reflect principles already inherent in our law. In view of concerns in some of these areas in recent years, the Government believes that it would be particularly helpful to give these important principles the same legal status as other rights in the Convention by ratifying and incorporating Protocol 7. There is, however, a difficulty with this because a few provisions of our domestic law, for example in relation to the property rights of spouses, could not be interpreted in a way which in compatible with Protocol 7. The Government intends to legislate to remove these inconsistencies when a suitable opportunity occurs, and then to sign and ratify the Protocol.

4.16   The Secretary of State will be able to amend the Human Rights Act by Order so as to insert into it the rights contained in any Protocols to the Convention which the United Kingdom ratifies in future. The Order will be subject to approval by both Houses of Parliament. The Bill also enables any reservation to a Protocol to be added, but as with the existing reservation it will have to be reviewed every five years if not withdrawn earlier.

Appendix Four
Extracts from Hansard

This is a selection of some of the statements made during the Parliamentary debates on the Human Rights Act 1998 by introducing ministers. The extracts are given section by section in the following format:

Place, [Stage]
Hansard reference
Speaker: text

For example:

House of Commons, Committee Stage
Hansard HC, 20 May 1998, col. 981
The Secretary of State for the Home Department (Mr Jack Straw): . . .
I wish future Judicial Committees of the House of Lords luck in working through these debates. One sometimes wonders about the wisdom of the *Pepper* v *Hart* judgment in terms of the work that it has given the higher judiciary.

Unless the wording of a provision changed after a ministerial explanation was given, we have given final section numbers rather than clause numbers.

For reasons of space, we have only given the ministerial rationale underlying individual sections (and the ministerial understanding of the margin of appreciation) where it illustrates underlying policy motives, or may be admissible under the rule in *Pepper* v *Hart* [1993] AC 593. (See Preface, pp. xii and xiii.)

Other passages which may be of particular interest to practitioners are as follows:

(a)   The introduction by Lord Irvine of Lairg LC to the purposes of the Act and its place in the British constitution (Hansard HL, 3 November 1997, col. 1227–38).

(b)   The introduction by the Home Secretary (Jack Straw) to the purposes of the Act (Hansard HC, 16 February 1998, col. 769–82).

(c)   The introduction by the Parliamentary Under-Secretary of State for the Home Department (Mike O'Brien) to the purposes of the Act (Hansard HC, 16 February 1998, col. 858–61).

(d)   General remarks by Jack Straw in committee on 'the British approach' to incorporation (Hansard HC, 3 June 1998, col. 419 ff.)

(e)   Arguments in favour of the Act on second reading in the House of Lords by Lord Bingham of Cornhill CJ (Hansard HL, 3 November 1997, col. 1245–6). Lord Scarman (retired Law Lord and long-time advocate of incorporation) (Hansard HL, 3 November 1997, col. 1256) and Lord Cooke of Thordon (retired senior New Zealand judge who has sat on appellate committees of the House of Lords) (Hansard HL, 3 November 1997, col. 1271–3). Of particular interest is Lord Cooke's analysis of section 3 of the Act, and the difference it will make to statutory interpretation (at col. 1272–3):

> [Section 3] will require a very different approach to interpretation from that to which United Kingdom courts are accustomed. Traditionally, the search has been for the true meaning; now it will be for a possible meaning that would prevent the making of a declaration of incompatibility. . . . The shift of the criterion to a search for possible compatible meanings will confront the courts with delicate responsibilities. Even for lawyers, a must is a must. For surely the difference between mandatory and directory provisions can have no place in interpreting the Human Rights [Act], which will itself be primary legislation. Consider, say, an Act making a certain kind of disclosure a criminal offence, enacting one specific defence, but not specifically excluding a defence under art. 10 (freedom to impart information). Without expressing any opinion as to the outcome, one can see that there will be a new kind of problem. In effect, the courts are being asked to solve these problems by applying a rebuttable presumption in favour of the Convention rights.

LONG TITLE

Bill does not make European Convention 'part of our law' — meaning of 'give further effect'

House of Lords, Report Stage
Hansard HL, 29 January 1998, col. 421
The Lord Chancellor (Lord Irvine of Lairg): . . . The word 'further' is included in the Long Title because, in our national arrangements, the Convention can, and is, already applied in a variety of different circumstances and is relied on in a range of ways by our own courts.

The Bill will greatly increase the ability of our courts to enforce Convention rights, but it is not introducing a wholly new concept. As I have said before, the Bill as such does not incorporate Convention rights into domestic law but, in accordance with the language of the Long Title, it gives further effect in the United

Kingdom to Convention rights by requiring the courts in [s. 3(1)], 'So far as it is possible to do so' to construe — in the language of the statute, to read and give effect to — primary legislation and subordinate legislation in a way which is compatible with the Convention rights. That is an interpretative principle. . . .

I have to make this point absolutely plain. The European Convention on Human Rights under this [Act] is not made part of our law. The [Act] gives the European Convention on Human Rights a special relationship which will mean that the courts will give effect to the interpretative provisions to which I have already referred, but it does not make the Convention directly justiciable as it would be if it were expressly made part of our law. I want there to be no ambiguity about that. . . . [col. 422] The short point is that if the Convention rights were incorporated into our law, they would be directly justiciable and would be enforced by our courts. That is not the scheme of this [Act]. If the courts find it impossible to construe primary legislation in a way which is compatible with the Convention rights, the primary legislation remains in full force and effect. All that the courts may do is to make a declaration of incompatibility.

SECTION 1. THE CONVENTION AND THE FIRST PROTOCOL

Section 1 sets out which Convention rights are incorporated. Controversial issues were the non-incorporation of art. 13 and the addition, at a late stage, by a free vote in the House of Commons, of the Sixth Protocol. Only those matters are considered here.

Failure to incorporate art. 13

House of Lords, Second Reading
Hansard HL, 3 November 1997, col. 1308
The Parliamentary Under-Secretary of State, Home Office (Lord Williams of Mostyn): . . . Our view is, quite unambiguously, that art. 13 is met by the passage of the [Act].

House of Lords, Committee Stage
Hansard HL, 18 November 1997, col. 475
The Lord Chancellor: . . . The [Act] gives effect to art. 1 by securing to people in the United Kingdom the rights and freedoms of the Convention. It gives effect to art. 13 by establishing a scheme under which Convention rights can be raised before our domestic courts. To that end, remedies are provided in [s. 8]. If the concern is to ensure that the [Act] provides an exhaustive code of remedies for those whose Convention rights have been violated, we believe that [s. 8] already achieves that and that nothing further is needed.

We have set out in the [Act] a scheme to provide remedies for violation of Convention rights and we do not believe that it is necessary to add to it. We also believe that it is undesirable to provide for arts 1 and 13 in the [Act] in this way.

The courts would be bound to ask themselves what was intended beyond the existing scheme of remedies set out in the [Act]. It might lead them to fashion remedies other than the [s. 8] remedies, which we regard as sufficient and clear. We believe that [s. 8] provides effective remedies before our courts. . . .

Lord Lester of Herne Hill: Is it the intention of the Government that the courts should not be entitled to have regard to art. 13 and the case law of the Strasbourg Court on that article in cases where it would otherwise be relevant? . . . Is it the intention of the Government that in cases where the European Court has said that the right provision is art. 13 and not art. 6 our courts should wear blinkers and are not allowed to look at art. 13 or the Court's case law?

The Lord Chancellor: One always has in mind *Pepper* v *Hart* when one is asked questions of that kind. I shall reply as candidly as I may. [Section 2(1)] provides:

> A court or tribunal determining a question which has arisen under this Act in connection with a Convention right must take into account any . . . judgment, decision, declaration or advisory opinion of the European Court of Human Rights.

That means what it says. The court must take into account such material. . . .

My response to the second part of the question posed by the noble Lord, Lord Lester, is that the courts may have regard to art. 13. In particular, they may wish to do so when considering the very ample provisions of [s. 8(1)].

. . . to incorporate expressly art. 13 may lead to the courts fashioning remedies about which we know nothing other than the [s. 8] remedies which we regard as sufficient and clear. Until we are told in some specific respect how [s. 8] is or may reasonably be anticipated to be deficient we maintain our present position.

House of Commons, Committee Stage
Hansard HC, 20 May 1998, col. 979

Secretary of State for the Home Department (Mr Jack Straw): We decided it was inappropriate to include art. 13, for the following reasons.

First and foremost, it is the Bill that gives effect to art. 13, so there was an issue of duplication. The Bill sets out clearly how the Convention rights will be given further effect in our domestic law, and what remedies are to be available when a court or tribunal finds that a person has been the victim of an unlawful act. . . . In our judgment, [the existing provisions of the Act] afford ample protection for individuals' rights under the Convention. In particular, [s. 8(1)] gives the courts considerable scope for doing justice when unlawful acts have been committed. Indeed, no one has been able to suggest any respect in which the [Act] is deficient in providing effective remedies to those who have been victims of an unlawful act. . . . If we were to include art. 13 in the Bill in addition to the remedies provided in [ss. 3, 6, 7 and 8], the question would inevitably arise what the courts would make of the amendment, which, on the face of it, contains nothing new. I suggest that the amendment would either cause confusion or prompt the courts to act in ways not intended by the Bill — for example, by creating remedies beyond those available in s. 8. Whatever the outcome, the result would be undesirable. . . . [col. 981] The Convention has been international law for 50 years, and any tribunal will consider the bare text of any original Convention by considering the way in which its application has developed there is, indeed, a requirement to do so so, in practice, the courts must take account of the large body of Convention jurisprudence when considering remedies. Obviously, in doing so, they are bound to take judicial notice of art. 13, without specifically being bound by it.

That is my judgment about the way in which the law will work. I wish future Judicial Committees of the House of Lords luck in working through these debates. One sometimes wonders about the wisdom of the *Pepper* v *Hart* judgment in terms of the work that it has given the higher judiciary. It is a fine point, but since we saw that there was no purpose, and indeed that there were some dangers, in including art. 13, we thought that it was best omitted. . . . [col. 986] As far as I am concerned, we are indeed legislating by black-letter law on the face of the Bill. [col. 987] We could have a separate debate about the wisdom of the decision in *Pepper* v *Hart*: I know why the Judicial Committee made that decision and, to some extent, there is common sense in seeking to tease out the meaning of words where they are ambiguous, but I have always taken the view that what Parliament passes is not what Ministers say, but what is on the face of a Bill. That is of profound importance to the manner in which we make legislation.

Incorporation of arts. 1 and 2 of the Sixth Protocol

House of Lords, Report Stage
Hansard HL, 29 October 1998, col. 2084
Lord Williams of Mostyn: My Lords, I beg to move that the House do agree with the Commons in their Amendment [to add arts 1 and 2 of the Sixth Protocol to the list of Convention rights in sch. 1]. . . . that would make it impossible for Parliament to reintroduce the death penalty in future, except for acts committed in time of war or imminent threat of war, without denouncing the Convention itself. . . . [I]f those articles were added to the [Act], when we had not signed or ratified the sixth protocol, there would be a certain degree of lack of kilter with our international obligations. . . .

Amendment No. 54 inserts a new subsection into [s. 21 — interpretation] which provides that any liability to the death penalty under the service discipline Acts is to be treated as a liability to life imprisonment or some lesser penalty. This general statement will be supplemented by detailed amendments to the service discipline Acts when the next legislation to consolidate those Acts is announced.

Amendment No. 55 provides that the new subsection inserted by Amendment No. 54 comes into force, when the Human Rights Bill receives Royal Assent. . . . that is consistent with our intention to proceed without delay to sign and ratify the sixth protocol.

Amendment No. 57 provides that the new subsection inserted by Amendment No. 54 has effect in any place in which the service discipline Acts have effect. This is needed because the Acts, unlike the Human Rights Bill, are not limited in their territorial extent to the United Kingdom. It is consistent with our intention, subject to their agreement, to extend the ratification of the sixth protocol to the Channel Islands and the Isle of Man.

SECTION 2. INTERPRETATION OF CONVENTION RIGHTS

House of Lords, Second Reading
Hansard HL, 3 November 1997, col. 1230
The Lord Chancellor (Lord Irvine of Lairg): . . . [Section 2] requires courts in the United Kingdom to take account of the decisions of the Convention institutions in Strasbourg in their consideration of Convention points which come before them. It is entirely appropriate that our courts should draw on the wealth of existing jurisprudence on the Convention.

House of Commons, Second Reading
Hansard HC, 16 February 1998, col. 780
The Secretary of State for the Home Department (Mr Jack Straw): . . . [Section 2] ensures that, in giving effect to those rights, our domestic courts and tribunals have regard to Strasbourg jurisprudence.

Amendment seeking to make decisions of the European Convention bodies 'binding' undesirable

House of Lords, Report Stage
Hansard HL, 19 January 1998, col. 1270
The Lord Chancellor (Lord Irvine of Lairg): As other noble Lords have said, the word 'binding' is the language of strict precedent but the Convention has no rule of precedent. . . . We take the view that the expression 'take in account' is clear enough. Should a United Kingdom court ever have a case before it which is a precise mirror of one that has been previously considered by the European Court of Human Rights, which I doubt, it may be appropriate for it to apply the European court's findings directly to that case; but in real life cases are rarely as neat and tidy as that. The courts will often be faced with cases that involve factors perhaps specific to the United Kingdom which distinguish them from cases considered by the European court. . . . [col. 1271] it is important that our courts have the scope to apply that discretion so as to aid in the development of human rights law.

There may also be occasions when it would be right for the United Kingdom courts to depart from Strasbourg decisions. We must remember that the interpretation of the Convention rights develops over the years. Circumstances may therefore arise in which a judgment given by the European Court of Human Rights decades ago contains pronouncements which it would not be appropriate to apply to the letter in the circumstances of today in a particular set of circumstances affecting this country. The [Act] would allow our courts to use their common sense in applying the European Court's judgment to such a case. We feel that to accept this amendment removes from the judges the flexibility and discretion that they require in developing human rights law. . . . [Section 2] requires the courts to pay heed to all the judgments of the European Court of Human Rights regardless of whether they have been given in cases involving the United Kingdom.

SECTION 3. LEGISLATION

House of Lords, Second Reading
Hansard HL, 3 November 1997, col. 1230
The Lord Chancellor (Lord Irvine of Lairg): . . . [Section 3] provides that legislation, whenever enacted, must as far as possible be read and given effect in a way which is compatible with the Convention rights. This will ensure that, if it is possible to interpret a statute in two ways — one compatible with the Convention and one not — the courts will always choose the interpretation which is compatible. In practice, this will prove a strong form of incorporation . . . however, the Bill does not allow the courts to set aside or ignore Acts of Parliament. [Section 3] preserves the effect of primary legislation which is [col. 1231] incompatible with the Convention. It does the same for secondary legislation where it is inevitably incompatible because of the terms of the parent statute. . . .

[col. 1294] The [Act] sets out a scheme for giving effect to the Convention rights which maximises the protection to individuals while retaining the fundamental principle of Parliamentary sovereignty. [Section 3] is the central part of this scheme. [Section 3(1)] requires legislation to be read and given effect to so far as it is possible to do so in a way that is compatible with the Convention rights. [Section 3(2)] provides that where it is not possible to give a compatible construction to primary legislation or to subordinate legislation whose incompatibility flows from the terms of the parent Act, that does not affect its validity, continuing operation or enforcement. This ensures that the courts are not empowered to strike down Acts of Parliament which they find to be incompatible with the Convention rights. Instead, [s. 4] together with [s. 10] introduces a new mechanism through which the courts can signal to the Government that a provision of legislation is, in their view, incompatible. It is then for government and Parliament to consider what action should be taken. I believe that this will prove to be an effective procedure and it is also one which accords with our traditions of Parliamentary sovereignty. That is why the [Act] adopts it.

House of Commons, Second Reading
Hansard HC, 16 February 1998, col. 780
The Secretary of State for the Home Department (Mr Jack Straw): . . . [Section 3] provides that legislation, whenever enacted, must as far as possible be read and given effect in such a way as to be compatible with Convention rights. We expect that, in almost all cases, the courts will be able to interpret legislation

compatibly with the Convention. However, we need to provide for the rare cases where that cannot be done. Consistent with maintaining Parliamentary sovereignty, [section 3] therefore provides that if a provision of primary legislation cannot be interpreted compatibly with the Convention rights, that legislation will continue to have force and effect.

House of Commons, Committee Stage
Hansard HC, 3 June 1998, col. 421

The Secretary of State for the Home Department (Mr Jack Straw): . . . we want the courts to strive to find an interpretation of legislation that is consistent with Convention rights, so far as the plain words of the [col. 422] legislation allow, and only in the last resort to conclude that the legislation is simply incompatible with them. . . . there was a time when all the courts could do to divine the intention of Parliament was to apply themselves to the words on the face of any Act. Now, following *Pepper* v *Hart*, they are able to look behind that and, not least, to look at the words used by Ministers. I do not think the courts will need to apply themselves to the words that I am about to use, but, for the avoidance of doubt, I will say that it is not our intention that the courts, in applying [s. 3], should contort the meaning of words to produce implausible or incredible meanings. I am talking about plain words in what is actually a clear [Act] with plain language — with the intention of Parliament set out in Hansard, should the courts wish to refer to it. . . . Ever since the *Wednesbury* decision, the courts have chided others for being unreasonable, so it is difficult to imagine them not being reasonable. If we had used just the word 'reasonable', we would have created a subjective test. 'Possible' is different. It means, [col. 423] 'What is the possible interpretation? Let us look at this set of words and the possible interpretations.'

SECTIONS 4 AND 5. DECLARATIONS OF INCOMPATIBILITY

House of Lords, Second Reading
Hansard HL, 3 November 1997, col. 1231

The Lord Chancellor (Lord Irvine of Lairg): . . . [Section 4] provides for the rare cases where the courts may have to make declarations of incompatibility. Such declarations are serious. That is why [s. 5] gives the Crown the right to have notice of any case where a court is considering making a declaration of incompatibility and the right to be joined as a party to the proceedings, so that it can make representations on the point.

A declaration of incompatibility will not itself change the law. The statute will continue to apply despite its incompatibility. But the declaration is very likely to prompt the Government and Parliament to respond.

House of Commons, Second Reading
Hansard HC, 16 February 1997, col. 780

The Secretary of State for the Home Department (Mr Jack Straw): . . . A declaration of incompatibility will not affect the continuing validity of the legislation in question. That would be contrary to the principle of the [Act]. However, it will be a clear signal to Government and Parliament that, in the court's view, a provision of legislation does not conform to the standards of the Convention. To return to a matter that I discussed earlier, it is likely that the Government and Parliament would wish to respond to such a situation and would do so rapidly. We have discussed how that would operate and no doubt there will be further detailed discussions in committee on the floor of the House.

House of Commons, Third Reading
Hansard HC, 21 October 1998, col. 1306
Jack Straw: . . . The right hon. and learned Gentleman asked me what would happen with the lower courts, and whether they would follow the judgment. No, they would not, because [s. 4(6)] is clear; a declaration does not affect the validity, continuing operation or enforcement of the provisions in respect of which it is given. There is absolute clarity there. In a judicial and political sense, the status quo ante would apply. Then, obviously, the Government would have to consider, and in most cases they would consider the position pretty rapidly. No time limit is set down, but the reverse could not apply. We could not, for example, say that the declaration of incompatibility would have force unless or until the Government said the reverse. That would create considerable uncertainty.

SECTION 6. ACTS OF PUBLIC AUTHORITIES

House of Lords, Second Reading
Hansard HL, 16 November 1997, col. 1231
The Lord Chancellor (Lord Irvine of Lairg): . . . [Section 6] makes it unlawful for a public authority to act in a way which is incompatible with the Convention.

House of Commons, Second Reading
Hansard HC, 16 February 1998, col. 780
The Secretary of State for the Home Department (Mr Jack Straw): . . . [Section 6] makes it unlawful for public authorities to act in a way that is incompatible with a Convention right, unless they are required to do so to give effect to primary legislation.

House of Lords, Second Reading
Hansard HL, 16 November 1997, col. 1231
The Lord Chancellor (Lord Irvine of Lairg): . . . We decided . . . that a provision of this kind should apply only to public authorities, [col. 1232] however defined, and not to private individuals. . . . We also decided that we should apply the Bill to a wide rather than a narrow range of public authorities, so as to provide as much protection as possible to those who claim that their rights have been infringed.

[Section 6] is designed to apply not only to obvious public authorities such as government departments and the police, but also to bodies which are public in certain respects but not others. Organisations of this kind will be liable under [s. 6] of the Bill for any of their acts, unless the act is of a private nature. Finally, [Section 6] does not impose a liability on organisations which have no public functions at all.

House of Lords, Committee Stage
Hansard HL, 24 November 1997, col. 784

The Lord Chancellor: I want to tackle the concerns of the press directly. They are essentially twofold. First, will the courts develop a law of privacy, and, secondly, is the PCC itself to be regarded as a public authority which should act consistently with the convention? First, as I have often said, the judges are pen-poised regardless of incorporation of the convention to develop a right to privacy to be protected by the common law. This is not me saying so; they have said so. It must be emphasised that the judges are free to develop the common law in their own independent judicial sphere. What I say positively is that it will be a better law if the judges develop it after incorporation because they will have regard to arts 8 and 10, giving art. 10 its due high value. . . . [col. 785]

I would not agree with any proposition that the courts as public authorities will be obliged to fashion a law on privacy because of the terms of the Bill. That is simply not so. If it were so, whenever a law cannot be found either in the statute book or as a rule of common law to protect a convention right, the courts would in effect be obliged to legislate by way of judicial decision and to make one. That is not the true position. If it were — in my view, it is not — the courts would also have in effect to legislate where Parliament had acted, but incompatibly with the convention. Let us suppose that an Act of Parliament provides for detention on suspicion of drug trafficking but that the legislation goes too far and conflicts with art. 5. The court would so hold and would make a declaration of incompatibility. The scheme of the Bill is that Parliament may act to remedy a failure where the judges cannot.

In my opinion, the court is not obliged to remedy the failure by legislating via the common law either where a convention right is infringed by incompatible legislation or where, because of the absence of legislation — say, privacy legislation — a convention right is left unprotected. In my view, the courts may not act as legislators and grant new remedies for infringement of convention rights unless the common law itself enables them to develop new rights or remedies. I believe that the true view is that the courts will be able to adapt and develop the common law by relying on existing domestic principles in the laws of trespass, nuisance, copyright, confidence and the like, to fashion a common law right to privacy. . . . I repeat my view that any privacy law developed by the judges will be a better law after incorporation of the convention because the judges will have to balance and have regard to arts 10 and 8, giving art. 10 its due high value. What I have said is in accord with European jurisprudence.

I tend to believe that the important function of the PCC to adjudicate on complaints from the public about the press may well be held to be a function of a public nature, so that . . . the PCC might well be held to be a public authority under the Human Rights [Act]. [col. 796] . . . There are some bodies which are obviously public authorities such as the police, the courts, government departments and prisons. They are obviously public authorities under [s. 6(1)]. However, under [s. 6(3)(c)] the term 'public authority' includes, 'any person certain of whose functions are functions of a public nature'. . . . [One should] abstain from asking . . . the question: is this a public authority just looking at the body in the round? That is what [s. 6(1)] invites us to do. However, [s. 6(3)(c)] asks whether the body in question has certain functions — not all — which are functions of a public nature. If it has any functions of a public nature, it qualifies as a public authority. However, it is certain acts by public authorities which this Act makes unlawful. In [s. 6(5)] the [Act] provides: 'In relation to a particular act, a person is not a public authority by virtue only of subsection (3)(c) if the nature of the act is private'. Therefore Railtrack, as a public utility, obviously qualifies as a public authority because some of its functions, for example its functions in relation to safety on the railway, qualify it as a public authority. However, acts carried out in its capacity as a private property developer would no doubt be held by the courts to be of a private nature and therefore not caught by the [Act].

. . . we took a policy decision to avoid a list. . . . There are obvious public authorities — I have mentioned some — which are covered in relation to the whole of their functions by [s. 6(1)]. Then there are some bodies some of whose functions are public and some private. If there are some public functions the body qualifies as a public authority but not in respect of acts which are of a private nature. Those statutory principles will have to be applied case by case by the courts when issues arise.

What we have sought to do in [s. 6] is to set out a principle: first, that the effects of [ss. 6 to 8] should apply in the first place to bodies which are quite plainly public authorities such as government departments; and, secondly, to other bodies whose functions include functions of a public nature, and therefore the focus should be on their functions and not their nature as an authority. In the latter case the provisions of the Bill would not apply to the private acts of the bodies in question. That is the principled approach that we have chosen.

House of Lords, Committee Stage
Hansard HL, 24 November 1997, col. 758
The Parliamentary Under-Secretary of State, Home Office (Lord Williams of Mostyn): . . . 'public authority' is plainly defined in [s. 6]. . . . one will be dealing with two types of public authority — those which everyone would recognise as being plainly public authorities in the exercise of their functions, and those public authorities which are public authorities because, in part of their functions, they carry out what would be regarded as public functions. Examples vary, but I believe that the courts will have in mind changing social economic and cultural conditions when they come to consider particular decisions on particular aspects of a public authority.

. . . [Section 6(3)(c)] provides that a 'public authority' includes, 'any person certain of whose functions are of a public nature'. [Section 6(5)] provides that: 'In relation to a particular act, a person is not a public authority by virtue only of subsection (3)(c) if the nature of the act is private'. I believe that my noble and learned friend the Lord Chancellor gave an illustration on an earlier occasion. For example, Railtrack has statutory public powers and functions as the safety regulatory authority; but, equally, it may well carry out private transactions, such as the disposal of, the acquisition of, or the development of property.

If one follows the scheme through, we suggest that it is perfectly capable of being understood. The amendment would exempt from the prohibition in [col. 759] [s. 6(1)] a public authority falling within [s. 6(3)] in respect of its private acts. However, I venture to suggest to the Committee that that is already achieved, we say satisfactorily, by subsection (5). The other public authorities specified in [s. 6(3)] are courts and tribunals which, we think, are in a very similar position to obvious public authorities, such as government departments, in that all their acts are to be treated as being of such a public nature as to engage the convention.

House of Commons, Second Reading
Hansard HC, 16 February 1998, col. 775

The Secretary of State for the Home Department (Mr Jack Straw): . . . the media and the Churches . . . have concerns that centre on the provisions of [s. 6], relating to public authorities, so I must briefly explain the principles underlying that clause.

Under the convention, the Government are answerable in Strasbourg for any acts or omissions of the state about which an individual has a complaint under the convention. The Government have a direct responsibility for core bodies, such as central Government and the police, but they also have a responsibility for other public authorities, in so far as the actions of such authorities impinge on private individuals.

The Bill had to have a definition of a public authority that went at least as wide and took account of the fact that, over the past 20 years, an increasingly large number of private bodies, such as companies or charities, have come to exercise public functions that were previously exercised by public authorities. Under United Kingdom domestic common law, such bodies have increasingly been held to account under the processes of judicial review. . . . it was not practicable to list all the bodies to which the Bill's provisions should apply. Nor would it have been wise to do so. What was needed instead was a statement of principle to which the courts could give effect. [Section 6] therefore adopts a non-exhaustive definition of a public authority. Obvious public authorities, such as central government and the police, are caught in respect of everything they do. Public — but not private — acts of bodies that have a mix of public and private functions are also covered.

House of Commons, Second Reading
Hansard HC, 16 February 1998, col. 860

Sir Brian Mawhinney: Does a body that spends taxpayers' money, or fulfils a statutory function, or has Government appointees on its governing body constitute a public authority for the purposes of the Bill?

The Parliamentary Under-Secretary of State for the Home Department (Mr Mike O'Brien): That will be a matter for the courts, but it would appear to be likely to be so.

Definition of persons for s. 6(3)

House of Lords, Committee Stage
Hansard HL, 24 November 1997, col. 803
Lord Williams of Mostyn: . . . [Section 6(3)(c)] refers to 'any person'. . . . the term is well known as a term of art in our law. It is defined in the Interpretation Act 1978 and is relied upon throughout the statute book as including any person or body of persons corporate or unincorporate. I suggest that that is clearly wide enough to cover the natural or legal person to which the amendment refers.

Status of media bodies

House of Commons, Second Reading
Hansard HC, 16 December 1998, col. 778
Mr David Ruffley (Bury St Edmunds): In the context of arts 8 and 10, would the BBC and independent television companies be public authorities for the purposes of [s. 6]?
The Secretary of State for the Home Department (Mr Jack Straw): That is ultimately a matter for the courts, but our judgment is that the BBC will be regarded as a public authority under [s. 6]; independent television companies will not, but the Independent Television Commission will be.

Parliamentary sovereignty

House of Commons, Second Reading
Hansard HC, 16 February 1998, col. 773
The Secretary of State for the Home Department (Mr Jack Straw): The [Act] makes the position clear, in [s. 6(3)] and elsewhere. [Section 6] excludes the Houses of Parliament from the category of public authorities, for very good reasons. What the [Act] makes clear is that Parliament is supreme, and that if Parliament wishes to maintain the position enshrined in an Act that it has passed, but which is incompatible with the convention in the eyes of a British court, it is that Act which will remain in force.

There is, however, a separate question, which is why, in most instances, Parliament and Government will wish to recognise the force of a declaration of incompatibility by the High Court. Let us suppose that a case goes to Strasbourg, where the European Court decides that an action by the British Government, or the British Parliament, is outwith the convention. According to 50 years of practice on both sides, we always put the action right, and bring it into line with the convention. One of the questions that will always be before Government, in practice, will be, 'Is it sensible to wait for a further challenge to Strasbourg, when the British courts have declared the provision to be outwith the convention?'

House of Commons, Committee Stage
Hansard HC, 20 May 1998, col 1018
The Secretary of State for the Home Department (Mr Jack Straw): There will be occasions — it is the nature of British society — on which various institutions that are private in terms of their legal personality carry out public functions. That includes the churches in the narrow circumstances that I have described. I would suggest that it also includes the Jockey Club. . . . The Jockey Club is a curious body; it is entirely private, but exercises public functions in some respects, and to those extents, but to no other, it would be regarded as falling within [s. 6].

SECTION 7. PROCEEDINGS

'Victims', standing and third party interventions

House of Lords, Second Reading
Hansard HL, 3 November 1997, col. 1232
The Lord Chancellor (Lord Irvine of Lairg): If people believe that their convention rights have been infringed by a public authority, what can they do about it? Under [s. 7] they will be able to rely on convention points in any legal proceedings involving a public authority; for example as part of a defence to criminal or civil proceedings, or when acting as plaintiff in civil proceedings, or in seeking judicial review, or on appeal. They will also be able to bring proceedings against public authorities purely on convention grounds even if no other cause of action is open to them.

House of Commons, Second Reading
Hanard HC, 16 February 1998, col. 780
The Secretary of State for the Home Department (Mr Jack Straw): . . . [Section 7] enables individuals who believe that they have been a victim of an unlawful act of a public authority to rely on the convention rights in legal proceedings. They may do so in a number of ways: by bringing proceedings under the [Act] in an appropriate court or tribunal; in seeking judicial review; as part of a defence against a criminal or civil action brought against them by a public authority; or in the course of an appeal. [Section 7] ensures that an individual will always have a means by which to raise his or her convention rights. It is intended that existing court procedures will, wherever possible, be used for that purpose.

House of Commons, Second Reading
Hansard HC, 16 February 1998, col. 856
The Parliamentary Under-Secretary of State for the Home Department (Mr Mike O'Brien): . . . My hon. Friend . . . asked us to consider allowing organisations that are not themselves victims to bring class actions and to anticipate issues. We considered doing that, but decided to follow the convention practice and enable victims of breaches to raise issues as they occur.

Effect of Section 7 rules on standing and third-party interventions

House of Lords, Second Reading
Hansard HL, 24 November 1997, col. 830
The Lord Chancellor (Lord Irvine of Lairg): The purpose of the [Act] is to give greater effect in our domestic law to the convention rights. It is in keeping with this approach that persons should be able to rely [col. 831] on the convention rights before our domestic courts in precisely the same circumstances as they can rely upon them before the Strasbourg institutions. The wording of [s. 7] therefore reflects the terms of the convention, which stipulates that petitions to the European Commission (or to the European Court once the Eleventh Protocol comes into force) will be ruled inadmissible unless the applicant is the victim of the alleged violation.

I acknowledge that a consequence of that approach is that a narrower test will be applied for bringing applications by judicial review on convention grounds than will continue to apply in applications for judicial review on other grounds. But interest groups will still be able to provide assistance to victims who bring cases under the [Act] and to bring cases directly where they themselves are victims of an unlawful act.

I also point out that [s. 7], consistently with the position in Strasbourg, also treats as victims those who are faced with the threat of a public authority proposing to act in a way which would be unlawful under [s. 6(1)]. So potential victims are included. Interest groups will similarly be able to assist potential victims to bring challenges to action which is threatened before it is actually carried out.

Lord Goodhart: Can the noble and learned Lord the Lord Chancellor say what is the position of a public interest group which, having perfectly properly brought proceedings under [s. 11] of the [Act] on grounds [col. 832] which do not involve convention rights, then finds that in those same proceedings it is unable to raise issues of convention rights because of [s. 7]?

The Lord Chancellor: . . . I do not believe, for reasons I shall explain in a moment, that that consequence will follow.

. . . Essentially we believe the victim/potential victim test to be right. If there is unlawful action or if unlawful action is threatened, then there will be victims or potential victims who will complain and who will in practice be supported by interest groups. If there are no victims, the issue is probably academic and the courts should not be troubled.

We are right to mirror the law as Strasbourg applies it.

. . . in relation to third-party intervention. The European Court of Human Rights rules of procedure allow non-parties such as national and international non-governmental organisations to make written submissions in the form of a brief. There is no reason why any change to primary legislation in this [Act] is needed to allow the domestic courts to develop a similar practice in human rights cases, which is the answer to the noble Lord's question on how I would respond to the point that an interest group would have the right to be heard in a judicial review case under the English domestic test but that, if there was not a victim, could the individual interest group be heard on the convention point? So now . . . I address an answer to that question.

This is a development — that is to say, allowing third parties to intervene and be heard — which has already begun in the higher courts of this country in public law cases. Provisions as to standing are quite different. They determine who can become parties to the proceedings. The standing rule which the Bill proposes in relation to convention cases *simpliciter* is identical to that operated at Strasbourg; and why not? Is that not right in principle? It would not, however, prevent the acceptance by the courts in this country of non-governmental organisational briefs here any more than it does in Strasbourg.

Your Lordships' House, in its judicial capacity, has recently given leave for non-governmental organisations to intervene and file amicus briefs. It has done that in [col. 833] *R* v *Khan* for the benefit of Liberty and it has done that in *R* v *Secretary of State for the Home Department, ex parte Venables* for the benefit of Justice. So it appears to me . . . that the natural position to take is to adopt the victim test as applied by Strasbourg when complaint is made of a denial of convention rights, recognising that our courts will be ready to permit amicus written briefs from non-governmental organisations; that is to say briefs, but not to treat them as full parties. [col. 834] . . . [Section 7(1)(b)] does not touch a third party who has not *ex hypothesi* been the victim of the infringement of a convention right. It in no way precludes a third party from making submissions about the implication of convention rights in written briefs if a written brief is invited or accepted by the court, as I believe will happen.

As regards oral interventions by a third party, I dare say that the courts will be equally hospitable to oral interventions provided that they are brief.

. . . It is no part of the intention of this [Act] to alter the standing rules in relation to judicial review in either England or Scotland. It is part of the intention of this [Act] to import the Strasbourg victim test in relation to complaints based solely on denial of convention rights.

House of Commons, Committee Stage
Hansard HC, 20 May 1998, col. 1084
The Parliamentary Under-Secretary of State for the Home Department (Mr Mike O'Brien): . . . It is clear that [in s. 7(5)] we are appropriating the text of art. 34 and the jurisprudence that goes with it. The intention is that a victim under the [Act] should be in the same position as a victim in Strasbourg. A local [col. 1085] authority cannot be a victim under s. 7 because it cannot be a victim in Strasbourg under current Strasbourg jurisprudence. . . . On the definition, the convention provides that

The Commission may receive petitions . . . from any person, non-governmental organisation or group of individuals claiming to be a victim of a violation by one of the High Contracting Parties of the rights set forth in this Convention.

Applying the victim requirement, the basic approach of the Commission and the Court has been to require that the applicant must claim to be directly affected in some way by the matter complained of. In some cases, they have interpreted fairly flexibly the requirement for the applicant to be directly affected, although the jurisprudence on the issue is not always entirely consistent. . . . Applications have been allowed not only by the person immediately affected — sometimes referred to as the direct victim — but by indirect victims. Where there has been an alleged violation of the right to life and the direct victim is dead, for example, close relatives of the deceased can be treated as victims on the basis that they were indirectly affected by the alleged violation. . . . Obviously, [family members] can be victims in appropriate circumstances. For example, a decision to deport someone might allow the family of the person to claim to be a victim of a violation of article 8 — the right to respect for family life. . . . I can confirm that we have no intention of restricting guardians *ad litem* or [col. 1086] others who could normally undertake cases from doing so. Likewise, a case can be brought on behalf of a dead victim by his or her family or relatives. The best known case, of which we have all heard, is the 'Death on the Rock' case, brought on behalf of a dead IRA terrorist shot in Gibraltar. That is the sort of area that we are considering. A person may be able to claim that he or she is directly affected as a consequence of a violation of the rights of someone else. Where complaints are brought by persons threatened by deportation, that may arise.

. . . Interest groups, such as professional associations and NGOs, can bring an application in Strasbourg only if they can demonstrate that they themselves are victims of a breach — that is, that they are in some way affected by the measure complained of. It is not enough that the actual victim, whether a member of the organisation or not, consents to them acting on his behalf. In *B v United Kingdom*, both Mrs B and the Society for the Protection of the Unborn Child brought an application complaining of the way in which the law affected electoral expenses. The Commission ruled the application by SPUC inadmissible because it was not directly affected by the law — only Mrs B had been prosecuted. On the other hand, in *Council of Civil Service Unions v United Kingdom*, the Commission accepted that the CCSU was itself a victim of the GCHQ ban and could therefore bring an application, although it was rejected on different grounds. An NGO may represent its members in certain contexts and, in that case, it needs to identify them and produce the evidence of authority. In such circumstances, the NGO does not, however, thereby become a party itself.

Our courts will develop their own jurisprudence on the issue, taking account of Strasbourg cases and the Strasbourg jurisprudence. As a Government, our aim is to grant access to victims.

House of Commons, Committee Stage
Hansard HC, 24 June 1998, col. 1083
The Parliamentary Under-Secretary of State for the Home Department (Mr Mike O'Brien): . . . The purpose of the [Act] is to give effect in our domestic

law to the Convention rights. It is in keeping with that approach that people should be able to rely on those rights before our courts in the same circumstances as they can rely on them before the Strasbourg institutions. [Section 7] accordingly seeks to mirror the approach taken by Strasbourg — reliance on the Convention rights is restricted to victims or potential victims of unlawful acts and the definition of a victim for this purpose is tied to art. 34 of the Convention as amended by the 11th protocol. . . .

I acknowledge that, as a consequence, a narrower test will be applied for bringing applications by judicial review on Convention grounds than in applications for judicial review on other grounds. However, interest groups will still be able to provide assistance to victims who bring cases under the Bill, including the filing of amicus briefs. Interest groups will also be able to bring cases directly where they are victims of an unlawful act.

I do not believe that the different tests for Convention and non-Convention cases will cause undue difficulty for the courts, or prevent interest groups from helping individuals who are victims of unlawful acts.

. . . the [Act] does not prevent interest groups from providing assistance to a victim once a case is brought.

Limitation periods

(Section 7(5) of the Act was added by amendment during the House of Commons committee stage.)

House of Commons, Committee Stage
Hansard HC, 20 May 1998, col. 1094
The Parliamentary Under-Secretary of State for the Home Department (Mr Mike O'Brien): . . . proceedings brought on Convention grounds alone and not under any pre-existing cause of action . . . should be no different from other civil proceedings in having a limitation period. . . . our amendment relates only to proceedings under [s. 7(1)(a)]. If a plaintiff proceeded under [s. 7(1)(b)] — that is to say, he brought proceedings under an existing cause of action and relied on his Convention rights as an additional argument in support of his case — the limitation period would be the one that applies in the normal way to the existing cause of action.

The Government amendment provides that proceedings under [s. 7(1)(a)] must be brought within one year, beginning with the date on which the act complained of took place, or within such longer period as the court or tribunal considers equitable, having regard to all the circumstances. However, that time limit is subject to any stricter time limit in relation to the procedure in question. The most obvious such case is judicial review. Assuming that the new rules of court that will be needed for the [Act] provide that a procedure analogous to judicial review may [col. 1095] be used for cases under [s. 7(1)(a)], it is reasonable that the time limit for that procedure — which is three months — should continue to apply. It would not be right for applicants who choose to bring their claims by way of judicial review to benefit from the longer 12-month period proposed for claims under the [Act]. . . . There is no off-the-shelf answer to the question of how long the limitation period for claims under [s. 7(1)(a)] should be. What we have tried to do in our amendment is to strike a balance between the legitimate needs of the plaintiff and the legitimate needs of the defendant, which is what all limitation periods should do. . . . We believe that the right balance is provided by a 12-month period, with a power to extend it for the benefit of the complainant. . . . We recognise . . . that there may be circumstances where a rigid one-year cut-off could lead to injustice. [Section 7(5)] does not therefore seek to provide a rigid limit, but enables a court to extend the period where it is appropriate to do so. There will be cases in which an individual has a good reason for delay. In judicial review cases, for example, the courts have extended time where the applicant has been seeking redress by other proper means, such as by pursuing internal grievance procedures, or where he has had to apply for legal aid. I have no doubt that the courts will continue to exercise their discretion so as to prevent prejudice to one party or the other where an application is made to extend time. . . . We do not wish to narrow the range of circumstances which might influence the court. . . . [col. 1097] It is not our intention to create a vast array of novel features that would allow litigants to pursue cases in courts in a way that the courts and Parliament had not intended. However, someone with a genuine human rights grievance will be entitled to pursue it under [s. 7(1)(a)], whether or not he is within the time limit for judicial review. We accept that that should be so. The . . . one-year time limit for [s. 7(1)(a)] [is] so that the courts have time to make a judgment. We have not sought to constrain that time too much because [s. 7(5)(b)] allows the courts to decide when they wish to go beyond the 12-month period, should it be equitable to do so.

We are conscious that it is important that the person is allowed to pursue any action under [s. 7(1)(a)]. We do not want to create an artificial time limit of three months . . . without giving the level of flexibility that is needed [which] would tie the procedure too tightly to the judicial review procedure. The courts will develop their own jurisprudence on this issue, over time.

SECTION 8. REMEDIES

House of Lords, Second Reading
Hansard HL, 3 November 1997, col. 1232
The Lord Chancellor (Lord Irvine of Lairg): . . . If a court or tribunal finds that a public authority has acted in a way which is incompatible with the Convention . . . [u]nder [s. 8] it may provide whatever remedy is available to it and which seems just and appropriate. That might include awarding damages against the public authority.

House of Lords, Committee Stage
Hansard HL, 24 November 1997, col. 844

The Lord Chancellor: [Section 8] provides the courts and tribunals with wide powers to grant such relief or remedy which they consider just and appropriate where they find that a public authority has acted unlawfully by virtue of [s. 6(1)] of the [Act]. [Section 8(2) and (3)] . . . [is] a comprehensive and comprehensible code. However, it is necessary to put down certain limits on what remedies a court or tribunal can provide. Subsection (2) . . . provides one such restriction. . . . [quoted] . . . Quite clearly, this means that a criminal court will not be able to award damages for a Convention breach, even if it currently has the power to make a compensation order unless it also has the power to award damages in civil proceedings. . . .

[col. 855] So as to make the intention plain, it is not the [Act's] aim that, for example, the Crown Court should be able to make an award of damages where it finds, during the course of a trial, that a violation of a person's Convention rights has occurred. We believe that it is appropriate for an individual who considers that his rights have been infringed in such a case to pursue any matter of damages through the civil courts where this type of issue is normally dealt with; in other words, to pursue the matter in the courts that are accustomed to determining whether it is necessary and appropriate to award damages and what the proper amount should be. For that reason, we regard the inclusion of subsection (2) as an entirely proper part of the scheme.

We say that the Crown Court, in cases of crime, should not award damages. The remedy that the defendant wants in a criminal court is not to be convicted. We see very considerable practical difficulties about giving a new power to award damages to a criminal court in Convention cases. It would seem to me to open up the need for representation in the Crown Court to any person who it might appear in the course of criminal proceedings might be at risk of damages. We believe that that would be potentially disruptive of a criminal trial. Similarly, a magistrates' court is a criminal court. . . . We believe that it is appropriate that the civil courts, which traditionally make awards of damages, should, alone, be enabled to make awards of damages in these Convention cases.

House of Lords, Committee Stage
Hansard HL, 18 November 1997, col. 479
The Lord Chancellor (Lord Irvine of Lairg): . . . I cannot conceive of any state of affairs in which an English court, having held an Act to be unlawful because of its infringement of a Convention right, would under [s. 8(1)], be disabled from giving an effective remedy. I believe that the English law is rich in remedies and I cannot conceive of a case in which English law under [s. 8(1)] would be unable to provide an effective remedy.

However, during the earlier course of the debate I did not say that art. 13 was incorporated. The debate is about the fact that it is not incorporated. . . . in my view the English courts . . . would be able to have regard to art. 13.

House of Lords, Report Stage
Hansard HL, 19 January 1998, col. 1266
The Lord Chancellor (Lord Irvine of Lairg): My Lords, I have not the least idea what the remedies the courts might develop outside [s. 8] could be if art. 13 was

included. . . . [Section 8(1)] is of the widest amplitude. No one is [col. 1267] contending that it will not do the job. When we have challenged the proponents of the amendment on a number of occasions in Committee to say how [s. 8] might not do the job, they have been unable to offer a single example. Therefore, the argument is all one way. What we have done is sufficient.

House of Commons, Second Reading
Hansard HC, 16 February 1998, col. 780
The Secretary of State for the Home Department (Mr Jack Straw): . . . [Section] 8 deals with remedies. . . . If a court or tribunal finds that a public authority has acted unlawfully, it may grant whatever remedy is available to it that it considers just and appropriate.

House of Common, Committee Stage
Hansard HC, 20 May 1998, col. 979
Mr Garnier: Will the right hon. Gentleman give one or two examples of the remedies he envisages [under art. 13] that would go beyond those set out in [s. 8]?
The Secretary of State for the Home Department (Mr Jack Straw): In considering article 13, the courts could decide to grant damages in more circumstances than we had envisaged. We had to consider that matter carefully, because of the effect on the public purse. . . . We had to think carefully about the scope of the remedies that we should provide.

House of Commons, Committee Stage
Hansard HC, 24 June 1998, col. 1113
The Parliamentary Under-Secretary of State for the Home Department (Mr Mike O'Brien): . . . The Civil Liability (Contribution) Act 1978 provides a right to contribution when more than one person is liable for the same damage. We see no reason why that standard provision should not apply when damages are awarded against a public authority under [s. 8] of the [Act]. . . . the terms of the 1978 Act . . . apply to the award of such damages. . . .
 [col. 1114] the requirement to take into account the principles applied in Strasbourg . . . allows the court to have regard to the conduct of the applicant.

SECTION 10. REMEDIAL ORDERS

(In the original Bill, the provisions which were eventually enacted as s. 10 and sch. 2 were set out as clauses 10, 11 and 12. The circumstances in which a remedial order could be made was also amended during the passage of the Bill, so that this may now be done only in 'compelling' circumstances. Because of these substantial changes, references in relation to this section have been retained as references to clauses of the Bill except where referring to language which was adopted as part of the final section, where references have been given to the final provision).

House of Lords, Second Reading
Hansard HL, 3 November 1997, col. 1231
The Lord Chancellor (Lord Irvine of Lairg): . . . if legislation has been declared incompatible, a prompt Parliamentary remedy should be available. Clauses 10 to 12 of the Bill provide how that is to be achieved. A Minister of the Crown will be able to make what is to be known as a remedial order. The order will be available in response to a declaration of incompatibility by the higher courts. It will also be available if legislation appears to a Minister to be incompatible because of a finding by the European Court of Human Rights.

We recognise that a power to amend primary legislation by means of a statutory instrument is not a power to be conferred or exercised lightly. Those clauses therefore place a number of procedural and other restrictions on its use. First, a remedial order must be approved by both Houses of Parliament. That will normally require it to be laid in draft and subject to the affirmative resolution procedure before it takes effect. In urgent cases, it will be possible to make the order without it being approved in that way, but even then it will cease to have effect after 40 days unless it is approved by Parliament. So we have built in as much Parliamentary scrutiny as possible.

In addition, the power to make a remedial order may be used only to remove an incompatibility or a possible incompatibility between legislation and the Convention. It may therefore be used only to protect human rights, not to infringe them. And the Bill also specifically provides that no person is to be guilty of a criminal offence solely as a result of any retrospective effect of a remedial order.

House of Commons, Second Reading
Hansard HC, 16 February 1998, col. 773
The Secretary of State for the Home Department (Mr Jack Straw): . . . occasions on which the courts will declare an Act of this Parliament to be incompatible are rare; there will be very few such cases. Secondly, the purpose of remedial action is to try to resolve the current paralysis, which is to nobody's advantage. It is not to take away anyone's rights; it is to confer rights.

Rationale behind and intended effect of s. 10(1)(a)

House of Lords, Report Stage
Hansard HL, 29 January 1998, col. 393
Lord Williams of Mostyn : . . . Amendments Nos. 41 — [the words after 'right' in s. 10(1)(a)] and 42 [which inserted the words after 'rights' in s. 10(1)(b)] place limits on the power of a Minister to make a remedial order under Clause 10 following a declaration of Convention incompatibility by a court. Both are specific responses to concerns expressed by your Lordships in Committee. . . .

House of Commons, Committee Stage
Hansard HC, 20 June 1998, col. 42
The Secretary of State for the Home Department (Mr Jack Straw): . . . [O]ur intention is not that the procedure under clause 10 should be used to by-pass

the will of the House, but simply to deal with practical problems that may arise.
. . . Even on the most dismal interpretation of clause 10, the will of the House still
prevails. It may be a truncated procedure, but it certainly does not give the courts
the power to say what the law of the land should be . . .

Meaning of 'compelling' in s. 10(2)

House of Commons, Committee Stage
Hansard HC, 24 June 1998, col. 1140
The Secretary of State for the Home Department (Mr Jack Straw): I am
answering ad lib and without the benefit of a legal dictionary, but the situation that
I described in the Chahal case, where the liberty of a subject would be adversely
affected by a delay in producing primary legislation, was a compelling case. I am
not certain that it would be an exceptional case, because one could ask, 'To what
is it exceptional?' but it would certainly be a compelling case. Frankly, only in
that situation would remedial orders be necessary and appropriate.

House of Commons, Third Reading
Hansard HC, 21 October 1998, col. 1300
The Secretary of State for the Home Department (Mr Jack Straw): The
Government thought — there was no great argument about the matter, but it was
important that we should deal with all the arguments — that it was important to
enshrine Parliament's sovereignty in the Bill. We therefore developed the scheme
of declarations of incompatibility. We did not propose that the Judicial Committee
of the House of Lords should have the power to override Acts of Parliament by
stating that, because they were incompatible with the Convention, they were
unenforceable and of no effect.

[col. 1301] We said that the Judicial Committee of the House of Lords would
be able to declare whether, in its opinion, an Act of Parliament was incompatible
with the Convention, and subsequently to refer the matter back to the Government,
which is answerable to Parliament. In the overwhelming majority of cases,
regardless of which party was in government. I think that Ministers would examine
the matter and say, 'A declaration of incompatibility has been made, and we shall
have to accept it. We shall therefore have to remedy the defeat in the law spotted
by the Judicial Committee of the House of Lords.' Therefore — as has been
discussed in previous debates, and will be discussed again today — we have
included in the Bill procedures for remedial orders. It is also always open to
Ministers to introduce amending legislation in the normal way.

It is possible that the Judicial Committee of the House of Lords could make a
declaration that, subsequently, Ministers propose, and Parliament accepts, should
not be accepted. . . . the issue of abortion . . . provides a good example. . . .

Mr Mike O'Brien: [col. 1330] The requirement for compelling reasons in
[s. 10(2)] is itself a response to concern expressed here and in another place about

the remedial order provisions. It is there to make it absolutely clear that a remedial order is not a routine response in preference to fresh primary legislation. We would not want to go further . . . and limit 'compelling reasons' to [likely jeopardy to national security, public health or the liberty of the individual]. There may be other circumstances that constitute compelling reasons sufficient to justify a remedial order: for example, a decision of the higher courts in relation to basic provisions of criminal procedure affecting the way in which, perhaps, all criminal cases must be handled. An example is a provision that might invalidate a crucial part of the codes of practice under the Police and Criminal Evidence Act 1984, or provisions relating to the detention of suspects. Therefore, there are a number of issues where we would want to proceed with care. We also might need to respond very quickly simply to avoid the criminal justice system in such cases either collapsing or not being able to deliver justice and proper convictions.

'Compelling' is a strong word. We see no need to define it by reference to particular categories. In both the outstanding cases . . . put to me, our view is likely to be that those would not create the compelling reasons that would justify a remedial order. In any event, on those issues — electoral law and chastising children — everyone would expect primary legislation rather than a remedial order. . . .

[col. 1331] It would be open to the Government to take no action in response to a declaration of incompatibility . . . but, where a declaration is made, a Government who are committed to promoting human rights, as we are, will want to do something about the law in question. It is possible for primary legislation to be introduced and passed quickly, but the pressures on the timetable can make it very difficult to find a slot.

The power to make a remedial order is there for cases where there is a very good reason to amend the law following a declaration of incompatibility or a finding by the Strasbourg court, but no suitable legislative vehicle is available. Where a remedial order is made or proposed, we accepted that the procedures for Parliamentary scrutiny needed to be strengthened. That is why the requirement to provide a document containing all the relevant information and a statement providing a summary of any representations on an order or draft order was added to [sch. 2] in Committee.

Mr Straw: [col. 1357] Three sets of changes have been made as a result of concerns expressed. . . . The first concerns remedial orders. We continue to believe that it should be possible to amend Acts of Parliament by a remedial order so as to bring them into line with the Convention rights, but we have . . . considerably restricted the circumstances in which they can be made, and we have significantly enhanced the Parliamentary opportunities for scrutiny of those orders.

[col. 1358] We have explained that any response to a declaration of incompatibility by the courts, whether by fresh primary legislation or by a remedial order, is a matter on which the Government will propose, but it is for Parliament to dispose. One of the [Act's] many strengths is that it promotes human rights while maintaining the sovereignty of Parliament and the separation of powers which underpins our constitutional arrangements.

SECTION 11. SAVING FOR EXISTING HUMAN RIGHTS PROTECTION

House of Lords, Report Stage
Hansard HL, 29 January 1998, col. 410
Lord Williams of Mostyn: . . . [Section 11] is simply to provide a saving for other human rights. It is there to ensure that if a person has existing rights, nothing in this [Act] shall detract from them in any way. . . . [col. 411] There are, of course, two kinds of relationship created in the [Act] between Convention and domestic law: the interpretive principle in [ss. 3 to 5], and the right to rely on Convention rights against a public authority in [ss. 6 to 9]. We do not wish to have any misunderstanding.

House of Commons, Second Reading
Hansard HC, 16 February 1998, col. 738
The Secretary of State for the Home Department (Mr Jack Straw): . . . [Section 11] confirms that a person's reliance on a Convention right does not restrict any other right or freedom that he enjoys under United Kingdom law.

SECTION 12. THE PRESS

[The provision enacted as s. 12 was introduced as new clause 13 in committee in the House of Commons on 2 July 1998, by Jack Straw.]

When restrictions on press freedom permissable

House of Commons, Committee Stage
Hansard HC, 2 July 1998, col. 535
The Secretary of State for the Home Department (Mr Jack Straw): . . . Subsection (1) provides for the new clause to apply in any case where a court is considering granting relief — for example, an injunction restraining a threatened breach of confidence; but it could be any relief apart from that [col. 536] relating to criminal proceedings — which might affect the exercise of the art. 10 right to freedom of expression. It applies to the press, broadcasters or anyone whose right to freedom of expression might be affected. It is not limited to cases to which a public authority is a party. We have taken the opportunity to enhance press freedom in a wider way than would arise simply from the incorporation of the Convention into our domestic law.

Subsection (2) provides that no relief is to be granted if the person against whom it is sought — the respondent — is not present or represented, unless the applicant has taken all practicable steps to notify the respondent or there are compelling reasons why the respondent should not be notified. The courts are well able to deal with the first limb of that exception relating to whether all practical steps have been taken to notify the respondent, and in the case of broadcasting authorities and the press, rarely would an applicant not be able to serve notice of the proceedings on the respondent.

The latter circumstance — compelling reasons — might arise in a case raising issues of national security where the mere knowledge that an injunction was being sought might cause the respondent to publish the material immediately. We do not anticipate that that limb would be used often. In the past, such applications have been rare, but there has been at least one recent case involving the Ministry of Defence.

. . . the provision is intended overall to ensure that *ex parte* injunctions are granted only in exceptional circumstances. Even where both parties are represented, we expect that injunctions will continue to be rare, as they are at present.

. . . we believe that the courts should consider the merits of an application when it is made and should not grant an interim injunction simply to preserve the status quo ante between the parties.

[col. 537] . . . we believe that the new clause would protect a respondent potential publisher from what amounts to legal or legalised intimidation. We have already discussed the difficulty of getting interlocutory relief. It will be very difficult to get it unless the applicant can satisfy the court that the applicant is likely to establish that publication should not be allowed. That is a much higher test than that there should simply be a prima facie case to get the matter into court. . . .

[I was asked about a case where] a respondent who succeeded in preventing an injunction at the interlocutory stage and then published but it turned [col. 538] out that there had been some breach of the law. [I was] asked whether that could be weighed in the balance in respect of damages. . . .

Subsection (4) requires the court to have particular regard to the importance of the art. 10 right to freedom of expression. Where the proceedings concern journalistic, literary or artistic material, the court must also have particular regard to the extent to which the material has or is about to become available to the public — in other words, a question of prior publication — and the extent to which publication would be in the public interest. If the court and the parties to the proceedings know that a story will shortly be published anyway, for example, in another country or on the Internet, that must affect the decision whether it is appropriate to restrain publication by the print or broadcast media in this country.

Under subsection (4), the court must also have particular regard to any relevant privacy code. Depending on the circumstances, that could be the newspaper industry code of practice operated by the Press Complaints Commission, the Broadcasting Standards Commission code, the Independent Television Commission code, or a broadcaster's internal code such as that operated by the BBC. The fact that a newspaper has complied with the terms of the code operated by the [col. 539] PCC — or conversely, that it has breached the code — is one of the factors that we believe the courts should take into account in considering whether to grant relief.

Definition of public interest

House of Commons, Second Reading
Hansard HC, 2 July 1998, col. 539
The Secretary of State for the Home Department (Mr Jack Straw): . . . The courts are well versed in making judgments about the balance between a private

interest of an applicant before them and the wider public interest. That is inherent in any case in a clash between art. 10 and art. 8. It is also inherent in the way in which the courts until now have dealt with many issues surrounding proceedings for defamation. The European Commission and the European Court of Human Rights have devoted quite a lot of time and effort to developing the concept of the public interest. Without being too tautologous, one of the points of the public interest is, to quote the words of the Strasbourg court in *Handyside* v *United Kingdom* in 1976, that 'freedom of expression constitutes one of the essential foundations of a democratic society, one of the basic conditions for its progress, and for the development of every man' — and these days, I have no doubt, every woman. That is a brief sketch of a subject on which I have every confidence in the courts' ability to make good judgments in particular cases. . . .

[col. 540] There is no direct qualification to the word 'public' in the new clause. Ultimately, it would be a matter for the courts to decide, based on common sense and proportionality. The fact that the information was available across the globe in very narrow circumstances would be weighed in the balance. . . . The courts would be bound to take such facts into account. . . . they would also take into account the extent to which the information was available in another country or on the Internet, but in each case, the courts would have to apply balance and proportionality.

House of Commons, Committee Stage
Hansard HC, 2 July 1998, col. 562
The Parliamentary Under-Secretary of State for the Home Department (Mr Mike O'Brien): . . . I am perhaps tempting further interventions by going into the issue of what the public interest is, but the basic question is whether the public should have particular information. For example, information might have an effect on proper political discourse, or a matter of public policy. It might also affect individual behaviour. For example, information about BSE might have affected decisions on whether to eat beef. Those are areas in which there is a proper public interest in the press revealing information. The judge would have to ask the same question put by the hon. and learned Member for Harborough: is a matter only of interest to the public, or is it a matter of public interest? There should be some good reason why the public should know. [col. 563] It is arguable whether there should be a good reason for the public not to know something. That takes us into realms of philosophy and jurisprudence, and I do not want to go too far into them. However, judges will debate that matter among themselves as they reach their decisions.

Intended effect of subsection (3)

House of Commons, Committee Stage
Hansard HC, 2 July 1998, col. 562
The Parliamentary Under-Secretary of State for the Home Department (Mr Mike O'Brien): . . . We suggest . . . that the law on granting injunctions is

flexible in privacy cases, and we are tightening it to ensure that the applicant will in all cases need to establish a stronger case.

Subsection (4): 'conduct connected with such material'

House of Commons, Committee Stage
Hansard HC, 2 July 1998, col. 540
The Secretary of State for the Home Department (Mr Jack Straw): . . . The reference in the new clause to 'conduct connected with such material' is intended for cases where journalistic inquiries suggest the presence of a story, but no actual material yet exists — perhaps because the story has not yet been written.

Subsection (5)

House of Commons, Committee Stage
Hansard HC, 2 July 1998, col. 540
The Secretary of State for the Home Department (Mr Jack Straw): . . . Subsection (5) provides that references to a court include references to a tribunal, and that references to relief include references to any remedy or order, other than in criminal proceedings. We drafted the amendment with civil, rather than criminal, proceedings against the media in mind. Without such an exclusion, judges wanting to impose reporting restrictions in a criminal trial would, for example, have to consider any relevant privacy code, although plainly it would not be appropriate in that context.

Nevertheless, as public authorities, the criminal courts will of course, in the same way as other courts, be required not to act in a way that is incompatible with arts 8 and 10 and other Convention rights. The special provision that we are making in [s. 12] does not therefore exempt criminal courts from the general obligations imposed by other provisions of the Bill. However, had we included criminal proceedings under [s. 12], we would have made the running of criminal trials very complicated.

SECTION 13. THE CHURCHES

(The provision enacted as s. 13 was introduced as new clause 9 in committee in the House of Commons on 20 May 1998 by Jack Straw.)

House of Commons, Committee Stage
Hansard HC, 20 May 1998, col. 1020
The Secretary of State for the Home Department (Mr Jack Straw): . . . [Section 13] would come into play in any case in which a court's determination of any question arising out of the [Act] might affect the exercise by a religious organisation of the Convention right of freedom of thought, conscience and religion. In such a case, it provides for the court to have particular regard — not

[col. 1021] just to have regard, going back to the earlier debate, but to have particular regard — to the importance of that right. Its purpose is not to exempt Churches and other religious organisations from the scope of the [Act] — they have not sought that — any more than from that of the Convention. It is to reassure them against the [Act] being used to intrude upon genuinely religious beliefs or practices based on their beliefs. I emphasise the word 'practices', as well as 'beliefs'.

There is ample reassurance available on this point from Convention jurisprudence. Apart from stating the importance of the courts having due regard to art. 9, [s. 13] is designed to bring out the point that art. 9 rights attach not only to individuals but to the Churches. The idea that Convention rights typically attach only to individuals and not the Churches caused considerable anxiety. I understood that, and that is why the new clause has been phrased so that the Churches have its protection as well as individuals.

There is Convention jurisprudence to the effect that a Church body or other association with religious objectives is capable of possessing and exercising the rights in art. 9 as a representative of its members. [Section 13] will emphasise that point to our courts. The intention is to focus the courts' attention in any proceedings on the view generally held by the Church in question, and on its interest in protecting the integrity of the common faith of its members against attack, whether by outsiders or by individual dissidents. That is a significant protection.

. . . [Section 13] refers to the exercise of the right to freedom of thought, conscience and religion by a 'religious organisation', but leaves that expression undefined . . . [the reason is] partly that no definition is readily available, at home or in Strasbourg.

We considered the issue with great care, and took the advice of Parliamentary counsel. I have already referred to the difficulty arising from this point in the amendments made in another place in discriminating between some religions and others. We are seeking to reflect precisely the Strasbourg case law. The Convention institutions have not offered a definition, but we are confident that the term 'religious organisation' is recognisable in terms of the Convention. . . .

The key concept that we are talking about is organisations with religious objectives.

[col. 1022] . . . [s. 13] is flexible enough to cover cases involving religious charities where Church issues form a backdrop to the case. . . . it applies to a court's determination of any question arising under the Human Rights [Act] that might affect the exercise by a religious organisation of the rights guaranteed by art. 9. It is therefore not tied to circumstances in which a religious organisation is directly involved, as a body, in the court proceedings.

If a case is brought against a charity, and the charity can show that what it is doing is to maintain and practise the religious beliefs which it shares with its parent Church, we consider that [s. 13] would come into play so as to ensure that due consideration was given to those beliefs. . . .

[col. 1023] Nothing in the [Act] applies to any organisation unless the organisation is a public body — charities are not of themselves public bodies. . . . Provided the employment practices of a charity came within the general law — nothing to do with the Convention — [the Act] would have no effect.

SECTION 19. STATEMENTS OF COMPATIBILITY

Statements of compatibility

House of Lords, Second Reading
Hansard HL, 3 November 1997, col.1233
The Lord Chancellor (Lord Irvine of Lairg): . . . [Section 19] imposes a new requirement on government Ministers when introducing legislation. In future, they will have to make a statement either that the provisions of the legislation are compatible with the Convention or that they cannot make such a statement but nevertheless wish Parliament to proceed to consider the Bill.

Ministers will obviously want to make a positive statement whenever possible. That requirement should therefore have a significant impact on the scrutiny of draft legislation within government. Where such a statement cannot be made, Parliamentary scrutiny of the Bill would be intense.

House of Lords, Second Reading
Hansard HL, 27 November 1997, col. 1228
Lord Williams of Mostyn: The design of the Bill is to give the courts as much space as possible to protect human rights, short of a power to set aside or ignore Acts of Parliament. In the very rare cases where the higher courts will find it impossible to read and give effect to any statute in a way which is compatible with Convention rights, they [col. 1229] will be able to make a declaration of incompatibility. Then it is for Parliament to decide whether there should be remedial legislation. Parliament may, not must, and generally will, legislate. If a Minister's prior assessment of compatibility (under [s. 19]) is subsequently found by declaration of incompatibility by the courts to have been mistaken, it is hard to see how a Minister could withhold remedial action.

House of Commons, Second Reading
Hansard HC, 16 February 1998, col. 780
The Secretary of State for the Home Department (Mr Jack Straw): . . . [Section 19] is a further demonstration of our determination to improve compliance with Convention rights. It places a requirement on a Minister to publish a statement in relation to any Bill that he or she introduces. The statement will either be that the provisions of the legislation are compatible with Convention rights or that he or she cannot make such a statement, but that the Government nevertheless wish to proceed with the Bill.

I am sure that Ministers will want to make a positive statement whenever possible. The requirement to make a statement will have a significant impact on the scrutiny of draft legislation within Government and by Parliament. In my judgment, it will greatly assist Parliament's consideration of Bills by highlighting the potential implications for human rights.

COMMENT ON THE MARGIN OF APPRECIATION

House of Commons, Committee Stage
Hansard HC, 3 June 1998, col. 424
The Secretary of State for the Home Department (Mr Jack Straw): . . . [Section 8] would require the courts, in considering whether legislation was compatible with Convention rights, to have full regard to the margin of appreciation accorded to states by Strasbourg institutions. Presumably, that is intended to signal to the courts that they should recognise the primary responsibility of Governments for detailed decisions on how Convention rights are given effect in domestic law. [col. 424] The doctrine of the margin of appreciation — it is an important one — recognises that a state is allowed a certain measure of discretion, subject to European supervision, when it takes legislative, judicial or administrative action in respect of some Convention rights. In other words, it is best placed to decide in the first place whether — and, if so, what — action is required.

My first point about the margin of appreciation is that it is more relevant to some Convention rights than to others. It is especially relevant to arts 8 to 11, which enable restrictions to be placed on rights where that is necessary in a democratic society, for any one of a number of reasons. It is less relevant to some of the other articles, for example, art. 2 on the right to life and art. 3 on the prohibition on torture or inhuman and degrading treatment or punishment. The doctrine of the margin of appreciation means allowing this country a margin of appreciation when it interprets our law and the actions of our Governments in an international court, perhaps the European Court of Human Rights. Through incorporation we are giving a profound margin of appreciation to British courts to interpret the Convention in accordance with British jurisprudence as well as European jurisprudence.

One of the frustrations of non-incorporation has been that our own judges . . . have not been able to bring their intellectual skills and our great tradition of common law to bear on the development of European Convention jurisprudence. . . .

The margin of appreciation is laid down in many commission and court judgments. Therefore, it is spelt out in the meaning of [s. 2].

Appendix Five
Rules of Procedure of the European Court of Human Rights

RULES OF COURT
(4 November 1998)

REGISTRY OF THE COURT
STRASBOURG

CONTENTS

Chapter VIII — Judgments

Chapter IX — Advisory Opinions

Chapter X — Legal Aid

TITLE III — Transitional Rules

TITLE IV — Final Clauses

The European Court of Human Rights,
Having regard to the Convention for the Protection of Human Rights and
Fundamental Freedoms and the Protocols thereto,
Makes the present Rules:

Rule 1
(Definitions)

For the purposes of these Rules unless the context otherwise requires:

(a)   the term 'Convention' means the Convention for the Protection of Human Rights and Fundamental Freedoms and the Protocols thereto;

(b)   the expression 'plenary Court' means the European Court of Human Rights sitting in plenary session;

(c)   the term 'Grand Chamber' means the Grand Chamber of seventeen judges constituted in pursuance of Article 27 § 1 of the Convention;

(d)   the term 'Section' means a Chamber set up by the plenary Court for a fixed period in pursuance of Article 26(b) of the Convention and the expression 'President of the Section' means the judge elected by the plenary Court in pursuance of Article 26(c) of the Convention as President of such a Section;

(e)   the term 'Chamber' means any Chamber of seven judges constituted in pursuance of Article 27 § 1 of the Convention and the expression 'President of the Chamber' means the judge presiding over such a 'Chamber';

(f)   the term 'Committee' means a Committee of three judges set up in pursuance of Article 27 § 1 of the Convention;

(g)   the term 'Court' means either the plenary Court, the Grand Chamber, a Section, a Chamber, a Committee or the panel of five judges referred to in Article 43 § 2 of the Convention;

(h)   the expression '*ad hoc* judge' means any person, other than an elected judge, chosen by a Contracting Party in pursuance of Article 27 § 2 of the Convention to sit as a member of the Grand Chamber or as a member of a Chamber;

(i)   the terms 'judge' and 'judges' mean the judges elected by the Parliamentary Assembly of the Council of Europe or *ad hoc* judges;

(j)   the term 'Judge Rapporteur' means a judge appointed to carry out the tasks provided for in Rules 48 and 49;

(k)   the term 'Registrar' denotes the Registrar of the Court or the Registrar of a Section according to the context;

(l)   the terms 'party' and 'parties' mean

— the applicant or respondent Contracting Parties;

— the applicant (the person, non-governmental organisation or group of individuals) that lodged a complaint under Article 34 of the Convention;

(m)   the expression 'third party' means any Contracting State or any person concerned who, as provided for in Article 36 §§ 1 and 2 of the Convention, has exercised its right or been invited to submit written comments or take part in a hearing;

(n)   the expression 'Committee of Ministers' means the Committee of Ministers of the Council of Europe;

(o)   the terms 'former Court' and 'Commission' mean respectively the European Court and European Commission of Human Rights set up under former Article 19 of the Convention.

TITLE I
ORGANISATION AND WORKING OF THE COURT

Chapter I
Judges

Rule 2
(Calculation of term of office)

1. The duration of the term of office of an elected judge shall be calculated as from the date of election. However, when a judge is re-elected on the expiry of the term of office or is elected to replace a judge whose term of office has expired or is about to expire, the duration of the term of office shall, in either case, be calculated as from the date of such expiry.

2. In accordance with Article 23 § 5 of the Convention, a judge elected to replace a judge whose term of office has not expired shall hold office for the remainder of the predecessor's term.

3. In accordance with Article 23 § 7 of the Convention, an elected judge shall hold office until a successor has taken the oath or made the declaration provided for in Rule 3.

Rule 3
(Oath or solemn declaration)

1. Before taking up office, each elected judge shall, at the first sitting of the plenary Court at which the judge is present or, in case of need, before the President of the Court, take the following oath or make the following solemn declaration:

'I swear' — or 'I solemnly declare' — 'that I will exercise my functions as a judge honourably, independently and impartially and that I will keep secret all deliberations.'

2. This act shall be recorded in minutes.

Rule 4
(Incompatible activities)

In accordance with Article 21 § 3 of the Convention, the judges shall not during their term of office engage in any political or administrative activity or any professional activity which is incompatible with their independence or impartiality or with the demands of a full-time office. Each judge shall declare to the President of the Court any additional activity. In the event of a disagreement between the President and the judge concerned, any question arising shall be decided by the plenary Court.

Rule 5
(Precedence)

1. Elected judges shall take precedence after the President and Vice-Presidents of the Court and the Presidents of the Sections, according to the date of their

election; in the event of re-election, even if it is not an immediate re-election, the length of time during which the judge concerned previously held office as a judge shall be taken into account.

2.   Vice-Presidents of the Court elected to office on the same date shall take precedence according to the length of time they have served as judges. If the length of time they have served as judges is the same, they shall take precedence according to age. The same Rule shall apply to Presidents of Sections.

3.   Judges who have served the same length of time as judges shall take precedence according to age.

4.   *Ad hoc* judges shall take precedence after the elected judges according to age.

Rule 6
(Resignation)

Resignation of a judge shall be notified to the President of the Court, who shall transmit it to the Secretary General of the Council of Europe. Subject to the provisions of Rules 24 § 3 *in fine* and 26 § 2, resignation shall constitute vacation of office.

Rule 7
(Dismissal from office)

No judge may be dismissed from his or her office unless the other judges, meeting in plenary session, decide by a majority of two-thirds of the elected judges in office that he or she has ceased to fulfil the required conditions. He or she must first be heard by the plenary Court. Any judge may set in motion the procedure for dismissal from office.

Chapter II
Presidency of the Court

Rule 8
(Election of the President and Vice-Presidents of the Court and the Presidents and Vice-Presidents of the Sections)

1.   The plenary Court shall elect its President, two Vice-Presidents and the Presidents of the Sections for a period of three years, provided that such period shall not exceed the duration of their terms of office as judges. They may be re-elected.

2.   Each Section shall likewise elect for a renewable period of three years a Vice-President, who shall replace the President of the Section if the latter is unable to carry out his or her duties.

3.   The Presidents and Vice-Presidents shall continue to hold office until the election of their successors.

4.   If a President or a Vice-President ceases to be a member of the Court or resigns from office before its normal expiry, the plenary Court or the relevant Section, as the case may be, shall elect a successor for the remainder of the term of that office.

5.   The elections referred to in this Rule shall be by secret ballot; only the elected judges who are present shall take part. If no judge receives an absolute majority of the elected judges present, a ballot shall take place between the two judges who have received most votes. In the event of a tie, preference shall be given to the judge having precedence in accordance with Rule 5.

Rule 9
(Functions of the President of the Court)

1.   The President of the Court shall direct the work and administration of the Court. The President shall represent the Court and, in particular, be responsible for its relations with the authorities of the Council of Europe.

2.   The President shall preside at plenary meetings of the Court, meetings of the Grand Chamber and meetings of the panel of five judges.

3.   The President shall not take part in the consideration of cases being heard by Chambers except where he or she is the judge elected in respect of a Contracting Party concerned.

Rule 10
(Functions of the Vice-Presidents of the Court)

The Vice-Presidents of the Court shall assist the President of the Court. They shall take the place of the President if the latter is unable to carry out his or her duties or the office of President is vacant, or at the request of the President. They shall also act as Presidents of Sections.

Rule 11
(Replacement of the President and the Vice-Presidents)

If the President and the Vice-Presidents of the Court are at the same time unable to carry out their duties or if their offices are at the same time vacant, the office of President of the Court shall be assumed by a President of a Section or, if none is available, by another elected judge, in accordance with the order of precedence provided for in Rule 5.

Rule 12
(Presidency of Sections and Chambers)

The Presidents of the Sections shall preside at the sittings of the Section and Chambers of which they are members. The Vice-Presidents of the Sections shall take their place if they are unable to carry out their duties or if the office of President of the Section concerned is vacant, or at the request of the President of the Section. Failing that, the judges of the Section and the Chambers shall take their place, in the order of precedence provided for in Rule 5.

Rule 13
(Inability to preside)

Judges of the Court may not preside in cases in which the Contracting Party of which they are nationals or in respect of which they were elected is a party.

Rule 14
(Balanced representation of the sexes)

In relation to the making of appointments governed by this and the following chapter of the present Rules, the Court shall pursue a policy aimed at securing a balanced representation of the sexes.

Chapter III
The Registry

Rule 15
(Election of the Registrar)

1.   The plenary Court shall elect its Registrar. The candidates shall be of high moral character and must possess the legal, managerial and linguistic knowledge and experience necessary to carry out the functions attaching to the post.

2.   The Registrar shall be elected for a term of five years and may be re-elected. The Registrar may not be dismissed from office, unless the judges, meeting in plenary session, decide by a majority of two-thirds of the elected judges in office that the person concerned has ceased to fulfil the required conditions. He or she must first be heard by the plenary Court. Any judge may set in motion the procedure for dismissal from office.

3.   The elections referred to in this Rule shall be by secret ballot; only the elected judges who are present shall take part If no candidate receives an absolute majority of the elected judges present, a ballot shall take place between the two candidates who have received most votes. In the event of a tie, preference shall be given, firstly, to the female candidate, if any, and, secondly, to the older candidate.

4.   Before taking up office, the Registrar shall take the following oath or make the following solemn declaration before the plenary Court or, if need be, before the President of the Court:

'I swear' — or 'I solemnly declare' — 'that I will exercise loyally, discreetly and conscientiously the functions conferred upon me as Registrar of the European Court of Human Rights.'

This act shall be recorded in minutes.

Rule 16
(Election of the Deputy Registrars)

1.   The plenary Court shall also elect two Deputy Registrars on the conditions and in the manner and for the term prescribed in the preceding Rule. The procedure for dismissal from office provided for in respect of the Registrar shall likewise apply. The Court shall first consult the Registrar in both these matters.

2.   Before taking up office, a Deputy Registrar shall take an oath or make a solemn declaration before the plenary Court or, if need be, before the President of the Court, in terms similar to those prescribed in respect of the Registrar. This act shall be recorded in minutes.

Rule 17
(Functions of the Registrar)

1.   The Registrar shall assist the Court in the performance of its functions and shall be responsible for the organisation and activities of the Registry under the authority of the President of the Court.

2.   The Registrar shall have the custody of the archives of the Court and shall be the channel for all communications and notifications made by, or addressed to, the Court in connection with the cases brought or to be brought before it.

3.   The Registrar shall, subject to the duty of discretion attaching to this office, reply to requests for information concerning the work of the Court, in particular to enquiries from the press.

4.   General instructions drawn up by the Registrar, and approved by the President of the Court, shall regulate the working of the Registry.

Rule 18
(Organisation of the Registry)

1.   The Registry shall consist of Section Registries equal to the number of Sections set up by the Court and of the departments necessary to provide the legal and administrative services required by the Court.

2.   The Section Registrar shall assist the Section in the performance of its functions and may be assisted by a Deputy Section Registrar.

3.   The officials of the Registry, including the legal secretaries but not the Registrar and the Deputy Registrars, shall be appointed by the Secretary General of the Council of Europe with the agreement of the President of the Court or of the Registrar acting on the President's instructions.

Chapter IV
The Working of the Court

Rule 19
(Seat of the Court)

1.   The seat of the Court shall be at the seat of the Council of Europe at Strasbourg. The Court may, however, if it considers it expedient, perform its functions elsewhere in the territories of the member States of the Council of Europe.

2.   The Court may decide, at any stage of the examination of an application, that it is necessary that an investigation or any other function be carried out elsewhere by it or one or more of its members.

Rule 20
(Sessions of the plenary Court)

1.   The plenary sessions of the Court shall be convened by the President of the Court whenever the performance of its functions under the Convention and under these Rules so requires. The President of the Court shall convene a plenary session if at least one-third of the members of the Court so request, and in any event once a year to consider administrative matters.

2.   The quorum of the plenary Court shall be two-thirds of the elected judges in office.

3.   If there is no quorum, the President shall adjourn the sitting.

Rule 21
(Other sessions of the Court)

1.   The Grand Chamber, the Chambers and the Committees shall sit full time. On a proposal by the President, however, the Court shall fix session periods each year.

2.   Outside those periods the Grand Chamber and the Chambers shall be convened by their Presidents in cases of urgency.

Rule 22
(Deliberations)

1.   The Court shall deliberate in private. Its deliberations shall remain secret.

2.   Only the judges shall take part in the deliberations. The Registrar or the designated substitute, as well as such other officials of the Registry and interpreters whose assistance is deemed necessary, shall be present. No other person may be admitted except by special decision of the Court.

3.   Before a vote is taken on any matter in the Court, the President may request the judges to state their opinions on it.

Rule 23
(Votes)

1.   The decisions of the Court shall be taken by a majority of the judges present. In the event of a tie, a fresh vote shall be taken and, if there is still a tie, the President shall have a casting vote. This paragraph shall apply unless otherwise provided for in these Rules.

2.   The decisions and judgments of the Grand Chamber and the Chambers shall be adopted by a majority of the sitting judges. Abstentions shall not be allowed in final votes on the admissibility and merits of cases.

3.   As a general rule, votes shall be taken by a show of hands. The President may take a roll-call vote, in reverse order of precedence.

4.   Any matter that is to be voted upon shall be formulated in precise terms.

Chapter V
The Chambers

Rule 24
(Composition of the Grand Chamber)

1.   The Grand Chamber shall be composed of seventeen judges and three substitute judges.

2.   The Grand Chamber shall be constituted for three years with effect from the election of the presidential office-holders referred to in Rule 8.

3.   The Grand Chamber shall include the President and Vice-Presidents of the Court and the Presidents of the Sections. In order to complete the Grand Chamber, the plenary Court shall, on a proposal by its President, divide all the other judges into two groups which shall alternate every nine months and whose membership shall be geographically as balanced as possible and reflect the different legal systems among the Contracting Parties. The judges and substitute judges who are to hear each case referred to the Grand Chamber during each nine-month period shall be designated in rotation within each group; they shall remain members of the Grand Chamber until the proceedings have been completed, even after their terms of office as judges have expired.

4.   If he or she does not sit as a member of the Grand Chamber by virtue of paragraph 3 of the present Rule, the judge elected in respect of any Contracting Party concerned shall sit as an *ex officio* member of the Grand Chamber in accordance with Article 27 §§ 2 and 3 of the Convention.

5.   (a)   Where any President of a Section is unable to sit as a member of the Grand Chamber, he or she shall be replaced by the Vice-President of the Section.

   (b)   If other judges are prevented from sitting, they shall be replaced by the substitute judges in the order in which the latter were selected under paragraph 3 of the present Rule.

   (c)   If there are not enough substitute judges in the group concerned to complete the Grand Chamber, the substitute judges lacking shall be designated by a drawing of lots amongst the members of the other group.

6.   (a)   The panel of five judges of the Grand Chamber called upon to consider requests submitted under Article 43 of the Convention shall be composed of
   — the President of the Court,
   — the Presidents or, if they are prevented from sitting, the Vice-Presidents of the Sections other than the Section from which was constituted the Chamber that dealt with the case whose referral to the Grand Chamber is being sought,
   — one further judge designated in rotation from among the judges other than those who dealt with the case in the Chamber.

   (b)   No judge elected in respect of, or who is a national of, a Contracting Party concerned may be a member of the panel.

   (c)   Any member of the panel unable to sit shall be replaced by another judge who did not deal with the case in the Chamber, who shall be designated in rotation.

Rule 25
(Setting up of Sections)

1.   The Chambers provided for in Article 26(b) of the Convention (referred to in these Rules as 'Sections') shall be set up by the plenary Court, on a proposal by its President, for a period of three years with effect from the election of the presidential office-holders of the Court under Rule 8. There shall be at least four Sections.

2.   Each judge shall be a member of a Section. The composition of the Sections shall be geographically and gender balanced and shall reflect the different legal systems among the Contracting Parties.

3.   Where a judge ceases to be a member of the Court before the expiry of the period for which the Section has been constituted, the judge's place in the Section shall be taken by his or her successor as a member of the Court.

4.   The President of the Court may exceptionally make modifications to the composition of the Sections if circumstances so require.

5.   On a proposal by the President, the plenary Court may constitute an additional Section.

Rule 26
(Constitution of Chambers)

1.   The Chambers of seven judges provided for in Article 27 § 1 of the Convention for the consideration of cases brought before the Court shall be constituted from the Sections as follows.

   (a)   The Chamber shall in each case include the President of the Section and the judge elected in respect of any Contracting Party concerned. If the latter judge is not a member of the Section to which the application has been assigned under Rule 51 or 52, he or she shall sit as an *ex officio* member of the Chamber in accordance with Article 27 § 2 of the Convention. Rule 29 shall apply if that judge is unable to sit or withdraws.

   (b)   The other members of the Chamber shall be designated by the President of the Section in rotation from among the members of the relevant Section.

   (c)   The members of the Section who are not so designated shall sit in the case as substitute judges.

2.   Even after the end of their terms of office judges shall continue to deal with cases in which they have participated in the consideration of the merits.

Rule 27
(Committees)

1.   Committees composed of three judges belonging to the same Section shall be set up under Article 27 § 1 of the Convention. After consulting the Presidents of the Sections, the President of the Court shall decide on the number of Committees to be set up.

2.   The Committees shall be constituted for a period of twelve months by rotation among the members of each Section, excepting the President of the Section.

3.   The judges of the Section who are not members of a Committee may be called upon to take the place of members who are unable to sit.

4.   Each Committee shall be chaired by the member having precedence in the Section.

Rule 28
(Inability to sit, withdrawal or exemption)

1.   Any judge who is prevented from taking part in sittings shall, as soon as possible, give notice to the President of the Chamber.

2.   A judge may not take part in the consideration of any case in which he or she has a personal interest or has previously acted either as the Agent, advocate or adviser of a party or of a person having an interest in the case, or as a member of a tribunal or commission of inquiry, or in any other capacity.

3.   If a judge withdraws for one of the said reasons, or for some special reason, he or she shall inform the President of the Chamber, who shall exempt the judge from sitting.

4.   If the President of the Chamber considers that a reason exists for a judge to withdraw, he or she shall consult with the judge concerned; in the event of disagreement, the Chamber shall decide.

Rule 29
(Ad hoc judges)

1.   If the judge elected in respect of a Contracting Party concerned is unable to sit in the Chamber or withdraws, the President of the Chamber shall invite that Party to indicate within thirty days whether it wishes to appoint to sit as judge either another elected judge or, as an *ad hoc* judge, any other person possessing the qualifications required by Article 21 § 1 of the Convention and, if so, to state at the same time the name of the person appointed. The same rule shall apply if the person so appointed is unable to sit or withdraws.

2.   The Contracting Party concerned shall be presumed to have waived its right of appointment if it does not reply within thirty days.

3.   An *ad hoc* judge shall, at the opening of the first sitting fixed for the consideration of the case after the judge has been appointed, take the oath or make the solemn declaration provided for in Rule 3. This act shall be recorded in minutes.

Rule 30
(Common interest)

1.   If several applicant or respondent Contracting Parties have a common interest, the President of the Court may invite them to agree to appoint a single elected judge or *ad hoc* judge in accordance with Article 27 § 2 of the Convention. If the Parties are unable to agree, the President shall choose by lot, from among the persons proposed as judges by these Parties, the judge called upon to sit *ex officio*.

2. In the event of a dispute as to the existence of a common interest, the plenary Court shall decide.

TITLE II
PROCEDURE

Chapter 1
General Rules

Rule 31
(Possibility of particular derogations)

The provisions of this Title shall not prevent the Court from derogating from them for the consideration of a particular case after having consulted the parties where appropriate.

Rule 32
(Practice directions)

The President of the Court may issue practice directions, notably in relation to such matters as appearance at hearings and the filing of pleadings and other documents.

Rule 33
(Public character of proceedings)

1. Hearings shall be public unless, in accordance with paragraph 2 of this Rule, the Chamber in exceptional circumstances decides otherwise, either of its own motion or at the request of a party or any other person concerned.

2. The press and the public may be excluded from all or part of a hearing in the interest of morals, public order or national security in a democratic society, where the interests of juveniles or the protection of the private life of the parties so require, or to the extent strictly necessary in the opinion of the Chamber in special circumstances where publicity would prejudice the interests of justice.

3. Following registration of an application, all documents deposited with the Registry, with the exception of those deposited within the framework of friendly-settlement negotiations as provided for in Rule 62, shall be accessible to the public unless the President of the Chamber, for the reasons set out in paragraph 2 of this Rule, decides otherwise, either of his or her own motion or at the request of a party or any other person concerned.

4. Any request for confidentiality made under paragraphs 1 or 3 above must give reasons and specify whether the hearing or the documents, as the case may be, should be inaccessible to the public in whole or in part.

Rule 34
(Use of languages)

1. The official languages of the Court shall be English and French.

2. Before the decision on the admissibility of an application is taken, all communications with and pleadings by applicants under Article 34 of the

Convention or their representatives, if not in one of the Court's official languages, shall be in one of the official languages of the Contracting Parties.

3.   (a)   All communications with and pleadings by such applicants or their representatives in respect of a hearing, or after a case has been declared admissible, shall be in one of the Court's official languages, unless the President of the Chamber authorises the continued use of the official language of a Contracting Party.

(b)   If such leave is granted, the Registrar shall make the necessary arrangements for the oral or written translation of the applicant's observations or statements.

4.   (a)   All communications with and pleadings by Contracting Parties or third parties shall be in one of the Court's official languages. The President of the Chamber may authorise the use of a non-official language.

(b)   If such leave is granted, it shall be the responsibility of the requesting party to provide for and bear the costs of interpreting or translation into English or French of the oral arguments or written statements made.

5.   The President of the Chamber may invite the respondent Contracting Party to provide a translation of its written submissions in the or an official language of that Party in order to facilitate the applicant's understanding of those submissions.

6.   Any witness, expert or other person appearing before the Court may use his or her own language if he or she does not have sufficient knowledge of either of the two official languages. In that event the Registrar shall make the necessary arrangements for interpreting or translation.

Rule 35
(Representation of Contracting Parties)

The Contracting Parties shall be represented by Agents, who may have the assistance of advocates or advisers.

Rule 36
(Representation of applicants)

1.   Persons, non-governmental organisations or groups of individuals may initially present applications under Article 34 of the Convention themselves or through a representative appointed under paragraph 4 of this Rule.

2.   Following notification of the application to the respondent Contracting Party under Rule 54 § 3 (b), the President of the Chamber may direct that the applicant should be represented in accordance with paragraph 4 of this Rule.

3.   The applicant must be so represented at any hearing decided on by the Chamber or for the purposes of the proceedings following a decision to declare the application admissible, unless the President of the Chamber decides otherwise.

4.   (a)   The representative of the applicant shall be an advocate authorised to practise in any of the Contracting Parties and resident in the territory of one of them, or any other person approved by the President of the Chamber.

(b)   The President of the Chamber may, where representation would otherwise be obligatory, grant leave to the applicant to present his or her own case, subject, if necessary, to being assisted by an advocate or other approved representative.

(c)   In exceptional circumstances and at any stage of the procedure, the President of the Chamber may, where he or she considers that the circumstances or the conduct of the advocate or other person appointed under the preceding sub-paragraphs so warrant, direct that the latter may no longer represent or assist the applicant and that the applicant should seek alternative representation.

5.   The advocate or other approved representative, or the applicant in person if he or she seeks leave to present his or her own case, must have an adequate knowledge of one of the Court's official languages. However, leave to use a non-official language may be given by the President of the Chamber under Rule 34 § 3.

Rule 37
(Communications, notifications and summonses)

1.   Communications or notifications addressed to the Agents or advocates of the parties shall be deemed to have been addressed to the parties.

2.   If, for any communication, notification or summons addressed to persons other than the Agents or advocates of the parties, the Court considers it necessary to have the assistance of the Government of the State on whose territory such communication, notification or summons is to have effect, the President of the Court shall apply directly to that Government in order to obtain the necessary facilities.

3.   The same rule shall apply when the Court desires to make or arrange for the making of an investigation on the spot in order to establish the facts or to procure evidence or when it orders the appearance of a person who is resident in, or will have to cross, that territory.

Rule 38
(Written pleadings)

1.   No written observations or other documents may be filed after the time-limit set by the President of the Chamber or the Judge Rapporteur, as the case may be, in accordance with these Rules. No written observations or other documents filed outside that time-limit or contrary to any practice direction issued under Rule 32 shall be included in the case file unless the President of the Chamber decides otherwise.

2.   For the purposes of observing the time-limit referred to in paragraph 1, the material date is the certified date of dispatch of the document or, if there is none, the actual date of receipt at the Registry.

Rule 39
(Interim measures)

1.   The Chamber or, where appropriate, its President may, at the request of a party or of any other person concerned, or of its own motion, indicate to the parties

any interim measure which it considers should be adopted in the interests of the parties or of the proper conduct of the proceedings before it.

2.   Notice of these measures shall be given to the Committee of Ministers.

3.   The Chamber may request information from the parties on any matter connected with the implementation of any interim measure it has indicated.

Rule 40
(Urgent notification of an application)

In any case of urgency the Registrar, with the authorisation of the President of the Chamber, may, without prejudice to the taking of any other procedural steps and by any available means, inform a Contracting Party concerned in an application of the introduction of the application and of a summary of its objects.

Rule 41
(Case priority)

The Chamber shall deal with applications in the order in which they become ready for examination. It may, however, decide to give priority to a particular application.

Rule 42
(Measures for taking evidence)

1.   The Chamber may, at the request of a party or a third party, or of its own motion, obtain any evidence which it considers capable of providing clarification of the facts of the case. The Chamber may, *inter alia*, request the parties to produce documentary evidence and decide to hear as a witness or expert or in any other capacity any person whose evidence or statements seem likely to assist it in the carrying out of its tasks.

2.   The Chamber may, at any time during the proceedings, depute one or more of its members or of the other judges of the Court to conduct an inquiry, carry out an investigation on the spot or take evidence in some other manner. It may appoint independent external experts to assist such a delegation.

3.   The Chamber may ask any person or institution of its choice to obtain information, express an opinion or make a report on any specific point.

4.   The parties shall assist the Chamber, or its delegation, in implementing any measures for taking evidence.

5.   Where a report has been drawn up or some other measure taken in accordance with the preceding paragraphs at the request of an applicant or respondent Contracting Party, the costs entailed shall be borne by that Party unless the Chamber decides otherwise. In other cases the Chamber shall decide whether such costs are to be borne by the Council of Europe or awarded against the applicant or third party at whose request the report was drawn up or the other measure was taken. In all cases the costs shall be taxed by the President of the Chamber.

Rule 43
(Joinder and simultaneous examination of applications)

1.   The Chamber may, either at the request of the parties or of its own motion, order the joinder of two or more applications.

2.   The President of the Chamber may, after consulting the parties, order that the proceedings in applications assigned to the same Chamber be conducted simultaneously, without prejudice to the decision of the Chamber on the joinder of the applications.

Rule 44
(Striking out and restoration to the list)

1.   When an applicant Contracting Party notifies the Registrar of its intention not to proceed with the case, the Chamber may strike the application out of the Court's list under Article 37 of the Convention if the other Contracting Party or Parties concerned in the case agree to such discontinuance.

2.   The decision to strike out an application which has been declared admissible shall be given in the form of a judgment. The President of the Chamber shall forward that judgment, once it has become final, to the Committee of Ministers in order to allow the latter to supervise, in accordance with Article 46 § 2 of the Convention, the execution of any undertakings which may have been attached to the discontinuance, friendly settlement or solution of the matter.

3.   When an application has been struck out, the costs shall be at the discretion of the Court. If an award of costs is made in a decision striking out an application which has not been declared admissible, the President of the Chamber shall forward the decision to the Committee of Ministers.

4.   The Court may restore an application to its list if it concludes that exceptional circumstances justify such a course.

Chapter II
Institution of Proceedings

Rule 45
(Signatures)

1.   Any application made under Articles 33 or 34 of the Convention shall be submitted in writing and shall be signed by the applicant or by the applicant's representative.

2.   Where an application is made by a non-governmental organisation or by a group of individuals, it shall be signed by those persons competent to represent that organisation or group. The Chamber or Committee concerned shall determine any question as to whether the persons who have signed an application are competent to do so.

3.   Where applicants are represented in accordance with Rule 36, a power. of attorney or written authority to act shall be supplied by their representative or representatives.

Rule 46
(Contents of an inter-State application)

Any Contracting Party or Parties intending to bring a case before the Court under Article 33 of the Convention shall file with the registry an application setting out

(a)   the name of the Contracting Party against which the application is made;

(b)   a statement of the facts;

(c)   a statement of the alleged violation(s) of the Convention and the relevant arguments;

(d)   a statement on compliance with the admissibility criteria (exhaustion of domestic remedies and the six-month rule) laid down in Article 35 § 1 of the Convention;

(e)   the object of the application and a general indication of any claims for just satisfaction made under Article 41 of the Convention on behalf of the alleged injured party or parties; and

(f)   the name and address of the person(s) appointed as Agent; and accompanied by

(g)   copies of any relevant documents and in particular the decisions, whether judicial or not relating to the object of the application.

Rule 47
(Contents of an individual application)

1.   Any application under Article 34 of the Convention shall be made on the application form provided by the registry, unless the President of the Section concerned decides otherwise. It shall set out

(a)   the name, date of birth, nationality, sex, occupation and address of the applicant;

(b)   the name, occupation and address of the representative, if any;

(c)   the name of the Contracting Party or Parties against which the application is made;

(d)   a succinct statement of the facts;

(e)   a succinct statement of the alleged violation(s) of the Convention and the relevant arguments;

(f)   a succinct statement on the applicant's compliance with the admissibility criteria (exhaustion of domestic remedies and the six-month rule) laid down in Article 35 § 1 of the Convention; and

(g)   the object of the application as well as a general indication of any claims for just satisfaction which the applicant may wish to make under Article 41 of the Convention; and be accompanied by

(h)   copies of any relevant documents and in particular the decisions, whether judicial or not, relating to the object of the application.

2.   Applicants shall furthermore

(a)   provide information, notably the documents and decisions referred to in paragraph 1(h) above, enabling it to be shown that the admissibility criteria (exhaustion of domestic remedies and the six-month rule) laid down in Article 35 § 1 of the Convention have been satisfied; and

(b)   indicate whether they have submitted their complaints to any other procedure of international investigation or settlement.

3.   Applicants who do not wish their identity to be disclosed to the public shall so indicate and shall submit a statement of the reasons justifying such a departure from the normal rule of public access to information in proceedings before the Court. The President of the Chamber may authorise anonymity in exceptional and duly justified cases.

4.   Failure to comply with the requirements set out in paragraphs 1 and 2 above may result in the application not being registered and examined by the Court.

5.   The date of introduction of the application shall as a general rule be considered to be the date of the first communication from the applicant setting out, even summarily, the object of the application. The Court may for good cause nevertheless decide that a different date shall be considered to be the date of introduction.

6.   Applicants shall keep the Court informed of any change of address and of all circumstances relevant to the application.

Chapter III
Judge Rapporteurs

Rule 48
(Inter-State applications)

1.   Where an application is made under Article 33 of the Convention, the Chamber constituted to consider the case shall designate one or more of its judges as Judge Rapporteur(s), who shall submit a report on admissibility when the written observations of the Contracting Parties concerned have been received. Rule 49 § 4 shall, in so far as appropriate, be applicable to this report.

2.   After an application made under Article 33 of the Convention has been declared admissible, the Judge Rapporteur(s) shall submit such reports, drafts and other documents as may assist the Chamber in the carrying out of its functions.

Rule 49
(Individual applications)

1.   Where an application is made under Article 34 of the Convention, the President of the Section to which the case has been assigned shall designate a judge as Judge Rapporteur, who shall examine the application.

2.   In their examination of applications Judge Rapporteurs

(a)   may request the parties to submit, within a specified time, any factual information, documents or other material which they consider to be relevant;

(b)   shall, subject to the President of the Section directing that the case be considered by a Chamber, decide whether the application is to be considered by a Committee or by a Chamber.

3.   Where a case is considered by a Committee in accordance with Article 28 of the Convention, the report of the Judge Rapporteur shall contain

(a)   a brief statement of the relevant facts;

(b)   a brief statement of the reasons underlying the proposal to declare the application inadmissible or to strike it out of the list.

4.   Where a case is considered by a Chamber pursuant to Article 29 § 1 of the Convention, the report of the Judge Rapporteur shall contain

(a)   a statement of the relevant facts, including any information obtained under paragraph 2 of this Rule;

(b)   an indication of the issues arising under the Convention in the application;

(c)   a proposal on admissibility and on any other action to be taken, together, if need be, with a provisional opinion on the merits.

5.   After an application made under Article 34 of the Convention has been declared admissible, the Judge Rapporteur shall submit such reports, drafts and other documents as may assist the Chamber in the carrying out of its functions.

Rule 50
(Grand Chamber proceedings)

Where a case has been submitted to the Grand Chamber either under Article 30 or under Article 43 of the Convention, the President of the Grand Chamber shall designate as Judge Rapporteur(s) one or, in the case of an inter-State application, one or more of its members.

Chapter IV
Proceedings on Admissibility

Inter-State applications

Rule 51

1.   When an application is made under Article 33 of the Convention, the President of the Court shall immediately give notice of the application to the respondent Contracting Party and shall assign the application to one of the Sections.

2.   In accordance with Rule 26 § 1 (a), the judges elected in respect of the applicant and respondent Contracting Parties shall sit as *ex officio* members of the Chamber constituted to consider the case. Rule 30 shall apply if the application has been brought by several Contracting Parties or if applications with the same object brought by several Contracting Parties are being examined jointly under Rule 43 § 2.

3.   On assignment of the case to a Section, the President of the Section shall constitute the Chamber in accordance with Rule 26 § 1 and shall invite the respondent Contracting Party to submit its observations in, writing on the admissibility of the application. The observations so obtained shall be communicated by the Registrar to the applicant Contracting Party, which may submit written observations in reply.

4.   Before ruling on the admissibility of the application, the Chamber may decide to invite the parties to submit further observations in writing.

5.   A hearing on the admissibility shall be held if one or more of the Contracting Parties concerned so requests or if the Chamber so decides of its own motion.

6.   After consulting the Parties, the President of the Chamber shall fix the written and, where appropriate, oral procedure and for that purpose shall lay down the time-limit within which any written observations are to be filed.

7.   In its deliberations the Chamber shall take into consideration the report submitted by the Judge Rapporteur(s) under Rule 48 § 1.

Individual applications

Rule 52
(Assignment of applications to the Sections)

1.   Any application made under Article 34 of the Convention shall be assigned to a Section by the President of the Court, who in so doing shall endeavour to ensure a fair distribution of cases between the Sections.

2.   The Chamber of seven judges provided for in Article 27 § 1 of the Convention shall be constituted by the President of the Section concerned in accordance with Rule 26 § 1 once it has been decided that the application is to be considered by a Chamber.

3.   Pending the constitution of a Chamber in accordance with the preceding paragraph, the President of the Section shall exercise any powers conferred on the President of the Chamber by these Rules.

Rule 53
(Procedure before a Committee)

1.   In its deliberations the Committee shall take into consideration the report submitted by the Judge Rapporteur under Rule 49 § 3.

2.   The Judge Rapporteur, if he or she is not a member of the Committee, may be invited to attend the deliberations of the Committee.

3.   In accordance with Article 28 of the Convention, the Committee may, by a unanimous vote, declare inadmissible or strike out of the Court's list of cases an application where such a decision can be taken without further examination. This decision shall be final.

4.   If no decision pursuant to paragraph 3 of the present Rule is taken, the application shall be forwarded to the Chamber constituted under Rule 52 § 2 to examine the case.

Rule 54
(Procedure before a Chamber)

1.   In its deliberations the Chamber shall take into consideration the report submitted by the Judge Rapporteur under Rule 49 § 4.

2.   The Chamber may at once declare the application inadmissible or strike it out of the Court's list of cases.

3. Alternatively, the Chamber may decide to

(a) request the parties to submit any factual information, documents or other material which it considers to be relevant;

(b) give notice of the application to the respondent Contracting Party and invite that Party to submit written observations on the application;

(c) invite the parties to submit further observations in writing.

4. Before taking its decision on admissibility, the Chamber may decide, either at the request of the parties or of its own motion, to hold a hearing. In that event, unless the Chamber shall exceptionally decide otherwise, the parties shall be invited also to address the issues arising in relation to the merits of the application.

5. The President of the Chamber shall fix the procedure, including time-limits, in relation to any decisions taken by the Chamber under paragraphs 3 and 4 of this Rule.

Inter-State and individual applications

Rule 55
(Pleas of inadmissibility)

Any plea of inadmissibility must, in so far as its character and the circumstances permit, be raised by the respondent Contracting Party in its written or oral observations on the admissibility of the application submitted as provided in Rule 51 or 54, as the case may be.

Rule 56
(Decision of a Chamber)

1. The decision of the Chamber shall state whether it was taken unanimously or by a majority and shall be accompanied or followed by reasons.

2. The decision of the Chamber shall be communicated by the Registrar to the applicant and to the Contracting Party or Parties concerned.

Rule 57
(Language of the decision)

1. Unless the Court decides that a decision shall be given in both official languages, all decisions shall be given either in English or in French. Decisions given shall be accessible to the public.

2. Publication of such decisions in the official reports of the Court, as provided for in Rule 78, shall be in both official languages of the Court.

Chapter V
Proceedings after the Admission of an Application

Rule 58
(Inter-State applications)

1. Once the Chamber has decided to admit an application made under Article 33 of the Convention, the President of the Chamber shall, after consulting the

Contracting Parties concerned, lay down the time-limits for the filing of written observations on the merits and for the production of any further evidence. The President may however, with the agreement of the Contracting Parties concerned, direct that a written procedure is to be dispensed with.

2.   A hearing on the merits shall be held if one or more of the Contracting Parties concerned so requests or if the Chamber so decides of its own motion. The President of the Chamber shall fix the oral procedure.

3.   In its deliberations the Chamber shall take into consideration any reports, drafts and other documents submitted by the Judge Rapporteur(s) under Rule 48 § 2.

Rule 59
(Individual applications)

1.   Once the Chamber has decided to admit an application made under Article 34 of the Convention, it may invite the parties to submit further evidence and written observations.

2.   A hearing on the merits shall be held if the Chamber so decides of its own motion or, provided that no hearing also addressing the merits has been held at the admissibility stage under Rule 54 § 4, if one of the parties so requests. However, the Chamber may exceptionally decide that the discharging of its functions under Article 38 § 1 (a) of the Convention does not require a hearing to be held.

3.   The President of the Chamber shall, where appropriate, fix the written and oral procedure.

4.   In its deliberations the Chamber shall take into consideration any reports, drafts and other documents submitted by the Judge Rapporteur under Rule 49 § 5.

Rule 60
(Claims for just satisfaction)

1.   Any claim which the applicant Contracting Party or the applicant may wish to make for just satisfaction under Article 41 of the Convention shall, unless the President of the Chamber directs otherwise, be set out in the written observations on the merits or, if no such written observations are filed, in a special document filed no later than two months after the decision declaring the application admissible.

2.   Itemised particulars of all claims made, together with the relevant supporting documents or vouchers, shall be submitted, failing which the Chamber may reject the claim in whole or in part.

3.   The Chamber may, at any time during the proceedings, invite any party to submit comments on the claim for just satisfaction.

Rule 61
(Third-party intervention)

1.   The decision declaring an application admissible shall be notified by the Registrar to any Contracting Party one of whose nationals is an applicant in the case, as well as to the respondent Contracting Party under Rule 56 § 2.

2. Where a Contracting Party seeks to exercise its right to submit written comments or to take part in an oral hearing, pursuant to Article 36 § 1 of the Convention, the President of the Chamber shall fix the procedure to be followed.

3. In accordance with Article 36 § 2 of the Convention, the President of the Chamber may, in the interests of the proper administration of justice, invite or grant leave to any Contracting State which is not a party to the proceedings, or any person concerned who is not the applicant, to submit written comments or, in exceptional cases, to take part in an oral hearing. Requests for leave for this purpose must be duly reasoned and submitted in one of the official languages, within a reasonable time after the fixing of the written procedure.

4. Any invitation or grant of leave referred to in paragraph 3 of this Rule shall be subject to any conditions, including time-limits, set by the President of the Chamber. Where such conditions are not complied with, the President may decide not to include the comments in the case file.

5. Written comments submitted in accordance with this Rule shall be submitted in one of the official languages, save where leave to use another language has been granted under Rule 34 § 4. They shall be transmitted by the Registrar to the parties to the case, who shall be entitled, subject to any conditions, including time-limits, set by the President of the Chamber, to file written observations in reply.

Rule 62
(Friendly settlement)

1. Once an application has been declared admissible, the Registrar, acting on the instructions of the Chamber or its President, shall enter into contact with the parties with a view to securing a friendly settlement of the matter in accordance with Article 38 § 1 (b) of the Convention. The Chamber shall take any steps that appear appropriate to facilitate such a settlement.

2. In accordance with Article 38 § 2 of the Convention, the friendly settlement negotiations shall be confidential and without prejudice to the parties' arguments in the contentious proceedings. No written or oral communication and no offer or concession made in the framework of the attempt to secure a friendly settlement may be referred to or relied on in the contentious proceedings.

3. If the Chamber is informed by the Registrar that the parties have agreed to a friendly settlement, it shall, after verifying that the settlement has been reached on the basis of respect for human rights as defined in the Convention and the protocols thereto, strike the case out of the Court's list in accordance with Rule 44 § 2.

Chapter VI
Hearings

Rule 63
(Conduct of hearings)

1. The President of the Chamber shall direct hearings and shall prescribe the order in which Agents and advocates or advisers of the parties shall be called upon to speak.

2.   Where a fact-finding hearing is being carried out by a delegation of the Chamber under Rule 42, the head of the delegation shall conduct the hearing and the delegation shall exercise any relevant power conferred on the Chamber by the Convention or these Rules.

Rule 64
(Failure to appear at a hearing)

Where, without showing sufficient cause, a party fails to appear, the Chamber may, provided that it is satisfied that such a course is consistent with the proper administration of justice, nonetheless proceed with the hearing.

Rule 65
(Convocation of witnesses, experts and other persons; costs of their appearance)

1.   Witnesses, experts and other persons whom the Chamber or the President of the Chamber decides to hear shall be summoned by the Registrar.

2.   The summons shall indicate
   (a)   the case in connection with which it has been issued;
   (b)   the object of the inquiry, expert opinion or other measure ordered by the Chamber or the President of the Chamber;
   (c)   any provisions for the payment of the sum due to the person summoned.

3.   If the persons concerned appear at the request or on behalf of an applicant or respondent Contracting Party, the costs of their appearance shall be borne by that Party unless the Chamber decides otherwise. In other cases, the Chamber shall decide whether such costs are to be borne by the Council of Europe or awarded against the applicant or third party at whose request the person summoned appeared. In all cases the costs shall be taxed by the President of the Chamber.

Rule 66
(Oath or solemn declaration by witnesses and experts)

1.   After the establishment of the identity of the witness and before testifying, every witness shall take the following oath or make the following solemn declaration:
   'I swear' — or 'I solemnly declare upon my honour and conscience' — 'that I shall speak the truth, the whole truth and nothing but the truth.'
This act shall be recorded in minutes.

2.   After the establishment of the identity of the expert and before carrying out his or her task, every expert shall take the following oath or make the following solemn declaration:
   'I swear' — or 'I solemnly declare' — 'that I will discharge my duty as an expert honourably and conscientiously.'
This act shall be recorded in minutes.

3.   This oath may be taken or this declaration made before the President of the Chamber, or before a judge or any public authority nominated by the President.

Rule 67
(Objection to a witness or expert; hearing of a person for information purposes)

The Chamber shall decide in the event of any dispute arising from an objection to a witness or expert. It may hear for information purposes a person who cannot be heard as a witness.

Rule 68
(Questions put during hearings)

1. Any judge may put questions to the Agents, advocates or advisers of the parties, to the applicant, witnesses and experts, and to any other persons appearing before the Chamber.

2. The witnesses, experts and other persons referred to in Rule 42 § 1 may, subject to the control of the President of the Chamber, be examined by the Agents and advocates or advisers of the parties. In the event of an objection as to the relevance of a question put, the President of the Chamber shall decide.

Rule 69
(Failure to appear, refusal to give evidence or false evidence)

If, without good reason, a witness or any other person who has been duly summoned fails to appear or refuses to give evidence, the Registrar shall, on being so required by the President of the Chamber, inform the Contracting Party to whose jurisdiction the witness or other person is subject. The same provisions shall apply if a witness or expert has, in the opinion of the Chamber, violated the oath or solemn declaration provided for in Rule 66.

Rule 70
(Verbatim record of hearings)

1. The Registrar shall, if the Chamber so directs, be responsible for the making of a verbatim record of a hearing. The verbatim record shall include

(a) the composition of the Chamber at the hearing;

(b) a list of those appearing before the Court, that is to say Agents, advocates and advisers of the parties and any third party taking part;

(c) the surnames, forenames, description and address of each witness, expert or other person heard;

(d) the text of statements made, questions put and replies given;

(e) the text of any decision delivered during the hearing by the Chamber or the President of the Chamber.

2. If all or part of the verbatim record is in a non-official language, the Registrar shall, if the Chamber so directs, arrange for its translation into one of the official languages.

3. The representatives of the parties shall receive a copy of the verbatim record in order that they may, subject to the control of the Registrar or the President of the Chamber, make corrections, but in no case may such corrections affect the

sense and bearing of what was said. The Registrar shall lay down, in accordance with the instructions of the President of the Chamber, the time-limits granted for this purpose.

4.   The verbatim record, once so corrected, shall be signed by the President and the Registrar and shall then constitute certified matters of record.

Chapter VII
Proceedings before the Grand Chamber

Rule 71
(Applicability of procedural provisions)

Any provisions governing proceedings before the Chambers shall apply, *mutatis mutandis*, to proceedings before the Grand Chamber.

Rule 72
(Relinquishment of jurisdiction by a Chamber in favour of the Grand Chamber)

1.   In accordance with Article 30 of the Convention, where a case pending before a Chamber raises a serious question affecting the interpretation of the Convention or the protocols thereto or where the resolution of a question before it might have a result inconsistent with a judgment previously delivered by the Court, the Chamber may, at any time before it has rendered its judgment, relinquish jurisdiction in favour of the Grand Chamber, unless one of the parties to the case has objected in accordance with paragraph 2 of this Rule. Reasons need not be given for the decision to relinquish.

2.   The Registrar shall notify the parties of the Chamber's intention to relinquish jurisdiction. The parties shall have one month from the date of that notification within which to file at the Registry a duly reasoned objection. An objection which does not fulfil these conditions shall be considered invalid by the Chamber.

Rule 73
(Request by a party for referral of a case to the Grand Chamber)

1.   In accordance with Article 43 of the Convention, any party to a case may exceptionally, within a period of three months from the date of delivery of the judgment of a Chamber, file in writing at the Registry a request that the case be referred to the Grand Chamber. The party shall specify in its request the serious question affecting the interpretation or application of the Convention or the protocols thereto, or the serious issue of general importance, which in its view warrants consideration by the Grand Chamber.

2.   A panel of five judges of the Grand Chamber constituted in accordance with Rule 24 § 6 shall examine the request solely on the basis of the existing case file. It shall accept the request only if it considers that the case does raise such a question or issue. Reasons need not be given for a refusal of the request.

3.   If the panel accepts the request, the Grand Chamber shall decide the case by means of a judgment.

Chapter VIII

Judgments

Rule 74

(Contents of the judgment)

1.   A judgment as referred to in Articles 42 and 44 of the Convention shall contain

(a)   the names of the President and the other judges constituting the Chamber concerned, and the name of the Registrar or the Deputy Registrar;

(b)   the dates on which it was adopted and delivered;

(c)   a description of the parties;

(d)   the names of the Agents, advocates or advisers of the parties;

(e)   an account of the procedure followed;

(f)   the facts of the case;

(g)   a summary of the submissions of the parties;

(h)   the reasons in point of law;

(i)   the operative provisions;

(j)   the decision, if any, in respect of costs;

(k)   the number of judges constituting the majority;

(l)   where appropriate, a statement as to which text is authentic.

2.   Any judge who has taken part in the consideration of the case shall be entitled to annex to the judgment either a separate opinion, concurring with or dissenting from that judgment, or a bare statement of dissent.

Rule 75

(Ruling on just satisfaction)

1.   Where the Chamber finds that there has been a violation of the Convention, it shall give in the same judgment a ruling on the application of Article 41 of the Convention if that question, after being raised in accordance with Rule 60, is ready for decision; if the question is not ready for decision, the Chamber shall reserve it in whole or in part and shall fix the further procedure.

2.   For the purposes of ruling on the application of Article 41 of the Convention, the Chamber shall, as far as possible, be composed of those judges who sat to consider the merits of the case. Where it is not possible to constitute the original Chamber, the President of the Court shall complete or compose the Chamber by drawing lots.

3.   The Chamber may, when affording just satisfaction under Article 41 of the Convention, direct that if settlement is not made within a specified time, interest is to be payable on any sums awarded.

4.   If the Court is informed that an agreement has been reached between the injured party and the Contracting Party liable, it shall verify the equitable nature of the agreement and, where it finds the agreement to be equitable, strike the case out of the list in accordance with Rule 44 § 2.

Rule 76
(Language of the judgment)

1.   Unless the Court decides that a judgment shall be given in both official languages, all judgments shall be given either in English or in French. Judgments given shall be accessible to the public.

2.   Publication of such judgments in the official reports of the Court, as provided for in Rule 78, shall be in both official languages of the Court.

Rule 77
(Signature, delivery and notification of the judgment)

1.   Judgments shall be signed by the President of the Chamber and the Registrar.

2.   The judgment may be read out at a public hearing by the President of the Chamber or by another judge delegated by him or her. The Agents and representatives of the parties shall be informed in due time of the date of the hearing. Otherwise the notification provided for in paragraph 3 of this Rule shall constitute delivery of the judgment.

3.   The judgment shall be transmitted to the Committee of Ministers. The Registrar shall send certified copies to the parties, to the Secretary General of the Council of Europe, to any third party and to any other person directly concerned. The original copy, duly signed and sealed, shall be placed in the archives of the Court.

Rule 78
(Publication of judgments and other documents)

In accordance with Article 44 § 3 of the Convention, final judgments of the Court shall be published, under the responsibility of the Registrar, in an appropriate form. The Registrar shall in addition be responsible for the publication of official reports of selected judgments and decisions and of any document which the President of the Court considers it useful to publish.

Rule 79
(Request for interpretation of a judgment)

1.   A party may request the interpretation of a judgment within a period of one year following the delivery of that judgment.

2.   The request shall be filed with the Registry. It shall state precisely the point or points in the operative provisions of the judgment on which interpretation is required.

3.   The original Chamber may decide of its own motion to refuse the request on the ground that there is no reason to warrant considering it. Where it is not possible to constitute the original Chamber, the President of the Court shall complete or compose the Chamber by drawing lots.

4.   If the Chamber does not refuse the request, the Registrar shall communicate it to the other party or parties and shall invite them to submit any written comments

within a time-limit laid down by the President of the Chamber. The President of the Chamber shall also fix the date of the hearing should the Chamber decide to hold one. The Chamber shall decide by means of a judgment.

Rule 80
(Request for revision of a judgment)

1.   A party may, in the event of the discovery of a fact which might by its nature have a decisive influence and which, when a judgment was delivered, was unknown to the Court and could not reasonably have been known to that party, request the Court, within a period of six months after that party acquired knowledge of the fact, to revise that judgment.

2.   The request shall mention the judgment of which revision is requested and shall contain the information necessary to show that the conditions laid down in paragraph 1 have been complied with. It shall be accompanied by a copy of all supporting documents. The request and supporting documents shall be filed with the Registry.

3.   The original Chamber may decide of its own motion to refuse the request on the ground that there is no reason to warrant considering it. Where it is not possible to constitute the original Chamber, the President of the Court shall complete or compose the Chamber by drawing lots.

4.   If the Chamber does not refuse the request, the Registrar shall communicate it to the other party or parties and shall invite them to submit any written comments within a time-limit laid down by the President of the Chamber. The President of the Chamber shall also fix the date of the hearing should the Chamber decide to hold one. The Chamber shall decide by means of a judgment.

Rule 81
(Rectification of errors in decisions and judgments)

Without prejudice to the provisions on revision of judgments and on restoration to the list of applications, the Court may, of its own motion or at the request of a party made within one month of the delivery of a decision or a judgment, rectify clerical errors, errors in calculation or obvious mistakes.

Chapter IX
Advisory Opinions

Rule 82

In proceedings relating to advisory opinions the Court shall apply, in addition to the provisions of Articles 47, 48 and 49 of the Convention, the provisions which follow. It shall also apply the other provisions of these Rules to the extent to which it considers this to be appropriate.

Rule 83

The request for an advisory opinion shall be filed with the Registry. It shall state fully and precisely the question on which the opinion of the Court is sought, and also

(a)   the date on which the Committee of Ministers adopted the decision referred to in Article 47 § 3 of the Convention;

(b)   the names and addresses of the person or persons appointed by the Committee of Ministers to give the Court any explanations which it may require.

The request shall be accompanied by all documents likely to elucidate the question.

Rule 84

1.   On receipt of a request, the Registrar shall transmit a copy of it to all members of the Court.

2.   The Registrar shall inform the Contracting Parties that the Court is prepared to receive their written comments.

Rule 85

1.   The President of the Court shall lay down the time-limits for filing written comments or other documents.

2.   Written comments or other documents shall be filed with the Registry. The Registrar shall transmit copies of them to all the members of the Court, to the Committee of Ministers and to each of the Contracting Parties.

Rule 86

After the close of the written procedure, the President of the Court shall decide whether the Contracting Parties which have submitted written comments are to be given an opportunity to develop them at an oral hearing held for the purpose.

Rule 87

If the Court considers that the request for an advisory opinion is not within its consultative competence as defined in Article 47 of the Convention, it shall so declare in a reasoned decision.

Rule 88

1.   Advisory opinions shall be given by a majority vote of the Grand Chamber. They shall mention the number of judges constituting the majority.

2.   Any judge may, if he or she so desires, attach to the opinion of the Court either a separate opinion, concurring with or dissenting from the advisory opinion, or a bare statement of dissent.

Rule 89

The advisory opinion shall be read out in one of the two official languages by the President of the Court, or by another judge delegated by the President, at a public hearing, prior notice having been given to the Committee of Ministers and to each of the Contracting Parties.

Rule 90

The opinion, or any decision given under Rule 87, shall be signed by the President of the Court and by the Registrar. The original copy, duly signed and sealed, shall be placed in the archives of the Court. The Registrar shall send certified copies to the Committee of Ministers, to the Contracting Parties and to the Secretary General of the Council of Europe.

Chapter X
Legal Aid

Rule 91

1. The President of the Chamber may, either at the request of an applicant lodging an application under Article 34 of the Convention or of his or her own motion, grant free legal aid to the applicant in connection with the presentation of the case from the moment when observations in writing on the admissibility of that application are received from the respondent Contracting Party in accordance with Rule 54 § 3 (b), or where the time-limit for their submission has expired.

2. Subject to Rule 96, where the applicant has been granted legal aid in connection with the .presentation of his or her case before the Chamber, that grant shall continue in force for purposes of his or her representation before the Grand Chamber.

Rule 92

Legal aid shall be granted only where the President of the Chamber is satisfied

(a) that it is necessary for the proper conduct of the case before the Chamber;

(b) that the applicant has insufficient means to meet all or part of the costs entailed.

Rule 93

1. In order to determine whether or not applicants have sufficient means to meet all or part of the costs entailed, they shall be required to complete a form of declaration stating their income, capital assets and any financial commitments in respect of dependants, or any other financial obligations. The declaration shall be certified by the appropriate domestic authority or authorities.

2. The Contracting Party concerned shall be requested to submit its comments in writing.

3. After receiving the information mentioned in paragraphs 1 and 2 above, the President of the Chamber shall decide whether or not to grant legal aid. The Registrar shall inform the parties accordingly.

Rule 94

1. Fees shall be payable to the advocates or other persons appointed in accordance with Rule 36 § 4. Fees may, where appropriate, be paid to more than one such representative.

2. Legal aid may be granted to cover not only representatives' fees but also travelling and subsistence expenses and other necessary expenses incurred by the applicant or appointed representative.

Rule 95

On a decision to grant legal aid, the Registrar shall

(a) fix the rate of fees to be paid in accordance with the legal-aid scales in force;

(b) the level of expenses to be paid.

Rule 96

The President of the Chamber may, if satisfied that the conditions stated in Rule 92 are no longer fulfilled, revoke or vary a grant of legal aid at any time.

TITLE III
TRANSITIONAL RULES

Rule 97
(Judges' terms of office)

The duration of the terms of office of the judges who were members of the Court at the date of the entry into force of Protocol No. 11 to the Convention shall be calculated as from that date.

Rule 98
(Presidency of the Sections)

For a period of three years from the entry into force of Protocol No. 11 to the Convention,

(a) the two Presidents of Sections who are not simultaneously Vice-Presidents of the Court and, the Vice-Presidents of the Sections shall be elected for a term of office of eighteen months;

(b) the Vice-Presidents of the Sections may not be immediately re-elected.

Rule 99
(Relations between the Court and the Commission)

1. In cases brought before the Court under Article 5 §§ 4 and 5 of Protocol No. 11 to the Convention the Court may invite the Commission to delegate one or more of its members to take part in the consideration of the case before the Court.

2. In cases referred to in the preceding paragraph the Court shall take into consideration the report of the Commission adopted pursuant to former Article 31 of the Convention.

3. Unless the President of the Chamber decides otherwise, the said report shall be made available to the public through the Registrar as soon as possible after the case has been brought before the Court.

4.   The remainder of the case file of the Commission, including all pleadings, in cases brought before the Court under Article 5 §§ 2 to 5 of Protocol No. 11 shall remain confidential unless the President of the Chamber decides otherwise.

5.   In cases where the Commission has taken evidence but has been unable to adopt a report in accordance with former Article 31 of the Convention, the Court shall take into consideration the verbatim records, documentation and opinion of the Commission's delegations arising from such investigations.

Rule 100
(Chamber and Grand Chamber proceedings)

1.   In cases referred to the Court under Article 5 § 4 of Protocol No. 11 to the Convention, a panel of the Grand Chamber constituted in accordance with Rule 24 § 6 shall determine, solely on the basis of the existing case file, whether a Chamber or the Grand Chamber is to decide the case.

2.   If the case is decided by a Chamber, the judgment of the Chamber shall, in accordance with Article 5 § 4 of Protocol No. 11, be final and Rule 73 shall be inapplicable.

3.   Cases transmitted to the Court under Article 5 § 5 of Protocol No. 11 shall be forwarded by the President of the Court to the Grand Chamber.

4.   For each case transmitted to the Grand Chamber under Article 5 § 5 of the Protocol No 11, the Grand Chamber shall be completed by judges designated by rotation within one of the groups mentioned in Rule 24 § 3, the cases being allocated to the groups on an alternate basis.

Rule 101
(Grant of legal aid)

Subject to Rule 96, in cases brought before the Court under Article 5 §§ 2 to 5 of Protocol No. 11 to the Convention, a grant of legal aid made to an applicant in the proceedings before the Commission or the former Court shall continue in force for the purposes of his or her representation before the Court.

Rule 102
(Request for interpretation or revision of a judgment)

1.   Where a party requests interpretation or revision of a judgment delivered by the former Court, the President of the Court shall assign the request to one of the Sections in accordance with the conditions laid down in Rule 51 or 52, as the case may be.

2.   The President of the relevant Section shall, notwithstanding Rules 79 § 3 and 80 § 3, constitute a new Chamber to consider the request.

3.   The Chamber to be constituted shall include as *ex officio* members

(a)   the President of the Section; and, whether or not they are members of the relevant Section,

(b)   the judge elected in respect of any Contracting Party concerned or, if he or she is unable to sit, any judge appointed under Rule 29;

(c)   any judge of the Court who was a member of the original Chamber that delivered the judgment in the former Court.

4.   (a)   The other members of the Chamber shall be designated by the President of the Section by means of a drawing of lots from among the members of the relevant Section.

(b)   The members of the Section who are not so designated shall sit in the case as substitute judges.

TITLE IV
FINAL CLAUSES

Rule 103
(Amendment or suspension of a Rule)

1.   Any Rule may be amended upon a motion made after notice where such a motion is carried at the next session of the plenary Court by a majority of all the members of the Court. Notice of such a motion shall be delivered in writing to the Registrar at least one month before the session at which it is to be discussed. On receipt of such a notice of motion, the Registrar shall inform all members of the Court at the earliest possible moment.

2.   A Rule relating to the internal working of the Court may be suspended upon a motion made without notice, provided that this decision is taken unanimously by the Chamber concerned. The suspension of a Rule shall in this case be limited in its operation to the particular purpose for which it was sought.

Rule 104
(Entry into force of the Rules)

The present Rules shall enter into force on 1 November 1998.

Appendix Six
Convention for the Protection of Human Rights and Fundamental Freedoms as amended by Protocol No. 11 (Date of entry into force 1 November 1998)

The governments signatory hereto, being members of the Council of Europe,

Considering the Universal Declaration of Human Rights proclaimed by the General Assembly of the United Nations on 10th December 1948;

Considering that this Declaration aims at securing the universal and effective recognition and observance of the Rights therein declared;

Considering that the aim of the Council of Europe is the achievement of greater unity between its members and that one of the methods by which that aim is to be pursued is the maintenance and further realisation of human rights and fundamental freedoms;

Reaffirming their profound belief in those fundamental freedoms which are the foundation of justice and peace in the world and are best maintained on the one hand by an effective political democracy and on the other by a common understanding and observance of the human rights upon which they depend;

Being resolved, as the governments of European countries which a re like-minded and have a common heritage of political traditions, ideals, freedom and the rule of law, to take the first steps for the collective enforcement of certain of the rights stated in the Universal Declaration,

Have agreed as follows:

Article 1
Obligation to respect human rights

The High Contracting Parties shall secure to everyone within their jurisdiction the rights and freedoms defined in Section I of this Convention.

Section I — Rights and freedoms

Article 2
Right to life

1   Everyone's right to life shall be protected by law. No one shall be deprived of his life intentionally save in the execution of a sentence of a court following his conviction of a crime for which this penalty is provided by law.

2   Deprivation of life shall not be regarded as inflicted in contravention of this article when it results from the use of force which is no more than absolutely necessary:

    a   in defence of any person from unlawful violence;

    b   in order to effect a lawful arrest or to prevent the escape of a person lawfully detained;

    c   in action lawfully taken for the purpose of quelling a riot or insurrection.

Article 3
Prohibition of torture

No one shall be subjected to torture or to inhuman or degrading treatment or punishment.

Article 4
Prohibition of slavery and forced labour

1   No one shall be held in slavery or servitude.

2   No one shall be required to perform forced or compulsory labour.

3   For the purpose of this article the term 'forced or compulsory labour' shall not include:

    a   any work required to be done in the ordinary course of detention imposed according to the provisions of Article 5 of this Convention or during conditional release from such detention;

    b   any service of a military character or, in case of conscientious objectors in countries where they are recognised, service exacted instead of compulsory military service;

    c   any service exacted in case of an emergency or calamity threatening the life or well-being of the community;

    d   any work or service which forms part of normal civic obligations.

Article 5
Right to liberty and security

1   Everyone has the right to liberty and security of person. No one shall be deprived of his liberty save in the following cases and in accordance with a procedure prescribed by law:

    a   the lawful detention of a person after conviction by a competent court;

    b   the lawful arrest or detention of a person for non-compliance with the lawful order of a court or in order to secure the fulfilment of any obligation prescribed by law;

c   the lawful arrest or detention of a person effected for the purpose of bringing him before the competent legal authority on reasonable suspicion of having committed an offence or when it is reasonably considered necessary to prevent his committing an offence or fleeing after having done so;

d   the detention of a minor by lawful order for the purpose of educational supervision or his lawful detention for the purpose of bringing him before the competent legal authority;

e   the lawful detention of persons for the prevention of the spreading of infectious diseases, of persons of unsound mind, alcoholics or drug addicts or vagrants;

f   the lawful arrest or detention of a person to prevent his effecting an unauthorised entry into the country or of a person against whom action is being taken with a view to deportation or extradition.

2   Everyone who is arrested shall be informed promptly, in a language which he understands, of the reasons for his arrest and of any charge against him.

3   Everyone arrested or detained in accordance with the provisions of paragraph 1.c of this article shall be brought promptly before a judge or other officer authorised by law to exercise judicial power and shall be entitled to trial within a reasonable time or to release pending trial. Release may be conditioned by guarantees to appear for trial.

4   Everyone who is deprived of his liberty by arrest or detention shall be entitled to take proceedings by which the lawfulness of his detention shall be decided speedily by a court and his release ordered if the detention is not lawful.

5   Everyone who has been the victim of arrest or detention in contravention of the provisions of this article shall have an enforceable right to compensation.

Article 6
Right to a fair trial

1   In the determination of his civil rights and obligations or of any criminal charge against him, everyone is entitled to a fair and public hearing within a reasonable time by an independent and impartial tribunal established by law. Judgment shall be pronounced publicly but the press and public may be excluded from all or part of the trial in the interests of morals, public order or national security in a democratic society, where the interests of juveniles or the protection of the private life of the parties so require, or to the extent strictly necessary in the opinion of the court in special circumstances where publicity would prejudice the interests of justice.

2   Everyone charged with a criminal offence shall be presumed innocent until proved guilty according to law.

3   Everyone charged with a criminal offence has the following minimum rights:

a   to be informed promptly, in a language which he understands and in detail, of the nature and cause of the accusation against him;

b   to have adequate time and facilities for the preparation of his defence;

c   to defend himself in person or through legal assistance of his own choosing or, if he has not sufficient means to pay for legal assistance, to be given it free when the interests of justice so require;

d   to examine or have examined witnesses against him and to obtain the attendance and examination of witnesses on his behalf under the same conditions as witnesses against him;

e   to have the free assistance of an interpreter if he cannot understand or speak the language used in court.

Article 7
No punishment without law

1   No one shall be held guilty of any criminal offence on account of any act or omission which did not constitute a criminal offence under national or international law at the time when it was committed. Nor shall a heavier penalty be imposed than the one that was applicable at the time the criminal offence was committed.

2   This article shall not prejudice the trial and punishment of any person for any act or omission which, at the time when it was committed, was criminal according to the general principles of law recognised by civilised nations.

Article 8
Right to respect for private and family life

1   Everyone has the right to respect for his private and family life, his home and his correspondence.

2   There shall be no interference by a public authority with the exercise of this right except such as is in accordance with the law and is necessary in a democratic society in the interests of national security, public safety or the economic well-being of the country, for the prevention of disorder or crime, for the protection of health or morals, or for the protection of the rights and freedoms of others.

Article 9
Freedom of thought, conscience and religion

1   Everyone has the right to freedom of thought, conscience and religion; this right includes freedom to change his religion or belief and freedom, either alone or in community with others and in public or private, to manifest his religion or belief, in worship, teaching, practice and observance.

2   Freedom to manifest one's religion or beliefs shall be subject only to such limitations as are prescribed by law and are necessary in a democratic society in the interests of public safety, for the protection of public order, health or morals, or for the protection of the rights and freedoms of others.

Article 10
Freedom of expression

1   Everyone has the right to freedom of expression. This right shall include freedom to hold opinions and to receive and impart information and ideas without interference by public authority and regardless of frontiers. This article shall not prevent States from requiring the licensing of broadcasting, television or cinema enterprises.

2   The exercise of these freedoms, since it carries with it dudes and responsibilities, may be subject to such formalities, conditions, restrictions or penalties as are prescribed by law and are necessary in a democratic society, in the interests of national security, territorial integrity or public safety, for the prevention of disorder or crime, for the protection of health or morals, for the protection of the reputation or rights of others, for preventing the disclosure of information received in confidence, or for maintaining the authority and impartiality of the judiciary.

Article 11
Freedom of assembly and association

1   Everyone has the right to freedom of peaceful assembly and to freedom of association with others, including the right to form and to join trade unions for the protection of his interests.

2   No restrictions shall be placed on the exercise of these rights other than such as are prescribed by law and are necessary in a democratic society in the interests of national security or public safety, for the prevention of disorder or crime, for the protection of health or morals or for the protection of the rights and freedoms of others. This article shall not prevent the imposition of lawful restrictions on the exercise of these rights by members of the armed forces, of the police or of the administration of the State.

Article 12
Right to marry

Men and women of marriageable age have the right to marry and to found a family, according to the national laws governing the exercise of this right.

Article 13
Right to an effective remedy

Everyone whose rights and freedoms as set forth in this Convention are violated shall have an effective remedy before a national authority notwithstanding that the violation has been committed by persons acting in an official capacity.

Article 14
Prohibition of discrimination

The enjoyment of the rights and freedoms set forth in this Convention shall be secured without discrimination on any ground such as sex, race, colour, language, religion, political or other opinion, national or social origin, association with a national minority, property, birth or other status.

Article 15
Derogation in time of emergency

1   In time of war or other public emergency threatening the life of the nation any High Contracting Party may take measures derogating from its obligations under this Convention to the extent strictly required by the exigencies of the

situation, provided that such measures are not inconsistent with its other obligations under international law.

2   No derogation from Article 2, except in respect of deaths resulting from lawful acts of war, or from Articles 3, 4 (paragraph 1) and 7 shall be made under this provision.

3   Any High Contracting Party availing itself of this right of derogation shall keep the Secretary General of the Council of Europe fully informed of the measures which it has taken and the reasons therefor. It shall also inform the Secretary General of the Council of Europe when such measures have ceased to operate and the provisions of the Convention are again being fully executed.

Article 16
Restrictions on political activity of aliens

Nothing in Articles 10, 11 and 14 shall be regarded as preventing the High Contracting Parties from imposing restrictions on the political activity of aliens.

Article 17
Prohibition of abuse of rights

Nothing in this Convention may be interpreted as implying for any State, group or person any right to engage in any activity or perform any act aimed at the destruction of any of the rights and freedoms set forth herein or at their limitation to a greater extent than is provided for in the Convention.

Article 18
Limitation on use of restrictions on rights

The restrictions permitted under this Convention to the said rights and freedoms shall not be applied for any purpose other than those for which they have been prescribed.

Section II — European Court of Human Rights

Article 19
Establishment of the Court

To ensure the observance of the engagements undertaken by the High Contracting Parties in the Convention and the Protocols thereto, there shall be set up a European Court of Human Rights, hereinafter referred to as 'the Court'. It shall function on a permanent basis.

Article 20
Number of judges

The Court shall consist of a number of judges equal to that of the High Contracting Parties.

Article 21
Criteria for office

1   The judges shall be of high moral character and must either possess the qualifications required for appointment to high judicial office or be jurisconsults of recognised competence.

2   The judges shall sit on the Court in their individual capacity.

3   During their term of office the judges shall not engage in any activity which is incompatible with their independence, impartiality or with the demands of a full-time office; all questions arising from the application of this paragraph shall be decided by the Court.

Article 22
Election of judges

1   The judges shall be elected by the Parliamentary Assembly with respect to each High Contracting Party by a majority of votes cast from a list of three candidates nominated by the High Contracting Party.

2   The same procedure shall be followed to complete the Court in the event of the accession of new High Contracting Parties and in filling casual vacancies.

Article 23
Terms of office

1   The judges shall be elected for a period of six years. They may be re-elected. However, the terms of office of one-half of the judges elected at the first election shall expire at the end of three years.

2   The judges whose terms of office are to expire at the end of the initial period of three years shall be chosen by lot by the Secretary General of the Council of Europe immediately after their election.

3   In order to ensure that, as far as possible, the terms of office of one-half of the judges are renewed every three years, the Parliamentary Assembly may decide, before proceeding to any subsequent election, that the term or terms of office of one or more judges to be elected shall be for a period other than six years but not more than nine and not less than three years.

4   In cases where more than one term of office is involved and where the Parliamentary Assembly applies the preceding paragraph, the allocation of the terms of office shall be effected by a drawing of lots by the Secretary General of the Council of Europe immediately after the election.

5   A judge elected to replace a judge whose term of office has not expired shall hold office for the remainder of his predecessor's term.

6   The terms of office of judges shall expire when they reach the age of 70.

7   The judges shall hold office until replaced. They shall, however, continue to deal with such cases as they already have under consideration.

Article 24
Dismissal

No judge may be dismissed from his office unless the other judges decide by a majority of two-thirds that he has ceased to fulfil the required conditions.

Article 25
Registry and legal secretaries

The Court shall have a registry, the functions and organisation of which shall be laid down in the rules of the Court. The Court shall be assisted by legal secretaries.

Article 26
Plenary Court

The plenary Court shall

a   elect its President and one or two Vice-Presidents for a period of three years; they may be re-elected;

b   set up Chambers, constituted for a fixed period of time;

c   elect the Presidents of the Chambers of the Court; they may be re-elected;

d   adopt the rules of the Court, and

e   elect the Registrar and one or more Deputy Registrars.

Article 27
Committees, Chambers and Grand Chamber

1   To consider cases brought before it, the Court shall sit in committees of three judges, in Chambers of seven judges and in a Grand Chamber of seventeen judges. The Court's Chambers shall set up committees for a fixed period of time.

2   There shall sit as an *ex officio* member of the Chamber and the Grand Chamber the judge elected in respect of the State Party concerned or, if there is none or if he is unable to sit, a person of its choice who shall sit in the capacity of judge.

3   The Grand Chamber shall also include the President of the Court, the Vice-Presidents, the Presidents of the Chambers and other judges chosen in accordance with the rules of the Court. When a case is referred to the Grand Chamber under Article 43, no judge from the Chamber which rendered the judgment shall sit in the Grand Chamber, with the exception of the President of the Chamber and the judge who sat in respect of the State Party concerned.

Article 28
Declarations of inadmissibility by committees

A committee may, by a unanimous vote, declare inadmissible or strike out of its list of cases an application submitted under Article 34 where such a decision can be taken without further examination. The decision shall be final.

Article 29
Decisions by Chambers on admissibility and merits

1   If no decision is taken under Article 28, a Chamber shall decide on the admissibility and merits of individual applications submitted under Article 34.

2   A Chamber shall decide on the admissibility and merits of inter-State applications submitted under Article 33.

3   The decision on admissibility shall be taken separately unless the Court, in exceptional cases, decides otherwise.

Article 30
Relinquishment of jurisdiction to the Grand Chamber

Where a case pending before a Chamber raises a serious question affecting the interpretation of the Convention or the protocols thereto, or where the resolution of a question before the Chamber might have a result inconsistent with a judgment previously delivered by the Court, the Chamber may, at any time before it has rendered its judgment, relinquish jurisdiction in favour of the Grand Chamber, unless one of the parties to the case objects.

Article 31
Powers of the Grand Chamber

The Grand Chamber shall

a   determine applications submitted either under Article 33 or Article 34 when a Chamber has relinquished jurisdiction under Article 30 or when the case has been referred to it under Article 43; and

b   consider requests for advisory opinions submitted under Article 47.

Article 32
Jurisdiction of the Court

1   The jurisdiction of the Court shall extend to all matters concerning the interpretation and application of the Convention and the protocols thereto which are referred to it as provided in Articles 33, 34 and 47.

2   In the event of dispute as to whether the Court has jurisdiction, the Court shall decide.

Article 33
Inter-State cases

Any High Contracting Party may refer to the Court any alleged breach of the provisions of the Convention and the protocols thereto by another High Contracting Party

Article 34
Individual applications

The Court may receive applications from any person, non-governmental organisation or group of individuals claiming to be the victim of a violation by one of the

High Contracting Parties of the rights set forth in the Convention or the protocols thereto. The High Contracting Parties undertake not to hinder in any way the effective exercise of this right.

Article 35
Admissibility criteria

1   The Court may only deal with the matter after all domestic remedies have been exhausted, according to the generally recognised rules of international law, and within a period of six months from the date on which the final decision was taken.

2   The Court shall not deal with any application submitted under Article 34 that
  a   is anonymous; or
  b   is substantially the same as a matter that has already been examined by the Court or has already been submitted to another procedure of international investigation or settlement and contains no relevant new information.

3   The Court shall declare inadmissible any individual application submitted under Article 34 which it considers incompatible with the provisions of the Convention or the protocols thereto, manifestly ill-founded, or an abuse of the right of application.

4   The Court shall reject any application which it considers inadmissible under this Article. It may do so at any stage of the proceedings.

Article 36
Third party intervention

1   In all cases before a Chamber of the Grand Chamber, a High Contracting Party one of whose nationals is an applicant shall have the right to submit written comments and to take part in hearings.

2   The President of the Court may, in the interest of the proper administration of justice, invite any High Contracting Party which is not a party to the proceedings or any person concerned who is not the applicant to submit written comments or take part in hearings.

Article 37
Striking out applications

1   The Court may at any stage of the proceedings decide to strike an application out of its list of cases where the circumstances lead to the conclusion that
  a   the applicant does not intend to pursue his application; or
  b   the matter has been resolved; or
  c   for any other reason established by the Court, it is no longer justified to continue the examination of the application.
However, the Court shall continue the examination of the application if respect for human rights as defined in the Convention and the protocols thereto so requires.

2   The Court may decide to restore an application to its list of cases if it considers that the circumstances justify such a course.

Article 38
Examination of the case and friendly settlement proceedings

1   If the Court declares the application admissible, it shall

a   pursue the examination of the case, together with the representatives of the parties, and if need be, undertake an investigation, for the effective conduct of which the States concerned shall furnish all necessary facilities;

b   place itself at the disposal of the parties concerned with a view to securing a friendly settlement of the matter on the basis of respect for human rights as defined in the Convention and the protocols thereto.

2   Proceedings conducted under paragraph 1.b shall be confidential.

Article 39
Finding of a friendly settlement

If a friendly settlement is effected, the Court shall strike the case out of its list by means of a decision which shall be confined to a brief statement of the facts and of the solution reached.

Article 40
Public hearings and access to documents

1   Hearings shall be in public unless the Court in exceptional circumstances decides otherwise.

2   Documents deposited with the Registrar shall be accessible to the public unless the President of the Court decides otherwise.

Article 41
Just satisfaction

If the Court finds that there has been a violation of the Convention or the protocols thereto, and if the internal law of the High Contracting Party concerned allows only partial reparation to be made, the Court shall, if necessary afford just satisfaction to the injured party.

Article 42
Judgments of Chambers

Judgments of Chambers shall become final in accordance with the provisions of Article 44, paragraph 2.

Article 43
Referral to the Grand Chamber

1   Within a period of three months from the date of the judgment of the Chamber, any party to the case may, in exceptional cases, request that the case be referred to the Grand Chamber.

2   A panel of five judges of the Grand Chamber shall accept the request if the case raises a serious question affecting the interpretation or application of the Convention or the protocols thereto, or a serious issue of general importance.

3   If the panel accepts the request, the Grand Chamber shall decide the case by means of a judgment.

Article 44
Final judgments

1   The judgment of the Grand Chamber shall be final.

2   The judgment of a Chamber shall become final

    a   when the parties declare that they will not request that the case be referred to the Grand Chamber; or

    b   three months after the date of the judgment, if reference of the case to the Grand Chamber has not been requested; or

    c   when the panel of the Grand Chamber rejects the request to refer under Article 43.

3   The final judgment shall be published.

Article 45
Reasons for judgments and decisions

1   Reasons shall be given for judgments as well as for decisions declaring applications admissible or inadmissible.

2   If a judgment does not represent, in whole or in part, the unanimous opinion of the judges, any judge shall be entitled to deliver a separate opinion.

Article 46
Binding force and execution of judgments

1   The High Contracting Parties undertake to abide by the final judgment of the Court in any case to which they are parties.

2   The final judgment of the Court shall be transmitted to the Committee of Ministers, which shall supervise its execution.

Article 47
Advisory opinions

1   The Court may, at the request of the Committee of Ministers, give advisory opinions on legal questions concerning the interpretation of the Convention and the protocols thereto.

2   Such opinions shall not deal with any question relating to the content or scope of the rights or freedoms defined in Section I of the Convention and the protocols thereto, or with any other question which the Court or the Committee of Ministers might have to consider in consequence of any such proceedings as could be instituted in accordance with the Convention.

3   Decisions of the Committee of Ministers to request an advisory opinion of the Court shall require a majority vote of the representatives entitled to sit on the Committee.

Article 48
Advisory jurisdiction of the Court

The Court shall decide whether a request for an advisory opinion submitted by the Committee of Ministers is within its competence as defined in Article 47.

Article 49
Reasons for advisory opinions

1   Reasons shall be given for advisory opinions of the Court.

2   If the advisory opinion does not represent, in whole or in part, the unanimous opinion of the judges, any judge shall be entitled to deliver a separate opinion.

3   Advisory opinions of the Court shall be communicated to the Committee of Ministers.

Article 50
Expenditure on the Court

The expenditure on the Court shall be borne by the Council of Europe.

Article 51
Privileges and immunities of judges

The judges shall be entitled, during the exercise of their functions, to the privileges and immunities provided for in Article 40 of the Statute of the Council of Europe and in the agreements made thereunder.

Section III — Miscellaneous provisions

Article 52
Inquiries by the Secretary General

On receipt of a request from the Secretary General of the Council of Europe any High Contracting Party shall furnish an explanation of the manner in which its internal law ensures the effective implementation of any of the provisions of the Convention.

Article 53
Safeguard for existing human rights

Nothing in this Convention shall be construed as limiting or derogating from any of the human rights and fundamental freedoms which may be ensured under the laws of any High Contracting Party or under any other agreement to which it is a Party.

Article 54
Powers of the Committee of Ministers

Nothing in this Convention shall prejudice the powers conferred on the Committee of Ministers by the Statute of the Council of Europe.

Article 55
Exclusion of other means of dispute settlement

The High Contracting Parties agree that, except by special agreement, they will not avail themselves of treaties, conventions or declarations in force between them for the purpose of submitting, by way of petition, a dispute arising out of the interpretation or application of this Convention to a means of settlement other than those provided for in this Convention.

Article 56
Territorial application

1   Any State may at the time of its ratification or at any time thereafter declare by notification addressed to the Secretary General of the Council of Europe that the present Convention shall, subject to paragraph 4 of this Article, extend to all or any of the territories for whose international relations it is responsible.

2   The Convention shall extend to the territory or territories named in the notification as from the thirtieth day after the receipt of this notification by the Secretary General of the Council of Europe.

3   The provisions of this Convention shall be applied in such territories with due regard, however, to local requirements.

4   Any State which has made a declaration in accordance with paragraph 1 of this article may at any time thereafter declare on behalf of one or more of the territories to which the declaration relates that it accepts the competence of the Court to receive applications from individuals, non-governmental organisations or groups of individuals as provided by Article 34 of the Convention.

Article 57
Reservations

1   Any State may, when signing this Convention or when depositing its instrument of ratification, make a reservation in respect of any particular provision of the Convention to the extent that any law then in force in its territory is not in conformity with the provision. Reservations of a general character shall not be permitted under this article.

2   Any reservation made under this article shall contain a brief statement of the law concerned.

Article 58
Denunciation

1   A High Contracting Party may denounce the present Convention only after the expiry of five years from the date on which it became a party to it and after six months' notice contained in a notification addressed to the Secretary General of the Council of Europe, who shall inform the other High Contracting Parties.

2   Such a denunciation shall not have the effect of releasing the High Contracting Party concerned from its obligations under this Convention in respect

of any act which, being capable of constituting a violation of such obligations, may have been performed by it before the date at which the denunciation became effective.

3   Any High Contracting Party which shall cease to be a member of the Council of Europe shall cease to be a Party to this Convention under the same conditions.

4   The Convention may be denounced in accordance with the provisions of the preceding paragraphs in respect of any territory to which it has been declared to extend under the terms of Article 56.

Article 59
Signature and ratification

1   This Convention shall be open to the signature of the members of the Council of Europe. It shall be ratified. Ratifications shall be deposited with the Secretary General of the Council of Europe.

2   The present Convention shall come into force after the deposit of ten instruments of ratification.

3   As regards any signatory ratifying subsequently, the Convention shall come into force at the date of the deposit of its instrument of ratification.

4   The Secretary General of the Council of Europe shall notify all the members of the Council of Europe of the entry into force of the Convention, the names of the High Contracting Parties who have ratified it, and the deposit of all instruments of ratification which may be effected subsequently.

Done at Rome this 4th day of November 1950, in English and French, both texts being equally authentic, in a single copy which shall remain deposited in the archives of the Council of Europe.

The Secretary General shall transmit certified copies to each of the signatories.

PROTOCOL [NO. 1] TO THE CONVENTION FOR THE PROTECTION OF HUMAN RIGHTS AND FUNDAMENTAL FREEDOMS, AS AMENDED BY PROTOCOL NO. 11

The governments signatory hereto, being members of the Council of Europe,

Being resolved to take steps to ensure the collective enforcement of certain rights and freedoms other than those already included in Section I of the Convention for the Protection of Human Rights and Fundamental Freedoms signed at Rome on 4 November 1950 (hereinafter referred to as 'the Convention'),

Have agreed as follows:

Article 1
Protection of property

Every natural or legal person is entitled to the peaceful enjoyment of his possessions. No one shall be deprived of his possessions except in the public interest and subject to the conditions provided for by law and by the general principles of international law.

The preceding provisions shall not, however, in any way impair the right of a State to enforce such laws as it deems necessary to control the use of property in accordance with the general interest or to secure the payment of taxes or other contributions or penalties.

Article 2
Right to education

No person shall be denied the right to education. In the exercise of any functions which it assumes in relation to education and to teaching, the State shall respect the right of parents to ensure such education and teaching in conformity with their own religious and philosophical convictions.

Article 3
Right to free elections

The High Contracting Parties undertake to hold free elections at reasonable intervals by secret ballot, under conditions which will ensure the free expression of the opinion of the people in the choice of the legislature.

Article 4
Territorial application

Any High Contracting Party may at the time of signature or ratification or at any time thereafter communicate to the Secretary General of the Council of Europe a declaration stating the extent to which it undertakes that the provisions of the present Protocol shall apply to such of the territories for the international relations of which it is responsible as are named therein.

Any High Contracting Party which has communicated a declaration in virtue of the preceding paragraph may from time to time communicate a further declaration modifying the terms of any former declaration or terminating the application of the provisions of this Protocol in respect of any territory.

A declaration made in accordance with this article shall be deemed to have been made in accordance with paragraph 1 of Article 56 of the Convention.

Article 5
Relationship to the Convention

As between the High Contracting Parties the provisions of Articles 1, 2, 3 and 4 of this Protocol shall be regarded as additional articles to the Convention and all the provisions of the Convention shall apply accordingly.

Article 6
Signature and ratification

This Protocol shall be open for signature by the members of the Council of Europe, who are the signatories of the Convention; it shall be ratified at the same time as or after the ratification of the Convention. It shall enter into force after the deposit of ten instruments of ratification. As regards any signatory ratifying subsequently, the Protocol shall enter into force at the date of the deposit of its instrument of ratification.

The instruments of ratification shall be deposited with the Secretary General of the Council of Europe, who will notify all members of the names of those who have ratified.

Done at Paris on the 20th day of March 1952, in English and French, both texts being equally authentic, in a single copy which shall remain deposited in the archives of the Council of Europe. The Secretary General shall transmit certified copies to each of the signatory governments.

PROTOCOL NO. 4 TO THE CONVENTION FOR THE PROTECTION OF HUMAN RIGHTS AND FUNDAMENTAL FREEDOMS, SECURING CERTAIN RIGHTS AND FREEDOMS OTHER THAN THOSE ALREADY INCLUDED IN THE CONVENTION AND IN THE FIRST PROTOCOL THERETO, AS AMENDED BY PROTOCOL NO. 11

The governments signatory hereto, being members of the Council of Europe,

Being resolved to take steps to ensure the collective enforcement of certain rights and freedoms other than those already included in Section 1 of the Convention for the Protection of Human Rights and Fundamental Freedoms signed at Rome on 4th November 1950 (hereinafter referred to as the 'Convention') and in Articles 1 to 3 of the First Protocol to the Convention, signed at Paris on 20th March 1952,

Have agreed as follows:

Article 1
Prohibition of imprisonment for debt

No one shall be deprived of his liberty merely on the ground of inability to fulfil a contractual obligation.

Article 2
Freedom of movement

1   Everyone lawfully within the territory of a State shall, within that territory, have the right to liberty of movement and freedom to choose his residence.

2   Everyone shall be free to leave any country, including his own.

3   No restrictions shall be placed on the exercise of these rights other than such as are in accordance with law and are necessary in a democratic society in the interests of national security or public safety, for the maintenance of *ordre public*, for the prevention of crime, for the protection of health or morals, or for the protection of the rights and freedoms of others.

4   The rights set forth in paragraph 1 may also be subject, in particular areas, to restrictions imposed in accordance with law and justified by the public interest in a democratic society.

Article 3
Prohibition of expulsion of nationals

1   No one shall be expelled, by means either of an individual or of a collective measure, from the territory of the State of which he is a national.

2   No one shall be deprived of the right to enter the territory of the state of which he is a national.

Article 4
Prohibition of collective expulsion of aliens

Collective expulsion of aliens is prohibited.

Article 5
Territorial application

1   Any High Contracting Party may, at the time of signature or ratification of this Protocol, or at any time thereafter, communicate to the Secretary General of the Council of Europe a declaration stating the extent to which it undertakes that the provisions of this Protocol shall apply to such of the territories for the international relations of which it is responsible as are named therein.

2   Any High Contracting Party which has communicated a declaration in virtue of the preceding paragraph may, from time to time, communicate a further declaration modifying the terms of any former declaration or terminating the application of the provisions of this Protocol in respect of any territory.

3   A declaration made in accordance with this article shall be deemed to have been made in accordance with paragraph 1 of Article 56 of the Convention.

4   The territory of any State to which this Protocol applies by virtue of ratification or acceptance by that State, and each territory to which this Protocol is applied by virtue of a declaration by that State under this article, shall be treated as separate territories for the purpose of the references in Articles 2 and 3 to the territory of a State.

5   Any State which has made a declaration in accordance with paragraph 1 or 2 of this Article may at any time thereafter declare on behalf of one or more of the territories to which the declaration relates that it accepts the competence of the Court to receive applications from individuals, non-governmental organisations or groups of individuals as provided in Article 34 of the Convention in respect of all or any of Articles 1 to 4 of this Protocol.

Article 6
Relationship to the Convention

As between the High Contracting Parties the provisions of Articles 1 to 5 of this Protocol shall be regarded as additional Articles to the Convention, and all the provisions of the Convention shall apply accordingly.

Article 7
Signature and ratification

1   This Protocol shall be open for signature by the members of the Council of Europe who are the signatories of the Convention; it shall be ratified at the same time as or after the ratification of the Convention. It shall enter into force after the deposit of five instruments of ratification. As regards any signatory ratifying subsequently, the Protocol shall enter into force at the date of the deposit of its instrument of ratification.

2   The instruments of ratification shall be deposited with the Secretary General of the Council of Europe, who will notify all members of the names of those who have ratified.

In witness whereof the undersigned, being duly authorised thereto, have signed this Protocol.

Done at Strasbourg, this 16th day of September 1963, in English and in French, both texts being equally authoritative, in a single copy which shall remain deposited in the archives of the Council of Europe. The Secretary General shall transmit certified copies to each of the signatory states.

PROTOCOL NO. 6 TO THE CONVENTION FOR THE PROTECTION OF HUMAN RIGHTS AND FUNDAMENTAL FREEDOMS CONCERNING THE ABOLITION OF THE DEATH PENALTY, AS AMENDED BY PROTOCOL NO. 11

The member States of the Council of Europe, signatory to this Protocol to the Convention for the Protection of Human Rights and Fundamental Freedoms, signed at Rome on 4 November 1950 (hereinafter referred to as 'the Convention'),

Considering that the evolution that has occurred in several member States of the Council of Europe expresses a general tendency in favour of abolition of the death penalty;

Have agreed as follows:

Article 1
Abolition of the death penalty

The death penalty shall be abolished. No-one shall be condemned to such penalty or executed.

Article 2
Death penalty in time of war

A State may make provision in its law for the death penalty in respect of acts committed in time of war or of imminent threat of war; such penalty shall be applied only in the instances laid down in the law and in accordance with its provisions. The State shall communicate to the Secretary General of the Council of Europe the relevant provisions of that law.

Article 3
Prohibition of derogations

No derogation from the provisions of this Protocol shall be made under Article 15 of the Convention.

Article 4
Prohibition of reservations

No reservation may be made under Article 57 of the Convention in respect of the provisions of this Protocol.

Article 5
Territorial application

1   Any State may at the time of signature or when depositing its instrument of ratification, acceptance or approval, specify the territory or territories to which this Protocol shall apply.

2   Any State may at any later date, by a declaration addressed to the Secretary General of the Council of Europe, extend the application of this Protocol to any other territory specified in the declaration. In respect of such territory the Protocol shall enter into force on the first day of the month following the date of receipt of such declaration by the Secretary General.

3   Any declaration made under the two preceding paragraphs may, in respect of any territory specified in such declaration, be withdrawn by a notification addressed to the Secretary General. The withdrawal shall become effective on the first day of the month following the date of receipt of such notification by the Secretary General.

Article 6
Relationship to the Convention

As between the States Parties the provisions of Articles 1 to 5 of this Protocol shall be regarded as additional articles to the Convention and all the provisions of the Convention shall apply accordingly.

Article 7
Signature and ratification

The Protocol shall be open for signature by the member States of the Council of Europe, signatories to the Convention. It shall be subject to ratification, acceptance or approval. A member State of the Council of Europe may not ratify, accept or approve this Protocol unless it has, simultaneously or previously, ratified the Convention. Instruments of ratification, acceptance or approval shall be deposited with the Secretary General of the Council of Europe.

Article 8
Entry into force

1   This Protocol shall enter into force on the first day of the month following the date on which five member States of the Council of Europe have expressed their consent to be bound by the Protocol in accordance with the provisions of Article 7.

2   In respect of any member State which subsequently expresses its consent to be bound by it, the Protocol shall enter into force on the first day of the month following the date of the deposit of the instrument of ratification, acceptance or approval.

Article 9
Depositary functions

The Secretary General of the Council of Europe shall notify the member States of the Council of:

a   any signature;

b   the deposit of any instrument of ratification, acceptance or approval;

c   any date of entry into force of this Protocol in accordance with Articles 5 and 8;

d   any other act, notification or communication relating to this Protocol.

In witness whereof the undersigned, being duly authorised thereto, have signed this Protocol.

Done at Strasbourg, this 28th day of April 1983, in English and in French, both texts being equally authentic, in a single copy which shall be deposited in the archives of the Council of Europe. The Secretary General of the Council of Europe shall transmit certified copies to each member State of the Council of Europe.

PROTOCOL NO. 7 TO THE CONVENTION FOR THE PROTECTION OF HUMAN RIGHTS AND FUNDAMENTAL FREEDOMS, AS AMENDED BY PROTOCOL NO. 11

The member States of the Council of Europe signatory hereto,

Being resolved to take further steps to ensure the collective enforcement of certain rights and freedoms by means of the Convention for the Protection of Human Rights and Fundamental Freedoms signed at Rome on 4 November 1950 (hereinafter referred to as 'the Convention'),

Have agreed as follows

Article 1
Procedural safeguards relating to expulsion of aliens

1   An alien lawfully resident in the territory of a State shall not be expelled therefrom except in pursuance of a decision reached in accordance with law and shall be allowed:

a   to submit reasons against his expulsion,

b   to have his case reviewed, and

c   to be represented for these purposes before the competent authority or a person or persons designated by that authority.

2   An alien may be expelled before the exercise of his rights under paragraph 1.a, b and c of this Article, when such expulsion is necessary in the interests of public order or is grounded on reasons of national security.

Article 2
Right of appeal in criminal matters

1   Everyone convicted of a criminal offence by a tribunal shall have the right to have his conviction or sentence reviewed by a higher tribunal. The exercise of this right, including the grounds on which it may be exercised, shall be governed by law.

2   This right may be subject to exceptions in regard to offences of a minor character, as prescribed by law, or in cases in which the person concerned was tried in the first instance by the highest tribunal or was convicted following an appeal against acquittal.

Article 3
Compensation for wrongful conviction

When a person has by a final decision been convicted of a criminal offence and when subsequently his conviction has been reversed, or he has been pardoned, on the ground that a new or newly discovered fact shows conclusively that there has been a miscarriage of justice, the person who has suffered punishment as a result of such conviction shall be compensated according to the law or the practice of the State concerned, unless it is proved that the non-disclosure of the unknown fact in time is wholly or partly attributable to him.

Article 4
Right not to be tried or punished twice

1   No one shall be liable to be tried or punished again in criminal proceedings under the jurisdiction of the same State for an offence for which he has already been finally acquitted or convicted in accordance with the law and penal procedure of that State.

2   The provisions of the preceding paragraph shall not prevent the reopening of the case in accordance with the law and penal procedure of the State concerned, if there is evidence of new or newly discovered facts, or if there has been a fundamental defect in the previous proceedings, which could affect the outcome of the case.

3   No derogation from this Article shall be made under Article 15 of the Convention.

Article 5
Equality between spouses

Spouses shall enjoy equality of rights and responsibilities of a private law character between them, and in their relations with their children, as to marriage, during marriage and in the event of its dissolution. This Article shall not prevent States from taking such measures as are necessary in the interests of the children.

Article 6
Territorial application

1   Any State may at the time of signature or when depositing its instrument of ratification, acceptance or approval, specify the territory or territories to which the Protocol shall apply and state the extent to which it undertakes that the provisions of this Protocol shall apply to such territory or territories.

2   Any State may at any later date, by a declaration addressed to the Secretary General of the Council of Europe, extend the application of this Protocol to any other territory specified in the declaration. In respect of such territory the Protocol shall enter into force on the first day of the month following the expiration of a period of two months after the date of receipt by the Secretary General of such declaration.

3   Any declaration made under the two preceding paragraphs may, in respect of any territory specified in such declaration, be withdrawn or modified by a notification addressed to the Secretary General. The withdrawal or modification shall become effective on the first day of the month following the expiration of a period of two months after the date of receipt of such notification by the Secretary General.

4   A declaration made in accordance with this Article shall be deemed to have been made in accordance with paragraph 1 of Article 56 of the Convention.

5   The territory of any State to which this Protocol applies by virtue of ratification, acceptance or approval by that State, and each territory to which this Protocol is applied by virtue of a declaration by that State under this Article, may be treated as separate territories for the purpose of the reference in Article 1 to the territory of a State.

6   Any State which has made a declaration in accordance with paragraph 1 or 2 of this Article may at any time thereafter declare on behalf of one or more of the territories to which the declaration relates that it accepts the competence of the Court to receive applications from individuals, non-governmental organisations or groups of individuals as provided in Article 34 of the Convention in respect of Articles 1 to 5 of this Protocol.

Article 7
Relationship to the Convention

As between the States Parties, the provisions of Article 1 to 6 of this Protocol shall be regarded as additional Articles to the Convention, and all the provisions of the Convention shall apply accordingly.

Article 8
Signature and ratification

This Protocol shall be open for signature by member States of the Council of Europe which have signed the Convention. It is subject to ratification, acceptance or approval. A member State of the Council of Europe may not ratify, accept or approve this Protocol without previously or simultaneously ratifying the Convention. Instruments of ratification, acceptance or approval shall be deposited with the Secretary General of the Council of Europe.

Article 9
Entry into force

1   This Protocol shall enter into force on the first day of the month following the expiration of a period of two months after the date on which seven member States of the Council of Europe have expressed their consent to be bound by the Protocol in accordance with the provisions of Article 8.

2   In respect of any member State which subsequently expresses its consent to be bound by it, the Protocol shall enter into force on the first day of the month following the expiration of a period of two months after the date of the deposit of the instrument of ratification, acceptance or approval.

Article 10
Depositary functions

The Secretary General of the Council of Europe shall notify all the member States of the Council of Europe of:

a   any signature;

b   the deposit of any instrument of ratification, acceptance or approval;

c   any date of entry into force of this Protocol in accordance with Articles 6 and 9;

d   any other act, notification or declaration relating to this Protocol.

In witness whereof the undersigned, being duly authorised thereto, have signed this Protocol.

Done at Strasbourg, this 22nd day of November 1984, in English and French, both texts being equally authentic, in a single copy which shall be deposited in the archives of the Council of Europe. The Secretary General of the Council of Europe shall transmit certified copies to each member State of the Council of Europe.

[DRAFT] PROTOCOL NO. 12 TO THE CONVENTION FOR THE PROTECTION OF HUMAN RIGHTS AND FUNDAMENTAL FREEDOMS

The member states of the Council of Europe signatory hereto,

Having regard to the fundamental principle according to which all persons are equal before the law and are entitled to the equal protection of the law;

Being resolved to take further steps to promote the equality of all persons through the collective enforcement of a general prohibition of discrimination by means of the Convention for the Protection of Human Rights and Fundamental Freedoms signed at Rome on 4 November 1950 (hereinafter referred to as 'the Convention');

Reaffirming that the principle of non-discrimination does not prevent States Parties from taking measures in order to promote full and effective equality, provided that there is an objective and reasonable justification for those measures,

Have agreed as follows:

Article 1
General prohibition of discrimination

1   The enjoyment of any right set forth by law shall be secured without discrimination on any ground such as sex, race, colour, language, religion, political or other opinion, national or social origin, association with a national minority, property, birth or other status.

2   No one shall be discriminated against by any public authority on any ground such as those mentioned in paragraph 1.

Article 2
Territorial application

1   Any state may, at the time of signature or when depositing its instrument of ratification, acceptance or approval, specify the territory or territories to which this Protocol shall apply.

2   Any state may at any later date, by a declaration addressed to the Secretary General of the Council of Europe, extend the application of this Protocol to any other territory specified in the declaration, in respect of such territory the Protocol shall enter into force on the first day of the month following the expiration of a period of three months after the date of receipt by the Secretary General of such declaration.

3   Any declaration made under the two preceding paragraphs may, in respect of any territory specified in such declaration, be withdrawn or modified by a notification addressed to the Secretary General. The withdrawal or modification shall become effective on the first day of the month following the expiration of a period of three months after the date of receipt of such notification by the Secretary General.

4   A declaration made in accordance with this article shall be deemed to have been made in accordance with paragraph 1 of Article 56 of the Convention.

5   Any state which has made a declaration in accordance with paragraph 1 or 2 of this article may at any time thereafter declare on behalf of one or more of the territories to which the declaration relates that it accepts the competence of the Court to receive applications from individuals, non-governmental organisations or groups of individuals as provided by Article 34 of the Convention in respect of Article 1 of this Protocol.

Article 3
Relationship to the Convention

As between the States Parties, the provisions of Articles 1 and 2 of this Protocol shall be regarded as additional articles to the Convention, and all the provisions of the Convention shall apply accordingly.

Article 4
Signature and ratification

This Protocol shall be open for signature by member states of the Council of Europe which have signed the Convention. It is subject to ratification, acceptance or approval. A member state of the Council of Europe may not ratify, accept or approve this Protocol without previously or simultaneously ratifying the Convention. Instruments of ratification, acceptance or approval shall be deposited with the Secretary General of the Council of Europe.

Article 5
Entry into force

1   This Protocol shall enter into force on the first day of the month following the expiration of a period of three months after the date on which ten member states of the Council of Europe have expressed their consent to be bound by the Protocol in accordance with the provisions of Article 4.

2   In respect of any member state which subsequently expresses its consent to be bound by it, the Protocol shall enter into force on the first day of the month following the expiration of a period of three months after the date of the deposit of the instrument of ratification, acceptance or approval.

Article 6
Depositary functions

The Secretary General of the Council of Europe shall notify all the member states of the Council of Europe of:

a   any signature;

b   the deposit of any instrument of ratification, acceptance or approval;

c   any date of entry into force of this Protocol in accordance with Articles 2 and 5;

d   any other act, notification or communication relating to this Protocol.

In witness whereof the undersigned, being duly authorised thereto, have signed this Protocol.

Done at ...., this .... day of .... 2000, in English and French, both texts being equally authentic, in a single copy which shall be deposited in the archives of the Council of Europe. The Secretary General of the Council of Europe shall transmit certified copies to each member state of the Council of Europe.

Appendix Seven
Finding European Convention on Human Rights
Jurisprudence

REFERENCING SYSTEM

Practitioners will need to understand the referencing system used for Strasbourg case law. All applications to Strasbourg once lodged are given a number with five digits, and then two digits representing the year of the application. Sometimes the issues before the Court are such as to demand confidentiality and so the applicant is referred to by a letter of the alphabet, for example, *W v United Kingdom* (Application No. 25678/90).

WHERE TO FIND CONVENTION CASE LAW

Paper

The draft Practice Directions for the Human Rights Act 1998 (see Appendix 2) issued at the time of writing outline the procedures for citing human rights material in court. The sources that are acceptable for the citation of authorities include the texts and collections outlined below.

The Council of Europe publishes individual judgments and decisions under the title 'Publications of the European Court of Human Rights'. Series A contains the official report of all the judgments of the Court of Human Rights up to 1995, along with the Commission Report on merits. Series B contains the pleadings and documents submitted by the parties. Cases up to November 1995 are referred to by an 'A Series Number'. From 1996 onwards the Court's judgments have been reported in *Reports, Judgments and Decisions of the European Court of Human Rights* (published by Carl Heymanns Verlag KG).

To find Commission admissibility decisions (i.e., before Protocol 11 brought about a change in the structure of the Court) there are several possible sources. Early decisions from 1969 can be found in the *Yearbook of the European*

Convention on Human Rights (YB). From 1975 onwards, Commission decisions are to be found in the *Decisions and Reports of the European Commission of Human Rights* (DR). With the abolition of the Commission in 1998 these admissibility decisions are no longer made.

The most easily available source of case law is the *European Human Rights Reports*, published by Sweet and Maxwell. The first volume was published in 1979 and there are now 28 volumes. As well as most of the substantive cases decided by the Court you can also find a selection of old Commission decisions at the back of the 1990 volumes onwards. There is a time delay of about 12 months between a judgment being given and its inclusion in the EHRR.

Butterworths Human Rights Cases also includes selected coverage of the most important cases from Strasbourg since 1997.

Electronic/Online

The most comprehensive source for decisions of the Strasbourg authorities is the Court's free website which can be found at *http://www.echr.coe.int*. Decisions of the now defunct Commission and the Court can be found on this site via the HUDOC search engine where you can search by party names, article number of the Convention and application number. This judgment database is updated regularly with most recent decisions added within 24 hours of the judgment being released. Also useful are the Case Law Information Notes which offer regular summaries of the cases admitted to the Court.

Several electronic publishers do (or are about to) provide case law via online subscription services. The full texts of Strasbourg authorities from JUSTIS (published by Context Electronic Publishers), LEXIS, Westlaw UK and Butterworths are also acceptable under the Draft Rules and Practice Directions for the Human Rights Act currently issued.

United Kingdom Human Rights Material

Two new series of human rights reports devoted to the United Kingdom commenced publication in early 2000: *UK Human Rights Reports* published by Jordans and *Human Rights Law Reports — UK Cases* published by Sweet and Maxwell. These will provide full text reports of English and Scottish cases on human rights issues. *Crown Office Digest* will have enhanced coverage of human rights cases after October 2000. It will provide digests of the large number of cases which are likely to be dealt with in the Crown Office List. *Blackstone's Human Rights Digest*, K. Starmer (London: Blackstone Press, 2000) will also provide a useful source and analysis of current information. The new looseleaf publication *Human Rights Practice* (eds. Simor and Emmerson) is due to published by Sweet and Maxwell in October 2000 and is likely to become an authoritative resource.

BIBLIOGRAPHIC MATERIALS AND RESOURCES

Books on Convention Case Law

D.J. Harris, M. O'Boyle and C. Warbrick, *Law of the European Convention on Human Rights* (London: Butterworths, 1995).

P. van Dijk and F. van Hoof (eds), *Theory and Practice of the European Convention on Human Rights*, 3rd ed. (The Netherlands: Kluwer, 1998)

A.H. Robertson and J.G. Merrils, *Human Rights in Europe: A Study of the European Convention on Human Rights*, 3rd ed. (Manchester: Manchester University Press, 1993).

P. Kempees, *A Systematic Guide to the Case-Law of the European Court of Human Rights, 1960–1994* (The Hague: Martinus Nijhoff, 1996) (two volumes).

V. Berger, *Case Law of the European Court of the Human Rights* (Dublin: Round Hall Press, 1989–95) (three volumes).

Lawson and Schermers, *Leading Cases of the European Court of Human Rights* (London: Aers Aequi Libri, 1997).

S. Farran, *The United Kingdom before the European Court of Human Rights: Case Law and Commentary* (London: Blackstone Press, 1996).

K. Reid, *A Practitioner's Guide to the European Convention on Human Rights* (London: Sweet and Maxwell, 1998).

F.G. Jacobs and R.C.A. White, *The European Convention on Human Rights*, 2nd ed. (Oxford: Clarendon Press, 1996).

M.W. Janis, R.S. Kay and A.W. Bradley, *European Human Rights Law: Text and Materials* (Oxford: Clarendon Press, 1995).

On the pre-Human Rights Act application of the Convention in domestic courts

M. Hunt, *Using Human Rights Law in English Courts* (Oxford: Hart, 1997).

R. Singh, *The Future of Human Rights in the United Kingdom* (Oxford: Hart, 1997).

On the Human Rights Act 1998

R. Clayton and H. Tomlinson, *Human Rights Law* (Oxford: Oxford University Press, 2000).

J. Coppel, *The Human Rights Act 1998: Enforcing the European Convention in the Domestic Courts* (London: John Wiley & Sons, 1999).

K. Starmer, *European Human Rights Law* (London: Legal Action Group, 1999).

D. Pannick and A. Lester, *Human Rights Law and Practice* (London: Butterworths, 1999).

S. Grosz, J. Beatson and P. Duffy, *Human Rights: The 1998 Act and the European Convention* (London: Sweet and Maxwell, 2000).

See also the forthcoming titles in Blackstone's Human Rights Series on the impact of the Human Rights Act 1998 on specific subject areas.

WEBSITES

UK Case Law

- *House of Lords judgments* from 1996. These are available 2 hours after the judgment is handed down.
- The Court Service — contains judgments from the Court of Appeal, Civil and Criminal Divisions; Queen's Bench Division; Commercial Court; Chancery Division and Companies Court. As well as selected judgments and practice directions from the Court of Appeal and the High Court this site includes a searchable database.
- *The Times* — reports available from January 1 1996. To find a Times law report you have to know its date. Go to *Back Issues*, enter the issue you want, then look under *Law Reports*.
- *Scottish Courts Website* — provides an access point to information relating to all civil and criminal courts within Scotland, including the Court of Session, the High Court of Justiciary, the Sheriff Courts and a number of other courts, commissions and tribunals as well as the District Courts. The information includes details of recent significant judgments and is regularly updated with any changes and other relevant information. It is fully searchable.
- *BAILII* — provides free, unlimited access to a growing number of reports and legislation from English and Irish courts.
- *Beagle* is an extremely useful site, where the decided cases are arranged alongside the relevant articles of the ECHR. The 'searches' section is updated regularly with cases which raise Convention issues and are searchable by article of the Convention/keywords. Links to the JSB's case digest.

UK Government Departments and Agencies

- *Lord Chancellor's Department* — good links to the main activities of the LCD including consultation papers, research, statute law database and a special human rights section.
- *Legal Services Commission*
- *Home Office*
- *Home Office Human Rights Unit* — The Human Rights Unit's main responsibility is to ensure the successful implementation of the Human Rights Act 1998, which incorporates into UK law rights and freedoms guaranteed by the European Convention on Human Rights. The Unit also maintains and develops the UK's position under various Human Rights Treaties. This site includes policy documents, contact details, activities and training opportunities.

UK Parliament

- *House of Commons* including *Hansard* (debates in Parliament) reproduced in full. The new edition of Hansard is made available each day at 12.30pm.
- *House of Lords* — includes *Hansard* and *Judicial business*. The House of Lords is the final court of appeal on points of law. This page contains information on the judicial work of the Lords and the full text of judgments delivered since 14 November 1996.

European Union institutions

- *European Commission* — includes access to the *Directorates General* and Agencies of the EU.
- *European Parliament* — you can search the legislative process of the EP by using the *Legislative Observatory*.
- *European Court of Justice* including recent *Judgments*.

European Convention on Human Rights

- *European Convention on Human Rights and Protocols*
- *ECHR homepage*
- *HUDOC* Search engine for Convention jurisprudence.
- *Information Notes* brief notes on recent Cases arranged by Article.

Other Commonwealth Jurisdictions

- Australia (*www.austlii.edu.au*) contains a full database of High Court decisions and a large amount of State and Federal material.
- Canada (*www.droit.umontreal.ca/doc/csc-scc/en/index.html*). Decisions of the Supreme Court of Canada from 1989 onwards are available.
- New Zealand (*www.brookers.co.nz*) is a searchable online database of Court of Appeal Judgments from 1995. Also try AUSTLII for more recent judgments.
- India (*www.supremecourtonline.com*) has a limited number of decisions available.
- South Africa (*www.law.wits.ac.za/archive.html*) has judgments of the Constitutional Court and related materials.
- United States (*www.law.cornell.edu*) contains both Supreme Court decisions and other US Courts.

Also visit:

Liberty (*www.liberty-human-rights.org.uk*) and Matrix (*www.matrixlaw.co.uk*) for further human rights interest issues.

Index